MW01038858

HARDY
WOMEN

ALSO BY PAULA BYRNE

The Adventures of Miss Barbara Pym

Kick: The True Story of Kick Kennedy, JFK's Forgotten Sister, and the Heir to Chatsworth

Belle: The True Story of Dido Belle

The Real Jane Austen: A Life in Small Things

Mad World: Evelyn Waugh and the Secrets of Brideshead

Perdita: The Life of Mary Robinson

The Genius of Jane Austen: Her Love of Theatre and Why She is a Hit in Hollywood

FICTION

Blonde Venus

Look to Your Wife

HARDY WOMEN

Mother, Sisters, Wives, Muses

Paula Byrne

WILLIAM
COLLINS

William Collins
An imprint of HarperCollins*Publishers*
1 London Bridge Street
London SE1 9GF

WilliamCollinsBooks.com

HarperCollins*Publishers*
Macken House,
39/40 Mayor Street Upper,
Dublin 1, D01 C9W8, Ireland

First published in Great Britain in 2024 by William Collins

1

Copyright © Paula Byrne 2024

Paula Byrne asserts the moral right to be identified
as the author of this work in accordance with
the Copyright, Designs and Patents Act 1988

A catalogue record for this book is available from the British Library

ISBN 978-0-00-832225-0 (Hardback)
ISBN 978-0-00-832226-7 (Trade Paperback)

All rights reserved. No part of this publication may be
reproduced, stored in a retrieval system, or transmitted, in any form or by
any means, electronic, mechanical, photocopying, recording or otherwise,
without the prior permission of the publishers.

This book is sold subject to the condition that it shall not, by way of trade or otherwise, be lent,
re-sold, hired out or otherwise circulated without the publisher's prior consent in any form of
binding or cover other than that in which it is published and without a similar condition
including this condition being imposed on the subsequent purchaser.

Typeset in Adobe Garamond Pro by
Palimpsest Book Production Ltd, Falkirk, Stirlingshire

Printed and Bound in the UK using 100% Renewable Electricity
at CPI Group (UK) Ltd

This book contains FSC™ certified paper and other controlled
sources to ensure responsible forest management

For more information visit: www.harpercollins.co.uk/green

Gertrude Bugler as Tess

For Andrew Schuman

Contents

PHASE THE THIRD:
THE WOMEN HE LOVED
AND THE WOMEN HE LOST

From now alway
Till my last day
What I discern I will not say.

(Thomas Hardy, 'He Resolves to
Say No More', in *Winter Words*)

I wonder at your complete understanding
of a woman's soul.

(Emily Pass of New York, aged 20, on
reading *Tess of the D'Urbervilles* in 1927)

He understands only the women
he *invents* – the others not at all.

(Emma Lavinia Hardy)

PROLOGUE

Raising Ghosts

It was a sight he would never forget. As an old man, filled with a mixture of erotic yearning and shame, he recalled 'what a fine figure she showed against the sky as she hung in the misty rain, and how the tight black silk gown set off her shape as she wheeled half-round and back'.[1] The details were forever branded on his memory: 'I saw – they had put a cloth over her face – how, as the cloth got wet, *her features came through it.* That was extraordinary.' Long after the large crowd of spectators who had gathered in front of the gatehouse to the Dorchester County Gaol had dispersed, the sixteen-year-old boy stayed on, mesmerised by the woman 'turning slowly round on the rope'.[2]

The young man was Thomas Hardy and he should have been at work at Hicks' architectural office in Dorchester, where he was apprenticed. Instead, he decided he would get himself a good view of the public execution. It was the first public hanging of a woman for twenty-three years. The prisoner was Elizabeth Martha Brown, who had been found guilty of killing her husband in a crime of passion.

In the summer of 1918, Hardy made a bonfire in his garden at Max Gate. Page after page of precious manuscripts, notebooks, reviews, newspaper cuttings and correspondence, thrown into the flames. His young (second) wife Florence was notably distressed by the holocaust, writing to their friend Sydney Cockerell of his insistence that drafts and notes for his recollections of the years between 1840 and 1892 should be destroyed.[3]

He had always been adamant that he did not want anyone to write about his personal life. During his lifetime, there was to be no authorised biography. He had been deeply troubled by the publication in 1911 of F. A. Hedgcock's *Thomas Hardy: penseur et artiste*, a critical study of the novels that included biographical details. 'Too personal, and in bad taste, even supposing it were true, which it is not!' he furiously exclaimed in the margin of his copy.[4]

His biographical paranoia was further fuelled by the revelations in the papers of his first wife, Emma, which he discovered after her sudden death in 1912. Her journals were titled 'What I Think of My Husband', and they were deeply distressing. He also discovered a memoir, which described his wife's early life and her courtship with Hardy. Always fiercely protective of his private life, he began to panic about his posthumous reputation. In the months leading up to the Great War, he asked Sydney Cockerell to be his literary executor, telling him that he had begun to jot down some dates 'to use if any preposterous stories should require contradiction'. Nevertheless, he assured his friend that he had nothing to hide, and that after his death he would 'sleep quite calmly at Stinsford, whatever happens'.[5] His wish was to be buried in the churchyard of the parish where he was born, close to his mother and to Emma.

Cockerell began encouraging him to write his memoirs. He was keen to read about the young Thomas Hardy: 'Write something down about yourself,' he urged, 'and especially about that youthful figure whose photograph I have got, and of whom you told me that you could think with almost complete detachment.'[6]

Florence aided and abetted. After her husband's death, she claimed that it was her 'strong request' that persuaded him to agree to write his own life. She insisted that although her husband 'had not sufficient admiration for himself' to write an auto-biography, his 'hand was forced'.[7] Hardy had a fear of the person 'who comes here and goes away to write down things'. The only solution was to write them down himself and to rely on Florence to be keeper of the flame. She could be trusted: her own diary merely recorded 'incidents' – 'no personalities'. It was, she told a friend, 'A dull affair no doubt – but when I remember the *awful* diary the first Mrs T. H. kept (which he burned) full of venom, hatred and abuse of him and his family I am afraid to do more than chronicle facts.'[8]

A month before Hardy received Cockerell's request, his beloved sister Mary had died. She had been 'almost my only companion in childhood', he confessed. The loss brought intimations of his own mortality and a flood of memories. Perhaps Cockerell was right. The war made the future seem dark and uncertain: 'It is a gloomy time', Hardy wrote, 'in which the world, having like a spider climbed to a certain height, seems slipping back to where it was long ago.'[9] A time for him to slip back into his own past. To tell his own story in his own words. This, though, was not exactly how things would transpire.

By 1917, the project, code name 'Materials', was underway. Secrecy was paramount. In a bizarre twist, Hardy decided to ghost-write his own autobiography.

And so one of the literary world's greatest deceptions was perpetrated. Hardy would write his memoirs for publication after his death, but they would be branded as an 'official' biography by Florence, who was a respected author in her own right. 'I realize that *on no account* must we mention the word "autobiog-raphy" or call them "autobiographical"', Florence explained.[10] They would write in third-person narrative: a further stratagem of emotional distancing. If this all sounds confusing, that was the intention. A further complication occurred when Florence (aided by the author and creator of *Peter Pan*, J. M. Barrie) edited the manuscript after Hardy's death, omitting various details and adding extra anecdotes and personal information.[11]

Hardy wrote down his memories in longhand, closely referring to his journals, letters, reviews, press cuttings and notebooks, before passing the pages to Florence, who would type them and then hand back the typescript for corrections. Hardy's own emendations were written in a disguised calligraphic hand. He would also dictate stories which Florence would type, and then return for corrections. Once satisfied, the manuscripts were then destroyed. In May 1919, Hardy wrote to his friend Sir George Douglas that he had been busy burning 'papers of the last 30 or 40 years'. In a telling phrase, he explained: 'they raise ghosts'.[12]

So who were the ghosts, and why was Thomas Hardy so keen to present his own whitewashed version of the facts of his life, and destroy almost every one of his private papers? Was it that fame and the tetchiness of old age had made him suspicious of the press and ultra-sensitive to gossip? The truth is, he had always been a man of mystery, a keeper of many secrets. More often than not, those secrets were connected to the women in his life. Now, the full extent of his evasions, his deliberate omissions and distortions, can be revealed for the first time, and they shed valuable light on his life and works.

This book draws on Hardy's extensive correspondence (now complete in eight volumes, the last of them, containing 650 letters unknown to previous biographers, published in 2012), as well as memoirs, newspaper stories and the novels themselves. New letters from Hardy's second wife, Florence, have recently been discovered. This book also benefits from access to some tantalising annotations in Hardy's religious books.

He was drawn to women, and especially to beautiful,

inaccessible women. In order to write, he required a female muse. As a young boy, he was surrounded by strong, determined women, mainly of a lower social class. His (almost obsessive) love for his mother, Jemima, is well documented, and explored most fully in his novel *The Return of the Native*. Familial love for his younger sisters, Mary and Kate, aroused a nurturing and protective instinct; he was a loving brother, guiding their reading and providing succour during difficult times in their lives. His maternal aunts, the formidable Hand sisters, were a source of inspiration, and he was intimately connected with his female cousins.

Many of the women he grew up with had troubled lives. He saw at first hand the effects of domestic violence, poverty, and hard drinking on the women in his family. He also witnessed the strength of the women who rose above their circumstances, who were enterprising, resilient, and an endless source of strange and fascinating stories.

Thomas Hardy would create some of the most memorable and enduring heroines in fiction: Bathsheba Everdene, Eustacia Vye, Tess Durbeyfield, Sue Bridehead. He was a pioneer of the idea of the modern woman. He could not have been the writer he was without the women who inspired his vision. But his relationship with the female sex was vexed and complicated. Into *Tess of the D'Urbervilles*, he poured all his deepest emotions. Over tea at Max Gate, he confessed to Frank Hedgcock – the academic researching the book that Hardy would come to regard as a betrayal – that, though he agreed with the general opinion that it was his best novel, he 'had put too much feeling in it to recall it with pleasure.' And back when the novel was published in 1891, he wrote to a painter friend: 'I'm glad you like *Tess* – though I have not been able to put on paper all that she is, or was, to me.'[13]

He lost his heart to Tess. No living woman could ever compete with her. The prominent American critic Irving Howe wrote that the act of creating her was Hardy's 'greatest tribute to the possibilities of human existence'. His first wife had a different view: 'He understands only the women he *invents* – the others not at all.'[14]

There are many excellent 'cradle to grave' biographies of Thomas Hardy.[15] We do not need another one. But the central importance of the women in his life is not always apparent when their appearances are dispersed across a comprehensive study that also takes on other influences, publication history and so forth. In addition, recent research, often by amateur Hardy enthusiasts, has added to the picture. It is also the case that the stories told by women who knew Hardy, or whose foremothers knew him, have often been ignored or simply not believed. For all these reasons, this 'partial life' of Hardy takes a fresh approach. Like *Tess of the D'Urbervilles*, it is divided by 'phases'. Phase one views him through the eyes of the strong women – some forty of them, along with one man – who were formative of his life and writing, then phase two reads his major novels prior to *Tess* from the point of view of the women he created. And in phase three, we meet his greatest loves, including the fictional Tess, the ghost of his first wife, and the actress who brought Tess into three dimensions. Most chapters are named for the women, many of whom did not have a voice and who were often deliberately omitted from Hardy's self-ghosted autobiography. This book seeks to bring them back to life: it is not only a new biography of Thomas Hardy, but also a glimpse into the hard lives of schoolteachers and other working women in the Victorian age.

'The doll of English fiction must be demolished, if England is to have a school of fiction at all', Hardy wrote.[16] But the women in his life paid a large price for his creation of heroines who are flesh and blood, not dolls. This, then, is the story of how the magnificent fictional women he invented would not have been possible without the hardship and hardiness of the real ones who shaped his passions and his imagination.

PHASE THE FIRST

The women who made him

CHILDHOOD

CHAPTER 1

Elizabeth Downton

Tender women that are bred delicately must not be governed
after the same manner that hardy country women must, for
one is commonly weak stomached, but the other is strong.[1]

It was a hot June day in rural Dorset in 1840, and a young
woman was in the throes of a difficult first labour. Her name
was Jemima, and she was reliant upon the care of her midwife,
who also happened to be a close neighbour and a friend. As was
conventional with difficult labours, a doctor was finally called
to assist with the last stages of the delivery, and the baby, a tiny,
delicate boy, was presumed dead and cast aside. But then a
minor miracle occurred. The midwife looked again for signs of
life and declared: 'Dead! Stop a minute: he's alive enough, sure!'[2]

The baby was named after his father, and his surname seemed
apt for the fighting spirit shown in the first few moments of his
life. He was Thomas Hardy. Tom or Tommy to his family.[3]
Hardy in spirit, though not in body. He would come to appreciate the qualities of resilience and strength that were
connotations of his family name – the impoverished but flinty
hero of his first novel was called Will Strong.

Another hot day while the baby slept in his crib, a large snake slithered in and curled itself around the boy's breast, 'comfortably asleep like himself'.[4] His mother gently removed it. The baby had come to no harm. Hardy owed his lucky escapes not to men, such as the doctor who had pronounced him dead, but to women: his mother and his midwife.

It seems likely that Hardy was born premature; he was delivered five and a half months after the marriage of his parents. He was also conceived out of wedlock, a fact that he tried to conceal, though unplanned pregnancies and their consequences became a theme of his work.

He was born in his family's cottage home in the tiny village of Higher Bockhampton, three miles from the county town of Dorchester. There were just eight houses in the hamlet. His midwife, or 'nurse' as he preferred to call her, lived with her soldier husband in one of the cottages; the other inhabitants were elderly, retired people, so much so that the hamlet was known as 'Veterans' Valley'.[5] Hardy preferred the more romantic nickname 'Cherry Alley', after the trees that lined the village street.[6] His family lived in the last cottage on the south side of the lane, close to the woods and the heath. It was a beautiful and isolated spot.

Hardy's nurse was called Elizabeth Downton, known locally as Lizzie. She was a hard-working, fearless woman, of the kind that Hardy would grow to admire. The day after her own baby was born, she walked eighteen miles without a complaint. She was, in his words, 'an excellent nurse, much in demand; of infinite kind-heartedness, humour, and quaintness'.[7] Midwifery was traditionally an all-female practice and a valuable way for local women to make a living. Wisdom regarding birthing practice was handed down through the female line. Midwives usually relied on word-of-mouth recommendations, though in more sophisticated places such as London, some printed their own business cards.

But in the eighteenth century, male doctors and male midwives, often taught by celebrity obstetrician Dr William Smellie, began infiltrating the delivery room, branding forceps (with disastrous effect in Laurence Sterne's famous novel *Tristram Shandy*). In rural Dorset, male doctors called 'surgeons' were only used in emergencies, as was the case with Thomas Hardy. Many rural midwives such as Elizabeth Downton were regarded as the village sage or wise woman. They gave advice on fertility, birth control, unplanned pregnancies, and marital and courtship issues. One day a local woman came to Lizzie for help. She had seen the ghost of a woman whom she was convinced was the spirit of her sweetheart's dead wife. Lizzie asked how long the wife had been dead and was told that it had been many years. 'Oh, that were no ghost', she said. 'Now if she'd only been dead a month or two, and you were making her husband your fancy-man, there might have been something in your story. But Lord, much can she care about him after years and years in better company!' Hardy, self-confessedly superstitious and fond of 'creepy stories', lapped up such folklore. Another story concerned a local girl who was engaged to be married and was given a watch from her betrothed. Soon after, he died of consumption, and in time the girl found herself another sweetheart. On the day of her wedding, she heard the watch *'going in her box'* though it had not been touched for years.[8]

Lizzie remained close to the family, and to the baby she had saved from death. She would defend Jemima in 'clashing cases' – presumably neighbours' quarrels. Throughout his life, Thomas Hardy viewed Lizzie Downton as a spiritual matriarch. He acknowledged that without her 'estimable commonsense', he might 'never have walked the earth'.[9] She could not have been further from the stereotypical, gin-swilling incompetent immortalised as Mrs Gamp in Charles Dickens' *Martin Chuzzlewit*.

In narrating the story of his birth, Hardy was keen to name

his saviour. It is telling that in his novels, every servant girl, no matter how lowly or insignificant, is named. Women were at the core of his childhood. His own mother, and his grandmother who lived in an annex to the cottage, were the most formative influence on the young boy. They nursed and raised the children – Tommy, then Mary, Henry and Kate. They ran the household: cooked, cleaned and sewed. And when they had a rare moment to sit down, they were storytellers.

CHAPTER 2

Elizabeth Swetman

Elizabeth Swetman owned thirty gowns.[1] Or so her grandson, Thomas Hardy, wanted the world to know. It is a curious detail in the life of a woman who was to endure much poverty and hardship, as if somehow her wardrobe was a talisman to protect her from harm. According to Hardy, his maternal grandmother was tall, handsome, and 'an omnivorous reader' who built herself a library with 'a stock of books of exceptional extent for a yeoman's daughter'.[2] He claimed that she knew the essays of Addison and Steele by heart, was familiar with the novels of Richardson and Fielding, and had read deeply in Milton's *Paradise Lost* and John Bunyan's *The Pilgrim's Progress*.

This portrayal of Betsy Swetman as a cultivated and finely dressed woman was not entirely accurate. Thomas Hardy was always sensitive about his origins. On his father's side, he claimed descent from the 'le Hardys of Jersey', and even considered changing his name to le Hardy.[3] His ancestors, he claimed, 'had all the characteristics of an old family of spent social energies'.[4] The idea of 'an old family' would always be important to Hardy, the self-made man.

He was seven years old when his maternal grandmother died, but her memory was kept alive by her five devoted daughters.

She was born Elizabeth Swetman, known to her family as Betty
or Betsy, and christened in the early spring of 1778 in the picturesque Dorset village of Melbury Osmond, seven miles from the
town of Yeovil. The name Melbury derives from the old English
word for 'multi-coloured hills'. The cluster of stone cottages with
thatched roofs were strewn with green creepers that turned
red-gold in the autumn. The winding road, flanked by grassy
banks, led to a shallow stream and a footbridge. In the spring
and summer, the village was covered in flowers and ferns.

Betsy was the fourth of five children. Tragedy struck when
her brother Thomas drowned in a well at the age of four when
she was a baby.[5] In the extended family, there were yeoman
farmers and even an uncle, Christopher Childs, who reached
into the wider world: he was among a group of 'gentlemen' who
founded a regional newspaper of liberal leaning, the *West Briton*.[6]
Thomas Hardy was proud that in old age Childs's portrait was
painted by a famous artist, Sir Charles Eastlake.[7] But most of
the family were confined to humble lives: a grandfather on poor
relief, father and brother working as agricultural labourers, sisters
who went into domestic service and, like many women of their
status and class, were never heard of again.[8] In the census of
1801, Betsy, twenty-three and not yet married, was living with
her parents and listed as a spinner.

The census identified most of the women living in the village
of Melbury Osmond as weavers, spinners or spoolers. The textile
cottage industry was a way for women to earn a wage; indeed,
the word 'spinster' derives from unmarried spinners, whose 'work'
supposedly made them financially independent, though in reality
they were paid a pittance. It was, nevertheless, supplementary
income for homes in which the menfolk relied on seasonal
agricultural labour. The work of spinning the Dorset wool or
linen flax on a wheel at home was an activity that was safe to
do with children nearby. Melbury Osmond was known for the

manufacture of 'dowlas', a strong coarse linen. There was also lively trade in horn buttons and plated buckles. Betsy possibly worked for a linen manufacturer called Thomas Cave, who ran a textiles business in the village.[9] One can imagine her spinning the flax into linen on her wheel, treadling with her feet as she wet the flax with her fingers to ensure the yarn was smooth and strong.

The village, its honey-coloured church and the local mansion, Melbury House, exerted a strong pull on Hardy's imagination. The Duke of Monmouth, illegitimate son of King Charles II, allegedly took refuge in the home of his Swetman ancestors during his rebellion. The legend inspired one of Hardy's short stories, 'The Duke's Reappearance'.[10] He was also enchanted by a family tradition that told of two Swetman sisters, Grace and Leonarde, narrowly avoiding being raped by soldiers after the Battle of Sedgemoor. They escaped from the upstairs rooms via a back staircase which led to the orchard.

Melbury Osmond was also notorious for being the home of an infamous devil mask, the 'Dorset Ooser'. Every child in the village was terrified of the Ooser.[11] The mask was carved from a single piece of wood, with a separate, moving jaw, held by leather hinges; human hair, a beard and a pair of bullock's horns completed the ghastly contraption. Hardy used it to frame his short story, 'The First Countess of Wessex'.

Another family anecdote that fascinated Hardy was a story about a fortune teller who set up home on land that, generations before, had been leased to the Swetmans. Betsy's father went on a Sunday to order the woman to pack up and leave: 'If you don't take yourself off, I'll have you burnt as a witch!' Calmly, she took his silk handkerchief out of his pocket and threw it into her fire, saying 'if that burn I burn'. The flames curled around the hanky, but it did not burn. John Swetman was so impressed by her magic that he left her alone. For Hardy, the tale was an illustration not only of folk traditions, but also of his great-grandfather's ill temper. Betsy's father was 'stern', 'severe' and 'unyielding'.[12]

Soon after the death of her mother, Betsy, now twenty-six, 'clandestinely' married a servant called George Hand. According to Hardy's recollections, her father was so angry about the marriage that he cut her off and never saw her again.[13] An important omission in this account was that Betsy was eight months pregnant when she married.[14] In poor rural communities, babies conceived out of wedlock were common enough; a pregnant bride was seen as a fertile bride, and not necessarily a source of shame or embarrassment. Nevertheless, this pregnancy and the pattern it set for her female children, would have serious ramifications. The little girl, Maria, was sent to Puddletown to live with her grandparents.

Betsy gave birth to another six children, though the marriage was deeply unhappy. Hand was a violent alcoholic and a womaniser. He took mistresses and refused to let his legitimate children be baptised, forcing Betsy to have the ceremony done privately. He died in 1822, probably of consumption, and left his wife penniless with six children to provide for, the youngest of them only six years old. He had been on poor relief; after his death, Betsy received a monthly 'dole' which was reduced as each of the children reached the age of thirteen, when they could be sent out to work.

When Betsy was banished by her father, she was said to have been allowed to take her books and clothes with her. Another of the traditions surrounding Hardy's grandmother was an interest in medical literature: 'From the old medical books in her possession she doctored half the village.'[15] Her 'sheet-anchor' was Nicholas Culpeper's *Complete Herbal*, a ground-breaking medical and herbal manual, first published in the age of Queen Elizabeth I and written specifically for the layperson. Whereas most medical treatises were written in Latin, Culpeper used the

vernacular and his books were published cheaply as self-help
medical guides, aimed at the poor who could not afford to
consult physicians.

According to Hardy, Betsy's fascination with local history
made her into an authority, consulted by parson and sexton, on
the position of particular graves in the cemetery. But her 'bright
intelligence', he lamented, 'did not serve her in domestic life'.[16]
For some time after her daughters left home and married, she
lived with her youngest son, William, in a cottage in Puddletown,
but she left there soon after he married. What happened to her
comprehensive 'stock of books' and her thirty gowns is not
entirely clear – which suggests that the extent of her library and
wardrobe may have been one of Hardy's embellishments intended
to make his heritage seem more elevated than it really was. In
a letter dating from 1842, Betsy wrote down a list of possessions
that she wished to leave to her children. It does not show signs
of high learning, and there is no mention of gowns or books:

> The small feather bed is for Chris – mine for you with the
> bolster and pillows – as the feathers are not as good as Jemimas
> was – I told Jemima I had given you that looking glass your
> uncle Henery gave me she said she wished to have that – then
> here are they two little French pictures and two little ones besides
> you must do as you like with it – there seven sheets 5 good ones
> and 2 old ones.[17]

Earlier that year, she had written to her daughter Mary:

> it is a true saying that poverty seperates chiefest friends – and
> I should not have been poor if right had took its place – you
> wished me to let you know what beef I had att Christmas it
> was a small bit of lean cut of the leg or shene – it would have
> been quite dear att 3d.[18]

This is the only time we hear her voice, and the misery of her poverty and her loneliness is clear. Records show that in 1846, the year before she died, she was again collecting poor relief.[19]

Betsy's sons, Henry and William, inherited their father's hard drinking: they both spent time in prison for misdemeanours associated with alcohol abuse.[20] But her four daughters, Maria, Jemima, Mary and Martha, were determined to leave Melbury Osmond and forge better lives for themselves. Opportunities were scarce for bright but poor young women in rural communities. As we have seen, most of the women in the village of Melbury Osmond were in the rag trade, but there was another route to a way out of a life of poverty. At the bottom of the village, along the winding road which led from the honey-coloured church, past the ford, and next to the cottage where Betsy Swetman was raised, was the entrance to Melbury House, the seat of the Earl of Ilchester, and the family of Fox-Strangways.

CHAPTER 3

Lady Susan Fox-Strangways

Melbury House exercised a powerful force over Thomas Hardy's imagination; in particular because of his fascination with the powerful women who had shaped its destiny. One of the most spectacular mansions in south-west England, dating from the fifteenth century, it boasted a striking hexagonal tower, which provided views of its wooded parkland and surrounding countryside overlooking the Vale of Blackmore. Unusually in an age in which grand family estates were passed down the male line, in 1726 Melbury was inherited jointly by two sisters, Susanna and Elizabeth Strangways.

When Elizabeth died, Melbury passed entirely to Susanna. Even though she had married, the property did not pass into her husband's hands, as was customary before the Married Women's Property Act of 1882. All of the estate income was to be paid to Susanna 'as if she were sole and unmarryed'. Her husband, Thomas Horner, was clearly and firmly instructed not to 'intermeddle' in her financial affairs.[1] He also took on her name, Strangways.

Lady Susanna's marriage to Thomas Horner was unhappy. Two sons died in infancy, and their only surviving child was a daughter, Elizabeth. In order to get away from her husband, she took her daughter to the Continent, where she engaged in an illicit affair with the dashing Henry Fox, younger brother of the wealthy Stephen Fox of Redlynch in Somerset. Henry, who had squandered his inheritance, was on the run from his creditors. Susanna paid them off, writing to his brother that she aimed to 'improve' him. Probably with Henry's collusion, Lady Susanna concocted a plot to marry her young daughter to Stephen, despite the fact that for ten years he had been the lover of the courtier and diarist John Hervey, eldest son among the seventeen children of the first Earl of Bristol and his second wife. Hervey was the most notorious bisexual of the age, satirised by the poet Alexander Pope under the names 'Lord Fanny' and 'Sporus' (the latter being an allusion to the husband of the Emperor Nero). Stephen and Hervey were so deeply infatuated that they set up home together, though the relationship was beginning to cool, Stephen feeling that he was too unsophisticated for the urbane Hervey, the latter reassuring him: 'I should like you rusty better than any other body polish'd.'[2]

Though Stephen Fox's heart belonged to men, and he was more than twice the age of Elizabeth, he was attracted to the match, probably on account of her vast inheritance. Thomas Hardy based his short story 'The First Countess of Wessex' on the family scandal. It glosses over the homosexual background, but makes no bones about money: 'Betty' is described as so rich that it was 'a misfortune that the child would inherit so much wealth. She would be a mark for all the adventurers in the kingdom.'[3] Indeed, Elizabeth had interest from the Duke of Leeds and Lord Middlesex, but her mother had set her sights on Stephen Fox, despite the fierce opposition of her husband. In 1735, Lady Susanna arranged a clandestine marriage in the library of Fox's London home. Lord Hervey was furious and broke off the long-term affair. In Hardy's melodramatic fictionalisation of the story, Betty's father is so distraught at the news of the marriage that he crashes to the floor in an apoplectic fit. Elizabeth, who was only thirteen, returned home with her mother to wait until she was sixteen, when she began her new life as Fox's wife, eventually gaining the title first Countess of Ilchester. Despite the scandal, and the opposition of Elizabeth's father, the couple went on to have nine children together and appeared to share a contented life, first at Fox's country house, Redlynch, and then at Melbury, where they moved following Lady Susanna's death. Fox took on his wife's name, as had Elizabeth's father before him.

Melbury House had been greatly modernised and improved by Susanna. Stonework was cleaned and repaired, the roof retiled, and interior improvements were made, pictures cleaned and floors re-laid. Payments in July 1742 include £8 to carpenter Joseph Childs, for wainscoting the full '120 yard[s]' of the gallery.[4] Joseph Childs was Thomas Hardy's great-great-grandfather. Housekeeping accounts from the house also reveal that a 'Betty Childs' was paid five shillings a day to wash and mangle, and nine shillings a day for helping to brew beer.[5]

Elizabeth Fox-Strangways' eldest child, a daughter called Susan, initiated a scandal of her own when she ran away from home to marry a handsome and highly regarded but penniless Irish actor called William O'Brien. The disgraced couple, ostracised from their family, emigrated to America. Their luck changed when, through the good offices of the Governor of New York, William was appointed Provost-Master-General of the Bermudas. Eventually, the family forgave them and they returned to England. O'Brien briefly re-established his theatrical career, this time as a playwright, but then they retired to Dorset. One day, the couple drove to Stinsford, a village just outside of Dorchester, fifteen miles from Melbury, and saw a dilapidated old manor house next door to the church. It belonged to the Fox-Strangways family, but was in bad repair. The couple fell in love with it and made it their home for the rest of their lives.[6]

Though Hardy was fascinated by all the ladies of Melbury House, he was especially enthralled by the great romance between the aristocratic lady and the Irish actor. The couple were childless, yet remained deeply and passionately in love until old age. After her husband's death, Lady Susan was distraught, telling a niece that William had been 'the object of my thoughts, affections and anxieties since nineteen years old, and must until death be the object of my regrets'.[7]

Lady Sue, as she was known locally, and her husband were very popular in the neighbourhood. An old man who had once been an under-gardener at Stinsford told a fascinated Thomas Hardy that the O'Briens 'kept a splendid house, with plenty of beer for the servants'.[8] Christmas festivities were elaborate, with the church choristers invited in to sing carols on Christmas Eve. Even as an elderly widow, Lady Sue would listen to the Christmas carols from the top of the stairs while the singers stood below her in the hall. She would then give a supper of beef and beer. One of the choristers who remembered her well was Thomas Hardy's father.[9]

From a very young age, Hardy felt deeply connected to the Strangways family. Not only were his grandfather and father members of the Stinsford choir who performed at the house, but both his grandmothers had seen and admired handsome William O'Brien and told stories of the famously devoted couple. As a boy attending services at Stinsford Church, he observed with 'romantic interest' the loving plaques erected in their honour on the north wall of the church. They had been put there by his Hardy grandfather, who was also given the job of making the vault that Lady Susan had requested be 'just large enough for our two selves only'.[10]

Polite society had been shocked by the marriage on the grounds of class miscegenation, and it was this aspect of the love story that stirred the feelings of Thomas Hardy. Lady Susan, an accomplished actress herself, had met O'Brien while performing amateur theatricals at Holland House, the home of her cousin Henry Fox. Though O'Brien was cultivated and his manners genteel, he was still considered to be low-born and Irish. People sneered that he played the gentleman so well on the stage that he fooled everyone off-stage. Horace Walpole thought the union 'the completion of disgrace – even a footman were preferable . . . I could not have believed that Lady Susan would have stooped so low.'[11] Hardy was irritated by Walpole's condescending comments, writing that 'in these modern days, the *stooping* might have been viewed inversely'.[12] To his mind, O'Brien was an 'accomplished and well-read man', whose marriage had 'annihilated a promising career'. In addition to writing the short story about Elizabeth, Hardy also penned two poems about Lady Susan and William O'Brien, one of which imagines him returning to the stage for one last night, while his devoted wife watches him, secretly, from the audience. Entitled 'The Noble Lady's Tale c. 1790', it ends with the 'yellowing marble' of the memorial tablet that Hardy's grandfather raised in 'Mellstock Quire' (i.e. Stinsford church), from which the 'two joined hearts enchased' meet the eyes of the congregation and give assurance that 'She knew her actor best'.[13]

The union also helped Hardy to discover one of his great themes, that of 'the poor man and his lady', as he titled his first novel. The O'Briens were living proof that true and lasting love did not discriminate between social class and status. The great country house and its symbiotic relationship to the villages and inhabitants was another theme that consumed his thinking, and shaped his art. The Strangways women had set their own standard. Exceptional in holding the power and the purse strings, they improved their estates, went their own way, and retained their names. And they were aware that the smooth running of their estates was dependent on good relations with the people who ran the household – the entourage of indoor and outdoor servants, the stewards, butlers, housekeepers, cooks and gardeners.

But Thomas Hardy's connection with Stinsford House ran a little closer to home than he cared to admit. He did his best not to reveal that his beloved mother, Jemima, was at the age of thirteen sent into domestic service with the Fox-Strangways family. She became a valued and trusted servant for thirteen years of her life. Her intelligence and her strength of character served her well, and enabled her to see a life very different from the one in which she was born – to enter another world that she was determined to impress upon her susceptible son.

CHAPTER 4

Jemima Hand

Jemima's path to becoming a respected servant at Stinsford House was not straightforward. Her early life was marred by poverty and violence, and her parents' chaotic and unhappy union left her with a deep fear of the institution of marriage, which she would pass on to her four children. The departure of Maria Hand to her grandparents in Puddletown left Jemima in the role of oldest sister and sometimes effective mother to her younger siblings.

While there are no explicit details about George Hand's brutality towards his family, there were hints of dark times. Hardy recalled his mother's deep emotional stress at the memory of her upbringing: 'Jemima saw during girlhood and young womanhood some very stressful experiences of which she could never speak in her maturer years without pain.'[1] Hardy's second wife, Florence, told the researcher Richard Little Purdy about the domestic violence endured by Betsy, and recounted that it was something Hardy had often talked about during their marriage.[2] Drinking and domestic violence went hand in hand, especially in rural areas marred by poverty, seasonal work, and unemployment.[3] If it were true that Hardy often talked about his grandfather's domestic violence it suggests that it left its own profound mark on him, and aroused his deepest pity for his grandmother and mother.

Jemima was in her ninth year when he died, old enough to see and hear the violence, and to be determined to avoid marriage at all costs. According to Hardy's second wife, Jemima heard from her mother the story of how she insisted on burying her husband alongside his mistress, and how her father had refused to allow his children to be baptised – details that Hardy would later use as plot points in his novels.[4] Few could blame Jemima for a jaundiced view of men; when one of her younger newly-wed sisters was beaten by her husband, Jemima took quick and effective action.

In the *Life*, Hardy recalled that Jemima turned to books to mollify her unhappy childhood. Like her mother, she immersed herself in 'every book she could lay hands on'. Dante was her favourite author. She was the exceptional child of the Hand family, the one with 'unusual ability and judgment'.[5] The girl who might have gone far if circumstances had been kinder. She was small in stature, with a Roman nose, grey eyes, and chestnut hair. What she lacked in conventional beauty, she more than compensated for in energy and vitality. Hardy recorded that her beauty lay in movement: 'walking buoyant through life: strangers approaching her from behind imagined themselves, even when she was nearly seventy, about to overtake quite a young woman.'[6]

Hardy made no mention of his mother's schooling, but one of the legacies of Lady Susanna Strangways Horner was her contribution to education for the poor in Melbury Osmond, Jemima's village. During her lifetime, Lady Susanna paid the salary of the schoolmaster, and in her will she decreed that she wished to provide a schoolhouse and a residence for the master.

At the age of thirteen, like her maternal aunts before her, Jemima was sent into domestic service. She began her new life as a maidservant for the Revd Charles Redlynch Fox-Strangways,

the brother of Lady Susan. He was rector of St Mary's Church
in the village of Maiden Newton. He and his wife had eight
children, so Jemima possibly lent a hand as a nursery maid.

Maidservants were notoriously unreliable, and most stayed
for months rather than years, often viewing the job as a means
to earn a living before finding a husband. Others found themselves pregnant, and were sacked or ran away. However, servants
who worked for the Strangways family were treated well, and
many of them stayed for several years. Lady Susan's devotion to
her maids is evident in her letters.[7] Trusted servants were treated
like members of the family; they were given hand-me-down
clothes, presents, and sometimes personal legacies when a family
member died. There was even a servants' library at Redlynch.

If a servant was considered intelligent, hard-working, and,
above all, honest, they were moved around the extended family,
which is what happened to Jemima Hardy when the Reverend
Charles died in 1837. Jemima finally landed a job at Stinsford
House, once home to Lady Susan, now lived in by the Reverend
Edward Murray, brother-in-law to the Earl of Ilchester. Hardy
could never publicly admit that his mother had been a servant:
the closest he came was to say that she had aspirations to be a
London cook. Jemima had spent time in London, more than
likely with the rector's family; Hardy recalled the church she
attended, St James's. He also claimed that his mother spent time,
before she was married, in Weymouth, where she once saw the
young Queen Victoria.

Jemima's experience as a valued servant, and her exposure to
a very different social class, shaped her vision and increased her
ambition. By now, she had been in domestic service for thirteen
years. Stinsford House led directly to the church, and the
Reverend Murray, her new employer, was a keen musician and
a supporter of the Stinsford choir. The leader of the choir, a
man called Thomas Hardy, would appear at the church every

Sunday, with his sons, James and young Tom, and a friend, James Dart. They would take up their position in the west gallery. The boys played violin and the father bass viol (cello).

Jemima, always sensitive to fine clothing, recalled the three Hardys arriving at church on a Sunday morning wearing top hats, stick-up shirt collars, dark blue coats with great collars and gilt buttons, deep cuffs and black silk stocks (neckerchiefs). There was something of the dandy in the younger son, with his dark curly hair, and blue eyes. Years later, Jemima would describe her attraction to his 'blue swallow tailed coat with gilt embossed buttons . . . red and black flowered waistcoat, Wellington boots and French-blue trousers'.[8]

Hardy romanticised the first meeting between his parents in a charming poem he called 'A Church Romance': 'One strenuous viol's inspirer seemed to throw / A message from his string to her below, / Which said: "I claim thee as my own forthright!"'[9] Jemima was fond of music and dancing, which strengthened their attachment. But it wasn't long before she fell into the trap of so many female domestic servants and found herself pregnant but unmarried. Her sweetheart, Thomas, proposed marriage, and was accepted. At the age of twenty-six (Hardy would add a year to her age, to cover the shame of conceiving a baby out of wedlock), her employment at Stinsford House came to an abrupt end.

CHAPTER 5

Mary Head

Jemima left domestic service for an establishment of her own: a modest cottage in the tiny hamlet of Higher Bockhampton. But she was not the only woman in the household. Also living in the cottage was her husband's mother, Mary. The cottage, perching on the edge of Puddletown Heath, had been her home for many years.

Hardy's grandmother was born Mary Head in the Berkshire village of Fawley. She had endured a miserable childhood, was orphaned at a young age, and did not like to talk about her early life. Hardy would recall that her memories of Fawley were so 'poignant' that once she had left home she could never bear to return to the village; an unimaginable thought to the boy who was devoted to the idea of childhood and home.[1] Mary spent some time in Reading, though Hardy is reticent about his grandmother's reasons for living in the town; there is a possibility that she was the same Mary Head who in 1796 found herself pregnant with an illegitimate child, which she gave away to be adopted.[2]

In 1799, Mary married Thomas Hardy, a builder, in Puddletown. By 1801, she had given birth to a daughter. They would go on to have seven children. They moved into the cottage at Higher

Bockhampton that had been built by her husband's father. At that time, it stood alone under the heath, surrounded by open countryside, three miles north-east of Dorchester. Built from cob, and thatched with wheat straw and local hazel, it was originally just three rooms: a family room and two bedrooms. The surroundings were as beautiful as the size was modest. Wild honeysuckle climbed the wall, and red roses, lilacs and herbs abounded. It stood in an acre of ground, with a fine apple orchard, where the Hardy family grew local cultivars – Gascoyne's Scarlet, Golden Pippin and Bockhampton Sweet. They kept a pig, hens and beehives, and benefited from their own well at the front of the cottage. Thorncombe Wood lay to the south, close to Rushy Pond and Black Heath. A path led to Puddletown Forest, a magical and mysterious place. To the east was the heath, beyond which lay the Frome Valley, which could be viewed from an ancient burial mound called Rainbarrow.

Mary was closest to her youngest son, named after his father, Thomas. He shared his mother's easy temperament and gentleness of manner. He was still living with his mother in the cottage when his father died in 1837. When he married Jemima, he moved his new wife into the main part of the house, building an annex next door so that Mary had her own front door and living accommodation. She had her privacy, but she was very much part of the family. Now she had to play second fiddle to the new mistress of the home she had lived in for almost forty years, though it was by no means an unusual arrangement. She was called 'Granny' and was a loving presence to her grandchildren.

Mary managed the accounts for the family business, and cooked meals on her range. The bread oven and ranges were fired by gorse (or furze, as it was known in the West Country), collected from the heath. The bread oven could hold as many as fourteen loaves, and she baked delicious cakes, pies and milk puddings.

Mary was a good storyteller. She would gather the children around the fire and they would listen, wide-eyed. One of her most vivid memories concerned the beheading of Marie Antoinette in 1793. She could remember what she was doing and where she was when she heard the news of the doomed queen: she was ironing a dress. Years later, she recalled the exact pattern of the muslin chemise. One hot thundery day, Granny remarked to the young boy: 'it was like this in the French Revolution.' She told stories of the Reign of Terror and the execution of King Louis. Later, she raised her children in the spectre of the Napoleonic Wars, fretting about the threat of invasion. If it happened, the French army would land on the south coast, close to home. Mary's husband signed up as a volunteer in the local militia. Granny's stories of the Napoleonic Wars would inspire her grandson to write his novel *The Trumpet-Major* – set in Dorset at the time when the invasion fear was at its height – and his interminable verse-drama *The Dynasts*.

The call to arms for the militia was specific in its requirements: all volunteers should be respectable and reliable, of the utmost good character.[3] Thomas, a local builder and owner of property, was a suitable candidate, except that, unknown to the authorities, he was involved in smuggling. The cottage's isolation made it an ideal location as a halfway house for smugglers, and in his private notebooks Hardy made detailed notes about his grandfather's nefarious activities.[4] In the dead of night, a whiplash across the window would awaken him, and he would go outside in his dressing gown to find not a soul around but a heap of barrels outside his door. Known as 'tubs', each one contained 4 gallons of brandy. Hardy's grandfather would set to work, stowing them away in a darkened closet. The next evening groups of 'dark, long-bearded fellows would arrive, & carry off the tubs in twos & fours slung over their shoulders'. After a while, the smugglers grew bolder, and would arrive in the day, frightening

Mary, who insisted that her husband should stop the racket. He agreed, but only after the christening party for one of his children, where they enjoyed a 'washing pan of pale brandy'. The smugglers only stopped when another cottage was built next door.

It was surely Mary who told the story to Tom, describing the strong smell of spirits pervading the house, and the barrels with wooden hoops. Hardy wrote that he remembered one of the tubs, which had been refashioned into a bucket. Many years later, in Jemima's time, a woman known as Mother Rogers would call at the Hardy household, her large hips bulging with brandy canisters made from bullocks' bladders, and ask if any of 'it' was wanted cheap.[5]

Mary told stories of new country dances and old, 'wild pouset-ting and allemanding', and of May Day with its striped pole decorated at the top with flower garlands, where the village girls whirled round, hoping to find husbands. And of winters when the snow was so deep that in order to get to church she had to walk on top of snow-encrusted hedges. Then there was the terrifying gibbet which she passed on her way from Fawley to Wantage. In her mind's eye she could still see it as it creaked and swayed under the flash of lightning. In her time, male criminals were 'gibbeted', that is to say, the body was left to hang in a cage as a warning, stiffened, clanging as the cage turned in the wind. The smell of the decaying bodies was revolting, and the corpses would be eaten by birds and bugs until only a skeleton remained. The practice was abolished in 1834, but the memory of it endured in the rural imagination. In *Jude the Obscure*, Hardy would use the gibbet as an important plot point, and he would also pay tribute to his granny by using the name of her birthplace, Fawley, as the hero's surname.

Hardy remembered Mary as 'gentle and kindly'. In his poem about her, she is sensitive, dreamy, almost other-worldly:

With cap-framed face and long gaze into the embers—
    We seated around her knees—
She would dwell on such dead themes, not as one who
  remembers,
    But rather as one who sees.[6]

In his memory, she is always 'Smiling into the fire', as he phrased it in a superb little poem remembering the footworn 'ancient floor' of the cottage: Granny was connected with the hearth and home, a warm and stable influence on the Hardy homestead, and yet somehow lost in her own imaginative world.[7] Later, Hardy would immortalise her as the hero's granny, Mrs Martin, in his novel *Two on a Tower*: a 'woman of eighty, in a large mob cap, under which she wore a little cap to keep the other clean'. She would sit staring into a wood fire, entranced by the flames: 'She was gazing into the flames with her hands upon her knees, quietly re-enacting in her brain certain of the long chain of episodes, pathetic, tragical, humorous, which had constituted the parish history for the last sixty years.' During her naps, she would return 'straight back' to 'her old country, again, as usual'.[8]

Glimpses of Mary's voice and dialect can be heard in Granny Martin, 'hardly a soul would be left alive to say to me dog how art?' and 'tell Hannah [the maid] to stir her stumps and serve supper'. She bewails the fact that she is not native to the village: ''Twas a pity I didn't take my poor name off this earthly calendar and creep under ground sixty long years ago, instead of leaving my own county to come here!'[9] She bakes special puddings, which she warms in a 'pipkin' before the wood fire, and, like Mary, gives room to the local church choir to hold rehearsals.

Mary had enough vigour to participate in her grandchildren's games. On a Sunday when it was too wet to walk to church, young Tommy would wrap himself in a tablecloth and read the service of Morning Prayer, standing on a chair, preaching to his

cousin, with 'his grandmother representing the congregation'.[10]
The family consensus was that he would grow up to be a parson.

In one of his earliest poems of memory, he describes a walk
with his granny in which she stops to describe the homestead
as it had been fifty years ago. It was then a wild, uncultivated
place, overgrown with 'bramble bushes, furze and thorn' where
'Snakes and efts / Swarmed in the summer days, and nightly
bats / Would fly about our bedrooms.' It was Granny who would
bequeath to him one of his treasured themes: that of Old Dorset,
with its ancient customs and traditions, and a concern for a
fast-disappearing way of life. Now, after fifty years, 'change has
marked / The face of all things'. Back then, there was just the
one cottage, the house that 'stood quite alone'.[11]

CHAPTER 6

Mary Hardy

Most of the women in Hardy's early life worked hard for a living. Rural communities depended upon female labour, and even when women married and had children, they were still expected to earn their crust and contribute to the family expenses.[1] Jemima Hardy, like her sisters, was the beneficiary of the demand for out-sourced labour. According to her son, she was 'exceptionally skilled' in 'tambouring' gloves and 'mantua making'.[2] Glove-making had long been a thriving cottage industry in the West Country.[3] 'Tambouring' was a skilled and delicate art: gloves would be stretched over a drum, or tambour, allowing for the gloveress to embroider the fabric. Typically, bag-women distributed the gloves to female outworkers in their homes for sewing and embroidering, before collecting them to be sold. As for mantua-making, several of Jemima's handmade gowns survive, among which is a sprigged muslin dress, embroidered with delicate flowers, which suggests her tiny frame and trim figure. When it was time for her son to be baptised, Jemima made and embroidered his christening robe.

When he was aged one, Jemima gave birth to another baby, a little girl called Mary. Tommy was still delicate and sickly, and his parents feared that he might not survive childhood. Shortly after Mary's birth, her maternal grandmother, Betsy wrote: 'I hope the little girl will not be so tiresome as Tomey'.[4] They would become extremely close siblings. After her death, Hardy would look back on their childhood, where she was robust and healthy, a country girl climbing apple trees, 'her foot near mine on the bending limb, / Laughing, her young brown hand awave.'[5]

For ten years, until another sibling arrived, it was just the two of them, the closest of companions. While Hardy remembered them climbing trees together, Mary recalled games with a dolls' tea service, suggesting that he happily entered into the kind of imaginary play more usually associated with little girls. She adored her brother unconditionally and remained one of his closest friends and allies. She took his side and she kept his secrets. Hardy's view of childhood was Wordsworthian, and he regarded his sister with the same love that William felt for Dorothy Wordsworth; their bond was almost a sacred one. Later, he confessed that she was 'almost my only companion in child-hood'.[6] It was their closeness in age, and their similar interests and temperaments, that bound them so tightly; like him, Mary was introspective and shy by nature.

Though Tommy loved playing outdoors, the family parlour was the heart of the household. In the centre of the room was a large inglenook fireplace, where water was boiled for tea, and food prepared. The warmth from the fire heated the bedrooms above. Hardy shared a bedroom (perhaps even a bed) with his sister. In his earliest years, and while his father was at work as a builder, he was surrounded by a household of loving women. Jemima's unmarried sister Mary had been brought in to help raise the small children, and it was they, with Granny's help, who picked vegetables from the kitchen garden, did the laundry, and supervised the children's education.

Tommy soon showed signs of precocity, which did not go unmissed by his doting mother. It was sister Mary who recorded, for posterity, on the copy of his first book, that her brother could read by the age of three.[7] But if he could read by such an early age, it was because he had access to books. The book was a collection of woodcuts and verses for children, entitled *The Cries of London*. It opens 'Come buy, come buy, for sell I must, / Rosemary and briar so sweet.'

Perhaps Jemima's fond memories of her time spent in London inspired her choice of book, but it was also a reminder that there were worlds elsewhere, far from Bockhampton. Three-year-old Tommy could supposedly tune a violin, to the delight of his musical father. The next year, he was given a toy concertina, and the siblings were subsequently given a small piano, at which Mary quickly became proficient (later, she learnt to play the organ). Music moved Tommy to tears, though he would try to conceal his emotion, sometimes by dancing. Looking back, he was troubled by his own sensitivity, wondering if it suggested a tendency to depression, of which he was ashamed and afraid to confess.[8]

During Tommy and Mary's early years, Jemima endured a serious miscarriage. On her sickbed, she begged her husband to marry her sister Mary in the event of her death. He refused, which caused Jemima great distress. Jemima remained poorly through the mid-1840s, formative years for Tommy and Mary, and it was feared that she would not recover. The miscarriage was a turning point in her personality. Her son would later recall that her vitality, good humour and devotion were dampened by a quick temper that emerged as a result of her travails.

Jemima's wretched childhood and thwarted life fired her determination that her children's lives would be better than hers had been. She had limited resources at hand, but her exposure to the libraries of the Fox-Strangways, and the civilised way of life that the family represented, were enough to show her the way to achieve her ambitions. Music and nature were all very well, but books were sacred objects, to be revered and respected. And for a clever boy and girl, without connections or wealth, education was the only way out of a 'small, sleepy place'.[9]

Jemima's fierce ambition for her children and her strength of character have left an uneasy legacy. Photographic images perpetuate the myth of her as a shrew or a termagant. Her strong hooked nose and pointed chin have led to unflattering descriptions. But Victorian photography encouraged a sobriety and severity of style, and was not intended to flatter its subject. Jemima was not a conventional beauty like her sisters, but what mattered were her fierce intelligence and her strength of character – traits that her son acknowledged she had passed on to him.

The loveliest image of Jemima as a mother is a miniature watercolour painting by her daughter.[10] If Mary ever felt excluded from the intense bond between mother and son, she left no written record of the fact. Instead she honoured the union, which presents Jemima, Madonna-like, cradling her boy, but there is a third person in this image – that of the unseen artist, Mary.

CHAPTER 7

Mother Christmas

It is Christmas Eve. Outside the air is cold, and the sky is full of stars. On a lonely lane in the countryside, silver and black stemmed birches, pale grey boughs of beech and a dark-creviced elm appear as shadowy outlines, and all is dark as the grave. A Christmas peal of bells rings out across the valley. And a small band of local men make their way by foot to a cottage. They are members of the parish choir, and they aim to get 'drunk as lords' in preparation for one of their busiest nights of the year.

Inside, an inviting scene beckons. The long, low cottage with thatched roof has been decorated for yuletide. The main room is decked with holly and evergreens, and a huge bunch of mistletoe hangs from a beam. The mistress of the house sits on a brown settle by the glowing wood fire, where she is smoking ham and flitches of bacon. The man of the house nurses his barrel of cider, for his colleagues must be fortified for the long night ahead. On a side table there is a large pile of battered Christmas carol books. After the ninth cup of cider, the men finally choose the carols, fasten their mufflers around their neck, and wind wisps of hay around their boots. A thin film of snow has fallen, and the hay keeps the snowflakes from the inside of their boots.

The choir consists of three generations of male singers, and a family friend. The grandfather plays the violoncello, the other three play violin. They stick to strings, because strings are 'soul-lifters'.[1] A group of local boys accompany them to hold the music books, carry the horn lanterns, and help with the singing. And now, at almost midnight, the choir sets off: 'They passed forth into the quiet night an ancient and time-worn hymn, embodying a quaint Christianity in words orally transmitted from father to son through several generations down to the present characters, who sang them out right earnestly.'[2]

These are details from Thomas Hardy's first published novel, *Under the Greenwood Tree*, in which he reimagines his family's Christmas Eve custom of village carol singing. By the time he was born, his grandfather had died, but Hardy's father continued the tradition. In the weeks before the festival, they would prepare by choosing and copying down carols. They would invite the other members to their cottage in Bockhampton for supper on these occasions, and then on Christmas Eve there would be a special supper and 'plenty of liquor'.[3] They would play at every house in the village, arriving home not long before dawn feeling as wrung out as damp dishcloths ('malkins') before playing again in the west gallery of Stinsford Church on Christmas morning.

Though Hardy would later dismiss the tendency for critics to conflate his real life with his novels, he admitted in a preface to *Under the Greenwood Tree* that his story of the choir was 'intended to be a fairly true picture'.[4] In his self-ghosted biography, he reaffirmed that the Christmas Eve tradition was kept up by his own father, 'much as described in *Under the Greenwood Tree*'.[5] The 'ecclesiastical bandsmen' were paid very little, but it was a labour of love. The musicians had to pay for fiddle-strings, rosin and music paper. These were supplied by a pedlar who travelled from village to village. Consternation was caused one Christmas when the pedlar was snowed up on the downs, and the musicians were forced 'to make shift with whipcord and twine for strings'.[6]

Hardy evokes with tenderness those ancient Christmas hymns passed down through the generations. The leader of the choir, Old William Dewy, who would 'starve to death for music's sake' was based on the grandfather he had never known. William, an alien in the new world of church barrel organs played by women, feels the old traditions slipping away, and is powerless against the march of progress. Somehow, he intuits that Fancy Day, the youthful new schoolmistress and organ player, presents a danger, but he clings to the way of life that has sustained him over the years: 'At the close, waiting yet another minute he said in a clear loud voice, as he had said in the village at that hour and season for the previous forty years, "A Merry Christmas to ye!"'[7]

In *Under the Greenwood Tree*, the Dewy family, like the Hardys, are at the centre of the Christmas festivities. Once the Christmas Eve carol singing – the domain of the men – is over, the family holds a Christmas Night party. Here, as in the Hardy household, it is the matriarch who is the head of ceremonies. The flagstone floor is swept clean and sprinkled with sand, the best knives and forks are brought out, and the key is left out in the tap of the cider barrel instead of being carried in a pocket. Mother manages every detail, from presiding over the bacon and ham, which is smoked on the open fire, to trimming her husband's whiskers, twirling like a 'turnstile' to see that everything is creditable. She loves a Christmas party, like anyone, but she also knows that she will be the one expected to clear up the mess in the morning: 'But Lord, 'tis such a sight of heavy work next day! What with the dirty plates, and knives and forks, and dust and smother, and bits kicked off your furniture, and I don't know what all, why a body could a'most wish there were no such things as Christmases.'[8]

Years later, Thomas Hardy would return to the theme of

Christmas as a time of happiness, a season full of mead, music and dancing by the open hearth with its 'charred log-ends' in a childhood home that was 'the House of Hospitalities'.[9] But there is sadness in the nostalgia: in another Christmas poem, the image of how by the end of the night everyone would be on their knees, like the ox and ass in the stable of Jesus, is nothing more than a memory of a long-lost world.[10] Christmas was his father's season, when the local people remembered with fondness the Stinsford choir. But the house of hospitality was his mother's realm; the delicious aroma of that wood-smoked bacon was seared forever upon his memory.

CHAPTER 8

Maria Sparks

As soon as Tommy was old enough to walk, he was taken to visit his cousins in Puddletown, nestled in the Piddle Valley, surrounded by rolling hills and woodland. It was a two and a half mile walk across the heath to the small town, which was a bustling place, full of artisans and craftsmen. Jemima's eldest sister Maria had been the first of the Hand girls to be wed. In 1828, she married James Sparks, a cabinet maker from Dorchester, and they made their home in Puddletown. Maria had five children, and they lived in a double cob-and-thatch house in Duck Street, which faced the River Piddle. It was known locally as Sparks Corner.

The eldest child, Rebecca, was an accomplished dressmaker, working from home to aid the family income, and helped by her sisters, Emma and Martha. There were two sons, James and Nathaniel, with whom Hardy seems to have been on friendly terms. Martha was the most beautiful of the Sparks girls. She was also considered the cleverest sister. That is, until a sixth child came along.

Tommy and his sister Mary were often to be found at the Sparks' cottage. Mary fondly recalled their cheerful home 'with the sparkling river in front, and in the near distance the old

Church tower with the clock and rambling chimes, around which so many of our people are sleeping.'[1] St Mary the Virgin was a lovely Norman church, where Hardy's musical cousin, Nathaniel Sparks, played the cello. Nearby was the square, scene of weekly markets dating back to the thirteenth century and an annual fair, as ancient as the time of Henry VIII.

There were several pubs and taverns, giving the town what Hardy would describe as a reputation for hard drinking. All his Hand uncles, Henry, William and Christopher, labourers and bricklayers, were fond of a drink. Hardy's grandmother, Betsy, now living in Puddletown, worried about her sons, and saw at first hand the unpleasant effects of their hard drinking, notably at a pub called The Cat. As the saying went about Puddletown Sundays:

Into Church
Out of Church
Into Cat
Out of Cat
Into Piddle.[2]

There were three big houses on the outskirts of Puddletown: Athelhampton, Islington House and Waterston Manor. Athelhampton was a splendid Tudor mansion that in 1848 was sold to a man called George Wood, who set about restoring the house, employing Hardy's father as a builder. Hardy would later paint a watercolour of it, while architectural features and stories associated with the house can be detected in several of his works, notably a ballad of unhappy marriage, 'The Dame of Athelhall', and a short story called 'The Waiting Supper', in which, after a party in the Great Hall, the heroine Christine dances on the lawn in the arms of her beloved Nicholas, only for them to be parted, in characteristic Hardyesque manner, by irony of circumstance and difference of social class.[3] Elements of both Athelhampton and Waterston Manor, owned by the Strangways, also shaped the imagining of Weatherbury Farm in *Far from the Madding Crowd*.

The big houses could only run efficiently with servants, and many people from Puddletown found work at the estates. Money was tight in the Sparks household, and two of Hardy's cousins, Emma and Martha, were sent into service when they were of age. Maria Sparks, who kept a strict eye on her girls, was in poor health, suffering from consumption. In 1851, she gave birth to her last child, a daughter named Tryphena, and known to the family as an 'exhibition baby' because she was born in the year of the Great Exhibition in London.

There was an age gap of twenty-one years between Tryphena and her eldest sister, Rebecca. Nathaniel, the sibling nearest to her, was eight years her senior. Maria Sparks would have been forty-six when she gave birth to her last child. Old to have a child, but by no means impossible. Tryphena's biographer suggests that she was in fact sister Rebecca's illegitimate child, though there is little evidence to support this theory.[4] In rural and working-class communities, though, it was not uncommon for women to raise an illegitimate grandchild as their own offspring – a subject explored in Hardy's poem 'A Hurried Meeting'.

We will be meeting Tryphena again.

———

In 1847, Jemima's other sister, Mary, became betrothed to a bootmaker called John Antell. She had been a maidservant in Puddletown. He was a swarthy, handsome man, highly intelligent, though self-taught, who considered himself wasted in the boot business. Antell's shoe shop was in the High Street, and his workshop at the rear of the building became an unofficial meeting place of lively talk and learning. Hardy came to know it well.

In the *Life*, Hardy barely mentions the existence of his cousins, preferring to project an image of an isolated childhood, which can hardly have been further from the truth. In addition to the Sparks cousins, and later the Antells, there were also cousins on his father's side who lived in Puddletown. But because of Jemima's close relationships with her sisters, Tommy and Mary were particularly close to their maternal cousins. Jemima was a caring and capable sister, who would leave her own home in Bockhampton to care for them during pregnancy and childbirth.

Tommy's 'expeditions' with his mother to Puddletown were a source of great pleasure. According to the *Life*, 'they were excellent companions, having each a keen sense of humour and a love of adventure'. Jemima loved a prank, and on one occasion she suggested that they should make a visit to Puddletown relatives in disguise. Mother and son pulled cabbage-nets over their faces to conceal their identity: 'Thus oddly dressed, they walked across the heath to visit a sister of Mrs Hardy, living at Puddletown, whose amazement was great when she set eyes upon these strange visitors at the door.'[5]

CHAPTER 9

Julia Martin

When Hardy was five, there was a change in the parish of Stinsford. The local manor house, Kingston Maurward, changed hands. The owner got married and sold up in order to cover family debts and provide annuities for his sisters. The new owners were to have a profound effect on the young Thomas Hardy.

The handsome stone-clad house was bought by Francis Pitney Broughton Martin and his wife, Julia Augusta. Julia was a beautiful, cultivated woman who had a passion for educating the rural poor. She was also childless. Hardy's father contracted estate work at the manor house, and it was probably there that she first saw his young son. Hardy recalled that she had grown passionately fond of him almost from his infancy, and would take him into her lap and kiss him, 'until he was quite a big child'. Far from feeling any sense of impropriety in the relationship, he confirmed that 'He quite reciprocated her fondness.'[1] Tommy made frequent visits to Kingston Maurward, where Julia Martin would fuss over the little boy with the intelligent face and bright eyes. He would draw watercolours of animals for her and would sing love ballads. She in turn taught him his letters.

When Tommy was seven, his aunt Mary Hand was married from the Hardy cottage. She had been the children's nursemaid from an early age, and her absence from the household left a large gap. Around the same age, he was breeched. This was an important ritual in the life of a child transitioning from early childhood to boyhood. Hitherto, he had been surrounded by women; his grandmother, mother, sister, and aunts. 'Breeching' was the time when the father of the house began to play a more active role in the raising of boys. Tommy was taken to the local tailor for his first pair of breeches, and his parents thought of sending him to school. It was fortuitous that a couple of years after Julia Martin arrived in Stinsford, she founded a new school in Lower Bockhampton, funding and overseeing a building that still stands today. Julia hired a teacher, Mr T. Fuller, who ran the school alongside his wife. As Hardy acknowledged, Julia Martin was a woman of great dignity with a 'tender heart'. Her devotion to her school rendered it 'far superior to an ordinary village school'.[2]

Hardy left little impression of his visits to Kingston Maurward. Nor, in his ghosted biography, does he mention Julia Martin by name. She is the 'lady of the manor', the 'Squire's wife', the 'landowner's wife', the 'manor lady' and 'her ladyship'. He knew his place. But he also recognised that there was something profound, even erotic, about their relationship. There was a sexual awakening of sorts not only in the kisses she pressed on his lips, but in the swish of her silk gown as she strode into church on Sundays. Many years later he recalled the 'thrilling "frou-frou" of her four grey silk flounces when she had used to bend over him, and when they brushed against the font as she entered church'.[3]

It may have been Julia Martin who initiated his erotic fascination with clothing. In 1845, there was an epidemic of silkworm diseases, which caused production of real silk to fall and prices to soar. Counterfeit silks were being newly produced in France, but the rustle of Julia Martin's silk dress, a crisp sound known as 'wire-ming', was an indication that Julia wore real silk from China. Hardy could not have known any of this, he was merely responding to the erotic rustle of the fabric, but the silk gown placed Julia Martin in a different category from any other woman he had met. His deep emotional connection was also perhaps the beginning of his endless fascination with the romantic relationship between classes, what he would call the 'poor man and his lady' theme.

When the school at Lower Bockhampton opened in 1848, Tommy was one of the first pupils. Indeed, he was the very first person to walk through the gates of the brand-new schoolhouse, a short walk from his home. To his mortification, he had arrived early and found himself 'awaiting tremulously and alone, in the empty room'.[4] Later, in his poem 'He Revisits His First School', he evokes the memories of that day, even down to his clean and scrubbed appearance: 'fresh, / Pink, tiny, crisp-curled'.[5]

His mother had marked the occasion by giving him Dryden's translation of Virgil, Dr Johnson's *Rasselas* and a volume of translations of two celebrated French novels, Bernardin de Saint-Pierre's *Paul and Virginia* and Sophie Cottin's *Elizabeth; or, The Exiles of Siberia*. The Virgil bears an inscription 'Thomas Hardy – the gift of his mother', in his own hand. He would later make the point that his mother showed excellent taste in literature at a time when it was still difficult to obtain books. He found in a closet *A History of the Wars*, which sowed the seed of his interest in Napoleon.

At school, he excelled in arithmetic and geography. Hardy made no mention of his first schoolmaster in his biography, though in a notebook reflecting on this time, he made a note that Fuller was a drunkard.[6] For pleasure, meanwhile, he obtained the historical novels of William Harrison Ainsworth, which inspired a longing for the sights of London.

To Julia Martin, Hardy must have seemed an exemplary pupil,

a vindication of her commitment. His sister Mary was also proving to be a clever girl, interested in drawing and music, and following in her brother's footsteps. But Julia was not reckoning on the strength of character of Jemima Hardy. That Hardy was keenly aware of the rivalry between the women is obvious, and he felt torn between them. Jemima removed her children from the church at Stinsford, probably transferring them to Low Church services at Fordington St George. Tommy would no longer be entranced by the rustle of Mrs Martin's silk skirts.

It was Jemima's first sally, but not her last. She was determined to separate Tommy from the influence of Mrs Martin, but she was shrewd enough to make the withdrawal gradual. Soon enough, a plan presented itself. Julia Martin might have been the lady of the manor, but she did not stand a chance against Jemima Hardy.

CHAPTER 10

Martha Sharpe

Hardy's strong emotional attachment to Julia Martin felt like a betrayal to his mother. It was his first attempt at a loosening of the maternal bond. Since his breeching, he was spending more time with his father, gathering apples from the orchard to be stored for cider-making, and occasionally accompanying him to the mason's yard. His proficiency as a fiddler meant that he was permitted to join his father in his musical endeavours entertaining the local people at weddings and parties.

Tom, as he was now known, seemed to be a solitary boy, with few schoolmates. Being bookish and clever set him apart from the other village boys, and he did not like to join in their games. In recalling his schoolboy days, Hardy noted a peculiarity in his personality: an aversion to being touched physically (though clearly this aversion did not apply to the embraces of Julia Martin).

So, although his attachment to his mother was still strong, there was a natural weaning due to time spent at school, reading and writing with Julia Martin at Kingston, and long hours spent with his father as part of his musical band. Once he played at a village wedding, where the bride, all in white, kissed him 'in her intense pleasure at the dance'. And at his first school, he was introduced to girls. It wasn't long before he developed a schoolboy crush on a pretty, 'delicate' girl called Fanny Hurden, who lived in Higher Bockhampton.[1] They became childhood sweethearts – his first experience of being in love. At some point, there was a quarrel, and he pushed the little girl into the school-room stove, burning her hands. He was filled with shame and remorse. Later, he would learn that she died at the age of eighteen. As an old man, he showed his friend and fellow poet Walter de la Mare Fanny's grave in Stinsford churchyard, and confessed his deep remorse: 'It was the one thing in life he told me that he could never, never forgive himself. And there had never come the opportunity, since she had died young.'[2] Hardy memorialised her as 'poor Fanny Hurd' in a poem called 'Voices from Things Growing in a Churchyard':

> A little girl here sepultured.
> Once I flit-fluttered like a bird
> Above the grass, as now I wave
> In daisy shapes above my grave.[3]

The relationship set a pattern to be repeated throughout his personal life: infatuation, rejection, loss, and then – often many years later – an answering in writing to the woman's voice calling from the grave.

Before long, he faced another loss. When he was nine, his mother took him out of school. They went to live in Hertfordshire. Jemima's sister Martha was pregnant, and Jemima proposed herself as a housekeeper and nurse. She set off in the winter of 1849, taking her elder son. Martha, the best-looking of the Hand sisters, had married a dashing young man called John Brereton Sharpe in 1841, and was about to give birth to her sixth child. Her daughter, Martha Caroline, had died the previous year at just one year of age, and a son, Alfred, had died at seven months old.[4] The visit was Hardy's first experience of travel, rendered especially memorable because he went partly by train.

Jemima told her son that she was taking him on the journey for her own 'protection', as he recalled, since she was 'an attractive and still young woman'.[5] The visit lasted almost a month, and Jemima, unwilling for her son to miss out on his learning, enrolled him in a local school as a day boy. Hardy recalled that the school was 'somewhat on the Squeers model', a reference to the cruel schoolmaster in Charles Dickens' *Nicholas Nickleby* who beats and starves his charges. Hardy also remembered that he was 'mercilessly tyrannised over by the bigger boys whom he could beat hollow in arithmetic and geography'.[6]

Hardy was mesmerised by Martha and her dashing husband. Sharpe was the son of a Hertfordshire farmer who served occasionally in the Hertfordshire Yeomanry Cavalry and also worked as an agricultural bailiff. His elder brother George was a doctor, who was later involved in a local scandal when he was caught moving his mother's remains, and Martha's deceased children, from their graves to another location in order that his father could be buried together with his wife and grandchildren.[7] Thomas Hardy kept in touch with George Sharpe, later on writing to ask for medical advice in relation to one of his characters.

John Sharpe was a charismatic, educated man, well-regarded in the Yeomanry. They wore a distinctive scarlet coat with white facing, and a dragoon helmet carrying the county badge of a hart – a pun on the pronunciation of Hertfordshire. John Sharpe has long been considered as the model for Sergeant Troy in *Far from the Madding Crowd*. The connection is strengthened by Hardy's claim that his 'handsome aunt', Martha Sharpe, was the model for Bathsheba Everdene.[8]

John Sharpe was a restless, impulsive man, never settling down in any fixed occupation. His family was ever expanding – Martha gave birth eleven times. A few years after the visit of Jemima and Tom, they emigrated to Canada, raising money for the passage from friends and family. At a time of economic depression in the rural economy, the promise of a new life in a new land was tempting.

On the journey home from Hertfordshire, Jemima and Tom spent the night in London. It was his first visit to the capital, and his mother's first for twelve years. The coaching inn at which they stayed, the Cross Keys, was the very one in which the poet Percy Shelley and the teenage author of *Frankenstein* Mary Godwin had their clandestine meetings before their elopement. Hardy, who later worshipped Shelley, would one day fantasise that the attic room, which was all they could afford, might have been the same 'occupied by our most marvellous lyricist'. Looking back, he was thrilled that the inn, with its oval staircase and skylight, seemed untouched since the time of 'the lovers' romantic experiences there'.[9] That night, Jemima searched through the wardrobes in case any man was hiding, ready to pounce when the lights were turned down.

In the morning, she showed her son the places she loved: the Pantheon and Cumberland Gate leading into Hyde Park. In preparation for the exciting visit to the capital city, Hardy had made a map of London, based on 'the streets, lanes, and purlieus described by Ainsworth in *Old St Paul's*', readying him to lead his mother on a walking tour, following in the footsteps of the book's hero from street to street.[10] This literary excursion was an inspiration, but Hardy was less enamoured of Smithfield Market, where oxen, sheep, lambs, pigs and calves were sold. For the boy who loved animals, it was 'pandemonium', and he long remembered 'its mud, curses and cries of ill-treated animals'.[11]

Nevertheless, the Hertfordshire visit had been a huge success. Martha gave birth to a healthy baby boy called Charles Brereton.

And, perhaps more crucially, Jemima had begun the process of separating her son from the influence of Julia Martin. Hardy was not to return to Mrs Martin's school in Bockhampton, but was considered strong enough to make the journey by foot to the Dorchester British School in Greyhound Yard. The decision to remove Tom from the village school would have repercussions for the family, since Hardy's father was employed by the Martins, as it would for the boy who was too young to understand the rivalry between the two women.

CHAPTER 11

Mary Antell

When Jemima Hardy saw her pregnant sister Mary's bruised face and blackened eye, she knew what had to be done. Mary had been beaten by her husband, and her sisters were not going to stand by and watch, as they had been forced to stand by when their mother was beaten by their drunken father. Domestic violence had punctuated their young lives. Men in their cups were all too apt to use their fists when they came home after a night in the pub, and few controlled their violent impulses, even when the wife was pregnant. 'He'll give it to 'ee o' Saturday nights!' a female friend warns Arabella in *Jude the Obscure*.[1]

Jemima and her sisters were also accustomed to their brothers' violence. Christopher Hand regularly beat his wife, Ruth, after a night's drinking, so much so that his mother feared for the unborn baby: 'I am afraid there will be something wrong in the child as he throws her in such ways sometimes – still he is very kind to her in all respects beside.'[2] It was not uncommon for women to miscarry as a result of spousal violence brought on by excessive alcohol.

As with many women of her class and generation, Betty took domestic violence in her stride, but not so Jemima, who, when forced into wedlock by an unwanted pregnancy, ensured that she had tied herself to a gentle man who seemed incapable of lifting a finger to his wife or children. Unlike her sisters, she was determined to escape the cycle of heavy drinking and beatings. On this occasion, Jemima and her sister Maria, who lived in Puddletown, marched over to Mary's house in the High Street, and beat John Antell until he begged for mercy and swore that he would not hurt his wife again.[3] His drinking problem sprang, in part, from his intellectual frustration. He was a voracious reader who taught himself Latin, Greek and Hebrew. Like Hardy, he had dreams of going to university. Hardy would come to know Antell well and saw at first hand his uncle's behaviour under the influence of drink. Florence Hardy claimed that Antell was 'partly' a model for Jude Fawley in *Jude the Obscure*.[4]

Whether Tom was aware of the physical confrontation between his mother and his uncle is unknown, but he witnessed a domestic incident when he was a boy. On a cold, snowy night, he and his father were returning home at three in the morning from a gentleman-farmer's party, when the tired musicians were confronted with a ghostly sight: 'they saw motionless in the hedge what appeared to be a white human figure without a head'. It proved to be 'a very tall thin man in a long white smock-frock, leaning against the bank in a drunken stupor, his head hanging forward so low that at a distance he had seemed to have had no head at all'.[5] Tom and his father, fearing that the man would freeze to death, took him to the cottage where he lived. His wife, furious, greeted her husband 'with a stream of abuse', following which she knocked him down. Hardy's father remarked that it might have been better to have left the man to have taken his chances of being frozen to death rather than to be abused by his wife. A grim joke shared and understood by his son, who knew at first hand the force of an angry woman.

Jemima was indomitable when she wanted to make a point.

She showed a similar strength of character when she found herself up against Julia Martin. Hardy, who claimed that his mother was 'ambitious on his account though not on her own',[6] viewed his removal from the village school to the Dorchester School as evidence of her interest in giving him the best educational experience. His mother had made enquiries and discovered that the headmaster of the Dorchester School was an 'exceptionally able man, and a good teacher of Latin'.[7] Jemima did not inform Julia Martin that her son was leaving her school, and there was a falling-out.

Hardy took his mother's side. He claims that Julia Martin must have 'guessed' that he had only been sent to her school as a temporary measure, that she was 'too sensitive'. He was defensive of his mother, whom he claimed had no obligation to inform Julia of her decision to remove the boy: 'the Hardys being comparatively independent of the manor, as their house and the adjoining land were a family lifehold, and the estate work forming only a part of Mr Hardy's business'. But his father did lose work as a result of the fall-out, and was forced to go further afield, 'soon obtaining a mansion to enlarge . . . and thus not suffering much from the loss of business in the immediate vicinity of his home'.[8]

Another 'rock of offence' to the devout Julia Martin was the fact that Tom had been enrolled at a Nonconformist school. Hardy played down the 'unpleasant misunderstanding'. But in an unpublished note, written many years later, he recorded that his mother had 'openly defied' Julia Martin.[9] He also admitted that he 'secretly mourned the loss of his friend . . . to whom he had grown more attached than he cared to own'.[10]

Jemima had emerged victorious. For now, Tom was willing to abide by his mother's rules. His world was opening up, and as he approached his tenth year, he was excited by the prospect of a new school, and a new town to explore.

Jemima, ever ambitious for her family, expressed the wish for them all to move to Dorchester. She was convinced that her husband's business had a better chance to prosper in the county town, and she probably also wished to be closer to her son's new school. She was pregnant, too, so wanted to be less isolated. But this was a battle that she failed to win. Her husband was obdurate. The cottage at Bockhampton was the place of his birth, and even though conditions were cramped, he was determined to remain in his 'lonely spot between a heath and a wood'. Her husband lacked ambition, and was, according to his son, 'the furthest removed from a tradesman that could be conceived'. He was a man too deeply attached to the soil of the heath to care much for 'needers of brick and stone in the marketplace'. Jemima knew which battles to fight and she 'acquiesced at last with the cheerfulness natural to her, and made the best of it as she could'.[11]

From the moment he stepped through the Tudor archway in Greyhound Yard, which led to his new school, Thomas Hardy could see that he was a world away from his tiny village school in Bockhampton. By his own description, he was still small and delicate, but he had walked the three miles to Dorchester, and he would walk back at the end of the school day. Isaac Last's British School was Nonconformist, though Hardy claimed to have had little sense of the fact, other than wondering why the 'boring Church Catechism had vanished'.[12] He swiftly proved himself an 'apt student', who 'galloped unconcernedly over the ordinary school lessons'.[13] Last, seeing his potential, agreed to teach him Latin, which was an extra subject.

One of Hardy's school friends, Charles Lacey, remembered Mr Last as a 'severe disciplinarian' who would chase boys around the schoolroom with his cane until he was 'white in the face, the ink-pots flying in all directions as they leapt over the desks'.[14] Hardy makes no such reference, perhaps on account of his being a quiet and diligent pupil. Lacey described Hardy as 'one of the cleverest' boys, who was 'always ready to help other boys with their lessons'. Being clever and studious made him stand out, but he was still teased. There was a shop in South Street run by a woman called Sally Warren. Customers entered via a step. Lacey remembers the boys throwing Hardy's school cap down the steps and into the shop, and when Hardy tried to retrieve it, she would chase him with her broom.[15]

He was 'somewhat different from the rest of us boys, kind of dreaming, seeming to prefer to be by himself'.[16] While the other boys played, he would read a book or stand 'plunged in thought'. Because he was small in stature, his brightly coloured schoolbag, stuffed with books, seemed to be oversized, absurdly heavy for a young boy who walked six miles to and from school every day. His head seemed a little too large for his body. Though his bright eyes, curly fair hair and neat appearance made for an attractive boy, he did not care for company on the long walk home after school: 'He loved being alone, but often, to his concealed discomfort, some of the other boys would volunteer to accompany him on his homeward journey to Bockhampton. How much this irked him he recalled long years afterward.'[17] Hardy attributed some of this discomfort to his fear of physical contact: 'Hardy, how is it that you do not like us to touch you?' he was once asked.[18] The phobia did not, of course, extend to his mother. Jemima would be at the front gate, 'watching and waiting for Tom's coming'. As his schoolfellow also attested, 'They thought the world of each other, Tom and his mother.'[19]

Because of the long school journey, Jemima had arranged that her son should have his lunch break with relatives in Dorchester. James Sparks, married to her sister Maria, had two spinster sisters, Rebecca and Amelia, who lived together on High East Street. They were employed as shoebinders.[20] As busy working women, they failed to appreciate Tom's lunchtime antics of throwing buttered bread onto the ceiling and tossing sugar lumps into the air to catch. Many of the women in Dorchester worked for a living – as dressmakers, shoebinders, butter makers, house servants, laundresses, charwomen, glovers, schoolmistresses, housekeepers, barwomen, cooks, booksellers, stationers, fish-mongers, bakers, milliners, nurses, nursery maids. There was even a straw-bonnet maker.[21]

It was a place rich in historic associations, from prehistoric times to the days of the Romans, who built a garrison, an aque-duct, and an amphitheatre. Later, it was the site of the infamous 'Bloody Assizes' presided over by Judge Jeffreys after the Monmouth Rebellion, and later still the trial of the Tolpuddle Martyrs. By Hardy's time, it was growing and developing with a new Town Hall, completed in 1848, located in the same street as Rebecca and Amelia Sparks. A corn exchange was established on the ground floor, and a council chamber on the above. There were shops, banks, libraries, schools, markets, a hanging gaol, and hangman's cottage, where the rope was kept for executions. Young Tom would go there after dark 'to climb on the window-sill and peep through a chink in the blind at the dreaded executioner'. In later years, he would also tell stories of the cruel hangman who would also conduct public floggings and 'wait between each lash to let the flesh recover its feeling, while he squeezed the blood off the thongs'.[22]

Partly because of the Monmouth Rebellion, the town still held a strong anti-Catholic bias. In 1850, there was an upsurge in anti-Papal feeling when Cardinal Nicholas Wiseman was made the first Archbishop of Westminster, with the intention of re-establishing the Catholic hierarchy in England and Wales. In Dorchester, the Guy Fawkes celebrations of 1850 were particularly hostile, and though he was only ten, Hardy's father took him along to the 'No Popery' riots being held in the Maumbury Rings, the site of the old Roman amphitheatre. It was a disturbing sight. A procession of locals dressed as priests, nuns and monks marched around the town before reaching the amphitheatre, where 'highly realistic' effigies of the Pope and Cardinal Wiseman were burned. Hardy recalled the effigies burning 'on a huge rick of furze with a gallows above' and the fire that 'blazed till they were blown to pieces by fireworks contained within them'.[23] But the worst was yet to come. The wind got up and blew aside the cowl of one of the monk-garbed protestors. To the boy's bewilderment, he discovered the face of one of his father's workmen.[24]

Jemima, pregnant again after a period of nine years, was relaxing her hold on her eldest son. Her son was thriving at the British school. But if she thought that the Julia Martin episode was closed, then she was wrong. Tom was invited by a village girl to a harvest supper at one of the Kingston Maurward farms. He knew that Julia Martin would be present, and despite knowing that his mother would be angry, he so much longed to see her that 'he jumped at the offer'.[25] He had 'secretly mourned' her loss, unable to share his unhappiness with his mother and aware that it would have seemed perverse that 'at only nine or ten' his feelings for a woman who was 'nearly forty' were 'almost that of a lover'.[26]

By the time he reached the harvest celebrations, the supper was over, but there was ample time for singing and dancing. Julia's husband had invited some non-commissioned officers as dancing partners for the girls. The Martins and their guests had not yet arrived, which gave Hardy time to look around and take in the scene. Julia soon arrived with her husband and guests to lead the dances, and there was an emotional scene when she saw the boy: 'O Tommy, how is this! I thought you had deserted me!'[27] Through his tears, he assured her that he had not deserted her and would never do so. Julia arranged for him to dance with one of her nieces, who was Tom's age. But when she left, he was stranded. The village girls were dancing with the soldiers, and he was forced to wait until three in the morning. Nor had he eaten since the previous day and he was too fearful to ask for food or drink. The evening had turned into a disaster and was made worse by the scolding he received from his parents when he finally got home.[28]

Hardy felt that he had made a 'lover-like promise of fidelity to her ladyship'.[29] Soon after, the Martins sold Kingston Maurward and moved to London. Hardy did not keep his promise, and would fall in love repeatedly over the next few years. But he would not forget Julia Martin. They would meet again when he was old enough to be considered a lover, rather than a child.

CHAPTER 12

Louisa Harding

Hardy would long remember his first harvest supper. In his self-ghosted biography, he described the event, melodramatically, as the last at which the old traditional ballads were sung. He blamed the coming of the railway for the demise of the 'orally-transmitted ditties of centuries being slain at a stroke by the London comic songs that were being introduced'. Though he was ten years old when he attended the festivities, he could recall to an old age the young women in their light gowns sitting on a bench against the wall in the barn, leaning against each other as they warbled the Dorset version of the ballad: 'Lie there, lie there, thou-false-hearted man.'[1]

He would also remember the handsome uniforms of the soldiers who had been roped in for the dance. This, he claimed, began his 'extensive acquaintance with soldiers of the old uniforms'.[2] In Dorchester, Hardy had been struck by the erotic effect of dashing uniforms upon young women.[3] At the harvest supper, he had been surprised by the appearance of the soldiers as dancing partners, wondering whether Mrs Martin approved. His account of the harvest supper in the *Life* was, however, like so much of his autobiography, a highly sanitised version. In one of his surviving notebooks, regarding which he had given firm instructions to be destroyed after his death, he left a fascinating account of his inner feelings about the evening. His notes reveal the early stirrings of the class conflict that would dog his life and permeate his works:

A Farm of Labourers, as they appeared to me when a child in Martin's time . . . Susan Sq—, and Newnt (e.g leaning & singing at harvest-supper) their simple husbands: Newnt's lovers; Ben B's wife, & her lover, & her hypocrisy . . . the lech —'s boy T.M. . . .s. Also Walt, Betsy, & Eliza . . . & their char[acter]s, sensuous, lewd, & careless, as visible even to me at that time – all incarnadined by passion & youth – obscuring the wrinkles, creases, & cracks of life as then lived.[4]

This passage, meant for his eyes only, is an important insight into the mind of Hardy. Though a retrospective account, he does not romanticise the rural folk, but sees them as they appeared to him as a child of ten: 'simple', 'lecherous', 'sensuous, lewd and careless'. His choice of the word 'incarnadined' – pink and fleshy-coloured, brilliantly evokes their youth and vulgarity. Here he sees infidelity and sexual hypocrisy, not light gowns and traditional ballads.

There appears to be a sexual awakening in his appraisal of the erotic undertones of the harvest scene; but his romance with the 'lady of the manor', Julia Martin, is regarded on a higher, more romanticised level. It is she who accuses him of having deserted his love; his tears and remorse accompanied by the ballad soundtrack: 'Lie, there, thou false-hearted man.' But as much as he felt guilt and remorse for the truncated relationship, he supported his 'progressive' mother's decision to send him to the British school, especially when he began Latin lessons with Isaac Last. He devised a system for learning the genders by colouring the nouns in three different tints.[5]

But he also wanted to read for pleasure. He began reading Shakespeare's tragedies, 'for the plots only'. He was drawn to *Hamlet* by his love of the supernatural, but the ghost disappointed him for not playing up his part to the end, 'as he ought to have done'.[6] One day, he was browsing in a bookshop window in Dorchester, where he saw and coveted a copy of the *Boys' Own* book. He had no means of paying for it, and he knew that his mother would not approve of an encyclopaedia covering 'all the Diversions, Athletic, Scientific, and Recreative, of Boyhood and Youth'. He had been told by his mother never to accept financial reward for his musical gigs, but for once he broke the rules and collected the money that he needed to buy the book. Despite Jemima's disapproving shake of her head when she saw what he had done, Hardy treasured the book and kept it all his life.[7] The tiny rebellion was another attempt at loosening the apron strings, easier now that Jemima had a new baby demanding her attention.

When Hardy was thirteen, his schoolmaster set up an 'advanced' Academy.[8] Hardy became an exemplary pupil, being awarded prizes for progress and good behaviour. Advanced arithmetic, geometry, algebra and applied mathematics were on the curriculum, along with Latin. Hardy was proud of this schooling. In later life, he scribbled a hasty retort in the margin of a book that had described him as self-taught: 'an impertinent personality & untrue, as he [Hardy] was taught Latin & French at School and College'.[9]

He obtained the French lessons at his sister's school. Mary was now being educated in Dorchester, at the Ladies' School. Jemima was just as keen for her daughter to gain a good education as she was for her son, and she wanted Mary to have an independent life and career. Mary was an average student, but was encouraged by her brother to read and to draw, and she would become an accomplished watercolourist.

By now, Hardy's interest in girls was awakened. There were to be no more violent endings, such as pushing the love interest into a hot stove, but rather a romantic idealisation that he maintained for much of his life. Like the hero of *Under the Greenwood Tree*, Dick Dewy, partly modelled on himself, Hardy was susceptible to feminine beauty, prone to falling 'madly in love', as he phrased it, often at first sight.[10] One day, walking back from school, he saw a pretty girl on horseback who smiled at him. He was surprised at her acknowledgement as she was 'a total stranger'.[11] The next day he saw her with an old gentleman, probably her father, but there was no smile. For the next few days, he 'wandered about miserably' looking for her, and then finally saw her riding with another boy. He confided in his school friends, who sympathised, and some of the boarders promised to watch out for the girl. He described this abortive crush as a 'desperate attachment' and it set a pattern to be repeated throughout the course of his romantic life, and would be a theme of his writings.[12]

Other girls caught his eye. One was from Windsor. She aroused his interest because he was reading W. Harrison Ainsworth's Gothic novel about the doomed marriage of Henry VIII and Anne Boleyn, *Windsor Castle*. But when he discovered that she had no interest in the beheading of Anne Boleyn or the horned spirit of the forest, Herne the Hunter, he lost interest.[13] Hardy would later describe the 'unexplained mystery' of Herne the Hunter as 'most artistically treated'.[14] He would tell Ainsworth's biographer that this bestselling historical novelist was 'the most powerful literary influence of his boyhood'.[15] Among the other titles he read was *The Tower of London*, which told of many a grim execution and was illustrated with wood engravings by George Cruikshank that drew the eye to axe, block and women dressed in black preparing to meet a gruesome end.

And then there were 'four village beauties, to whom he lost

his heart'.[16] Emily Dart was an illegitimate relation of his, Rachel Hurst had 'rich colour, and vanity, and frailty', while Alice Paul was blessed with a 'mass of flaxen curls'.[17] The fourth was a beautiful girl called Elizabeth Bishop, with 'bay-red hair', the daughter of a Stinsford gamekeeper. Hardy later made her the subject of his lyric 'To Lizbie Browne'. She was another of his unrequited loves, who married young, and was lost to him. In the poem, he praises her white skin and arch smile, and laments that he never kissed her lips: 'I should have thought, / "Girls ripen fast," / And coaxed and caught / You ere you passed.' Hardy said that she despised him on account of the age difference (he was three years her junior), but in his poem it is the male narrator who says, 'I let you slip'.[18]

Meanwhile, he formed a trio of youth leaders to teach in the parish Sunday School. One of his pupils was a dairymaid, a 'pink and plump damsel' who had a facility for memorising whole chapters of the Bible, which bored Hardy, but also impressed him. He claimed that she was the model for Marian in *Tess of the D'Urbervilles*. He also added that she 'was by no means a model of virtue in her love-affairs'.[19]

One of the churchwardens was a 'well-to-do farmer' called Stephen Harding. Hardy fell in love with one of his six daughters, Louisa. He met her on a lane on his walk home from school, but he was too shy to speak. Later, she went to boarding school in Weymouth, and he followed her there, discovering the church she attended, and 'thither he went, Sunday after Sunday'. At the time, all he ever received was a bashful smile. When he moved to London as a young man, he would make a point of seeing her on his return visits to Dorset.[20] He described her as 'well-to-do', implying that he was punching above the weight of his own class. This sense of inferiority was corroborated by Ernest Harding, Louisa's cousin: 'You see, to my family, Hardy was just a village boy, although it was recognised that he was an unusual type, and different to the other boys.'[21] Louisa's sister, Julia, would remember Hardy as 'odd-looking', 'solemn' and always carrying a satchel of books.[22]

Hardy kept the ghost of Louisa Harding alive. In his memory, she always remained an ethereal figure in 'gauzy muslin'.[23] She never married, and when she died in 1913, he wrote several poems about her and sought out her unmarked grave in Stinsford churchyard. It was yet another relationship that seemed to grow more meaningful after the woman had died, as with Fanny Hurden. And it was evident that girls of Louisa's social class were unavailable to a village boy, no matter how 'studious' or 'unusual' he might be regarded.

Hardy's youthful infatuations were a natural weaning away from the tight, emotional grip of Jemima. And there were instances where he found his mother's ambitions for him more than a little cloying. One never-to-be-forgotten memory was a sunny day in late childhood when he was lying on his back on the ground, with his straw hat covering his face. The lining had worn out, and the sun's rays 'streamed through the interstices of the straw'. Hardy began to ruminate on his life, concluding that he was 'useless'. Other boys he knew were always talking of what they would do when they were men, but he 'did not want at all to be a man, or to possess things, but to remain as he was, in the same spot, and to know no more people than he already knew (about half a dozen)'. In short, he had discovered that 'he did not wish to grow up'.[24]

Hardy shared his 'conclusions on existence' with his mother, believing that she would endorse his views. To his consternation, she was 'very much hurt'. He ascribed her feelings to the events of his traumatic birth; that she had been 'at death's door in bringing him forth'. But the fact that Jemima never let him forget what he said suggests that there were other reasons for her dismay. Her beloved son must have appeared to her to be replicating her husband's lack of ambition. In summer weather, he too had a habit of 'lying on a bank of thyme or camomile with the grasshoppers leaping over him'.[25] Hardy, wishing to stay forever in his village, was just the same as Jemima's husband, with his refusal to move to Dorchester to expand his business. This was not what she wanted for her clever son, and she made her feelings clear. Hardy was also clear in his later recollections that his inertia was evidence of 'that lack of social ambition which followed him through life'. His point was that he felt this way 'when he was in perfect health and happy circumstances'.[26] It had nothing to do with a sense of pessimism or depressed feelings. It was all that he wanted. To stay where he was, in the same spot, with the same people. That his mother did not share in his feelings came as a shock. It was another weakening of the link between them.

Hardy, now sixteen, was coming to the end of his formal schooling, and it was time for him to look for a worthy occupation for his talents. It was his father's connections that would lead him to the next stage of his life.

CHAPTER 13

Mary Channing

He was a deeply sensitive boy, with a strong affinity for the natural world and a love of all creatures great and small. His horror of animal cruelty would stay with him all his life. One cold winter's day, when he was a boy, he stood in the garden with his father, where they suddenly saw a little bird that was half frozen. With his usual specificity of observation, he recognised it as a member of the thrush family, a fieldfare. His father picked up a stone, idly, and threw it in the direction of the bird, 'possibly not meaning to hit it', but the bird fell dead. Tommy took up the fieldfare, 'light as a feather, all skin and bone, practically starved'.[1] He never forgot the feel of the dead creature in his hand.

In another boyhood memory, he was crossing the ewe-lease (sheep pasture) on the heath when he dropped to his hands and knees to pretend to munch grass. He wanted to see what the sheep would do. When he looked up from pretending to be a sheep, he found that he was surrounded in a circle by the herd 'gazing at him with astonished faces'.[2] Getting a close, worm's-eye view of nature was important. Many years later, he attended an exhibition of paintings at the English Art Club and was unimpressed: 'If I were a painter. I would paint a picture of a room as viewed by a mouse from a chink under the skirting.'³

As a young boy, he would walk in the woods, and with his eyes closed try to identify a particular tree by listening to the wind whispering through the leaves. *Under the Greenwood Tree* begins: 'To dwellers in a wood, almost every species of tree has its voice as well as its feature. At the passing of the breeze the fir-trees sob and moan . . . the holly whistles as it battles with itself: the ash hisses amid its quivering: the beech rustles.'⁴

Sometimes his father would walk with him to Rainbarrows, and take out his telescope, pointing out various landmarks and the lush landscape of the Frome Valley. Such love of nature inevitably made William Wordsworth a literary hero. At the age of sixteen, Hardy composed his first serious poem, 'Domicilium', in what the autobiography would call a 'Wordsworthian' style: an idyllic homestead, the cottage overgrown with 'wild honey-sucks', 'red roses' and 'lilacs', nestled in the bosom of apple trees and high beeches. The flowers that do best are 'hardy flowers / As flourish best untrained'.⁵ Hardy was proud of his name, with its connotations of strength and virility. His pun on his own name suggests that he, too, would flourish best if 'untrained' and free.

But there is perhaps another connotation here of the 'hardy' trait, one that offers a clue to his unfolding character. Coupled with the Wordsworthian romance of his childhood was the dark enchantment of Shakespeare's *A Midsummer Night's Dream*. Rushy Pond on the heath was, according to legend, excavated by fairy shovels. The forest is a place of magic; of fairies, sprites and love potions, but there is an insalubrious underbelly to the enchanted wood. It is also a place of savage cruelty and the ill treatment of women, presided over by a capricious wood-sprite and shape-shifter, Puck. So too, Hardy's upbringing in rural Dorset offered a potent mix of natural beauty and childlike innocence with a seam of violence and horror. Though he could be stirred by the fate of the lowly earthworm, he thought nothing of dipping his toy sword into a pail of fresh pig's blood to ape the corn-law protestors. He could be moved to tears by the music of his father's violin, yet be riveted by the grisly true tales and weird superstitions told by his mother, whom he described as 'a woman with an extraordinary store of local memories reaching back to the days when the ancient ballads were everywhere heard at country feasts, in weaving shops, and at spinning wheels'.[6] In this, Jemima Hardy was a model for Mrs Durbeyfield in *Tess of the D'Urbervilles*, with her 'fast-perishing lumber of superstitions, folk-lore, dialect, and orally transmitted ballads'.[7] The young Thomas Hardy was certainly not unusual in wanting to hear Gothic ghost stories or old folklore legends, but some of the morbid stories told by his mother, his grandmother and Lizzie Downton left a lasting, troubling legacy.

There was the pond called 'Heedless William', named after an unlucky traveller who drowned in an accident. And the tale of the male sorcerer from Blackmoor Vale, who could conjure up the face of one's enemy in a glass of water. And a witch called Diana Chester who 'used to work her spells by the Devil'.[8] Jemima believed in the devil. When Hardy was a boy, he gambled and won a prize of a hen, but his mother was angry, and told him it was in a 'direct attempt by the devil' to lead him astray. She told him a story of a haunted barn in her old childhood village. One day, a drunken man entered the barn and fell asleep in a cow's crib. When he awoke, he saw a lady in a white riding habit riding round on a buck, holding the horns as reins. The wind of her speed blew so strong upon him that he sneezed and woke up, at which point she vanished into thin air.[9]

Hardy also liked hearing about the legend of the Cerne Giant, who lived on the hills, was waited upon by wild animals, and stole the famer's sheep to eat, one a day. He planned to descend upon Cerne, ravish the maidens, and kill all the young men. Goaded to 'desperate courage', the men waylaid and killed the giant, afterwards cutting his effigy on the hill. The 180-foot figure is of a naked man, with explicit phallic imagery, wielding a giant club.

Jemima also told tales of the fortune teller in her hometown of Melbury, which Hardy later transcribed into his secret notebooks. Known as the 'Planet ruler', dressed in a uniform of white stockings and black coat and trousers, the fortune teller would greet the local people with the words: 'The Lord hath sent us a fine morning' or 'the Lord hath thought proper to send us rain'. Those having their fortunes would be charged sixpence, and would give the hour and day of birth, and then he would return with a half-sheet of paper which predicted the ruling of the planets.[10] He kept his astrological diagrams in his lodgings in Beaminster. The fortune teller once predicted that Jemima's sister Martha, whose horoscope he cast, would have a large family, and would travel. True enough, she had a large family and emigrated to Ontario, Canada.

Best of all were Jemima's divination stories. She told of maids who stayed up until the clock struck midnight on Midsummer's evening, when they would get their first glance of the man they would marry, sometimes placing their shoes in the form of the letter T ('I put my shoes in the form of a T / And trust my true love for to see').[11] Another custom was to 'dig a hole in the grass plot' and 'place your ear thereon precisely at 12. The occupation of your future husband will be revealed by the noises heard.'[12]

In his notebooks, Hardy made note of a marriage game played at Bockhampton to divine the occupation of a maid's husband: 'All kinds of materials are put into a circle (wood, iron, brick, etc): girls blindfolded, turned round, & made to crawl from centre. Whichever material they crawl to will bear upon their future husbands.'[13] There was another 'old custom' that Hardy heard and then later transcribed into his private notebook: on All-Hallows' Eve, 'Kill a pigeon: stick its heart full of pins. Roast the heart in the candle flame. Faithless lovers will twist & toss with nightmare [sic] in his sleep.'[14]

All these stories drew him in, and he worried that local folklore and superstitions would be lost to future generations. Many of them would find their way into his fiction. Hardy believed in ghosts. He was convinced that he saw the ghost of his grandfather in the Stinsford churchyard. His childhood was a place where the oral tradition reigned supreme, where fables, folktales and ballads fired his imagination just as much as did his tenderness for the humble earthworm and his relish for his native heath and vales. This was the paradox of the young Thomas Hardy: a youth equally inspired by the poetry of Wordsworth and the story of Diana Chester who worked her spells by the devil.

And then there were the true stories told by his parents: of public whippings, murders and executions by hanging. They too would leave a lasting legacy.

Jemima did not sugar-coat her lurid tales for the sake of her small children. She told her son about a child who was whipped at a cart-tail in Yeovil for stealing a book.[15] For book-loving Jemima, this story must have sent shivers down her spine. And there was a suicide of a young (nameless) local girl, who was buried on Hendford Hill, near Yeovil, on a bleak mountaintop. The girl was not even given a coffin, her body thrown into a makeshift, unblessed grave. A stake was driven through the heart, and then earth was heaped over the body. Her only mourner was another anonymous girl who threw flowers on the exposed form.[16]

One in particular of Jemima's grisly stories left an indelible mark on the young Hardy. He recalled being a very small child of maybe four or six when she told him the tale of James Blomfield Rush. In fact, Hardy was nine when the crime was committed. Rush, known to the newspaper and the broadsheets as 'the killer in the fog', had murdered in cold blood his land-lord, Isaac Jermy. The rest of the family was home when the murder took place; Jermy's son was also killed and his wife and maid were shot and badly injured, but survived.

Hardy was puzzled when, discussing the case, his mother made the ambiguous remark 'the governess hanged him'.[17] The boy was confused, as he took her phrase literally. How could a governess hang a grown man? He discovered that Rush was convicted by the testimony of the 'governess' – a woman with whom he was having an affair and who was pregnant with his child. Her name was Emily Sandford. When Emily told Rush that she was pregnant, he jilted her, so she was out for revenge. She informed on him, and Rush was sentenced to death by hanging.

The trial, the gruesomeness of the murders, and the revelations of Emily Sandford, were widely discussed and fodder for the broadsheets. Sometimes known as 'murder ballads' or 'gallows ballads', they were sold on the day of execution or following a prisoner's confession. The ballads were passed around, sung aloud (often to the same tune as popular hymns), and were offered as warnings against crime and wrongdoing. These narrative songs were told from the perspective of the murderer, who now repents his crime and awaits death.

Another infamous case, which inspired several broadsheet ballads, was that of the Norwich murderer, William Sherward, who was hanged in 1852. Sherward killed his wife, mutilated her dead body, and boiled her head in a saucepan.

Hardy's father also told his son stories of the hangman's noose, though he was most interested in cases of those who were wrongly accused. He told his son about a young boy, suspected, Mr Hardy thought wrongly, of being a rioter. The boy was so 'light with hunger' that weights were attached to his feet to ensure that strangulation would occur. The detail of the weights seemed particularly shocking, though it was not uncommon for weights to be attached to the feet of women and boys to ensure a quick, more humane, death. Nor does it seem to be true that the boy was indeed innocent. Hardy, or his father, were probably conflating two local stories, and it seems probable that the young man was guilty of arson.[18]

It was also the case that, by the time Hardy was born, death by hanging was becoming less common. Transportation was a more likely outcome. But when an execution occurred, it made the newspapers and broadsheets, and was the talk of the town. One case lingered long in Hardy's imagination, though it happened many years before he was born, in 1706. An ancestor had been present at the execution and had handed down the gruesome details. It was the case of a Dorset girl called Mary Channing, who had been wrongly accused of the murder by poison of her husband. She had recently given birth, but she was shown no mercy, and sentenced to death by hanging and burning. Her execution took place in the Roman amphitheatre of Maumbury Ring, in the centre of Dorchester, where the ten-year-old Thomas would witness anti-Catholic protestors. The gladiatorial venue offered the crowd a good view.

Mary was just nineteen when she was executed. What made her case all the more poignant was that she had a sweetheart, whom she dearly loved. Her excessive affection had drawn criticism from her neighbours, and her parents had forced her into an arranged marriage with the local grocer, a man she did not love. After thirteen weeks of unhappy marriage she had poisoned her husband with mercury. At her trial, she had defended herself ably, but her reputation was tarnished, and the jury took only thirty minutes to find her guilty. In desperation she 'pleaded her belly' and her execution was delayed until after she had given birth. In those days, women who killed their husbands were given the added conviction of 'petty treason'. Male criminals found guilty of 'uxoricide' were usually sentenced to death by hanging. Women found guilty of mariticide were given a more severe punishment of partial hanging and then burning at the stake.[19] Mary's husband, Thomas Channing, had reportedly requested a last wish: to be kissed by his wife for one final time. Hardy's ballad, 'The Mock Wife', depicts the story of this 'last kiss'.

Mary was taken from prison to a gallows surrounded by a pile of faggots. She was partially strangled, and then burnt to death in the presence of ten thousand spectators. Tradition reported that at a certain stage of the burning, her heart burst out and leapt from her body. In his private notebooks, Hardy made notes on the case, pointedly writing that her guilt was 'not proven'. He lingered on the gory details: that she had reportedly 'writhed and shrieked' on recovering consciousness during the burning, and that 'one of the constables thrust a swab in her mouth to stop her cries'. As she was swabbed, 'milk from her bosoms . . . squirted out' into the faces of the baying spectators.[20] Hardy also noted that the smell of burning meat shocked the crowd, putting them off their roast dinners. These details were stored up and used in *The Mayor of Casterbridge*.

CHAPTER 14

Martha Clark

On Christmas Day in 1778, a baby was christened at St John the Baptist Church at Symondsbury in Dorset, the second of five girls. Her name was Martha Hussey, and she would give birth to one of the most notorious women of the West Country.[1] Martha Hussey married John Clark, an itinerant farm labourer and dairyman, who travelled around the region in search of work. There is no baptismal record for their daughter, named Martha after her mother, but sometimes known as Elizabeth. This second Martha only appears in public records in 1831, when she married a widower, almost twenty years her senior, a butcher called Bernard Bern. She was illiterate and signed her name on the marriage register with a cross.

Upon her marriage, Martha Clark took on a nine-year-old stepdaughter and an eight-year-old stepson. She gave birth to a baby boy named William, quickly followed by a second son, Thomas. When William was just a toddler, he contracted an illness, probably smallpox or measles. He died, as did his brother, twelve days later. Six months after that, the stepson died. More tragedy followed when Bernard fell into financial difficulties and left home. He died sometime in either 1841 or 1842, and Martha began a new life as a housekeeper at Blackmanston Farm in Steeple Dorset.

It was while she was working there that Martha met and fell deeply in love with John Brown, a handsome shepherd, six feet tall with long thick hair. Though nineteen years her junior, he married Martha in 1852, and they moved to Birdsmoorgate, a small hamlet in the Marshwood Vale, where John worked as a 'tranter' (carrier of goods) – the same occupation as Reuben Dewy in *Under the Greenwood Tree*. The couple adopted the illegitimate daughter of a relative and settled down to married life. While John travelled around with his horse and cart, Martha ran a small chandlery and grocery shop from her home.

She was a handsome woman with short black curly hair. Later, she was described as having a 'quiet appearance'. Sometime in 1855, she discovered that her husband was having an affair with their neighbour, Mary Davis, who was married to a carpenter much older than herself. Torrid details would emerge. Martha, suspecting her husband of infidelity, listened outside the window of Mary's cottage, and heard her husband's voice from within, speaking 'disgusting language jocularly incident to such improper interviews'. Martha may have looked quiet, but she clearly had a fierce temper. She beat Mary Davis so violently that she was summoned before the magistrates and bound over to keep the peace. John was not only unfaithful but was a heavy drinker, and the marriage was marked by violent outbursts, where he would beat his wife with a whip.

John was often away from home with his deliveries, and he would sometimes stay overnight at the home of his friend and fellow tranter, George Fooks. On the morning of 5 July 1856, George made an early call at Birdsmoorgate, and had breakfast with the Browns, before the two men set off on a long trip to Beaminster to deliver poles. About half a mile from his house, John gave a lift to Mary Davis, who was working at a nearby farm. After a long day, John and George stopped off at the local inn, the Cross Keys Inn, and slaked their thirst, staying for over an hour. They left and headed for another inn, the George. Later that evening, John made a purchase at a local saddlery, said goodbye to George, and headed home. That was the last time John Brown was seen alive.

In the early hours of the following morning, Martha ran to the house of her husband's cousin, Richard Deamon, and banged on his window, begging for help, saying that John had been in an accident with his horse. It was 5 a.m., and Richard came over to find his cousin lying on the floor, his body resting on a green cushion, his head tied with a handkerchief. He took his hand, and knew immediately that he was dead, though the hand was still warm. Blood gushed from the back of his head, though his face and shirt were untouched. One of his boots was unlaced. Martha told Richard Deamon that her husband returned home injured at two o'clock in the morning, and that she had dragged him into the house but been unable to revive him.

Deamon was suspicious. He went to the horse field and found no evidence of a disturbance. The horse's bridle was safely stored under a hay rick, and John Brown's hat in perfect condition. There was no blood near the gate. The only sign of any disturbance was a pool of vomit, and a piece of cord, as if someone had laid down on the ground.

When he returned to the house, he saw that there was no blood anywhere save in the living room. A coroner's inquest was held the following day at the Rose and Crown Inn, where the presiding doctor examined the body and discovered six blows to the head. Later, Elizabeth Sampson, who owned the field where John Brown kept his horse, confessed that at 2 a.m., she had heard three loud screams or groans, gradually growing quieter. But even before this testimony, Martha had been charged with murder and taken away to Dorchester Gaol.

Two weeks later, one of the most publicised and controversial trials of the time took place in Dorchester Crown Court. It hit the national newspapers. The press could not get enough of the sensational story. Details were exaggerated. How Martha was forty and her husband only nineteen. How his hair was covered in brains and blood. How Martha was a jealous woman.

. The surgeon testified that the head wounds were consistent with the striking of a blunt instrument or hatchet. It was inconceivable that it was a head injury caused by a horse. He went into fine details of the extensive injuries to the brain and neck, causing gasps to the crowded courtroom. Martha changed her testimony and claimed that her husband fell down the stairs, denying 'by oath' that she ever struck him. Only one man stood by her, a local farmer who described her as 'a kind and inoffensive woman'. The jury (all men) declared a verdict of 'Guilty'. Everyone in the courtroom knew what would happen next. Judge Channell reached for the black cap, put it over his wig, with one of the corners facing outwards, and sentenced Martha Brown to death by hanging.

On 7 August, two days before her execution, she made a full confession to the prison chaplain. It was made public and appeared in the *Weymouth Journal*. The details were a shocking account of domestic brutality. Her husband had arrived home late, and drunk. He was not wearing his hat, and he had vomited through excess drink. She asked after the whereabouts of his hat, which started a quarrel. He was swearing and abusive and asked for some cold tea. She asked him if he had been to see Mary Davis, and the row escalated. He kicked out the bottom of the chair she was sitting on, and they had an argument which lasted until 3 a.m. Martha brought some supper, which he refused to eat, striking her a severe blow across the side of her head, which dazed her. Then he drew his whip from the mantelpiece, a heavy hand whip, with a plaited head, and lashed her three times. When she screamed in pain, he threatened to knock her brains through the window. He told her that he wished he would find her dead in the morning, and gave her one more beating, a fierce kick to the left side of her body.

John sat down and unlaced his boot, and Martha took her chance, grabbing a hatchet that was lying nearby where she had been breaking down lumps of coal for the fire to keep his supper warm. All the rage and fury and pain he had caused swept over her, and she smashed the hatchet into his head. She could not remember how many times she struck, but he fell at the first blow, and never moved again. Once she had stopped her frenzied attack, she was immediately overcome with remorse. She had never hit him before and had borne his physical abuse – 'but when he hit me so hard at this time I was almost out of my senses, and hardly knew what I was doing'.

Her account rings true: the details of the heavy whip with the plaited head, the account of the warmed-up supper and the unlaced boot. After this startling confession, there was much public sympathy for Martha Brown, and efforts were made to save her life. Her case sparked debates about capital punishment and the treatment of women in the justice system. Earlier that same year, Lord Grey had granted a reprieve to a woman named Celestina Sommer who had killed her own daughter by cutting her throat. Known as the Islington murderess, she became an international cause célèbre. Sommer was extremely beautiful, and many people believed that she was reprieved for that reason, but her case highlighted the growing dissatisfaction with the death penalty.

The news of Celestina Sommer's reprieve came on the very day of her execution, and she was sentenced to life in prison. Hope remained high that the West Country's Martha Brown might also be saved. Her case brought attention to Dorset. Petitions were circulated and two prominent local men, one the vicar who had obtained the confession, travelled to London to obtain a pardon from the Secretary of State. It was to no avail.

Her executioner was the infamous William Calcraft. He employed the 'short-drop' method, in which the drop through the trapdoor was about three feet. The drop was not always sufficient to cause instant death, meaning that strangulation was slow. Calcraft would sometimes pull on the legs of his victim to hasten death. Some believed that he did so in order to entertain the crowd. The bodies were left hanging until certain death was assured.

That same year, Calcraft had spectacularly bungled the public execution of a notorious criminal, William Bousfield. Calcraft released the bolts of the trapdoor, and the condemned man began to hang, but he suddenly raised his leg to support himself on the platform. Calcraft threw himself around Bousfield's legs, the sheer weight eventually succeeding in strangling him. The story became the subject of a popular ballad.

Female murderers were a rarity. It is estimated that out of a possible 450 hangings performed by Calcraft, only thirty-five were women. Esher Hibner, known to the press as the 'Evil Monster', had to be restrained with a straitjacket at her execution as it was feared she would attack Calcraft. As she swung, the crowd cheered 'Three cheers for the Hangman'.[2]

On this day, William Calcraft seemed nervous. Martha was no hardened, seasoned criminal, but a woman who had snapped after years of domestic abuse. A woman that had immense public support. The night before the execution took place, she was visited by her family members, and the father of her husband. Until the last, she hoped for a reprieve.

The next morning a large crowd of more than four thousand people gathered at the new entrance of the Dorset County Gaol. One of those who got up early and found himself a bird's eye view, close to the scaffold was sixteen-year-old Thomas Hardy.

APPRENTICESHIP

CHAPTER 15

Mary Moule

They were known to Thomas Hardy as the 'Seven Brethren', and they lived in the Dorset village of Fordington, close to Dorchester and two miles from Bockhampton. Their reputation preceded them. Henry, George, Frederick, Horatio, Charles, Arthur, and Handley Moule: the strikingly good-looking and clever sons of the celebrated Reverend Henry Moule. Their father was the vicar of St George's, a fine fifteenth-century church, standing high on a hill overlooking the Fordington village green. The Reverend Moule was a writer, a brilliant orator, and the inventor of the first sanitary toilet. The Moule brothers were to play a crucial part in the life of Thomas Hardy. Their influence was far-reaching, though their backgrounds were very different.

The Reverend Henry Moule had arrived as the incumbent of the parish of Fordington in 1829, with his wife, Mary, and their two young sons. The rest of their sons were born and raised in the vicarage. Hardy's description of them as the seven brethren was an allusion to a story in the gospels, but there were in fact eight sons. Christopher, the seventh, had died aged fifteen months. This was a profound loss to Mary, who described him as 'beautiful with the light of mind and of love shining in his eyes'. She visited his grave often, praying and giving thanks. In memory of her dead baby, she told the brothers that they must consider themselves to be 'eight, eight forever'.[1]

The vicarage was a low, long building entered via stone steps through a door in the wall, which led onto the front garden. At the back of the vicarage were extensive gardens, a winding gravel path, and flower beds. Sycamore trees dotted the lawn, and there was an open field behind with views of the spires of Dorchester. To the left of the garden were open arable fields and a view of the sea, the isle of Portland, joined to the mainland by Chesil Beach, and to the east, the Isle of Wight. The horizon was dotted with prehistoric funeral barrows, cut clear against the sky. The church, at the top of the village, looked down on the water-meadows of the River Frome, and in the distant was the blue line of the Purbeck Hills.

The vicarage was also used as a school for boys preparing for Oxford and Cambridge. The dining room, which ran the length of the house, was used as a schoolroom, leading to a playroom where the boys played indoor games, and on winter evenings took part in singing. The most gifted of the seven brethren was Horatio, who by the age of twelve was an accomplished musician and organist, playing in the village church.

The Reverend Moule had a study where he talked to his sons about Christian history and gave them lessons in Greek. Mary Moule had a 'Little Parlour' where she taught the young boys to read – or went to escape the noise of the schoolroom. The Reverend made improvements to the schoolroom, building a fireplace at either end and filling three walls with books. It was the heart of the house; not just a schoolroom but the family library, and a space to read, and play games in the holidays. The open fields that backed onto the garden were used for cricket in the summer months.

In his first years at Fordington, the vicar was extremely unpopular. He was known to be a fervent 'Evangelist' and lover of the gospels, which meant he was feared by his parishioners and distrusted by the local gentry. As the family were soon to discover, the outskirts of Fordington were deprived, poverty-stricken areas, where 'vice and misery' flourished. Cuckolds Row had a particularly notorious reputation, as its name suggests. During the early years of Moule's incumbency, there were riots and ricket-burnings, scenes of political unrest and violence. Many of the rural poor were anti-religious and held the new vicar in contempt. His youngest son, Handley, remembered that his father 'had much to bear in the way of opposition, and even of personal insult'.[2] Crowds gathered at the churchyard gates to toss insults at the vicar and his family as they entered the church on Sundays.

Henry and Mary Moule ignored the insults and set about building two schools and organising a Sunday School. They worked alongside the poor, visiting every house and beginning weekday services and 'cottage lectures'. In protest against the vices he saw arising from the Dorchester Races, Henry successfully petitioned to end the races. One of his responsibilities was to act as curate to the Dorchester barracks. Having no church premises, services were conducted in the Riding School. The Reverend would walk to the barracks early in the morning to conduct his service. One morning, a young woman, visiting her brother in Dorchester, attended the 'rough and ready' service. It was her first sight of the Reverend Moule, and she thought him a 'fine, noble-looking young man'. He preached at the drumhead, to the congregation of soldiers standing in the sawdust. A guinea lay on the drumhead, which he gathered up at the end of the service before hurrying back to Fordington Church. The woman was Jemima Hand, and she never forgot that day.[3]

With his usual vigour and energy, Moule raised funds to build the soldiers a new church in west Fordington. But he was still unpopular in his parish and it would take twenty years to turn the public tide in his favour. There were two severe outbreaks of cholera in Fordington, in 1849 and 1854. It was then that the Reverend Moule showed the extent of his formidable talents and courage. Despite the danger to himself and his family, he visited the sick and conducted services in the open fields. Lack of sanitation intensified the horrors of the epidemic, and one Sunday in extremely hot weather, Moule sent two of his sons on horseback to ride up to the millers on the river and beg them to let loose the water to sluice the River Frome. One of the reasons that the village of Fordington was affected so badly by cholera was because a large number of infected convicts from London had been sent to live in empty barracks in Dorchester. Their clothes were sent to Fordington to be laundered, bringing the disease with them, and infecting the inhabitants.

Thomas Hardy would long recall the cholera years at Fordington. He remembered that every morning a man would wheel out the clothing and bedlinen of those who had died in the night. The Reverend had set a large copper pot on the mead to boil the clothes if they could be salvaged and burnt if they could not. Hardy remembered that Moule arranged to have large fires kindled in Mill Street to carry off infection.[4]

Moule's indefatigable efforts during the pandemic ensured that the disease was contained and did not reach Dorchester. After the pandemic ended, Moule was presented with gifts and testimonials from the Mayor of Dorchester. More importantly, he became loved and admired by his parishioners for his compassion and courage, as did his wife, Mary. Despite her family duties, rearing her children and educating the small boys, and supervising the Sunday School, she was indefatigable in her efforts during the pandemic. She prepared remedies and treatments at the vicarage and assisted the sick.

Mary was just as dedicated as her husband. Having lost one child, she must have greatly feared losing another. Her Bible, almost falling to pieces with usage, contained a note alluding to her fear of the cholera pandemics, and her faith in God 'amidst its dangers'.[5] She showed remarkable courage and fortitude in her efforts to combat the disease.

Their efforts during the cholera years made them local heroes. Following the 'Great Stink' of 1858, Moule turned his efforts to sanitary science, and in 1860, patented an earth composting closet system, which he hoped would save his parishioners from future cholera outbreaks. Moule published many works on the subject,[6] and his earth closet system was adopted in rural districts, private houses, hospitals, and extensively in the British Raj.

Moule was becoming much celebrated, publishing many works of verse, sermons, and educational and religious pamphlets. He also published works about the value of manure for gardens (*Manure for the Million*) and wrote a book about his own kitchen gardens. He was most famous for publishing his *Eight Letters to Prince Albert* in 1855, prompted by the squalid conditions of Fordington. It's hardly surprising that Thomas Hardy would later apply to him a phrase of Matthew Arnold's: 'energy is genius'.[7]

Mary, meanwhile, was adored by her sons. Born Mary Evans, she was educated at schools in London, which left her with a love of literature and 'perfect handwriting'.[8] Handley thought she would have been capable of becoming a literary critic or a writer, if circumstances had permitted. He had a difficult childhood, suffering from severe cornea trouble that affected his eyesight. His brothers Horace and Charles would read to him in the Nursery, where he was overseen by a formidable but devoted nurse, Susan Northover. Handley's bed was in his mother's room, where he stayed for several years, under her watchful eye. Sometimes, afraid of the dark, he would creep out of bed at night, and listen to the sounds of family prayer, which ended at nine thirty following the Lord's Prayer. Handley was puzzled that his mother spent so long in prayer, knowing her innate goodness. She would read the bed-psalm to her son, and in her gentle voice would 'lay me down and sleep'. Mary Moule became her son's eyes, and would read to him for hours on end, pouring 'beautiful and instructive' words into his 'darkened' eyes. To his delight, she read novels aloud, such as *Uncle Tom's Cabin*.[9]

The Moule sons were destined for Cambridge, following in the footsteps of their learned father. Henry Moule was a severe figure and disciplinarian, and Mary's gentleness and deep love for her sons compensated for his exacting conduct. His sons respected him more than they loved him. One of his sons recalled that they revered and feared their father too much for 'the easy demonstration of affection'.[10] This aspect of the Reverend Moule was to have serious consequences for one of his sons, who would become Hardy's closest friend and mentor. Later when the Reverend was a grandfather, and had mellowed with age, his sons were delighted by the loving and more openly demonstrative relationship he had with his grandchildren.

During his years as an apprentice in Dorchester, Thomas Hardy would come to know the Moule family well. For a time, he attended services at Fordington, long remembering the rich delivery of the vicar who spoke without notes. Though he was not technically a parishioner of St George's he felt 'virtually', though not 'topographically', a member of the congregation. And for 'many years of his life' Hardy would regard himself as a virtual member of the Reverend Moule's home.[11] The vicarage and its inhabitants showed Hardy a very different kind of existence to one he had known at Bockhampton. The Reverend Moule would also play an unexpected part in one of the most influential experiences of his life.

CHAPTER 16

Patty Sparks

Shortly before his sixteenth birthday, Thomas Hardy made an expensive purchase. He bought a leather-lined desk from William Treves' furniture shop in Dorchester. He treasured it and kept it in perfect condition all his life.[1] It was a symbolic gesture: he was about to leave school and start an apprenticeship. He had been introduced to a business acquaintance of his father: a local architect called John Hicks. Young Hardy made a sufficiently favourable impression that he was offered an apprenticeship for three years.

In his self-ghosted autobiography he said, somewhat apologetically, that he was a 'child till he was sixteen, a youth till he was five-and-twenty, and a young man till he was nearly fifty'.[2] Perhaps to celebrate his transition from childhood to youth, and his entrance into the world as an apprentice, as well as buying the desk, he sat for his studio portrait at John Pouncy's of Dorchester in High West Street. The young Thomas Hardy was probably one of the first clients of this new business.

John Pouncy, a self-made man and an acquaintance of Hicks, was born in Cuckolds Row in Fordington. He had assisted the Reverend Henry Moule during the cholera outbreaks. He was exactly the sort of man that Hardy admired. Originally a house painter and decorator, he was a pioneer in the development of photography, inventing a technique to prevent prints from fading.[3] His *Dorsetshire Photographically Illustrated* (1857) featured eighty illustrations of local scenes, alongside historical narrative and literary quotations from nature poets, such as William Cowper, James Thomson and Wordsworth. Photographs of Melbury House and Stinsford House were among the illustrations. Pouncy may well have been a model for Hardy's hero, William Dare, a photographic inventor in *A Laodicean*.

Pouncy sold his *cartes de visites* in batches of ten. Each photograph was the size of a visiting card, and cards were commonly traded among friends and visitors in the 1860s. Albums for the collection and display of cards became a common fixture in Victorian parlours. Over the years, Hardy would regularly sit for his studio portrait, and would present his sweethearts with a *carte de visite* as a token of affection.

Hardy was articled to John Hicks for three years. In those days, apprenticeships came at a price. The cost was a hundred pounds, but business-minded Jemima suggested a 'ready-money' agreement, and had the fee reduced to forty. Hardy claimed that he 'cheerfully agreed' to go to Mr Hicks, despite having the occasional thought of entering the church. And if his parents thought his studying days were over, they were wrong. He was, he said, 'a born bookworm' and, despite his new position, 'that alone was unchanging'.[4]

He devised a programme of self-study, but the education he received at Hicks' was in all likelihood the best he ever had, and for the first time he made real friends. His fellow apprentice, Henry Bastow, had been schooled in London, and, like Hardy, regretted breaking off his studies to take up architecture. The young men were healthily competitive, and they began to read together. Hicks, who was a genial, well-educated man, with a knowledge of the classics, encouraged the lads in their studies.

Hardy recalled that throughout the three years of his apprenticeship they gave more time to books than to drawing.

He would rise early and read for three hours between five and eight (or four and eight in the summer months). In this way, he got through several books of the *Aeneid*, and 'some Horace and Ovid', and took up Greek, which he had not learnt at school. Now he pored over the *Iliad* before breakfast. On the walk to Dorchester, Hardy would practise Latin by reciting aloud. During office hours, the two young men would test themselves on Greek and Latin, and Hicks would join in; he was 'ahead of them in Greek, though they could beat him in Latin'. Learning this way, for the sheer pleasure and the enjoyment of competition, was invaluable for Hardy. Sometimes arguments arose: 'the clash of polemics between the two pupils sometimes reached such a pitch of clamour that the architect's wife would send down a message . . . imploring them not to make so much noise'.[5]

His apprenticeship brought him into contact with a wider circle of friends. There were two clever Scottish friends of Bastow, devout Baptists, who 'could rattle off at a moment's notice the Greek original of any passage in the New Testament'. Clever as they were, Hardy thought that he possessed a 'breadth of mind that they lacked'.[6] More importantly, his sixteenth year was marked by the beginnings of his friendship with the Moule brothers.

Scholars and biographers have puzzled over how Hardy first met the Moules. The likeliest explanation is that Jemima knew Mary Moule. Hardy's own recollection was that he began to get to know the family when the eldest brother, Henry, gave him lessons in watercolour painting. Following Henry's death, Hardy recalled him standing beside him while he attempted a sketch from nature: 'He must have been about thirty, and had already become an adept in out-door painting. As I was but a youth, and by no means practised in that art, he criticised my performance freely.'[7] Henry Moule came to know the Bockhampton garden well enough to admire Jemima's 'old-fashioned flowers'.[8] It was probably he who introduced Hardy to his brother, Horace.

This formative time of Hardy's life was marked by two significant, and humiliating, events. One of them he never spoke about, and the other he spoke about only to his second wife. The first concerned an embarrassing incident with one of his female Sparks cousins. The incident was shrouded in mystery, but Hardy was turned out of the house for inappropriate behaviour. He was attending a Christmas Mummers' rehearsal at Sparks' Corner, and drink was flowing at the beer-barn next door. Hardy was said to have 'made violent approaches' to one of his cousins.[9] It was unclear which cousin it was, but a couple of hints suggest it was Martha, known to the family as Patty. She was the 'the flower of our flock', according to her sister Rebecca. She had been a lady's maid in London, and, for a brief time, in Paris. With her striking looks and sophistication, she looked the part of a lady. She was six years older than her cousin, and it was unlikely that she would have taken the pass very seriously. Hardy later visited her in London. Her nephew would later report that Tom wanted to marry her, but his mother and aunt were against the match.[10] Patty later married and emigrated to Australia, taking with her a book given to her by Hardy and inscribed 'to dear Patty'.[11]

According to the Sparks family, Maria was so angered by her nephew's behaviour that she threw Thomas out of the house and forbade him from visiting. If this story is true, Hardy did not stay away long, and his infraction did not prevent him from later falling in love with Patty's youngest sister. As we will see, the young Hardy was attracted to women of his social class who had risen to the status of lady's maid.

That summer of 1856 found Hardy in another humiliating

experience when he was at Stinsford church with his mother, listening to the sermon given by the Reverend Arthur Shirley. Shirley had long been the nemesis of the Hardy family, since they held him responsible for disbanding the Stinsford string musical choir and replacing them with a barrel organist (events that would inspire *Under the Greenwood Tree*). The Reverend Shirley was also responsible for starting the village school with Julia Martin and would have presumably known about her rift with the Hardys.

On one occasion, the Reverend Shirley's oratorical ineptitude had left the boy in a fit of giggles, which he struggled to control. Hardy knew that he was behaving 'mischievously' when he imagined that the vicar was 'preaching mockingly' and was 'tottering on the verge of laughter'.[12] Hardy may well have drawn attention to himself for his fit of giggles in church, and aroused the vicar's ire. If so, the Reverend Shirley took his revenge when he gave a sermon preaching against the rural class seeking to improve themselves by rising into the professional classes. Hardy felt that the sermon was aimed at him – he would never forgive Shirley.[13] The incident felt like a humiliating public dressing-down.

His new life as an architect's assistant was already pulling him towards a new sophisticated circle, including Hicks, Bastow and the Moule brothers. His infatuation with Louisa Harding, who was of a higher social class, and the rejection that ensued, had already been a stern reminder of his status as a builder's son. If he had ever truly felt conscious of the class system, it was now, in the words of the Reverend Shirley. At Bockhampton, his intelligence, smart clothes, and satchel full of books, had set him apart as someone superior to his classmates, but now he felt the sting of the class divide, and it was something that never fully left him.

CHAPTER 17

Martha Brown

At 7 a.m. on the morning of 9 August 1856, the under-sheriff, the sheriff and the javelin men met at the county hall and proceeded to the gaol by the old entrance. It was the job of the under-sheriff to knock on the door. The governor answered: 'Who is there?'

'The sheriff of Dorset, who demands the body of Elizabeth Martha Brown now under the sentence of death, that execution may be done on her.'[1]

The sheriff proceeded to the cell, leaving the other officers behind. Precisely at eight o'clock, the prison bell pealed forth 'its solemn and warning knell'. Martha Brown appeared. She shook hands with the warden and the other officers and left the prison, heading towards the scaffold. It was built on the gate-house of the gaol, some distance from the cells, but she had refused the offer of the prison van. The newspapers reported that she walked very, very slowly, her hands joined together in prayer.

By now, thick hazy rain was falling, but this did not deter the large crowd of several thousand. Martha's dignity and fortitude were remarkable. She talked quietly with the chaplain, Dacre Clemetson, who had tried so hard to win her a reprieve.

On either side of her were two female attendants, entirely over-come. Martha did not shed a tear: 'On her way to the scaffold, her demeanour was extraordinary . . . the culprit bore her awful position with the greatest resignation and composure.'

As she approached the place of execution, she mounted the steps, leaving behind her weeping attendants. Her tread was firm, and at the pinioning station she was given a cordial to drink, and then her arms were fixed to her sides with leather straps. Martha had dressed herself carefully, in an elegant black silk dress. There were whispers that this was the mourning dress that she had bought for her husband's funeral.

At this point, the Reverend Clemetson was so overcome with emotion that he could go no further. Another clergyman stepped forward to accompany her on her final journey to the gallows. Her step still firm, she walked up another flight of stairs (nineteen in number), to the roof of the gatehouse, with its view across the North Square of the town. She crossed the platform. It was only as she approached the gallows that her step faltered.

William Calcraft placed the rope over the beam and put a white hood over her face. The hood was to prevent the victim from seeing the executioner pull the lever, and to prevent the crowd from seeing the agony on the victim's face. He adjusted the noose to fit around her neck and left the scaffold. Then to the crowd's astonishment, he reappeared. He had forgotten to tie her dress in advance (a usual procedure for fear that flesh might be exposed to the crowd). He left the scaffold again, and drew the bolt. Martha Brown fell with great force, 'and after a few struggles ceased to exist'.

The young boy watching the execution would remember every detail. This was the day that sowed the seed for his greatest novel.

In November 1904, *The Sketch* printed a paragraph about *Tess*

of the D'Urbervilles in relation to Martha Brown. Without
evidence, it suggests that the young boy actually knew Martha
Brown and her husband:

> When Hardy was a boy he used to come into Dorchester to
> school, and he made the acquaintance of a woman there who,
> with her husband, kept an inn. She was beautiful, good and
> kind, but married to a dissipated scoundrel who was unfaithful
> to her. One day she discovered her husband under circumstances
> which so roused her passion that she stabbed him with a knife
> and killed him.

Hardy cut out this paragraph and pasted it into a scrapbook
marked 'Personal'. He crossed out and altered the sentence
suggesting that he knew Martha Brown, and he also corrected
the sentence about the profession of the Browns. He then wrote
the word 'Corrected' at the top of the paragraph. So we must
assume that the latter part of the story in *The Sketch* was true:

> Young Hardy, with another boy, came into Dorchester and
> witnessed the execution from a tree that overlooked the yard in
> which the gallows was placed. He never forgot the rustle of the
> thin black gown the woman was wearing as she was led forth
> by the warders. A penetrating rain was falling; the white cap
> was no sooner over the woman's head than it clung to her
> features, and the noose was put round the neck of what looked
> like a marble statue. Hardy looked at the scene with the strange
> illusion of its being unreal, and was brought to his complete
> senses when the drop fell with a thud and his companion on a
> lower branch of the tree fell fainting to the ground. The tragedy
> haunted Hardy, and at last, provided the emotional inspiration
> and some of the matter for *Tess of the D'Urbervilles*.[2]

This account was told by Hardy to the *Sketch's* journalist, Neil Munro: it presents a far more detailed picture than that provided in his memoirs and correspondence. But it rings true: the two boys climbing a tree to get a good view, the second boy fainting away when Martha dropped to her death, Hardy describing her as a marble statue. His account also mirrors the contemporary newspaper accounts, with their emphasis on her stillness and composure.

The rustle of Martha Brown's silk dress echoes that of Julia Martin's silks as she used to bend over him. Throughout his novels, female dress would be an important sexual motif. Later, Hardy repeated the Martha Brown story to another friend, 'with a sort of gaiety'. Yet again, he drew attention to the wet gown and Martha's features showing through the execution hood.[3]

When Hardy's second wife, Florence, wrote about the Martha Brown execution, she appears to have blamed his parents, writing that it was a pity that he had been 'permitted' to see the hanging. She added: 'It may have given a tinge of bitterness and gloom to his life's work.'[4] Yet his accounts of the case do not appear to be either gloomy or bitter; there is guilt, yes, but there is also a strong undeniable sexual frisson and voyeuristic enjoyment.[5] The day marked the end of his childhood.

And by one of those chilling coincidences of the kind that would become a hallmark of his novels, the second clergyman who accompanied Martha Brown on her final steps to the gallows was none other than the Reverend Henry Moule.

CHAPTER 18

Kate Hardy

That October, Jemima gave birth to her fourth and last child, a daughter, Katharine, known to the family as Kate. Jemima, now in her forty-fourth year, was taking no chances with her health, and instructed a doctor to assist with her labour.[1] Even though there was a sixteen-year gap between Thomas and his sister, and he was now out in the world working as an apprentice, he took an interest in her, though they were never as close as he was to Mary.

In the meantime, Tom was already embarking on a life filled with more freedom and adventure than his sisters would ever know. He was getting closer to the Moule brothers, fishing in the Frome River with Charles Moule and swimming in the green waters of Weymouth Bay.[2] And soon he would meet the most brilliant and charismatic of the brothers, Horatio, known to his brothers as Horace. The musical prodigy, who played the church organ at the age of twelve, had gone up to Oxford in 1851 to read classics, before transferring to Cambridge, where his dissertation *Christian Oratory: An Enquiry into its History* won the Hulsean Prize. He was a shining comet in Hardy's young adulthood, and the object of his devoted hero-worship. His influence was profound and long-lasting.

Horace was eight years senior to Hardy. He assumed the role of mentor and teacher, a part that came naturally enough to this man of great learning, enthusiasm, kindness and sensitivity. Horace had been the beneficiary of a gifted teacher himself, the Reverend J. A. Leakey, his father's curate, and he passed on his love of learning to those willing to listen. At the time that Hardy first knew him, Horace was teaching in his father's small school at the vicarage. He was also helping to prepare his youngest brother, Handley, for the Cambridge examinations. Both Handley and Hardy remembered Horace's unusual methods. Handley recalled that Horace had a 'hundred charming ways of interesting and teaching me, alike in scholarship and in classical history'.[3] Both young men remembered that Horace liked to walk in the fields as he taught, 'translating Hesiod'. Handley recalled his brother drawing a plan of ancient Rome with pebbles on the lawn to bring his lessons alive. Horace's talent for teaching, according to Handley, was his 'subtle facility' for imparting 'a living interest in the subject-matter'. Handley said that his brother was a stickler for 'grammatical precision' but he got to the heart of Horace's gift when he described it as 'shedding an *indefinable glamour of the ideal* over all we read'.[4]

For reasons that became complicated as their friendship progressed, Hardy was less fulsome in his praise of Horace's teaching methods, as he was in his mentorship. In the *Life*, Hardy described Horace as a 'literary friend' who shared with him a love of books and influenced his reading. He described Horace as a 'fine Greek scholar', who was always ready to 'act the tutor in any classical difficulty'.[5] But something is being held back here. Horace was a generous friend, who gave him books, personally inscribed. Under Moule's influence, Hardy would in turn become a giver of books. He often sent texts and recommendations to his sister Mary. Meeting Horace was a pivotal moment: it made him question his life in architecture and 'biassed him still further in the direction of books'.[6]

Moule was an aspiring writer. He was a talented poet, and he was also beginning to write articles and reviews for a new London periodical. If Hardy questioned why such a brilliant and promising young man as Moule was content to teach in his father's school, Moule's literary ambitions would seem to present the explanation. Moule had also founded, and was president of, a literary society, which included his father's pupils, his friends, and his brothers, called the 'Fordington Times Society'. However, there was another reason why Moule was back living at home, under the watchful eyes of his parents. He was a heavy drinker and a depressive. He had been unable to finish his degree at either Oxford or Cambridge as a result of his problems. Moule also had a difficult relationship with his father. Like his brothers, he doted on his mother. Every year, on the anniversary of the death of her baby son, he would write her a special letter. But his relationship with Henry Moule was strained. Many of his emotional troubles were connected to his battles with his formidable father, who was vehemently opposed to alcohol and despairing of his troubled son.

Hardy was no stranger to alcoholic men, but they had hitherto fallen into a different category to that of the vicar's son, with his double university education. At the moment, Horace seemed to be conquering his demons, but he still seemed to find it difficult to commit to any one profession or to fulfil his enormous potential. Temperamentally, emotionally and politically, he was opposed to his father, and the cracks in their relationship were beginning to show. Horace had dedicated his prize-winning Cambridge thesis to his father, but the Reverend Moule was outraged when he discovered that his son had bought a controversial book, Gideon Algernon Mantell's *The Wonders of Geology*. Horace bequeathed the volumes to Hardy in April 1858.

Mantell was a doctor and a palaeontologist. His attempts to reconstruct the structure and life of the Iguanodon began the scientific study of dinosaurs. At the time of his death (he overdosed on opium), he was credited with discovering four of the five genera of dinosaurs then known. Little wonder that the Evangelical and biblically fundamentalist Reverend Moule was so horrified to find the volumes in his son's library. It would seem that Horace was close enough to Hardy to confide in him the scene of the angry confrontation with his father. Hardy would later recreate the scene in *Tess of the D'Urbervilles*.[7]

In the autumn of 1856, Kate Hardy was christened, with Thomas playing the fiddle at the service officiated by the Reverend Shirley. Arguments with his friend Bastow about adult versus infant baptism were stimulated by his thoughts on his own sister's baptism. It was also around this time that he made his first venture into print with an anonymous skit for the local newspaper on the disappearance of the alms-house clock, in South Street, which had been taken down to be cleaned, and then neglected to be reaffixed. Hardy's verse was anonymous, but he was rumbled by a post office clerk 'who watched the handwriting of letters posted till he had spotted the culprit'.[8] That Hardy wrote the skit in the persona of the ghost of the clock was, given his interest in folklore and witchcraft, hardly surprising.

As one new life began with the birth of Kate, another was taken away, as his grandmother died in January of 1857. This stimulated some lines of memory in the poem 'Domicilium'. After her death, the Hardy family renovated the cottage, moving the kitchen range and the bread oven, taking over Mary's quarters.

The death of his grandmother and the waning influence of Jemima, who had her hands full with the new baby, made him turn more fully to the influence of Horace Moule, whose writings for the new periodical, *The Saturday Review*, Hardy began to read. Previously he had subscribed to the *Popular Educator*, thanks to his mother, who paid the bill. It was published by John Cassell (he who rejected Jane Austen's *Pride and Prejudice*). Earlier, Cassell had published a periodical called *The Working Man's Friend*, sympathetic to the lives of the working class, and aiming to educate its readers. Hardy claimed that he began to learn German from the pages of the *Popular Educator*. Now the *Saturday Review* began to exert its influence on the young man, who seemed to be increasingly confused about his life as an architect. Horace was encouraging about Hardy's writing, but it would appear that he was not at all certain that a university path was right for him. Nevertheless, he continued to help Hardy with his Greek studies. Annotations in Hardy's Greek Grammar would appear to be those of Moule.

Above all, Horace was opening Hardy to a new intellectual world. They made an odd-looking couple: Horace tall, handsome and distinguished looking, Hardy small of stature, and self-conscious in his demeanour. Yet behind the appearances, it was Hardy who was determined and resilient, and Horace who was fragile and full of self-loathing.

CHAPTER 19

Sarah Ann Guppy

'They have done for me at last, Hardy . . . my backbone is shot through.' The musket ball, fired at a range of only fifteen metres, entered the left shoulder, passed through a lung, and then into his spine. The Battle of Trafalgar was won, but at a terrible price: the death of the commander, Lord Horatio Nelson. He was carried down to the lower deck, where in his dying hours, he heard the news of the British victory. In great pain, and in full knowledge that he could not be saved, he called for his right-hand man, Flag Captain Thomas Hardy. Fearing the worst, he asked, 'Will no one bring Hardy to me? He is surely dead?' For an hour, brave Captain Hardy continued fighting above deck, but then he was brought to Nelson, who gave him his final instructions, asking him not to throw his body into the sea but to bury him next to his parents. He talked of his mistress, Lady Hamilton, and begged Hardy to take care of her. And in his final moments, he asked Hardy for one last mark of affection: 'Kiss me, Hardy.' Hardy bent down and bestowed a kiss on his forehead. 'Now I am satisfied. Now I have done my duty.' Hardy stood over his dying friend and kissed him again. 'God bless you, Hardy.' And then Hardy left him for ever.[1]

Captain Thomas Hardy was a famous name not just in his

native Dorset, but throughout Great Britain, where he was a national hero.

His famous portrait, with large telescope in hand, was known to the writer Thomas Hardy, who believed that he was related to Captain Hardy, and who felt a 'strong family likeness'.[2] Since childhood, he had loved stories about the Napoleonic Wars, which were in his grandmother's living memory. When Hardy was a boy at the village school, he had found in a closet and taken away a *History of the Napoleonic Wars*, its loose leaves unbound: the torn pages of these contemporary numbers with their melodramatic prints of serried ranks, crossed bayonets, huge knapsacks, and dead bodies, were the first to set him on the train of ideas that led to *The Trumpet-Major*, and *The Dynasts*. In the Hardy household at Bockhampton was a prized possession of a 'big brass telescope', which Hardy recalled was 'inherited from some collateral ancestor who had been captain of a merchant craft'. Hardy's father had a habit of going alone to the heath or the woods and peering for a long time through the telescope.[3]

One morning Tom Hardy was studying in his bedroom before setting off for work in Dorchester, when he suddenly remembered that a man was to be hanged at eight o'clock. He ran to fetch the family telescope, and hastened to a hill on the heath, a quarter of a mile from his home.

The sun behind his back shone straight on the white stone facade of the gaol, the gallows upon it, and the form of the murderer in white fustian, the executioner and officials in dark clothing and the crowd below being invisible at this distance of nearly three miles. At the moment of his placing the glass to his eye the white figure dropped downwards, and the faint note of the town clock struck eight.[4]

He recalled that the whole thing was so sudden that the telescope nearly fell from his hands, an echo of his friend falling from the lower branch of the tree at the moment of Martha

Brown's death. The hanged man was a nineteen-year-old itinerant labourer named James Searle or Seal. He had murdered a young woman called Sarah Ann Guppy. The man had crept into her house at Stoke Abbotts and tortured her before slitting her throat with a cheese knife, and inflicting other injuries to her hand, arm and breast. He then set fire to the house. In most accounts from the time, the victim was wrongly named or not even named at all.[5]

Later, in his first published novel, *Desperate Remedies*, Hardy would re-enact this death; the sudden drop, the setting of the town hall, the voyeuristic guilt. Hardy's account of suddenly remembering the execution was to take place does not, however, ring true. The grisly details of Searle's crimes against Sarah Ann were much discussed. The case once again stirred the public debate about capital punishment. Hardy once again makes his voyeurism seem to be an accident, a whim, when, in the light of all the publicity leading up to the execution, this does not seem to have been the case.

Little was known about the victim of the brutal murder, other than that Sarah Ann was said to be mentally impaired. But the case shocked Dorset and much was made of the fact that the murderer looked young and innocent. The execution took place on 10 August, two years almost to the day after the hanging of Martha Brown. Hardy, now eighteen, once again felt a deep sense of shame and remorse. The telescope gave him a 'bird's eye view' – a phrase that he often used in relation to animals and nature, and it framed the execution like a picture. The excitement that had built, the act of rushing to grab the large brass telescope, then running to the vast open heath to find the perfect view, the sudden drop, and the striking of the town clock, left him feeling empty and isolated: 'He seemed alone on the heath with the hanged man, and crept homeward wishing he had not been so curious.'[6]

Hardy's description of his father's 'big brass telescope that had been handed on in the family'[7] and its connection to a 'collateral ancestor' who was a naval captain irresistibly recalls Captain Thomas Hardy and his portrait prop. But Hardy's voyeuristic view of the execution was anything but heroic or noble. Throughout his work, he would present horrific and disturbing events through the prism of a telescopic frame. And Captain Hardy and his telescope would remain a favourite. When Hardy was a wealthy writer, living in Max Gate, he would walk every morning to see the famous Captain Hardy monument, 'a noticeable object on the sky-line to the south-west'. Designed to look like a spyglass, it was 72 feet high, standing on Black Down, between Dorchester and Bridport, overlooking the English Channel. The author would 'see what the weather was likely to be by observing this tower in the distance'.[8] Anxious to claim descent from brave Captain Hardy, no matter how tenuous the link, Hardy liked to point out this large erection to his visitors.

CHAPTER 20

Horace

That year of 1858, the Hardys heard bad news about the Sharpe family, now settled in Canada. All the promises of riches, free land and a prosperous new life had come to nothing. Beautiful Martha, whom Hardy claimed was his model for Bathsheba Everdene, was now the mother of ten children, and worn down by her cares. Handsome John Sharpe, variously described as a soldier, corn dealer and merchant, had not been able to support his family, though he would eventually become a schoolteacher. Cold winters made conditions hard, and the Sharpes no longer had the economic and emotional support of friends and family. Martha, 'with her numerous duties & weak health', was worn down, and the family almost destitute.[1] Always the dutiful sister, Jemima asked her son to write a letter to the family for news and sent a present of three pounds. It was a large amount, and not a sum she could easily afford, as she was turning her mind to her daughter Mary's future career, for which financial help would be needed. Jemima had plans to send her to one of the newly established teacher training colleges, which would open up better prospects than the old method of training in the classroom – but at a cost.

Tom was now beginning to harbour a dream that had for

centuries been almost impossible for a boy of his background: going to Oxford. He had befriended a young man called Hooper Tolbort, who was also being informally tutored by Horace Moule. Tolbort, who had been taught by the Dorset schoolmaster and poet William Barnes, was a linguistic prodigy, who, unlike plodder Hardy, seemed effortlessly brilliant. He would later translate *The Arabian Nights* into Urdu, and *Robinson Crusoe* into Persian. Reforms at Oxford University, the bastion of privilege and wealth, meant that young men like Hardy and Tolbort could aspire to entrance by way of a new examination, known as the Oxford University Locals or the 'Middle Class Examination', that was made available in the year of 1858.

Now eighteen, Hardy began to wean himself from his home in Bockhampton, staying in lodgings in Dorchester during the week, only returning home for the weekends. His appetite for Oxford was whetted by a lecture given by Horace Moule to the Local Working Men's Improvement Society at the Town Hall. The title was 'Oxford and the Middle Class Examination'. Like his father, Horace was a passionate and charismatic speaker. There was a large audience, and the event was chaired by Hooper's schoolmaster William Barnes. The lecture moved from the history of the University of Oxford to the Oxford of the present day. Moule talked of the 'great struggle between Town and Gown of 1854' and spoke evocatively of the heart-stopping view of the town from Headington Hill, and the 'great achievement of Oxford celebrities' such as Sir Robert Peel, Dr Arnold and Professor Newman. He talked of the halls and of the foundation of the Bodleian Library, painting a picture of the beauties of Oxford that had until then excluded the sons of the poor. He spoke about the advantages of self-study, and the value of a foreign literature, such as Greek: 'In enlarging upon this point Mr. Moule warmed into an eloquence which carried his audience away with him and he sat down amid loud applause.'[2] He made a striking figure, this handsome young man, taking the trouble to speak to the Working Men's Society, and to show them that they too could aspire to the great universities.

Following the vote of thanks, which praised the speaker as a 'clever and promising young gentleman' of whom Dorchester should feel proud, Moule reflected that in the present climate of 'reform' he would like to urge his 'younger hearers' to pay attention to their own personal reformation: 'If every man would sweep before his own door the streets would be clean.'³ Hardy's hero and mentor was restoring all the hurt pride that had come when the Reverend Shirley insinuated that he was an upstart and a social climber.

So it must have come as a shock when Hardy asked Moule for advice about applying for the examination. Moule advised Hooper to sit for the Oxford examination, which he did, duly taking first place among nine hundred boys. But it was becoming clear that Moule did not have the same great expectations for Tom Hardy. The examination had four requirements: mathematics, English, languages and physics. Students could be tested in Latin, Greek, French and German. The latter part of the exam was easy for Hooper, but not for Hardy. In a passage from the *Life*, Hardy went to great lengths to explain the reasons why Moule dissuaded him from Oxford, and all his pain and frustration can be felt in the obfuscation of his language. He refrains from mentioning the new Middle Class Examination, writing instead that Moule merely discouraged him from 'reading some Greek plays':

Moule's reluctant opinion was that if Hardy really had (as his father had insisted, and as indeed was reasonable since he never as yet had earned a farthing in his life) to make an income in some way by architecture in 1862, it would be hardly worth while for him to read Aeschylus or Sophocles in 1859–61. He had secretly wished that Moule would advise him to go on with Greek plays, in spite of the serious damage it might do to his architecture, but he felt bound to listen to reason and prudence.[4]

For all the disappointment veiled here, Hardy made it clear that Moule's advice had altered the course of his life: 'The upshot might have been his abandonment of architecture for a University career . . . having every instinct of a scholar he might have ended his life as a Don.'[5]

Moule clearly did not think Hardy university material. But there may have been other factors at play. He did encourage his pupil in his writing, and clearly believed that his talents lay that way. The usual consequence for a university career was the church, and Hardy was beginning to experience some religious doubts, which Moule may have initiated by giving him books such as *The Wonders of Geology*, whose interest in dinosaurs questioned the fundamentalist view of creation and the biblical story of Adam and Eve. If Hardy had expressed a desire to be a 'Don', then it would have meant a life of celibacy, as Oxford dons were not permitted to marry. Perhaps Moule, with all his shrewdness and emotional intelligence, had seen that Hardy deeply admired women, and very much intended to be a married man. Whatever the reasons, Moule's advice left an indelible mark on Hardy, much of which was expressed in *A Pair of Blue Eyes* and *Jude the Obscure*. A version of Moule's impassioned speech to the Working Men's Improvement Society would appear in *Jude the Obscure*. Though Hardy 'dropped' the study of Greek plays and did not entirely abandon his dream of Oxford, he showed no resentment towards Moule. But his hero-worship of his friend and mentor was soon to be tarnished, as he began to witness a troubled side to Horace's character.

Hardy described his inner life, at this time, as divided into three strands, 'the professional life, the scholar's life, and the rustic life, combined in the twenty-four hours of one day'.[6] The three strands, for now, seemed to happily co-exist, but as he moved away from his home, the displacement he would feel would be immense and far-reaching. For now, though, he had his determination and his strength to sustain him.

More bad news came from Canada: Aunt Martha had died giving birth to her eleventh child, a little girl who was christened Amelia. Her passing was a reminder of life's arbitrary and cruel twists, especially for women in Victorian times.

CHAPTER 21

Margaret Duncan

It was Jemima Hardy's fervent wish that none of her four children should marry. Her plan was for them to live together in two separate households: Tom with Mary, and Henry with Kate. The reasons why Jemima was so dead set against the institution of marriage are difficult to disentangle. Her own marriage seemed contented enough, and she had wed a kind and gentle man, the polar opposite of her own father. She was too much of a pragmatist to believe in a romantic ideal of wedlock as a supreme state of happiness. She derived enormous pleasure and satisfaction from her own children, enjoying a particularly close relationship with her eldest son. But Jemima appeared to believe that she and her family were not temperamentally suited to marriage, and that it would lead to unhappiness. Hardy would later consider that his mother's judgement was correct. Jemima had witnessed misery in her mother's marriage and had seen her sister the victim of domestic abuse. The death of her most beautiful sister in childbirth, poor and far from home in the freezing temperatures of Canada, was also a factor. Nevertheless, her insistence that her children remain unmarried but living in the same household as man and wife, was singular.

Now that Tom was settled into his apprenticeship, Jemima

turned her mind to Mary's future. There were several methods available to becoming a trained mistress for elementary school in the mid-Victorian era. Firstly, there was the pupil-teacher scheme, sometimes called the Monitorial system, in which clever girls of thirteen or over stayed on at elementary school to become assistant teachers.[1] They usually remained in training until they were eighteen, as they gained experience teaching the younger children under supervision. The starting salary was ten pounds a year. The most proficient could then apply for a Queen's Scholarship, which funded their training at college. In fact, many young women carried on in their schools and did not receive college training. Charlotte Brontë was one such.

The pupil-teacher scheme was not the route that Mary Hardy was to take. Jemima had plans for her daughter to be trained at one of the new teacher training colleges that had been recently founded as an alternative to the Monitorial scheme. She was to attend the Salisbury Teacher Training College, formally known as the Diocesan Training College for Schoolmistresses. The first training college exclusively for women, it was founded in 1841 and run by a woman called Margaret Duncan. It had one of the finest reputations among the dozen or more training colleges open to women in England.

Teachers with a college education were usually higher paid, and this was clearly Jemima's intention for Mary. As she had not taught elementary school as a paid assistant, she was not eligible for the Queen's Scholarship, so the Hardys were required to pay Mary's fees as well as board and lodgings. She was admitted in the spring of 1860, and Tom accompanied her on her journey to Salisbury. She was the first of the Hardy children to leave home in a permanent sense, and it was a courageous step into the unknown for a young woman who was shy, introverted, and had little sense of what she should expect from her new situation.

As with Jude Fawley in *Jude the Obscure*, Hardy's first glimpse

of Salisbury Cathedral was 'through a driving mist that nearly
hid the top of the spire'.[2] Mary's college was located in the
Cathedral Close, nestling by the River Avon. It was a lovely
building, called the King's House, opposite the great Cathedral
itself. The Close, the largest in England, had a rich history. It
was picturesque, with verdant rolling lawns, and ancient buildings that dated back to the twelfth century. It was visited by
Handel, painted by Constable and Turner, and inspired writers
such as Anthony Trollope, Jemima Hardy's favourite novelist.

The college's reputation had been built by Margaret Duncan,
the first Lady Superintendent, who had been there since the
1840s. She was born in Scotland, and, though married with a
child, had arrived at the school with only her daughter in tow.
No mention was made of the husband she had left behind, other
than that he was a watchmaker. From the start, Margaret Duncan
won the admiration of the student teachers, having a reputation
as firm but fair. She was determined to give girls from deprived
backgrounds the best education available, and encouraged her
students to see each pupil as an individual who needed encouragement and praise, rather than being constantly punished for
their failure to learn by rote. The students were given instruction
in all the subjects they were expected to teach: English, history,
geography, music, needlework, arithmetic, drawing, domestic
economy and scripture. Margaret Duncan elevated her profession, which was previously held in low esteem; in raising her
daughter alone and running one of the most highly regarded
training colleges, she challenged the conventions of her time
and transformed the idea that schoolteaching was merely a job
for gentlewomen in reduced circumstances. She believed firmly
in the school motto, taken from the book of Isaiah: 'In quietness
and confidence shall be your strength.'

Mary Hardy lacked confidence. Despite her mother's ambition, she was not a high-achieving student. Her State of

Acquirement on entrance to the college was 'Backward', and over the two years she would never rise above 'moderate' in academic subjects.[3] She was diligent and hard-working, and she knew that her parents' financial help had opened the college doors to her, but she did not have her brother's natural abilities. She arrived at college a term early, perhaps to make up time before the autumn start. Unsurprisingly for a family of spinners and dressmakers, she showed most prowess in the 'Industrial Department', which was primarily needlework, where she rose from 'very moderate' to 'good'. In the more academic subjects, she was 'persevering' and 'improving slowly'.[4]

Quiet and awkward as she was, Mary made good friends with a young woman who had come through the pupil-teacher scheme and achieved a Queen's Scholarship. Her name was Annie Lanham, and she would eventually marry into the Hardy family, wedding Mary's cousin, Nathaniel Sparks. Annie was, according to Mary, 'rather delicate and fragile and so unassuming, yet so intelligent and sensible'.[5] Her college record was, unsurprisingly, much stronger than Mary's. Annie's bedroom was next to Mary's, and every evening they would say goodnight to each other.[6] Annie was an orphan: her father, a Trowbridge cooper, and her mother died of consumption when she was a child. Annie and Mary, decidedly not of the middle class, despite Jemima's pretensions, were indicative of a newly educated class of women. Thanks to Margaret Duncan, they would go on to make careers for themselves.

CHAPTER 22

Mary Waight

Hardy had recently returned to Pouncy's to sit for another photograph. Now approaching his twenties, he presented a more confident figure than in his earlier sitting. Standing erect, with his hand resting on a small pile of books, he looked attractive with his dark brown hair and neat moustache. But his clothing, his smock jacket and shapeless trousers, still presented him as the apprentice architect of a provincial town.

Though Horace had persuaded him to abandon the idea of university, he was by no means sure that the life of an architect was for him. A part of him still harboured thoughts of the church, as his family had once suggested when he played the part of the vicar wrapped in a sheet, but his feelings about religion were complicated. It was during these final years of his apprenticeship that he developed a habit of underlining and annotating his Bible and religious books.[1] Some of the markings were perfunctory, dating his reading and his church attendances, but others denoted heightened states of emotion. Favourite passages were singled out, and sometimes he drew caricatures of people he knew, including a sketch of a bonneted Jemima, with her distinctive hooked nose. Hardy, a lover of music, was also drawn to the lyrical beauty of the psalms. His copy of the

Brady and Tate 'New Version' of the psalms has annotations beside those set to music and sung by the old Stinsford choir or by his mother. Of Psalm 16, for example, he noted, 'M[othe]r used to sing this: Protect me from my cruel foes, / And shield me, Lord, from harm.'[2]

Just after he accompanied Mary to Salisbury, he made a visit to Horace Moule, who, by a strange coincidence, had recently moved to Cathedral Close. He had taken lodgings and was living with and teaching two young men for entrance into Oxford and Cambridge. One of the pupils, Wynne Albert Bankes, wrote a record of some of the disturbing behaviour he witnessed at the hands of his tutor. It was no secret to the Moule family that their most brilliant son suffered from depression, exacerbated by a dependence on alcohol. Moule went on self-destructive binges when things got too much for him. He suffered from sleep deprivation and began taking opium to keep him awake for his long bouts of review writing, which could last up to seventy-two hours at a stretch. How much Tom Hardy knew about Horace's problems before 1860 is unclear, but he was shortly to experience the aftermath of one of his drink and drug binges.

Bankes hailed from an illustrious Dorset family. He was the same age as Thomas Hardy, born just a week before him – but with a very different early life. He was sent into the navy at the age of thirteen and sailed with the Baltic fleet for Russia. He was involved in the removal of the mutineers of the *Bounty*. By the age of seventeen he had seen Botany Bay, the South Sea Islands, Tasmania, New Zealand and much of Australia. When he was nineteen, he left the navy and began to read Greek and Latin with Horace Moule.

Bankes was a kind and compassionate young man, and as a former sailor he was no stranger to the effects of alcohol, but his diaries reflect his alarm at Moule's increasingly erratic behaviour. He recognised that Moule was a 'Dipsomaniac' and opium addict, who suffered hand tremors. Shortly after Hardy's visit to Salisbury, Moule and Bankes travelled to France for the summer, where Moule began drinking heavily. In Paris he missed a rendezvous and on making enquiries, Bankes discovered that his tutor had ordered a bottle of claret, cut off his whiskers, and disappeared. Fearing the worst, he began to make daily visits to the morgue. Horace's brothers, Henry and Charles, arrived in Paris to help with the search. After a week, they heard that Horace had somehow made his way back to England, where he made one of his habitual unkept promises to reform.

Shortly after Horace's reappearance from France, Hardy made a note in his Bible that he had attended the church in Fordington for evensong, and it may have been on this Sunday that Horace's father preached a poignant sermon on the text 'All the days of my appointed time will I wait, till my change come.' Hardy had been frequently exposed to the hard drinking of his Hand uncles, and John Antell, but this was the first time he had seen a man with all of Horace Moule's advantages in such a desperate and pitiful state due to the effects of alcohol. In his prayer book during the Salisbury trip, he noted that it was his first view of Salisbury Cathedral, and then put a cross next to these words of Psalm 119: 'Wherewithal shall a young man cleanse his way: even by ruling himself after thy word.' He underlined the words 'ruling himself'.[3] He was beginning to use his religious books – his Bible, a Book of Common Prayer and a copy of John Keble's popular book of Christian verse, *The Christian Year* – as a place of secrets, a repository of coded references to intimate matters.

Sometime during his apprenticeship in Dorchester, Hardy met a woman called Mary Waight. She was seven years his senior, and she worked as a shop assistant in an upmarket shop in town called The Mantle Showroom. The daughter of a printer and bookbinder, Mary was an attractive woman with light brown hair, blue eyes, and a lovely complexion. Hardy fell in love. According to her family, Mary was 'kind and generous' and a lover of 'beautiful things'.[4] She was always well dressed in clothing of 'very good material'. She was also a woman of strong character 'with very definite tastes, preferences and opinions'. In short, she was a woman very like Jemima Hardy. Mary accepted Hardy's signed photograph, but it would seem that when he proposed marriage, she rejected him, partly on the grounds of the age gap, but more likely because she had been swept off her feet by a man called George Oliver, whom she would eventually marry. Mary, however, continued to take an interest in Hardy, and although she rarely talked about the affair, he was on her mind in her dying days, and she kept his photograph.[5]

After Hardy had completed his fourth year with Hicks, in the summer of 1860, he was kept on as a paid assistant at the rate of fifteen shillings a week. It was another new experience: earning money of his own. His new-found independence was probably one of the reasons that he proposed marriage to Mary. Hardy, for his part, avoided all direct mention of Mary, but their abortive relationship set a peculiar pattern in his romantic life. In early 1862, he recorded the initials MW or M several times in his religious books. This kind of romantic entanglement, unmentioned in his memoirs, would continue until his marriage. As would his obsessive need for secrecy and subterfuge. Jemima would certainly not have approved of such a union, so there was some need for discretion, but his cryptic markings in his religious books seemed to suggest a sexual element to the relationship.

In April 1862, Hardy suddenly departed for London with no prearranged job or lodgings. He had the blessing of John Hicks and a return ticket to Dorchester, just in case he did not make his fortune. But it was an unexpected move. Although he did not seem unduly miserable about Mary's refusal, her rejection might well have been a factor in his abrupt decision to leave Hicks. In one of his better short stories, a young man who is jilted by his lover feels liberated into making the decision to leave Dorset for London:

> The No he had expected and got from her, in spite of a prelim-
> inary encouragement, gave Ned a new start in life. It had been
> uttered in such a tone of sad entreaty that he resolved to perse-
> cute her no more; she should not even be distressed by a sight
> of his form in the distant perspective of the street and lane. He
> left the place, and his natural course was to London.[6]

But there was perhaps another reason why Hardy set out for London. Mary Waight was not the only romantic entanglement in his life at this time. He had also become acquainted with another young woman, a lady's maid, who was working in London.

Like Ned in the story, he was ready for a 'new start in life'.

LONDON

CHAPTER 23

Amabel

Though Hardy had moved away from his home county of Dorset, London was closely associated with his mother. His childhood book *The Cries of London* had depicted colourful and vivid scenes of working-class life in the city, from street hawkers selling herbs, puddings and pies, to chimney sweeps, toymakers and pedlars. And he had grown up with his mother's exciting stories of her spell in London as a single working woman. Then there had been the memorable sightseeing trip at the age of nine.

One of the favourite romantic novels of his youth was Harrison Ainsworth's *Old St Paul's: A Tale of the Plague and the Fire*. The hero, Leonard Holt, is a grocer's apprentice, who is in love with his master's beautiful daughter, Amabel. The grocer boy has little chance with Amabel, who is in love with a rich scoundrel called Wyvil – who seduces her by tricking her into a sham marriage. He then reveals that he is in fact the wicked Earl of Rochester in disguise. Meanwhile, Holt, having lost Amabel, falls in love with a woman who is revealed to be an aristocrat, and therefore out of his reach. It is only by saving the life of King Charles II in the Great Fire of London that Holt is given a title and the poor man is able to marry his rich lady.

Now that he was older, London was a place with further

literary associations in addition to the historical novels of Harrison Ainsworth. It was, he recorded, the 'London of Dickens and Thackeray'.[1] And, above all, it was the place he associated with his new literary hero, Percy Bysshe Shelley. When Hardy had stayed at the Cross Keys coaching inn in Clerkenwell, at the age of nine, it was unlikely that he had been introduced to Shelley's poetry. It was only later that he was aware of the thrilling fact that he and his mother had perhaps slept in the same bedroom as the one where the married Shelley bedded the young Mary Godwin.

Hardy timed his arrival in London to coincide with the opening of the Great Exhibition of 1862.[2] It became something of a minor obsession. Held in South Kensington, beside the gardens of the Royal Horticultural Society on a large site now occupied by the Natural History Museum, it was a world's fair, showcasing 28,000 exhibitors from thirty-six countries. It represented a wide range of industry, technology and the arts and was a showcase for the advances made in the Industrial Revolution, with displays including electric telegraphs, machine tools and looms, and even the first plastic, Parkesine. The manufacture of ice by an early refrigerator caused a sensation. There was a comprehensive photographic exhibition, the latest Victorian craze, and a huge display of William Morris furniture. There were displays of musical instruments, silverware, porcelain, lace and tapestry, stained glass, musical toys, elaborately iced tiered cakes, and confectionery items. Exotic items, such as jewellery from an Egyptian tomb, astonished the crowds with its modern appearance. A huge attraction for Hardy were the art galleries and daily musical concerts. It attracted over six million visitors, though Queen Victoria, in mourning for Albert, failed to attend the grand opening.

When he first arrived in London, Hardy had in his pocket two letters of recommendation. One was from a client of his father's, but nothing came of the connection. He was luckier with the second, addressed to an architect of Old Bond Street, John Norton. Although he did not need an assistant, Norton took Hardy under his wing and treated him with great kindness. He told Hardy he would employ him on a nominal basis, to make drawings, until he found a proper job. John Norton changed the course of Thomas Hardy's life. He heard that there was an opening for a young draughtsman adept in the Gothic style at the offices of Arthur Blomfield of St Martin's Place. Blomfield was looking for someone to work on the restoration and design of churches and rectories. Norton gave Hardy a strong reference, and the matter was shortly settled. On 5 May 1862, Hardy began work as an assistant architect. Blomfield, a lithe, brisk Trinity College man of thirty-three, descended from the Bishop of London, became not only an employer but a friend – a friendship that was to last for forty years.

Blomfield was another brilliant, good-looking and charming man in the Horace Moule mould. He was an excellent amateur actor and singer, and a proficient watercolour painter. He had a great sense of humour and was a man of such energy that at Cambridge he and his older brother had been given the nick-names Thunder and Lightning. It was a stroke of good luck that brought Hardy into his orbit, but Blomfield clearly saw something special in the young West Country man, so different from the other men in the practice, most of whom were Eton and Oxbridge educated. Though Blomfield was often away on field visits, he cultivated an atmosphere of adventure and high spirits; no formal training was given. Hardy later described the environment as 'artists just awakening and feeling their way'.[3]

It was an exciting time to be a young man living and working in the metropolis. Hardy took lodgings in Kilburn, alongside another of Blomfield's apprentices, Philip Shaw. The two men got along very well together, though Shaw was of a higher social class.

His parents had given him a present of silver cutlery, which provoked the hostility of the men's landlady. Every evening she would rattle them noisily in her basket as she carried them up to dinner. Hardy called this performance 'the procession of the plate'.[4]

Hardy, by his own account, 'had not forgotten to pay a call on the lady of his earliest passion as a child'.[5] Though Julia Martin's interest in the boy had caused a rift between Julia and Jemima, Tom sought her out, discovering that she now lived in Bruton Street in Mayfair. He recognised William Adams, the old butler from Kingston Maurward, who opened the door. Hardy thought he was little altered by the passage of time. But what about the 'lady of his dreams'? Julia was now in her early fifties and was much altered. It was an awkward and embarrassing encounter, which Hardy ascribed to his being 'a young man of over twenty one, who was very much a handful in comparison with the rosy-cheeked innocent little boy'.[6] The meeting was stiff and cold, though eventually Julia, 'warming up', asked him to come again.

Julia was the first of the several higher-class women with whom Hardy would become infatuated, only to be later disenchanted, and disillusioned. And though he failed to take her up on her invitation for a return visit, the relationship was not entirely at an end, though he would never again see her in person.

Hardy's account of the visit is puzzling. Why was the meeting 'no less painful than pleasant' for her? He was a quiet and shy person, and not a 'handful', so it is unlikely that exuberance of spirits could account for her evident distress. The underlying reason for 'pain' of the encounter can be found in a poem that Hardy would later write about the reconciliation. It was evident that the 'pink-cheeked' youth could not hide his shock at the transformation wrought in the once beautiful woman of his dreams.

The poem describes her as not merely altered by the onset of middle age, but 'ruined' and 'Spoilt'. Her once light step is now 'mechanic' and she has lost her 'sweet' laugh. Not only is she physically changed, but, so too, her old-fashioned ideas have become 'custom-straitened'. Hardy, as ever sensitive to female clothing, and remembering the sexy swish of her silk dress with its ruffles and petticoats, now invokes her faded colours: 'I looked upon her gown, / Once rose, now earthen brown.' In his shock and agony, the narrator of the poem wants to 'creep / To some housetop, and weep.'

Hardy later illustrated the poem with a drawing of an hourglass, the sand trickling away. Two beautiful butterflies hover close to the glass, but one has fluttered to the floor and died, just as his love for her has died.

The Julia Martin figure bears the same name as the beautiful and unattainable woman in Ainsworth's *Old St Paul's*. She is his lost 'Amabel'. Though in his case, it is not the handsome Earl of Rochester that has seduced Amabel away from him, but the ravages of the tyrant Time:

> I marked her ruined hues,
>   Her custom-straitened views,
>   And asked, 'Can there indwell
>   My Amabel?'[7]

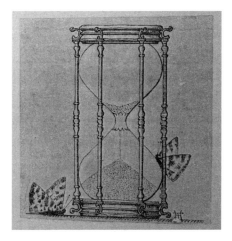

CHAPTER 24

The Tinted Venus

Hardy's first surviving letter was written to his beloved sister, Mary. For the first time we hear his voice, not mediated via the distancing third-person narration of the *Life*, but as a young man on the brink of an exciting new chapter in the busy metropolis. She was one of his first visitors to his lodgings in London. She was home from teacher training college for the summer break, before returning for her final term. Tom was keen to show her the sights. She attended the Exhibition and the West End theatre, and he introduced her to his roommate.

'My dear Mary', he wrote in the weeks after her visit: 'After the fire, a still small voice.' It was a rainy Sunday evening, and he had just returned from the service at St Mary's Kilburn. The passage from the Old Testament first book of Kings, he reminded her, was one of his favourites: 'And after the earthquake a fire; *but* the LORD *was* not in the fire: and after the fire a still small voice'.[1] Tom told Mary that Horace Moule had been to stay, and they had visited a Roman Catholic Jesuit chapel in Farm Street, Berkeley Square. Later, the two friends had supper in a hotel near Covent Garden, renowned for its Turkish baths, and considered a place for bachelors only. Horace, he told Mary, was considering a move to London. Other family news followed,

Tom had sought out their cousin, Martha Sparks, who was now working in Paddington as a lady's maid. He told Mary that he had taken Martha to the Exhibition in the evening.[2]

Possibly, romance was on his mind. At night, the atmosphere was appealing. There was a Great Fountain in the Eastern Dome, which puffed perfume into the air, and visitors were encouraged to dab their pocket handkerchiefs into the scented water. Strains of music wafted through the air from the musical concerts. A favourite exhibit was the sculpture gallery, where visitors flocked to see such figures as *The Reading Girl* – in loose drapery with one breast exposed – and John Gibson's sensational *Tinted Venus*. This full-size marble statue, naked to the waist, was tinted a warm ivory to represent real skin. The jewellery was gilt coloured. The eyes were painted blue, nipples roseate, hair blonde, and the hair net as golden as the apple held suggestively in hand. Critics denounced Venus as vulgar, more 'a naked, impudent Englishwoman' rather than a goddess.[3] But the crowds loved her, going in their thousands to pay homage to the lifelike statue. Hardy with his love of animals and his sharp eye could not have failed to notice the tortoise peeking out from the folds of her discarded gown.

The Sparks family believed that Tom had designs on Martha and would probably have proposed marriage had it not been for the intervention of Jemima. Hardy made Mary his confidante in matters of the heart. His phrase 'I have found Martha Sparks' suggests that her family deliberately had not disclosed Martha's whereabouts, but that he had made his own discreet enquiries. But there is no real evidence that Tom had a serious romantic interest in Martha. Besides, there was another young woman on his mind.

Tom fretted about his sister's health. Earlier in the year, Mary had suffered from a severe cold while at college. The nights were drawing in and the air was getting chilly. 'Be careful about getting cold again', he wrote, and 'do not go out in evenings'. He promised her a visit to Salisbury in a month's time, when he hoped to visit the cathedral, and apologised for the 'wretched composition of this epistle', as Philip Shaw was reading aloud from Ruskin's *Modern Painters*. Tom 'was obliged to make comments' on the Ruskin extracts, making it difficult to concentrate on letter-writing.[4]

Tom was showing his sister a side to himself that he kept concealed from his parents: not only his romances, of which he knew his mother would be deeply disapproving, but also his life as a lover of art and music. His mock-elevated language ('wretched composition of this epistle', 'obliged to make comments') was not the language of his parents, or their upbringing, and they both felt it, and it bound them more closely together. They also shared a sense of humour about their native tongue. Hardy insisted that his mother discouraged the use of dialect at home, and that both parents only used dialect when engaging with neighbours and tradesmen. This seems an unlikely claim. The affectionate portrayal of Mrs Dewy in *Under the Greenwood Tree* owes much to Jemima's colourful use of the vernacular. But it is in Tom's letters to Mary that he gives a glimpse into his working-class roots: 'I have a cowdid by head' (a head cold), he wrote. And that his father continued to 'talk broad' (in Hardy's phrase) is suggested by his parody of his father's use of dialect: 'she zid a lot of others be gone afore'. Later, perhaps as a rebuke to his younger self, they were inked over.[5] Living in London and about to embark upon a strict system of self-education and self-improvement, he was still at the stage where he could make jokes to his sister about their father's use of dialect, but it was language, in truth, that he was desperate to discard. Later, he would write with some bitterness that 'pretty and picturesque use of dialect words' are 'terrible marks of the beast' to 'the truly genteel'.[6]

Hardy's father had been to visit, curiously not in the company of his wife, but a 'Miss A.' who was looking for a situation, probably as a maidservant. Jemima's reluctance to visit her son is odd, given her fond memories of London, but it's possible that she was busy with her younger children, Harry and Kate. Tom told Mary that the visit 'went off all right' and that their father had 'enjoyed himself thoroughly'.[7] Tom had arranged tickets for the Opera at Covent Garden, but what his father really wanted to do was to see the famous triumph of civil engineering, the Thames Tunnel, built by Marc Isambard Brunel and his son Kingdom. The tunnel, built under the river between Rotherhithe and Limehouse, was originally intended for horse-drawn carriages, but was mainly used by pedestrians. It was a popular tourist attraction and considered one of the modern wonders of the world. Hardy told Mary that the tunnel was in the 'lowest and most crowded' part of London, but his father insisted and went with Miss A. Tom was probably at work, but one senses that he was beginning to feel more at home at the Opera House than in the East End.[8]

He had also attended a special evening at the Architectural Association. Blomfield had given him a ticket. Tom told Mary that the event was called a *Conversazione*, spelling out the pronunciation for her benefit ('Kon-ver-sat-zion-i'). There was a formal dress code, and Tom had borrowed a dress coat from Philip Shaw. The ladies, he told her, were in 'full dress', that is, hooped crinolines, which, in 1862, were at their fullest size. He drew a sketch of his borrowed coat for his sister's benefit. It was a tailcoat, and if he were to be accepted into the society, he would need one of his own, meaning added expenses.

Tom and Mary were in perfect sympathy. He could be himself when he was writing to her, because she alone understood that he was in the process of reinvention. Jemima had encouraged her children to 'better themselves' with little understanding of the emotional displacement and feelings of inadequacy that would ensue. She meant no harm, and she had their best interests at heart, but she would never understand the humiliation of having to borrow a frock coat in order to enter polite society, feeling like a brown bird in borrowed plumes. Nor would she understand her eldest son's powerful attraction to women. It would appear that, rather than leaving Dorchester to escape the rejection of Mary Waight, he had come to London to be close to another Dorset girl. Hardy had casually mentioned the name of a woman in his letter to Mary: 'Do you ever write to Eliza?'

CHAPTER 25

Eliza Bright Nicholls

In 1955, an elderly woman called Sarah Headley wrote a letter to Yale professor and Hardy bibliographer, Richard Little Purdy, in which she made the sensational claim that her aunt was once betrothed to Thomas Hardy during the early 1860s when Hardy was living in London. The name of the woman was Eliza Bright Nicholls.

According to Headley's testimony, Eliza was courted by Hardy for several years. They exchanged photographs, and Hardy gave Eliza some of his notebooks and an engagement ring. Purdy was intrigued enough to write back, and a correspondence began. Sarah Headley told him that the ring was lost or stolen, and that Eliza had destroyed Hardy's letters and manuscripts in later life. What she did have in her possession were photographs of Hardy and of her aunt Eliza. When Hardy ended the relationship, he returned Eliza's photograph. She could never bear to destroy his picture, so she kept it to the end of her life.

Scholars were initially sceptical about Sarah Headley's claim.[1] Hardy left no explicit reference to Eliza Nicholls, and the alleged destruction of his manuscripts and letters in her possession meant that there was no hard evidence. But she had the photograph:

taken in London in 1862, it was clearly authentic. How else could it have come into the possession of Eliza's niece?

Purdy met with Sarah Headley, and later purchased her photographs of Hardy and Eliza. He left notes of their conversations, including her account of the full extent of the attachment and the unhappy demise of the engagement.[2] For Purdy, it was remarkable to hold in his hand the very photograph that Hardy had returned when he called off the engagement. Eliza was clearly a beautiful woman. She is wearing a full crinoline dress, her expression serene. Headley recalled that she was cultivated and well read.

There was another twist to Sarah Headley's tale. She also had in her possession a photograph of Eliza's younger sister, Jane. Would Purdy like to see it? Could Jane Nicholls have been part of the story, too?

Sarah believed that Hardy had first met Eliza around 1863, when she was working in London. But back in 1861, when he was still with Hicks in Dorchester, Hardy's friend Henry Bastow had written to him: 'I suppose you have scarcely been gone and lost your heart yet, young man, – have you?' He went on to rib him: 'I still am of the opinion that you are not of a highly inflammable nature', but then he begged Hardy to let him know, when the time was right, 'who is the fair damsel'.[3] Could she have been the Eliza whose name he mentioned eighteen months later in his letter from London to his closest confidante, sister Mary?

———

Hidden away in a remote spot of Dorset, on a peninsula known as the Isle of Purbeck, stood Smedmore, one of the most romantic manor houses in England. Nestling among the hills, the elegant stone-fronted house had extensive gardens, with breathtaking views overlooking the sea. Its most famous feature, built in 1833, was Clavell Tower, a folly and observatory which sat atop Hen Hill, overlooking the sea.

Smedmore House was originally owned by the Clavell family, though following the death of the childless John Clavell in 1833, the estate passed to his niece, Louisa Pleydell Mansel. She had many children, the youngest of which was a daughter, Emma Georgina. In 1852, Emma married a barrister named Charles Hoare, and by 1853 was living in Orsett Terrace in the Bayswater district of London. In need of a lady's maid, Emma interviewed and appointed a Dorset girl called Eliza Bright Nicholls. She was born in 1840, the same year as Thomas Hardy, and raised in a coastguard's cottage close to the sea at Kimmeridge, not far from Smedmore House.

Though in service with the Hoare family in London, Eliza returned to Smedmore with them when they left town for the summer. It seems likely that it was there that she met the architect's apprentice: during his time with Hicks, he worked on several Purbeck churches. We know of their acquaintance because by April 1861 one of Eliza's books had passed into the hands of Thomas Hardy.

Eliza was very religious, and her mistress, Emma Hoare, had given her a copy of the popular devotional book, John Keble's *The Christian Year*. First published in 1827, this little collection of religious verses quickly became a bestseller. Though it was originally published anonymously, Keble's authorship was an open secret, and the success of the book was a contributory factor to his being awarded the Oxford Professorship of Poetry. Ninety-five editions of what has been described as 'the most popular volume of verse in the nineteenth century' were published during Keble's life.[4] The Church of England's *Hymns Ancient and Modern* included many of the poems, or selections from them, such as these much-loved lines from the opening poem:

New every morning is the love
Our wakening and uprising prove;
Through sleep and darkness safely brought,
Restored to life, and power, and thought . . .

The trivial round, the common task,
Would furnish all we ought to ask;
Room to deny ourselves, a road
To bring us daily nearer God.

Emma Hoare used her copy of *The Christian Year* as a calendar-cum-diary. She noted details of her wedding and honeymoon in 1852, and the move to Orsett Terrace, her new London home.

She then gave it to Eliza, who gave it to Thomas Hardy, who made his first entry on 1 April 1861.[5] Some months later, he in turn passed it on to his sister Mary, inscribing on the front endpaper her name and the date '11th Sunday after Trinity/61'. Keble's book of verse would become a repository of Hardy's secret relationship with Eliza Nicholls, shared between him and Mary. Eventually, Mary gave the book to her little sister Kate.

From 1860–61, Holy Reed Church in the hamlet of Coombe Keynes, near Purbeck, was restored by Hicks and his team. On 8 April, a week after scribbling his first annotation in *The Christian Year*, Hardy sketched the font. This places him firmly on Purbeck at exactly the time when he was intimate enough with Eliza to have received a gift of her Keble. Clavell Tower, with its romantic setting, would come to assume a symbolic significance for him. It is a presence in some of his greatest early love poems, which can only be because it was the backdrop to a courtship.

Hardy moved to London to further his career, to begin a system of self-improvement, and to loosen the suffocating grip of his mother. But there was also the pull of Eliza. In late March

1862, at exactly the time he was wrestling with the momentous decision to move to London, he marked up a verse in the book of Romans in his Bible with marginal strokes and underlining:

/ But I see another law in
/ my members, warring against
/ the law of my mind, and bring-
/ ing me into captivity to the
/ law of <u>sin which is in my mem-
/ bers</u>.[6]

The wrestling was also between his waxing sexual desires and his waning religious faith. Once he was in London, as soon as he could afford it, he moved from his initial lodgings in Kilburn to Westbourne Park Villas – a road located just a few hundred yards from the Hoares' residence in Orsett Terrace, giving him the opportunity to see the lady's maid whenever she was not working. A year into his time in London, he drew a line around another Bible verse and wrote the date 'Ap¹ 16/63'. The verse read 'Therefore to him that knoweth to do good, and doeth it not, to him it is sin.' As is apparent from *Tess of the D'Urbervilles*, sin and sex were often synonymous at this time.

For reasons only known to brother and sister, he was deter- mined to keep the relationship with Eliza Nicholls a secret. Despite the great lengths that Hardy went to to conceal the affair, destroying correspondence and journals, and using code or ellipsis in his personal books to obfuscate revealing details, it would appear that Sarah Headley was, indeed, telling the truth. And so was Eliza's youngest sister. Remarkably, though frail and elderly, she was still alive in the 1950s. Sarah contacted this other aunt for further details, and, again, the ring and the manuscripts were mentioned. Hardy, she said, was a frequent visitor at Eliza's parental home, a pub in Sussex, where her parents had moved following an accident that ended her father's career as a coastguard.[7] New evidence, to be discussed later, confirms that this was not a false memory or mere family fancy.

Hardy's desire to obliterate all mention of Eliza Nicholls established a pattern of his romantic entanglements: initial obsession, the gift of a ring and a photograph, failure to fully commit, followed by the destruction of evidence. The women he drew into his orbit were to endure not only rejection, but the witnessing of his extraordinary rise to fame. Further misery ensued when Hardy used the details of his romantic affairs as the subject of his published poems and novels.

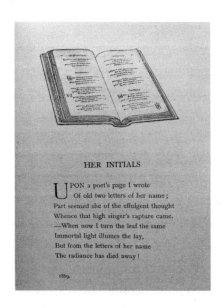

HER INITIALS

UPON a poet's page I wrote
    Of old two letters of her name;
Part seemed she of the effulgent thought
Whence that high singer's rapture came.
—When now I turn the leaf the same
Immortal light illumes the lay,
But from the letters of her name
The radiance has died away!

1869.

CHAPTER 26

The Courtesans

'Any spice in the papers?'

In February 1863, Arthur Blomfield changed premises from St Margaret Place to the upmarket neo-classical Adelphi Terrace. Hardy wrote to Mary to inform her of his new work address. He was full of excitement at the 'capital place' they now occupied: 'it is on the first floor and on a terrace that overlooks the river. We can see from our windows right across the Thames, and on a clear day every bridge is visible.'[1] The move had, however, been chaotic: 'We have not recovered from the confusion yet, and our drawings and papers are nohow.'[2]

Mary had scolded her brother for neglecting to write. She had come to depend upon his letters. Having finished her teacher training, she had successfully applied for a position as a probationary teacher at Denchworth Mixed School, near Wantage in Oxfordshire: 'The salary is 40 pounds a year,' she told him, 'with a garden & a house partly furnished. I have to play the Organ in Church.'[3] She was anxious and insecure about her musical abilities, but her new employer, the Reverend Thomas Rawlins, had reassured her that she could have organ lessons and plenty of practice before she was expected to perform in church.

Mary had started her new job in January, and Tom was anxious to hear her news: 'Tell me about the organ and how the Sundays go off – I am uncommonly interested. How is your friend the blind man &c School, clergyman &c. *Say how you are,* don't forget – . . . Is Katie coming up to live with you & when is Mother coming?'⁴ Jemima had hatched a plan for her younger daughter to go to live with her older one.

The truth was that Mary's life was narrowing in Denchworth, whereas in London her brother's prospects were widening. He told her that he had been a passenger on the new Underground Railway, and that he had seen Horace Moule, who had been ill (probably a euphemism for another alcoholic relapse). He also reported on great excitement about the imminent Royal Wedding. The marriage of the Prince of Wales, Albert Edward, to Princess Caroline of Denmark on 10 March 1863, was the grandest wedding yet held in St George's Chapel, Windsor. But for Queen Victoria, it was overshadowed by the death of her beloved Albert just over a year earlier. Prince Bertie was a playboy, with a taste for actresses. His affair with the actress Nellie Clifden and its fallout was hugely distressing to his father, who paid him a visit at Cambridge to issue a reprimand. Albert died shortly after this visit, and Queen Victoria remained convinced that Bertie was to blame, and that her beloved husband had died of a broken heart.

Hardy, caught up in the excitement of the public festivities that marked the wedding, headed out to see the illuminations in the city. A frightening scene ensued as thousands of people formed a 'great mass', leading to several spectators being crushed to death. Two of Hardy's friends were caught up in the crush and 'did not expect to get out alive'. Hardy, having started from the other end of the route, narrowly missed being crushed, only

The birthplace, painted by Mary Hardy, with Kate Hardy standing and Jemima Hardy reading

The Bockhampton cottage as it is today

Mother and child: Jemima and
baby Hardy, by sister Mary

First love? Louisa Harding

The origin of Sue Bridehead: sister Kate (extreme left) as schoolmistress

Sister: Mary Hardy

Sister: Kate Hardy

Cousin: Martha Sparks

More than cousin: Tryphena Sparks

Photograph sent from
Eliza Nicholls to Hardy

Watercolor of Eliza Nicholls as a teenager

Nude: *The Tinted Venus*

Actress: Mary Scott-Siddons

St Juliot Church, sketched by Emma with caption by Hardy

Where Hardy first met Emma: St Juliot Rectory, sketched by Emma

Boscastle Valley

The watercourse
looking up stream

Cottage in the lane

The lane

Thomas Hardy.

(Sketches made in the Vallency Valley –
_Boscastle, Cornwall, 1870–72.)

Courtship sketches

Beeny Cliff, where she rode, he walked – and the site of
the original 'cliffhanger' in *A Pair of Blue Eyes*

Her hair, her miniature portrait, in a precious locket

Emma Lavinia Gifford: the first Mrs Hardy

having his waistcoat buttons torn off, and his 'ribs bent in' before finding a haven in a doorway.[5] But the scene shook him.

Despite the lavish wedding celebrations, the Prince of Wales' affair with Nellie Clifden was fodder for the press. The image of stable family life, portrayed so effectively by the Queen and Prince Albert, was severely threatened by Bertie's affair with the low-born Irish actress. It was well known that the prince had lost his virginity to Nellie, and that his parents had been horrified by the fact that he was consorting with what they perceived to be a common prostitute.

Meanwhile, in the all-male environment of Blomfield's office in Adelphi Terrace, much of the daily banter centred upon the notable courtesans of the day. The morning rallying call was 'Any spice in the papers?'[6] and the lads would regale one another with the exploits of such ladies of ill repute as Cora Pearl, 'Skittles', Agnes Willoughby and Adah Menken.

The ravishingly beautiful brunette Cora Pearl (born Eliza Emma Crouch) plied her trade in the Argyll Subscription Rooms in Great Windmill Street, a so-called 'lust-casino' where, amid drinking and dancing, women could be bought by the hour. She became the mistress of the proprietor, Robert Bignell, and they later travelled to France, posing as husband and wife. Pearl fell in love with Paris, sending Bignell back to London and his Argyll Rooms. She rose to become one of the most famous courtesans of the day, mistress to several notable aristocrats, including the Prince of Orange, and Charles Duc de Morny, the half-brother of Napoleon III.

She was showered with jewels and given money, servants, horses and a private chef. At the height of her powers, she charged ten thousand francs for the pleasure of an evening with her, and her jewellery collection was estimated to be worth over one million francs. Her boudoir contained a custom-made bath of bronze, with her initials carved in gold. Pearl was famous for her dinner parties. One famous evening the guests awaited their final course; it was Cora Pearl, naked and garnished with parsley, delivered on a silver platter by four burly men.[7]

Pearl had left for Paris by the time Hardy was working for Blomfield, but she was always a talking point in the office, and Hardy later 'sought out' the infamous Argyll Rooms, where one of his colleagues back in Hicks' office had told him that he had once taken up with the *danseuses*. Hardy himself danced at the more staid Willis's Rooms, preferring the old-fashioned quadrille dancing to the degenerate 'waltzing step, to be followed by galloping romps to uproarious pieces'.[8]

He also frequented the pleasure gardens next to the River Thames that were known as the territory of the demi-monde. Thousands of prostitutes, many of them children, worked the streets of London, desperate in their poverty. 'The Social Evil', as it was called, was the subject of a show performed at the Cider Cellars in Leicester Square and in the Coal Hole Tavern, which Hardy also visited at this time. He recalled the 'judge and jury' mock trials where 'Lord Chief Justice Baron' (an actor called Renton Nicholson) would try a case of prostitution, the subject of much coverage in the press at the time. Nicholson also staged *poses plastiques* performances at his establishments, which consisted of barely clothed women posing in imitation of well-known works of art.

Agnes Willoughby, mentioned in Hardy's list of courtesans, was a sensational figure who enthralled mid-Victorian society. When William Wyndham, one of the richest heirs in England, who was obsessed by prostitutes, married her, he was declared of unsound mind by his uncle, who hoped to inherit his millions. The trial of the case in 1861 exposed all his eccentricities, such as his obsession with railways. He would befriend engine drivers and porters and pay them to allow him to play with the real trains. He would dress as a policeman and harangue the prostitutes in the Haymarket and Rotten Row. He was so smitten with Willoughby that he even installed her pimp in his London house. The trial was the longest and most expensive lunacy case in England, and caused a public sensation. It was difficult *not* to be aware of Agnes Willoughby.

Close to Adelphi Terrace was Holywell Street, the centre of Victorian London's pornography trade. It was soon to be renamed 'Bookseller's Row', but Hardy preferred the old name. In an interview late in life, he 'acknowledged himself a book-hunter', but did not elaborate on the kind of books he sought out there.[9] In his autobiography, Hardy gave the impression that he remained aloof from the smutty office talk and that the office lads exaggerated their knowledge of courtesans. But there is no doubting his knowledge of the geography of 'impurity' in Victorian London.

CHAPTER 27

Miss Hardy

Mary Hardy lived in cramped quarters above the schoolhouse, adjacent to the church. During her time at Denchworth, she kept a diary, which formed the material for an incomplete memoir. She was without family or friends (the plan for sister Kate to live with her had not yet materialised), and her prospects seemed limited: 'It was indeed now that I realised what life would be to me and although I felt no disappointment I was not cheered by the prospect.'[1] She found the village primitive: 'the only drinking water obtainable being from the brook', she wrote, 'which tells painfully on the health of the villagers.' Many of the villagers were too poor to eat meat, and Mary thought the village almost from another era: 'the traces of Catholicism have not yet died out, and some still say their prayers on the graves of their friends in the Churchyard'.[2]

Her main concern was not the teaching, but her secondary duty of playing the church organ at the restored church of St James the Great. The organ was new, and though she practised four times a day, she found the keys 'stiff and difficult to play at first'. Her only consolation was that the music practice helped her 'to forget the dullness of my surroundings'. After her death, her brother would recall her 'girlish consternation' when she was called upon to take the musical service in 'a strange church, in a strange parish'.[3]

Mary was fortunate, however, in the figure of the vicar, the Revd Thomas Rawlins, and his wife, who were congenial people. She was often invited to supper after a service, and she found the occasions 'the pleasantest part of my dull life, as I considered it'. Rawlins, perhaps perceiving her insecurity and shyness, provided valuable assistance in the school: 'I had nothing to complain of in the school, for I found it well in hand, well supplied with books etc and the queer children wonderfully forward having been brought on by the Vicar who came every morning to teach and whose influence and support assisted me continually.'[4]

Mary was also comforted by the fact that Denchworth was close to Fawley, the village in which her paternal grandmother was born. Mary made a visit to the market town of Wantage, the birthplace of King Alfred the Great, thinking fondly of 'Granny' who had come to Wantage several times on business for her uncle. In *Jude the Obscure*, Alfredston was based on Wantage. Then in April 1863, Tom made a visit to Denchworth, where he sketched Mary's school.

Both siblings had a keen interest in art. Tom, as part of his programme of self-education, had begun to frequent the National Gallery to study the Old Masters. Whenever he could, he went there for twenty minutes after lunch. His method was simple: 'confining his attention to a single master on each visit, and forbidding his eye to strain to any other'.[5] In May, he began a notebook, entitled, 'Schools of Painting'. He began to consider an alternative career: 'it was suggested to him that he might combine literature with architecture by becoming an art critic for the press'.[6] He paid particular attention to figures of beauty: Rubens for his 'sensuous women'; in the 'Roman School', Raphael ('ideal beauty, loftiness, & volupts.'); in the Neapolitan,

Antonio Solario ('heads beautiful'); 'German School' – 'All Germany in early days seems to have been one vast studio for Saints, Angels and Madonnas'; among the English, a favourite was George Romney, 'Lady Hamilton his chief model'.[7]

Before congratulating Mary on a drawing prize that she had won, he told her that he had entered a small competition on 'a design for a Country Mansion'. He won the prize. His delight was somewhat tempered by the discovery that the number of competitors was embarrassingly small – perhaps only two. Hardy's skill as a draughtsman was evident, but his sister was beginning to show genuine talent as a painter. However, her duties left little time for painting and drawing. Nevertheless, Mary took advantage of her proximity to Oxford, and visited the city several times in her first year at Denchworth. Tom was pleased that she was enjoying her precious free time: 'I am glad you have been to Oxford again,' he wrote. 'It must be a jolly place. I shall try to get down there some time or other.'[8] A painter of great promise, but with little encouragement, she depended on her brother's reassurance, which he duly gave: 'You have no right to say that you are not connected with art.' He bristled at the thought that she put herself down so easily: 'the only difference between a profesor [sic] and an amateur being that the former has the (often disagreeable) necessity of making it his means of earning bread and cheese – and thus often rendering what is a pleasure to other people a "bore" to himself.'

Conscious of the mentoring role that Horace played in his own life, he was happy to extend the courtesy to his sister: 'About Thackeray. You must read something of his. He is considered to be the greatest novelist of the day.' Hardy's letters to Mary are key to understanding his art, because he was able to share with her, freely and unadulterated, his view of the purpose of fiction:

looking at novel writing of the highest kind as a perfect and truthful representation of actual life – which is no doubt the proper view to take . . . because his novels stand so high as works of Art or Truth, they often have anything but an elevating tendency, and on this account are particularly unfitted for young people – from their very truthfulness. People say that it is beyond Mr Thackeray to paint a perfect man or woman – a great fault if novels are intended to instruct, but just the opposite if they are to be considered merely as Pictures. *Vanity Fair* is considered one of his best.[9]

Hardy claimed that his mother's favourite novel was *Vanity Fair* and perhaps he recommended the novel to Jemima, as he had done for his sister. Mary seemed to prefer art and music to fiction, perhaps because they gave her respite from her day-to-day duties as a schoolmistress.

Tom and Mary would be reunited in Bockhampton for Christmas: 'We must have a "bit of a lark"', he wrote, somewhat unconvincingly. He told Mary that he was learning shorthand ('I am able to write 40 words a minute'). Some of the words in his letter were obliterated, perhaps a mention of Eliza that he wanted to keep a secret?

Mary's loneliness was eased when arrangements were finalised for Katie to join her at Denchworth. The plan was for the older sister to teach the younger, in the hope of Kate qualifying via the Monitorial route. Kate later remembered sitting in the Chancel at St James' Church, listening to Mary practising the organ.[10]

By now Hardy was bored of his architectural work. He enjoyed the congenial office atmosphere created by Blomfield, but felt a fraud. He wanted a new direction. The summer of 1863 was the time that he felt that his literary career had begun.[11] He bought himself a ten-volume edition of Shakespeare and embarked on an extensive reading programme, 'with a growing tendency towards poetry'.[12]

Before he left for London, Horace had given him a very special present: a copy of Palgrave's *Golden Treasury*. Published in 1861, it was an anthology of great English poems, and it was one of Hardy's most precious books. Florence Hardy recalled that Hardy said, in the last year of his life, that his only ambition was to have some of his good poems in an anthology such as the *Golden Treasury*. Reading the lyric poetry of the age of Elizabeth, towards which Palgrave's selection was heavily weighted, awakened in him 'a true, or mature, consciousness of what poetry consists in'.[13] The anthology was the origin of his ambition to be a poet. Once again, Horace Moule had proved himself a guiding light. Hardy annotated many of his books, but the *Golden Treasury* was the most heavily annotated of all.[14] Inside the back flap of his copy, he pasted a poem by Moule, as a symbolic thank you.

Now that Moule was in London, a regular contributor to the *Saturday Review*, Hardy began to spend more time with him, soaking up all his clever friend had to offer. He sent all his own copies of 'The Saturdays' to Mary, for her to read and to keep safe. Moule advised him to read his review of the working-class, self-taught stone mason, Hugh Miller, who had carved out a reputation for himself as a geological writer. Moule wrote: 'Self-education is probably, at the best of times, a great deal harder than most of us are disposed to imagine.' In July, Moule wrote Hardy an affectionate and wise letter. 'My dear Tom, I cannot say enough in praise of yr analyses. They must do your head good.' Moule was delighted to hear about Tom's 'new scent', and the discipline it involved, but he implored him to have his own style. 'The grand object of all in <u>learning to write well</u> is to gain or to generate <u>something to say</u>.' But, in the end, he advised, you must 'write <u>your own style</u>, unless you wd be a mere imitator'. Moule suggested writing exercises designed to stimulate thought and originality rather than 'method and arrangement'. It was an important letter. Horace was taking Hardy seriously as a writer: 'Be a "full man" – "Put money in thy [mental] purse."' Moule advised Hardy to think about journalism, perhaps as a London correspondent for the *Dorset County Chronicle*: 'Yr chatty description of the Law Courts & their denizens is just in the style that wd go down well.'[15]

Above all, Moule was writing to him as an intellectual equal, and, more crucially, he was not squashing his ambitions, as he had squashed his desire to go to Oxford. It seems, for the first time, that Thomas Hardy truly began to believe that it was possible to pursue his dreams of earning a living by his pen. Exactly what kind of a writer was yet to be defined.

CHAPTER 28

Jane Nicholls

Though Hardy did his utmost to conceal his relationship with Eliza, he left various clues to her existence and her importance to him. Throughout his life, he associated the women he loved with their geographical location. It might be argued that his loves were the embodiment of places he found to be both sublime and exhilarating. For Eliza, it was Purbeck, with its glorious coastline and hills. And the folly of Clavell Tower. The demise of the affair, and its wretched fallout, would coincide with the birth of Hardy's life as a poet. She would inspire a sonnet sequence that put him on the path of greatness. It was a celebration of their passion and its slow death, underpinned by guilt and transgression. Without Eliza, it is difficult to see how Hardy could ever have penned his verse masterpiece, the *Poems of 1912–13*.

Around 1863, Eliza left Orsett Terrace, and took on a new position in the household of her employer's father, Archdeacon Hoare. A famous Evangelical preacher and writer, the archdeacon had retired to Godstone in Surrey. Eliza was sent to help in his final illness, and it was a mark of the Hoares' respect for her that she was entrusted with the job. Eliza's sister recalled that Hardy made many visits to Godstone. Eliza was now closer to her family, in Findon, West Sussex. Her father's public house, The Running Horse, looked out over the village green, the site of an annual sheep fair. That Hardy visited the Nicholls family in September 1863, is evident from a cryptic marking in his Bible 'F. . .n 19/9/63'.[1]

He used his religious books as diaries, but also as a repository for coded secrets, some of which he shared only with Mary. During the new year of 1864 there were several visits to Findon. Eliza, the eldest of six sisters, had one brother. Sarah Headley reported that Hardy played with the younger siblings and gave the boy a copy of *Tom Brown's Schooldays*.[2] At some point, Hardy gave Eliza a ring. They began a long correspondence, which she kept for a very long time. Perhaps influenced by the devout Eliza, he began turning the book of Ecclesiastes into stanzas in the form of the Elizabethan poet Edmund Spenser, but he soon abandoned the task, finding the original unmatchable.[3]

When he sketched the parish church of Eliza's family, he made no reference to Findon, simply writing, 'Ch near the Downs, From the Hill.' This evasiveness was of a piece with the extensive markings in his religious books and poetry collections during the first years of their courtship, which are inexplicit but revealing. In Eliza's copy of *The Christian Year*, he marked a heavy line down the margin of a stanza:

> For if one heart in perfect sympathy
> 　　Beat with another, answering love for love,
> Weak mortals, all entranced, on earth would lie,
> 　　Nor listen for those purer strains above.[4]

The relationship appeared to be at its height. Hardy's strong sexual desire is implied by conscience-racked markings in his religious books. Fear of pregnancy and being trapped into an unhappy marriage haunted his thoughts. Furthermore, Eliza's piety was troubling him at a time when he was questioning his faith.[5] Her strong Christian faith might have been a factor in his falling out of love with her; if so, a curious foreshadowing of his falling out of love with his first wife. Hardy scribbled the words 'Devotion' and 'Stoicism' alongside a sketch he made of Clavell Tower.[6] According to her family, Eliza was so devout that her employer, Mrs Hoare, refused to take her on a family holiday to Italy, because she feared that Eliza might convert to Roman Catholicism.

Hardy's ardour was beginning to cool, and he was about to make another serious error of judgement. During his frequent trips to Findon, he fell in love with Eliza's younger sister, Jane.[7] The misery that resulted from this development, and its unhappy outcome, only served to increase his paranoia about keeping the relationship secret.

Jane was younger and prettier than her sister, and seemingly less devout. Hardy maintained a lifelong habit of writing literary notebooks, most of which were destroyed before his death. In one of the few that have survived, begun at this time, he revealed deeply passionate and erotic thoughts. It provides a key into the mind of the young man as he experienced his first proper love affair with Eliza Nicholls. But it is not beyond the bounds of possibility that the notebook was also about his lust for Eliza's sister Jane.

The notebook was headed: 'Studies, Specimens Etc.' and it is the most openly sexualised of Thomas Hardy's writings. If as he claimed, he became a man at the age of twenty-five, then the subject matter of this notebook suggests his sexual awakening, clearly connected with Eliza and/or her sister, Jane. The notebook consists of eighty-six pages of transcribed quotations and literary exercises, often written in shorthand that he had been practising for three years: 'Thes' for Thesaurus, 'Dic' for Dictionary, 'Inv' for Inventions are all typical abbreviations.[8] Sometimes he underlined words or phrases that resonated or which he didn't fully understand.

But there is another aspect to the notebook that gives an insight into his emotional state. In a tremulous tone, Hardy pens erotic textual reworkings, often from biblical sources of the Old Testament: 'lips my lips' dwelling place: you raised up heats in me – hopes of haste . . . hasty pants: hasty treads: hasty heart: marches of pleasure, march into death, the grave: march through the years, march through your beauty.'⁹ This passage is headed 'Con from Hab', meaning concoctions from the book of Habakkuk. Another riff on a verse in the same book reads, 'violent kisses: delight too *violent* for me: violent days'.¹⁰

About a quarter of the notebook is given over to erotic fantasies. Hardy even used an architectural textbook as inspiration for his erotic phrases: 'soft suck of the mouth (lip) on mine, suck k—s from my mouth: sweet *bell* inside that told of waiting feasts . . . *coming & returning* of breast . . . *vein*-work in thy neck.'¹¹ Shorthand obscures sexual references. For example, 'sweet *ache* of neck, lip, soul' is rendered 'sweet *ache* of n—k, l—p, s—l'. Words such as 'love' and references to female body parts (lips, cheeks, breast) are often indicated by dashes and ellipses. Even when he was building his 'Thes[aurus]' in order to build his literary vocabulary, the emphasis is striking. Thus for the letter 'c': 'the long *cleaving*, eager *cleavings* together: the *close* of arms about me: soft *close* of thine eye: slow *closes* of thy lips on . . .; long low *close* of a k[iss] . . . *coil* of arms about me . . . fair *curves*, white *curves*: sweet *cut* of pain.' Similarly, when he gathers poetic quotations. Poring over his *Golden Treasury*, he found a lyric called 'Rosaline' extracted from the novel by Thomas Lodge that was Shakespeare's source for *As You Like It*. Into his notebook, he wrote '*centres* of delight', 'orbs' and 'feed perfection'. The words are taken from lines that read:

Her paps are centres of delight,
Her breasts are orbs of heavenly frame,
Where Nature moulds the dews of light
To feed perfection with the same.[12]

We will never know the extent to which such notebook entries are expressions of unfulfilled longing or coded records of new sexual delights.

His emotional confusion around this time is evident in a fragment dating from April 1865: 'There is not that regular gradation among womankind that there is among men. You may meet with 999 exactly alike, and then the thousandth – not a little better, but far above them. Practically therefore it is useless for a man to seek after this thousandth to make her his.'[13] On his twenty-fifth birthday, he became melancholy: 'Feel as if I had lived a long time, and done very little. Walked out at moonlight and wondered what woman, if any, I should be thinking about in five years' time.'[14]

Unable to confide in his mother, Hardy was grateful to Mary, the keeper of his secrets. Her reserved nature, her unshakeable confidence in him and her loyalty were much prized.

Reaching his quarter-century and feeling that he had 'done very little' galvanised Hardy and set him on his path to become a poet. He began building his poetry library in earnest. His guide to his mission of self-education was his beloved *Golden Treasury*, given to him by Horace Moule. All the greats were represented from Shakespeare, Spenser, Dryden and Milton to Scott, Wordsworth, Coleridge and Shelley. In his annotations in *The Golden Treasury* he began a lifelong habit of comparing lines of poetry with paintings, usually of women. Alongside Thomas

Gray's *The Progress of Poesy*, 'O'er her warm cheek and rising bosom move / The bloom of young desire and purple light of love', he noted that the lines reminded him of an Etty nude he had seen in the South Kensington Museum. The colour purple as a metaphor for love was used by several of the Romantic poets, and 'purple light' was often used by Hardy as an expression of lust or love.

William Etty, the son of a baker, was an obsessive painter of nudes, famous for his ability to create fleshy skin tones, which gave him a reputation for indecency. He insisted on drawing his nudes from real models in the studio and this gave rise to the press attacking him for his 'lascivious mind'.[15] By Victorian standards, Etty's nudes transgressed the boundary between idealism and realism: his women were too real, too fleshy, too naked.

Hardy's love for Percy Shelley had grown. In 1866, he bought an edition of *Queen Mab and Other Poems* in the cheap 'Cottage Library Series', which he carried around London in his pocket. J. M. Barrie later said of Hardy's copies of Shelley that 'There are a hundred, a thousand pencil marks on those two volumes that look now like love messages from the young poet of one age to the young poet of a past age.'[16]

His annotations reveal that he made personal connections between himself and Shelley. Round the title of *The Revolt of Islam*, he wrote 'Hyde Park – morning', perhaps suggesting a memory of walking there with Eliza (the park was but a short walk from Orsett Terrace and Westbourne Park Villas). Hardy's heavy annotations on this poem about an illicit love affair, and on *Prometheus Unbound*, suggest that they were not only 'love messages to Shelley' but also messages about being *in* love. He double-scored, for example, the hero's first description of his love, Cythna:

She moved upon this earth a shape of brightness,
A power, that from its objects scarcely drew
One impulse of her being – in her lightness
Most like some radiant cloud of morning dew
Which wanders through the waste air's pathless blue,
To nourish some far desert; she did seem
Beside me, gathering beauty as she grew,
Like the bright shade of some immortal dream
Which walks, when tempest sleeps, the wave of life's dark
    stream.[17]

Hardy also marked his copy where Shelley describes Cythna as her lover Laon's 'sole associate', wandering the earth with him. He pored over the account of their erotic reunion after they were separated and their final destiny of being united in the tomb.[18] In Hardy's mind, Shelley and his love for Eliza Nicholls were inextricably bound. His first published novel, in which the heroine Cytherea is in many respects based on Eliza Nicholls, owed a great debt to Shelley and was heavily peppered with quotations from his poetry.

As well as Shelley, there was George Meredith. His groundbreaking poetry collection *Modern Love* (1862) was an important influence on Hardy. Meredith, who was the real-life model for Henry Wallis' pre-Raphaelite portrait, *Death of Chatterton*, had married a beautiful widow, Mary Nicholls, the daughter of the comic novelist Thomas Love Peacock.

Mary grew close to Wallis, and when she became pregnant with his child, the couple ran away to Capri, leaving Meredith to raise their son, Arthur. His novel *The Ordeal of Richard Feverel* (1859) emerged from this betrayal. It shocked Victorian readers with its sexual frankness. Meredith's collection of sixteen-line sonnets *Modern Love* was also inspired by this experience: it explored the demise of a relationship. When it was published,

Meredith was accused of indecency. His depiction of his passionate love for his wife and her betrayal with another man were viewed as immoral subjects for poetry. The collection became known as 'Modern Lust'. This volume was a major influence on Hardy's own early sonnet sequence. Some years later, he would meet the infamous George Meredith, but for now the poet and novelist was just a name, albeit one he wanted to emulate. He was a key precedent for the possibility of becoming both a poet and a novelist.

Hardy didn't just want to read poetry, he wanted to *write* it. Encouraged by Blomfield, he had given several talks on poets and poetry for the other pupils in the office. His desire to make a living by his pen was stimulated by a successful foray into print. He wrote a skit called 'How I Built Myself a House' to amuse his friends, and had it accepted in *Chambers' Journal of Popular Literature* in March 1865. It brought him his first literary earnings: three pounds, fifteen shillings. Though he considered becoming an art critic or architectural reviewer, it was poetry that he viewed as the very highest form of literary endeavour.

Meredith's estranged wife Mary fared badly. The relationship with Henry Wallis did not last, and three years later she returned to London in poor health. Meredith refused to let her see their son until shortly before her death. Still humiliated by her desertion, he refused to go to Mary's funeral. But she lived on as the muse for his brilliant novel and his ground-breaking sonnet sequence.[19]

THE DEATH OF CHATTERTON, THE YOUNG POET.

CHAPTER 29

Mary Scott-Siddons

And still Hardy yearned for university. In the *Life*, he recalled his hopes for Cambridge, of how he wrote to 'a friend' about particulars of matriculation and then a curacy in a country village, thus 'combining poetry and the Church'.[1] He had been reading *Barchester Towers* (1857), so in all probability his thinking was affected by Trollope's depiction of English clergymen in a country village. In October, he sent a copy of the novel to Mary: 'you are probably by this time acquainted with Eleanor Bold etc. This novel is considered the best of Trollope's.'[2] Eleanor Bold is the heroine, an attractive, wealthy widow who is wooed by three suitors, the oleaginous chaplain Obadiah Slope, the artistic Bertie Stanhope, and the scholarly Reverend Arabin. Much of the novel centres on her choice of suitor – a plot line Hardy replicated in *Far from the Madding Crowd*. Hardy told his sister to take her time reading the novel.

The 'friend' that Hardy applied to for information about Cambridge matriculation was Horace, who had sent him the *Student's Guide to the University of Cambridge*.[3] But this was the period when Hardy's religious faith was disappearing, so this was a factor in allowing the scheme to 'drift out of sight'. Religious tests were still mandatory for college entrance, access predicated on adherence to the tenets of the Church of England. In all conscience, Hardy felt that it would be hypocritical to take the examination while 'holding the views' that he held on religion.[4]

The dream was slipping away from him, but, in a rather bizarre enactment of his desires he took the part of an Oxbridge undergraduate on the stage of the Haymarket Theatre. A blacksmith colleague who made the ironwork for Blomfield's church designs also designed and made stage furniture. That Christmas, pantomime season, he managed to get Hardy a one-night walk-on part in *Ali-Baba and the Forty Thieves* at Covent Garden.[5] Hardy played an extra in a crowd scene in the play's recreation of the Oxford and Cambridge boat race. One wonders how he felt wearing the costume of an undergraduate cheering the boats along the River Thames. He had conceived a notion of writing plays in blank verse and wanted to gain some technical skills, but a meeting with the stage-manager of the Haymarket came to nothing. His unfinished poem 'A Victorian Rehearsal' captures the backstage scenes: the cavernous, empty theatre and the actors in their shabby clothes under the dim stage lights.

Even with Horace Moule's encouragement, Hardy felt that he had to be realistic about his prospects. As ever, Mary was his confidante and it was to her that he turned, confirming his decision to abort his Cambridge plan: 'I find on adding up expenses and taking into consideration the time I should have to wait, that my notion is too far fetched to be worth entertaining any longer . . . it seems absurd to live on now with such a remote object in view.'[6] The myth, propounded by Hardy and others, that Moule was discouraging about university could not have been further from the truth. In a letter that Mary wrote to her brother many years later, on his receiving his honorary degree from Cambridge, she claimed that it was the late Horace Moule's 'dear soul' that was responsible for his degree.[7]

The theatre provided a much-needed escape from the dreariness of office life and his anxiety about his failures to get his poetry published. He was lucky that the stage offered a huge array of Shakespeare plays, and he took advantage of the cheap seats. He was obsessively reading Shakespeare. In a letter of 1916, he wrote that he read the plays 'more closely from 23 to 26' – the years of Eliza – 'than he had ever done since.'[8] With one of Blomfield's pupils, he attended production after production at Drury Lane, rushing to be among the first in the pit, carrying 'a good edition of the play'. He and his friend would balance their well-thumbed text 'edgewise on the bannister' in direct view of the players, 'a severe enough test for the actors if they noticed the two enthusiasts'.[9]

He was lucky enough to see Mary Scott-Siddons, great-granddaughter of the legendary Sarah Siddons. Hardy was mesmerised by the beauty and grace of the young actress playing the part of Rosalind in *As You Like It*. This was a 'breeches role', suggestively showing off the legs of a woman, customarily hidden beneath long skirts. For most of the play, Rosalind is disguised as a boy. The revered Sarah Siddons had refused to wear tights for the role, but her great-granddaughter was happy to do so. The reviews focused less on her acting skills than her 'pretty face' and her 'figure admirably suited to the part'. Papers such as the *Daily Telegraph* noted, salaciously, that she was 'saucy' and 'attractive' with 'the external requisites'.[10]

Hardy went back to see her Rosalind for a second time, and then was moved to write a sonnet in her honour, 'To an Impersonator of Rosalind'. And then another 'To an Actress'. The first poem imagines Shakespeare writing the part, but never dreaming how she could be brought to life so vividly on the stage: 'Glowing yet more to dream our ecstasy / When his Original should be forth shown.' The second is suffused with romantic sentiment: 'When now the knowing you is all of me.'

It was as if his world had been transformed by this one performance: 'And the old world of then is now a new.' He barely
recognises himself: 'Could *that* man be this I?'[11]

Mary Scott-Siddons had a troubled life. Her husband was a
heavy drinker and they eventually separated. Sadly, she did not
achieve success in America, as she had hoped. After returning
to England in 1879, she briefly took over the management of
the Haymarket. She continued to give dramatic readings but
did not sustain the success of her early days. In a typically
Hardyesque codicil to her story, he wrote a poem about her
many years later, a strange echo of the 'Amabel' poems about
Julia Martin. 'The Two Rosalinds' has the narrator walking
through the streets of London alone, when he sees a poster
listing a cast including Rosalind on a colonnade outside a theatre.
It stirs 'an ember': he recollects the Rosalind he saw when he
was a young man and is therefore tempted into the theatre. On
the way in, an old woman, hovering in half-light outside the
theatre, 'as 'twixt the live world and the tomb', offers him a play-
text. But he doesn't need 'a text or teacher / To revive and
re-illume' the play that meant so much to him when he saw
Mary Scott-Siddons take the lead. Inevitably, the second actress
fails to live up to her: 'how unfitted / Was *this* Rosalind!'
Disgusted, he leaves the production 'and with chilling disappointment' he goes into the street to 're-ponder the first'.

The old woman hawking the play-text is still there. 'So you
don't like her, sir?' she says, in response to his hasty exit. To his
astonishment, she then tells him that forty years ago in 1863 she
played the part of Rosalind: 'Thus I won Orlando to me / In
my then triumphant days when I had charm and maidenhood.'
She quotes from the play – '*Come woo me, woo me!*' – and strikes
the very 'attitude' of Mary Scott-Siddons. The narrator of the
poem is transported back:

It was when I had gone there nightly;
And the voice—though raucous now—was yet the old one.—
Clear as noon
My Rosalind was here.[12]

Whether or not Hardy invented the accidental meeting with the now aged actress, the poem captures the memory of the momentous occasion of seeing Shakespeare's heroine brought to life by a young woman of consummate beauty and energy.

Hardy soon forgot about his desire to dabble in the theatre, either as an actor or a writer of plays in blank verse. His life was to take an unexpected turn, which would send him home to Dorset. It would be many years before he returned to live in London. He was too closely bound to the ties of family and home to leave home in a permanent way.

CHAPTER 30

She

Hardy returned home to Bockhampton for Christmas of 1866, giving presents of books to his sisters; Palgrave's *Golden Treasury* for Mary, and a copy of an *Illustrated Natural History* for ten-year-old Katie. Once back in London his health suddenly deteriorated. He seemed plagued with doubts of varying kinds. This was the year of publication of Matthew Arnold's poem 'Dover Beach', with its image of the 'melancholy, long, with-drawing roar' of the retreating 'Sea of Faith'. And so it was for Hardy: the erosion of his faith, which had been coming on for some years, might have been a contributory factor in the end of the affair with Eliza. Hardy was also facing the unpleasant truth that her sister Jane did not return his affections. Perhaps there had been a brief flirtation, but he was betrothed to her elder sister, and claims of family took precedence. Besides, according to her niece, Jane's affections were engaged elsewhere.[1] It was a mess, and Hardy knew that he would have to face Eliza in Findon for the final time that winter. It was not a pleasant prospect.

Another worry was Horace. By now, he had left London and was teaching at Marlborough College. His bouts of depression and drinking had continued, but things had taken a new turn

that year, which alarmed Hardy. He explored some of his
concerns in his 1866 poem, 'A Confession to a Friend in Trouble':

> Your troubles shrink not, though I feel them less
> Here, far away, than when I tarried near;
> I even smile old smiles—with listlessness—
> Yet smiles they are, not ghastly mockeries mere.

The poem suggests the narrator's sense of alienation, and need
to distance himself from his friend: '*That I will not show zeal
again to learn / Your griefs, and, sharing them, renew my pain*'
(Hardy's emphasis). He feels guilty about even having this
disloyal thought, fleeting as it is. He berates himself for the
treacherous thought: 'Yet comrade old, can bitterer knowledge
be / Than that, though banned, such instinct was in me.'[2]

Another of his London poems, 'The Temporary the All',
depicts a bond of 'flowering youthtime' between two fellows
who 'despite divergence, / fused us in friendship'. The poem
explores an anxiety that would initiate a Hardy theme, the
triangular relationship between two male friends and a woman
who threatens to derail the friendship: can he continue to cherish
his friend when an 'all-eclipsing' female, 'my forefelt / Wonder
of women', enters his life?[3]

Hardy threw himself into work. In his rooms at Westbourne
Park Villas, after his day's toil at the office, he would read every
evening for six hours, before retiring to bed at midnight. And
he was writing poems; extraordinary poems. 'The Musing Maiden'
is about separation. The maiden is located in a rural place and
seeks to connect with her London-based lover, who observes the
boats from his window, just as Hardy did from his office at
Adelphi Terrace. The narrator watches the moon at night, as
a way to connect to his lover, since 'To mark the moon was
our delight'.[4]

But most of the Eliza poems are about the loss of love. He began a sonnet sequence, in the style of Meredith's *Modern Love*, depicting a relationship on the rocks. But there was a significant difference. Meredith's sonnets view the 'shipwreck' of the marriage from the perspective of the wronged husband. The poet's anger, his sense of betrayal, his misery, his revenge affair, are explored with raw and ruthless honesty, invoking and subverting the courtly love sonnet. Hosting a dinner, man and wife pretend to their guests that nothing is wrong: 'with sparkling surface-eyes we ply the ball'. The expression 'surface-eyes' is superb. But the narrator knows that they are playing 'a most contagious game / HIDING THE SKELETON, shall be its name'.[5]

Hardy made the decision that his sonnet sequence would be depicted from the woman's point of view. Her shame, her misery, her heartbreak. Of the fifteen sonnets that he preserved from the years 1865–7, seven are in a female voice. Four are in a sequence called 'She to Him'. And Hardy's final, agonising meeting with Eliza Nicholls that winter would inspire one of his greatest poems.

The blameless female narrator of 'She to Him' begins by asking her lover to remember her when she is old and her beauty has withered. 'Sportsman Time' – one of Hardy's great themes – will have been responsible for the loss of her youth. She asks her love to remember that she is 'One who would die to spare you touch of ill.'[6] The second poem continuing the theme, offers hope that her faithless lover will, after her death, see a face reminiscent of hers, be filled with remorse and come to realise that he has thrown away a prize:

Perhaps, long hence, when I have passed away,
Some other's feature, accent, thought like mine,
Will carry you back to what I used to say,
And bring some memory of your love's decline.[7]

As we reach Sonnet 3, the voice of the jilted lover becomes angrier: 'I will be faithful to thee; aye, will!' She begs him to consider that she is alone and friendless – 'I have no care for friends, or kin' – and is 'Numb as a vane that cankers on its point.' And she knows that she has lost his love: 'My old dexterities in witchery gone, / And nothing left for Love to look upon.'[8] The final sonnet, the most powerful, hints strongly of the man's betrayal and his transference of affection from one woman to another, a woman to whom she is closely bound:

This love puts all humanity from me;
I can but maledict her, pray her dead,
For giving love and getting love of thee –
Feeding a heart that else mine own had fed![9]

The 'She to Him' poems are dated 1866. A year later, the year of the final breakup with Eliza, Hardy wrote the searingly powerful 'Neutral Tones'. Even now it sends shock waves with its rawness and emotional intensity. It is an extraordinary achievement for a writer who was only beginning to feel his way as a poet. He was using all the pain and the guilt and the shame, turning it into art. The perspective appears to have shifted from the woman to the man, and we witness a face-off. Her eyes are fixed on him, her smile is 'the deadest thing'. We feel his discomfort, his desperation to run away, and her magnificent frosty dignity. She is neither timid nor broken, but fierce in her unrelenting, unyielding gaze:

We stood by a pond that winter day,
And the sun was white, as though chidden of God,
And a few leaves lay on the starving sod;
      —They had fallen from an ash, and were gray.

Your eyes on me were as eyes that rove
Over tedious riddles of years ago;
And some words played between us to and fro
      On which lost the more by our love.

The smile on your mouth was the deadest thing
Alive enough to have strength to die;
And a grin of bitterness swept thereby
      Like an ominous bird a-wing . . .

Since then, keen lessons that love deceives,
And wrings with wrong, have shaped to me
Your face, and the God-curst sun, and a tree,
      And a pond edged with grayish leaves.[10]

The anger attributed to God is anger at himself; the end of the affair and the end of his religious faith are woven together, as are the bleakness of the landscape and the spareness of the language, so much plainer than the usual fare of Victorian poetry. The monosyllables of 'On which lost the more by our love' render the stumbling speech that we have all experienced in such encounters.

He was just twenty-seven.

———

It seems hardly surprising, given the emotional intensity of poems such as these, that Hardy suffered a breakdown.

Blocking out the love affair, he later attributed this collapse to the poor quality of London air, arising from the 'stench' of the Thames in high summer, used as he was to 'pure country' air. In effect, he suggests that transplantation from his native Dorset, his home, was killing him. His health became so weakened that he had 'scarcely physical power left him to hold the pencil'.[11]

He would describe the effect of depression with great honesty: 'As to despondency I have known the very depths of it – you would be quite shocked if I were to tell you how many weeks & months in byegone years I have gone to bed wishing never to see daylight again.'[12] Other poems of the London years, 'Hap' and 'Revulsion', hint at acute mental distress. In the former, the narrator imagines 'some vengeful god' laughing at him: 'Thou suffering thing, / Know that thy sorrow is my ecstasy, / That thy love's loss is my hate's profiting!' In 'Revulsion' the first-person narrator heaps shame on himself: 'For winning love, we win the risk of losing.'[13]

Blomfield was sympathetic and suggested that Hardy should return to the countryside and recover his health. Fortunately, his old employer John Hicks came to the rescue. He was looking for an assistant qualified in church restoration. Hardy suggested himself, and left London to return to his parents' home. And what of Eliza? Her part in Hardy's life was not over. She kept his letters, his manuscripts, his ring, and his photograph, and she would faithfully collect all his works. She remained convinced that she was the model for the heroine of his first published novel. We can only guess how she felt when Hardy finally published the 1866–7 poems in his first verse collection, *Wessex Poems* (1898). In the preface, he sought to give the impression that the poems were not autobiographical: 'The Pieces are in a large degree dramatic or personative in conception, and this even when they are not obviously so.'[14] And yet he could not resist sending a secret code to his first great love by means of the illustration he supplied for the 'She to He' poems: it was a drawing of two lovers ascending a winding path towards Clavell Tower in Kimmeridge.

WEYMOUTH

There is more autobiography in a hundred lines
of Mr. Hardy's poetry than in all the novels.

(Florence Hardy)

CHAPTER 31

Tryphena Sparks

If Tom had experienced a difficult year, then so had sister Mary. A new teaching job had gone badly wrong, leading to her being fired in ignominious conditions. In June 1866, she left her position in Denchworth, moving to a school in New Waltham, ten miles out of Winchester. Her new boss was the Reverend Henry Carey, who, as it would turn out, was very different to her previous employer. Yet again, she was expected to teach in a tiny schoolroom; this one was just twenty-eight feet by eighteen. On her first day, she had sixty-six pupils, taught in two sessions. There was no pupil assistant or class monitor. The school logbook survives, a sad testimony to the difficulties she experienced. On the first day, Mary noted: 'There is hardly a trace of order or discipline.'[1] And things were about to get worse.

The following day, numbers increased to seventy, but the day after that a swathe of pupils failed to turn up because it was raining. School attendance was extremely erratic in a small country town. During the haymaking season the children were called upon to help in the fields, and when there was a local fair the children bunked off. The pupils were unmotivated and there was little support from the parents. Rather than being paid directly, mistresses were paid by new school managers, who kept a close eye on attendance and examination results. Struggling alone, Mary soon had no choice but to get out the cane for such offences as eating in class and being naughty in church. Sometimes, she resorted to collective punishment, keeping the whole class standing because they had been constantly 'stamping with their feet'.[2]

When the inspectors came in December, though they expressed support for her valiant efforts to discipline her pupils, test results were abysmal. Carey had no sympathy: 'Miss Hardy having failed to satisfy the Managers & having entirely lost the affection of the Scholars through excess of severity, it was thought expedient that her connexion with the school should cease at the end of the year.'[3]

Within three months of being fired, she found a new position as the mistress of a tiny school in the beautiful village of Minterne Magna, near the River Cerne and nestling among the chalk hills of the Dorset Downs. Close by was Dogberry Hill, one of the highest hills in the county and the site of a prehistoric hill fort. Soon after he returned to Dorset, Hardy visited his sister, making a sketch of Dogberry.

Though Mary's spell at Minterne was short, she had a happier time. The pupils were more orderly, and she was given a school monitor to help her keep order. Punishments were still meted out – on her third day she kept the pupils after class to finish their sums.[4] Another pupil was 'kept in and punished' for bad spelling, and four boys punished for 'using bad words'. Mary still had to endure the problem of the children being pulled out of school by their parents in wet weather or during the agricultural phases of the year, harvest and haymaking time: 'Very few children on account of gleaning'. But she was on home ground back in Dorset. She was paid in part by the owners of the local big house, which Hardy would use as the model for Great Hintock House in *The Woodlanders*.

Hardy returned to his former custom of walking to the Dorchester architect's office from his mother's house every day. Soon he felt 'completely restored'.[5] Hicks had several church restorations and new builds in mind. Most were local, but one was a restoration project far to the west in St Juliot in Cornwall.

Almost as soon as he was home, Hardy decided on a new writing project arising from his experiences in London. He felt that his 'desultory yet strenuous labours at literature' needed 'tangible results'. That writing verse had been 'waste of labour'. Like his admired Meredith, he would try his hand at a novel. He would take for his theme 'the life of an isolated student cast upon the billows of London with no protection but his brains' and he would also make use of his knowledge of 'West-country life in its less-explored recesses'. It would be a 'socialistic novel', he wrote later on, acknowledging his anachronistic use of the phrase. And it would be called:

The Poor Man and the Lady
By the Poor Man.[6]

He began in summer and had finished his first draft by October. That summer he frequently crossed the heath and the ewe-lease, then joined a track to the village of Puddletown, where his cousin Tryphena Sparks was teaching.

Tryphena (known as Tryffie to her family) was the youngest and prettiest of the Sparks sisters. She had always been a clever girl, becoming a school monitor at the age of eleven.[7] For her diligence in her duties, she was given a copy of a book called *Matty Greg: The Woman that Did What She Could*, a sentimental tale about an old country woman who befriends a local orphan boy, teaches him to read and to go to church, and reaps her reward. Like all the Hand women, she was a gifted needlewoman. When she was a young girl, she worked a beautiful sampler of the counties of England and Wales.[8]

By the age of sixteen, Tryphena had grown into an exceptionally beautiful young woman. She had dark, intelligent eyes and striking black eyebrows. Her hair was dark chestnut, which looked black in photographs. She had a cupid's bow mouth and a small, well-shaped nose. Her face would inspire several of Hardy's most beautiful heroines. And she was lively and good-humoured. One of her surviving letters to her brother James reveals her teasing nature: 'How's your sweetheart old blow porridge Bibican?' – suggesting his habit of blowing hot and cold in love affairs.[9]

The woman under whom she worked as a pupil teacher suffered from poor health, so delegated much of the teaching. Like her cousin Mary, Tryphena had her tribulations in the classroom: a parent calling her a fool, the anxiety caused by the Revised Code of 1862 which tied wages to performance, the risk of dismissal for a trivial matter. Her hope was to complete three years of pupil-training before applying for a two-year course at teacher training college, after which she would be fully qualified and financially independent.

When Hardy arrived back in Dorset in the summer of 1867, he offered to teach his sixteen-year-old cousin French. They took long walks on the heath and through the meadows together. And they fell in love. For Tryphena, every minute spent with cousin Tom was refuge from the stress of the classroom and her difficult home life – her short-tempered mother Maria was in failing health, so many domestic duties fell to Tryphena. It was easy to fall in love with her sensitive and worldly twenty-seven years old cousin, whose time in London had given him some polish and sophistication. Hardy gave her a photograph of himself that had been taken back in 1862. It showed him every bit the Londoner, with long dark overcoat, top hat in one hand and umbrella in other.

In November 1868, Maria Sparks died. It was Aunt Maria who had turned Thomas out of her house and put a stop to his romantic interest in Martha. According to Nathaniel Sparks, she also tried to put an end to his affair with Tryphena. Perhaps Hardy hoped that the death of his aunt would open a door for his blossoming romance with his cousin. In his poem 'Unrealized', he depicts a family breaking free following the death of a strict mother. The children run wild, play in the snow, get drunk at a Christmas show: 'Mother won't know.'

How we cried the day she died!
  Neighbours whispering low,
But we now do what we will –
  Mother won't know.[10]

After her mother's death, Tryphena went to live for a time with her aunt Mary, who had married John Antell the Puddletown shoemaker. Hardy spent much of his time in the workshop at the back of his uncle's shop on the High Street. At his best, the mercurial Antell was brilliant, exciting, knowledgeable not just about history and politics, but also about the countryside. At his worst, when he had been drinking, he was aggressive, ranting and exploding into bitterness about social injustice. 'Like JA, when drunk at Noah's Ark', Hardy would note when he was writing about a similar type of 'almost brutal, at least fierce' man in *Tess of the D'Urbervilles*.[11]

Tryphena had moved jobs to a school in the hamlet of Coryates, near Blackdown Hill, east of Dorchester and not far from Weymouth. The school was run by Elizabeth Samson, the unmarried daughter of its founder. She lived in a large manor house in the picturesque village of Upwey, and though she and Tryphena were of different social classes, they remained friends long after Miss Sparks had left the area.

Tryphena also befriended (and possibly lodged with) a family called Spiller. The husband was bailiff to local legend Catherine Hawkins, who was known as the female farmer, running her own farm of 525 acres. Hawkins was twenty-four when she married a Dorset farmer in 1857. He died suddenly, leaving Catherine a widow with five children. She was expected to sell the farm, but risked scandal when she decided that she would keep it in the family, employing several farm hands, a shepherd and a bailiff. Her story would help to inspire Hardy's female farmer, Bathsheba Everdene.

But right now he was writing a story of a fine lady who stoops to conquer a poor man. The social justice warrior John Antell might well have given Hardy useful copy. The manuscript of *The Poor Man and the Lady* was destroyed, but it's possible to piece together the story, not least because parts of it were recycled into *Desperate Remedies*, *Under the Greenwood Tree* and the short story 'An Indiscretion in the Life of an Heiress'. The novel's hero, Will Strong, is an architect, the son of a Dorset labourer. The name Strong is clearly a synonym for Hardy. A clever schoolboy, Strong is noticed by the local squire and his lady, who pay for him to be apprenticed as an architect's draughtsman. But Strong falls in love with the daughter of the house, much to the alarm of the squire, who banishes the young man to London. His class resentment fires his socialist views, and he is found, by his lover, making a radical political speech in Trafalgar Square. The lovers are temporarily reconciled, but parted by the daughter's parents. She dies, and Strong designs her funeral memorial.

In July 1868, on the advice of Horace, who read the manuscript and wrote a letter of introduction, Hardy sent the completed manuscript of *A Poor Man and His Lady* to the publishers, Macmillan. He told Alexander Macmillan that his main intention was to attack the manners of the upper classes, but to do so in a way that was so subtle that they would barely realise.[12]

The following month, his sister Mary came home for the summer and they set off together for a trip to the seaside.

CHAPTER 32

The Girl on the Steamboat

Weymouth, with its sparkling blue-green sea and pink rocks, its sandy beaches and mild weather, became one of the first modern tourist destinations. There were steamboat and paddleboat excursions, donkey rides for the children, bands playing waltzes, and brightly coloured bathing machines lining the sands for the crowds who flocked to swim in the sea. Its popularity had risen since the days when King George III made the resort his summer residence, delighting visitors with his love of sea-bathing. The writer Fanny Burney described the King being 'dipped' to the tune of 'God Save great George our King'.[1] George's brother the Duke of Gloucester built a grand residence in Weymouth. Tourists, including Jane Austen's siblings, flocked to see a glimpse of royalty, though Austen professed to show little interest in Weymouth or the royals: 'Weymouth is altogether a shocking place I perceive, without recommendations of any kind and worthy only of being frequented by the inhabitants of Gloucester.'

By mid-Victorian times, it was a thriving seaside town. The arrival of the railway in 1857 boosted numbers, enabling tourists to make day trips. It was a garrison town with an established naval presence and a busy harbour. Portland stone was shipped to London. There were passenger steamboats to Jersey and

Cherbourg, and the glorious Lulworth Cove, which boasted crystal-clear waters and spectacular views.

Among the tourists heading for Lulworth on a hot August day in 1868 were Tom and Mary Hardy. On the boat ride, Hardy caught a glimpse of a beautiful woman on the paddle-box steps, 'all laughter'. Though she seemed at one point to suffer sea sickness, her smile soon returned. When they alighted at the sandy, secluded beach, the mystery woman did not disembark, but headed back to Weymouth on the steamer. Hardy, true to form, felt for that split second that he had met a kindred spirit. He took a final glance: 'Saw her for the last time, standing on the deck, as the boat moved off. White feather in hat, brown dress. Dorset dialogue, Classic features, short upper lip. A woman I wd have married offhand, with probably disastrous results.'[2] Hardy was fascinated by the concept of love at first sight and the idea that one glance from a beautiful woman can turn your life upside down. But he was shrewd enough to know that his romantic recklessness could prove a recipe for disaster. He was drawn to Dorset beauties, but too ambitious to make a firm commitment to a local girl.

In his first published novel, set in Weymouth, Hardy describes the beauty of the sea at Lulworth (which he calls Lewborne Bay in the original version of the novel and Lulstead Cove when he revised it): 'Placidly spread out before her on the south was the open Channel, reflecting a blue intenser by many shades than that of the sky ahead.' The setting sun adds 'an orange tint to the vivid purple of the heather . . . the light so intensified the colours that they seemed to stand about the surface of the earth and float in mid-air like an exhalation of red'.[3]

Little did he know, but he was soon to return to Weymouth for an extended stay. The unexpected death of his employer John Hicks led to an offer of work from the firm who had taken over Hicks' practice, a man called Crickmay who was based in

Weymouth. Crickmay offered Hardy three months' work in the seaside town, which he gratefully accepted. Still in love with Tryphena, he could walk to Coryates, which was close enough that its local news was reported in the Weymouth newspapers. Hardy had once again suffered a time of 'mental depression over his work and prospects'.[4] The prospect of the bracing sea air, and sea-bathing was an inviting one. After coming away from the interview with Crickmay, Hardy felt 'much lightness of heart'.[5] He stood opposite the Burdon House Hotel on the Esplanade 'facing the beautiful sunlit bay' and listened to the Town's band playing 'charming new waltzes' by Johann Strauss II. He wandered over to the musicians and asked them the name of one particular waltz. He gives it in his evocative poem 'At a Seaside Town in 1869':

> The boats, the sands, the esplanade,
> > The laughing crowd;
> > Light-hearted, loud
> Greetings from some not ill-endowed:
>
> The evening sunlit cliffs, the talk,
> > Hailings and halts,
> > The keen sea-salts,
> The band, the Morgenblätter Waltz.[6]

He took lodgings and established a routine of beginning the day with a swim, 'rising and falling with the tide in the warmth of the morning sun'.[7] After work, he would row in the bay, every evening. It was an especially warm summer and he felt invigorated by the sea. 'Physically', he reported, 'he went back ten years in his age almost as by the touch of an enchanter's wand.'[8] Occasionally he was joined by old friends, such as Charles Moule. He later recalled them diving 'from a boat on summer mornings into the green water of Weymouth Bay'.[9] He went dancing in the Assembly rooms, finding the local girls 'heavier on the arm than their London sisters'.[10] Though Tryphena (whom he called Phena) was his sweetheart, he continued to flirt with others.

As the brief encounter with the girl on the steamboat indicated, he was as susceptible as ever to the charm of beautiful women. Hardy needed a muse to inspire his writing, and there was a sudden surge of creative outpourings, both in his poetry of this time and in the new novel he was writing. His poems written at Weymouth suggest that he experienced an intense love affair. He was certainly close enough to see a great deal of Tryphena. According to her daughter, Eleanor, the couple became engaged, and Hardy gave Phena a ring and a photograph.[11]

It was the second Mrs Hardy who noted that the ring Hardy gave to his first wife was intended for a local girl, the suggestion being that the local girl was Tryphena. But there was another girl to whom Hardy was connected during this time. Another girl expunged from his memoir. Was this the third time Hardy had given a ring to a woman before breaking off the engagement?

CHAPTER 33

The Ruined Maid

Hardy was grateful to Crickmay for giving him 'breathing-time' and the opportunity to have 'shelved further thoughts about himself'.[1] He had been depressed by the rejection of *The Poor Man and His Lady*. On 12 August he heard back from Alexander Macmillan, who praised Hardy's 'admirable' writing and presentation of 'country life among working men'. One particular scene, set in Rotten Row, was 'full of power and insight'. He had some reservations, objecting to several of the scenes, including one which depicted a man following his wife out of the house at midnight and striking her. Hardy had seen domestic violence at first hand, but to Macmillan this seemed implausible and distasteful. He told Hardy that he was not confident enough to publish, on account of his hostile portrayal of the upper classes: 'The utter heartlessness of *all* the conversation you give in drawing rooms and ballrooms about the working-classes, has *some* ground of truth I fear . . . but your chastisement would fall harmless from its very excess.' Macmillan made the not unreasonable point that Thackeray was far more effective in his condemnation of the aristocracy and gentry by also giving them redeeming features, rather than a 'wholesale blackening of a class' such as Hardy delivered. 'He [Thackeray] meant fair, you *mean mischief*.'

The publisher softened the blow by praising Hardy's considerable potential: 'If this is your first book I think you ought to go on. May I ask if it is? And – you are not a lady so perhaps you will forgive the question – are you young?'[2] Macmillan had shown the manuscript to a trusted friend, the journalist and politician John Morley, who also found the book patchy, but much of the writing 'strong and fresh'. In the end, Morley thought some of the scenes 'wildly extravagant' and that the writing was 'some clever lad's dream'. As rejection letters went, Macmillan's was kind and encouraging, and, above all, it was honest.

He suggested that Hardy should try Chapman & Hall (Charles Dickens' publisher), and provided him with a letter of introduction. Chapman arranged for a reader and in March invited Hardy back to London to discuss the novel. Hardy was invited to enter the backroom of the publishing offices to meet 'the gentleman who read your manuscript'. The room, he noted, was dusty and untidy, with piles of books and papers scattered all around. Hardy did not know the identity of the gentleman in front of him, but he was struck by his flamboyant appearance. He was tall and extremely handsome, with dark brown wavy hair and beard. He was wearing a frock coat, buttoned at the waist, but loose above. Hardy knew instantly that he was in the presence of a theatrical personality. The man spoke in a deep, sonorous voice, holding Hardy's manuscript aloft in his hand, while he delivered a dazzling 'lecture'.

To his complete astonishment the man was no other than his literary hero, George Meredith. Hardy was aware that Meredith was a self-made man, whose novels also explored inter-class liaisons. George Eliot praised his first novel, a comical oriental romance called *The Shaving of Shagpat*, 'as a work of genius, of poetical genius', but it was *The Ordeal of Richard Feverel* that had drawn critical acclaim, while setting Victorian tongues wagging in response to its sexual frankness and its depiction of a love affair between the son of a baronet and a lower-class girl. Then there was the 1861 novel *Evan Harrington*, which drew on Meredith's own background: the protagonist, like the author, is the son of a tailor. He rises to become a gentleman and aspires to marry the daughter of a baronet. Meredith's novels not only broke the boundaries of class; they were also progressive in depicting female characters who were independent and spirited. He was the perfect reader for *The Poor Man and His Lady*.

Naturally shy, Hardy was dazzled by Meredith's charisma and sense of the dramatic. He told Hardy that they would honour their promise to publish the novel, but he strongly advised against it. Meredith advised him 'not to nail his colours to the mast' so early in his career. His speech was electrifying, full of colour and excitement: the press would be 'about his ears like hornets'. He knew all about bad press, and how his own work had been criticised for its vulgarity and prurience. He warned the young man that the book might handicap him for a long time to come. He took Hardy to task for his portrayal of a female character, a dance-hall girl, who 'took in washing' for extra income and assisted her architect lover by designing ecclesiastic furniture. Meredith feared that this character was a step too far.[3]

He advised Hardy to rewrite the story, softening the satire, or, even better, set it aside and begin a new story with a more dramatic plot. Hardy was savvy enough to see that Meredith was giving good counsel, and that in taking so much trouble he was revealing himself to be a man of great generosity and wisdom. Despite this, Hardy carried on sending the novel out to other publishing houses, without success. Bitterly disappointed, he felt that Crickmay had offered him a lifeline.

When he had completed his work for Crickmay, he decided to stay on at Weymouth, where he began a second novel.

Following Meredith's advice 'too literally', he set about constructing a 'sensational' novel with a highly melodramatic plot line. Deep in his heart he felt that *The Poor Man and His Lady* was a much finer, more original piece of work, and that he had in fact been badly advised.

Nevertheless, Weymouth soothed and inspired him. All around, he saw young lovers – in *The Return of the Native*, Budmouth, the town's fictional counterpart, is a place where 'out of every ten folk, nine of 'em are in love'.[4] He set most of his new novel in the resort, first calling it Creston, then changing the name to Budmouth in later editions. And his new heroine was not a fine lady, but a maidservant. More accurately, a lady's maid. Eliza Nicholls always believed that she was the model for the heroine, Cytherea. But there was another lady's maid on his mind that autumn. In November 1869, Martha Sparks, Phena's beautiful sister, was involved in a scandal that ruined her career. She found herself pregnant. The father of the baby was the handsome butler of the household, William Duffield. They were both dismissed.

Martha Sparks was the exemplar of the country girl who had escaped the limitations of her rural community. She had made the most of her beauty and brains, becoming an upper servant in a wealthy establishment. And now she had risked it all. Luckily for Martha, Duffield did not abandon her.

As early as 1866, writing in his lodgings in Westbourne Park Villas, Hardy had attacked Victorian hypocrisy and the sexual double standard in his satirical poem, 'The Ruined Maid'. It dramatises a conversation between two country girls from the same village. 'Melia' is the ruined maid, who is better dressed and more sophisticated than her countrified friend. She has acquired polish, has learned to discard her country dialect, and seems to have a much better life than when she was back in the village digging up potatoes and dressed in rags. Her poverty-stricken home life which led to depression suggests that acute deprivation corrodes the soul. By going to town and being 'ruined' by a man, Amelia wins herself fine clothes and freedom from labour. 'We never do work when we're ruined', she says, implicitly denying that sex work is work. The poem raises the question of whether it is better to trade your sexuality for financial security or to endure a life of hard work, hunger, poverty and melancholy. Somehow, being an 'unruined' maid seems to be the worse option:

'I wish I had feathers, a fine sweeping gown,
And a delicate face, and could strut about Town!'—
'My dear—a raw country girl, such as you be,
Cannot quite expect that. You ain't ruined,' said she.[5]

Many years later, Hardy would take as his theme the 'ruin' of a 'pure' country girl who is very different from the pragmatic Amelia.

Martha Sparks married her fellow servant at Kensington Parish Church in the latter months of the pregnancy. It was a comedown for the woman Hardy had once hoped to marry, but she made the best of it. The couple moved to Essex and subsequently worked at a coffee shop in Notting Hill. Later, William Duffield joined the police force. Eventually, they emigrated to Australia.

CHAPTER 34

Cassie Pole

Tryphena had completed her three years of pupil-teacher training. She learned that she had achieved a place at Stockwell Normal College in London, to be taken up in January 1870. Teachers were required to have an unblemished moral character: no taint of scandal could accompany them. During her time in Weymouth, Tryphena had to be extremely careful as she was courted by cousin Tom. There could be no question of an extra-marital liaison, and it was far from certain that he had the financial security – or indeed, given his wandering eye, the commitment – to marry her. According to Tryphena's daughter, he gave her an engagement ring. Tryphena's nephew Nathaniel even recorded that 'Thomas Hardy first wanted to marry Martha! then he tried to marry Tryphena, but grandmother put a spoke in his wheel on the ground of its being against the laws of the church' (in fact, marriage between cousins was not against Anglican canon law).[1] Kate Hardy told Irene Willis that Tom gave Emma a ring intended for a local girl. But in later years Hardy's sister Kate and his second wife were less certain: they both said that the ring he gave to his first wife was originally intended for a 'local girl'.[2] Not necessarily, that is to say, a cousin.

The happy months at Weymouth in which Hardy worked on

his second novel were also marked by a burst of poetic creativity – in the form of love lyrics that seem to point to a new phase of emotional intensity. The balance of evidence suggests that they were inspired not by Tryphena but also another young woman with whom Hardy initiated a courtship. Like his cousin Martha, and Eliza Nicholls, she was a lady's maid. Her name was Catherine Pole.

Several years later, in 1874, an embarrassing incident took place at the vicarage in the Dorset village of West Stafford. Hardy was asked to dine with the rector and his wife. He gratefully accepted the offer. He found the vicar, Reginald Smith, and his wife, Genevieve, charming. Mrs Smith was well-travelled and cultivated, and Hardy wrote a thank you letter in which he spoke admiringly of her conversation and her 'varied knowledge and experiences'.[3] When the Smiths entertained, it was their custom to hire the services of the butler of the nearby Stafford House. The butler, Mr Pole, who was intensely old-fashioned, objected to waiting upon Thomas Hardy.[4] In part, this may have been because Hardy was the son of a builder, but there was another reason. Pole was angry that Hardy had jilted his daughter Catherine, known as Cassie. She was a lady's maid at Kingston Maurward and had met Hardy around 1868.[5]

It was another liaison about which he remained silent. But just before the Second World War, an American scholar interviewed a number of people who knew Hardy. He heard from three different sources, including Evangeline Smith, daughter of the rector of West Stafford, that Cassie had a relationship with Hardy and that he was aware of her eventual death at a pub called the New Chesterfield Arms kept by her husband just off Piccadilly in central London. In December 1894, Hardy was

alone in London, staying in lodgings close to his club, also just
off Piccadilly. Tragic coincidences – 'Satires of Circumstance',
as he called them – were at the heart of Hardy's imagination,
and this seems to have been one of them: his proximity to the
pub where Cassie was dying. It inspired a superbly controlled
poem of memory and regret called 'At Mayfair Lodgings':

How could I be aware,
The opposite window eyeing
As I lay listless there,
That through its blinds was dying
One I had rated rare
Before I had set me sighing
For another more fair?

Had the house-front been glass,
My vision unobscuring,
Could aught have come to pass
More happiness-insuring
To her, loved as a lass
When spouseless, all-alluring?
I reckon not, alas!

So, the square window stood,
Steadily night-long shining
In my close neighbourhood,
Who looked forth undivining
That soon would go for good
One there in pain reclining,
Unpardoned, unadieu'd.

Silently screened from view
Her tragedy was ending

> That need not have come due
> Had she been less unbending.
> How near, near were we two
> At that last vital rending,—
> And neither of us knew![6]

He is 'screened' from her death by the blinds on the window, but haunted by the light in the room behind them, where she is dying in pain. His wish for the house-front to have been of glass expresses his anguish that there was no pardon, no adieu. But if there had been a final meeting, would it really have been 'happiness-insuring' for her? 'Spouseless, all-alluring' is a give-away: his own marriage was in a dark place by this time, suggesting that beneath the surface of the poem is the wish that he had married her instead. By claiming that the relationship ended because she was 'unbending', he is evading his own guilt: the reality was that he jilted her for the woman he married.

There may be a further evasion. The autobiography is char-acteristically obfuscating: 'there seems to have occurred, according to remarks of his later, some incident of the kind possibly adumbrated in the verses called "At Mayfair Lodgings".'[7] But in an interview late in life he was more explicit about the poem:

> Vere Collins [interviewer]: Why and how 'need not the tragedy have come due'? Because she would have married him, and there would not now have been the tragedy of her dying apart from him?
>
> Hardy: Yes.[8]

And was his presence in London, just across the road from her deathbed, really a coincidence? Evangeline Smith reported that she told Hardy that Cassie was dying of cancer and gave him the address in London so that he could go to town specifically in order to make his goodbye.

Hardy's Weymouth poems explore the infatuation of a young man for a lovely woman. He woos her in a seaside town and falls out of love with her when he realises that she falls short of his romantic idealisation. As with the 'She to Him' sonnets, Hardy focuses on the breakup of the relationship. 'At a Seaside Town in 1869' is subtitled 'Young Lover's Reverie'. Hardy depicts a man who basks in the allure of a beautiful woman; 'All shone my love / That nothing matched the image of.' Their romance is kindled by the seashore. But she is lost to him: 'Yea, she is gone, is gone.'[9]

In 'Her Father', the narrator falls in love with a girl of 'pink and white' with 'crimson lips'. He has arranged to meet her privately, but to his disappointment, she is accompanied by her father, who puts an end to their love-making:

Her crimson lips remained unkissed,
Our fingers kept no tender hold,
His lack of feeling made the tryst
    Embarrassed, stiff and cold.[10]

In 'The Dawn after the Dance' Hardy describes the demise of a romantic relationship: 'Yes; last night we danced I know, Dear, as we did that year ago, Dear, / When a new strange bond between our days was formed and felt, and heard.' He clasps her to him 'just as always – just the olden love avow'. But he knows that the relationship has come to an end: 'And this long night's dance this year's end eve now finishes the spell.' The sweet cord between them has 'spun to breaking' and at the end of the poem the 'blind bleak windows' of the paternal home give the message that the 'vows of man and maid are frail as filmy gossamere'.[11]

The seaside and the dancing make these poems feel as if they are inspired by Tryphena, but the disapproving father points to Cassie Pole. In all probability, Hardy is combining his feelings for the two women and perhaps also indulging his fantasy of the girl on the steamboat. In the novel that he was writing simultaneously, the architect hero first sees the heroine, Cytherea, on a steamboat to the fictional rendition of Lulworth Cove. The relationship flourishes in a warm summer of glorious boating expeditions on the blue-green sea; he rows on the dimpled water as she sits in the stern with the tiller ropes in her hand: 'The curves of her figure welded with those of the fragile boat in perfect continuation, as she girlishly yielded herself to its heaving and sinking, seeming to form with it an organic whole.'[12]

Later, the couple experience their first erotic encounter on a graceful yellow cockle-shell boat: 'The boat was so small that at each return of the sculls, when his hands came forward to begin the pull, they approached so near to her bosom that her vivid imagination began to thrill her with a fancy that he was going to clasp his arms round her.' When he releases the tiller, he comes so close to her that his warm breath 'touched and crept round her face like a caress'. They decide to row some more and twice they embrace: 'Their hearts could hardly believe the evidence of their lips.'[13]

Cassie may well have been lovely to look at, but a contemporary who knew about the Thomas Hardy connection described her disparagingly: 'affected in manner, namby-pamby, not a very interesting girl. Just rather pretty.'[14] She was a redhead with blue eyes. Her cousin reported that Cassie believed she was the model for the heroine of *The Hand of Ethelberta*, who is described as having blue eyes (changed to brown in a later revision of the novel) and 'squirrel-coloured' hair (the indigenous red squirrel had not yet been displaced by the imported grey).

In a poem called 'At Waking', dated Weymouth 1869, the narrator imagines a vision of his beloved appearing to him at dawn. He realises that he no longer loves her. He suddenly sees in an insight that 'would not die' that all her charm is lost to him, she is 'one / Of the common crowd.' The poet covers his eyes. He cannot force the image out of mind that she is a 'sample' of 'earth's poor average kind / Lit up by no ample / Enrichments of mien or mind.' Finally, in the cold light of morning, he is forced to face the fact that he has fallen out of love:

> O vision appalling
> When the one believed-in thing
> Is seen falling, falling,
> With all to which hope can cling.[15]

She who was once the 'prize' is now a 'blank'. Once again, the breakdown of a relationship was inspiring extraordinary poetry, allowing him to look inward and also to recognise his own part in the romantic idealisation. The narrator offers no particular reading of why the girl has suddenly lost her allure. The realisation comes to him in a vision, despite his reluctance to admit the cold truth. If the poem was as autobiographical as Hardy implies – the use of the first-person narration adds to this impression – then it was a pattern all too familiar: falling in love quickly, entering into an understanding and making promises, a ring bought, and then the cold feet. The problem for him was how to break off the relationship without a repeat of the anguish of the breakup with Eliza Nicholls.

As Hardy approached his thirtieth birthday, he wrote in his notebook: 'A sweet face is a page of sadness to a man over thirty.'[16] But which sweet face was he to choose so as to avoid the sadness of prolonged bachelorhood? Phena left for London and Hardy returned home to Bockhampton. He had almost completed his church restoration work for Crickmay. But there was a job outstanding. In February of 1870, his employer asked him to go to Cornwall to take the particulars of a dilapidated church in the hamlet of St Juliot. He said goodbye to Cassie and set off early the next morning.

CORNWALL

CHAPTER 35

The Gifford Girls

The house was close to the Hoe, in the English coastal town of Plymouth, overlooking the sea. The Hoe was a large, expansive open space with green lawns, breathtaking views, and a famous lighthouse called the Smeaton Tower. According to legend, Sir Francis Drake spotted the Spanish Armada while playing a game of bowls there. He insisted on finishing his game (which he lost!), while waiting for the wind to change before setting off to defeat the Armada. It was also the harbour from which the Pilgrim Fathers set off on the *Mayflower*.

In the Victorian era, the Hoe was promoted as a pleasure and recreational space, where people could promenade, take boat trips, and be dipped into the sea. In November 1840, Emma Lavinia Gifford, born in her grandmother's seaside house, was the youngest daughter of a solicitor who hailed from a Bristol family. Her mother, also from Bristol, came from a family of merchants that had prospered during the era of the slave trade. Emma's grandmother was wealthy with a private income, and she encouraged her son, who was her favourite child, to give up his profession, which he disliked, and live a life of 'quiet culti-vation'.[1] The house had a large garden filled with fruit trees and flower beds. In her memoir, *Some Recollections*, Emma described

her 'happy childhood'. She had three brothers and a sister called
Helen. John Gifford was extremely fond of his garden, passing
on his love to his daughter. Her first memory was, when she
was three, being taken to a field of daisies: 'I can never forget
the ecstatic state it put me in.'[2] After the death, her future
husband, Thomas Hardy, would evoke this moment in his poem
'Rain on a Grave'.[3]

Underneath a magnificent elm, the family had erected long
garden seats with long tables for outdoor dining, close to fragrant
jasmine. The girls had a swing in the large courtyard, and water
casks for their collection of minnows, frogs and tadpoles.[4] There
was a poultry house full of 'fat noisy' chickens, a kitchen garden
and a garden of standard rose trees, which Emma named
'Rosewood'. On market days, she would accompany her mother
to the centre of town: 'Such a display of vegetables, fish, flowers,
dairy produce and meat etc. I have never seen such in England.'
She loved to see the fish-women calling to the buyers in the
street, bearing great wicker flasks filled with shiny fish, 'stiff,
with freshness and marvellously cheap'. Their voices were 'as
fresh and clear as the sea'.[5]

Emma's mother read her bible with 'exceeding diligence'. She
was also a hygiene obsessive. Her children had constant baths
in the house and out of it, dips in the open sea, and in the
Royal Public Baths in Union Street. Emma cherished the memories of the bathing attendant carrying swimming costumes and
dry towels, ushering the children into the little dressing rooms
which opened out on the opposite side to a high-walled space
full of seawater, and the 'shouting, laughing bathers – coolness,
freshness and saltness'.[6] She recalled being 'dipped' into the pools
under the Hoe when she was just a toddler. At first she was
terrified, but soon she learnt to love sea-bathing.

The Plymouth of her childhood was a much wilder place than
it later became. Her home was close to the Hoe, her 'glorious

playground'. As she grew older, she escaped to the outdoors and spent hours climbing the cliffs and rocks to inaccessible places, and descending the steps to the beach that had been named for Queen Victoria. Once, as a child, she hung over the 'devil's hole' on a dangerous steep crag, before being rescued by a local boatman. Quoting Coleridge, she explored caves and coves: '"Lightly then I flashed along" over those lovely slippery rocks with sure feet.'[7]

Later, the Gifford sisters attended a local school, run by 'dear refined single ladies of perfect manners'.[8] It overlooked the Hoe, below which military drills took place; the sisters would draw down the blinds, so that the young ladies were not tempted to gaze at the soldiers. Emma's summers were full of countryside walks, regattas, Devonshire cream teas, sketching parties and boating excursions. Even the rain, 'soft, almost imperceptible-sprinkling', produced not inconvenience but 'dewy complexions'. The streets of Plymouth, 'paved with marble', were pleasant and interesting; at the end of the old town was a dancing school, which Emma and Helen attended. Girls in muslin dresses would dance alongside the soldiers and sailors: 'Splendid sashes and stockings and shoes also adorned us, and our hair floated about in the rush of air made by our whirlings – never to be forgotten parties!'[9]

But there was a darker element to Emma's upbringing. Her beloved father was a binge drinker, and 'never a wedding, removal or death occurred in the family but he broke out again'. Emma claimed that her father's alcoholism was caused by a great sorrow in his life, the early death from scarlet fever of the girl he was going to marry. He married her sister but longed for the lovely golden-haired girl of eighteen he had lost. Emma claimed that her father would stroke her own golden hair, sighing. The story seems to have been an invention, an excuse for his hard drinking. Emma might also have liked the reference to her best feature, her blonde hair, which darkened to a deep corn colour as she grew into adulthood.

When temperate, her father was a dashing, charming figure. He was handsome, and cultivated, fond of declaiming Shakespeare, expert in his horticulture. Emma adored her grandmamma Gifford, a 'remarkably beautiful person as I remembered, even in age'. Beautifully dressed in black silk, summer and winter, the old lady would sit upright in an armchair at the side of the fire, her velvet slippered feet on a stool, her complexion almost wrinkle-free, her hair a chestnut brown, worn under a muslin and lace cap with satin ribbons: 'she made a most charming picture and dearly we loved her; her hands and feet were small and beautiful, and her voice sweet.'[10] She bequeathed Emma her diamond brooch, a present from her husband on her wedding day. Emma wore it all her life.

After her grandmother's death, the family moved to Bodmin in North Cornwall. Emma and her sister, Helen, stood out from the crowd, 'she dark and I fair, wearing our hair curling over our shoulders, well dressed but in mourning'. Emma longed for her beloved Plymouth: 'its loveliness of place, its gentleness, and the generosity of the people'.[11] The Giffords rented a house in the countryside, but money was tight, and Helen was sent to be a governess. Later on, Emma also had a six-month stint of governessing. As with Hardy's sisters and female cousins, teaching or becoming a lady's companion was the only option for an educated woman who wanted to be financially independent. But the sisters disliked governessing and returned home to Bodmin.

Before long, Helen left for Tintagel to become a companion to an eccentric woman of a county family. This would ultimately change the course of her sister's life. Helen adored her employer, and they knitted, gossiped, and took rides around the beautiful Cornish coast. The eccentric lady dressed as a peasant woman, only donning her finery when her lawyer called. Helen would return home and regale Emma with tales of Tintagel Castle and the rolling sea where the waves crashed against the cliffs. Tintagel had been associated since time immemorial with King Arthur – it was said that he was conceived there – and also with the legends of Tristan and Isolde. Emma was mesmerised by her sister's tales, and once, when she was recovering from an illness, Helen came to fetch her in a carriage filled with pillows, so she could recuperate at Tintagel.

Emma loved the remoteness and wildness of Tintagel, especially the waves in winter, which reached hundreds of feet up the dark rocks. She revelled in the cries of gulls and rooks. Once walking the cliffs in a storm, she was almost blown over the edge into the Atlantic. She had to cling on to the rocks. It was so remote that she barely saw another soul, other than a few old-fashioned people with old-world ways, who lived high on the cliffs in sheltered niches. She once met a little old woman in an old cottage spinning flax, and she gave Emma a lesson. Other cottagers gathered seaweed, which was then sold and used for manure.

The eccentric old lady of the house took a shine to Emma, and gave her books to read; Fanny Burney's *Evelina* and Dr Johnson's *Rasselas*. She told Emma about her girlhood and the balls she attended. She had a sister, who was also her rival, each trying to outdo one another by wearing glamorous ball gowns. The lady prophesied that one day when Emma married, there would be a great separation between the two sisters. This, as Emma wryly acknowledged, would come true. Other people seemed to want to tell her fortune, including her beloved servant Ann Chappell. One hot summer's day, Ann carried out tumblers of water, and asked the sisters to break an egg into them; the shape the egg took would determine their future husbands. To their amazement, Helen's egg revealed the shape of a church and a tower. Ann told Helen that she would marry a clergyman, which she did. When Emma took her turn, a large ink-bottle and an immense quill-pen shape appeared. Anne pronounced: 'You will marry a writer.'[12]

When Emma returned home, the eccentric old lady sent her a brown mare, which she named Fanny: 'I loved it well, rode much upon it and for many years it was the joy of my life.' When people teased her about marriage prospects she responded, 'I prefer my mare to any husband.'[13] Emma suffered from partial lameness as a child, and the horse was invaluable for exercise. The splendid air, she said, made her strong and healthy, with red cheeks.

One day, Helen was driving with the old lady in a new vehicle when she met with a bad accident. She fell from the high seat and banged her head on the granite road, falling unconscious and suffering from bad concussion. Emma nursed her through her long illness, feeling that her sister was never 'the same' thereafter. Nevertheless, Helen recovered and married a man, the Reverend Cadell Holder, who was thirty-five years her senior. He was Oxford educated, born in Barbados (he remembered the orange trees that grew beside his bedroom window). Helen's marriage meant an escape from her position as companion, and a chance to be mistress of her own household. The marriage also opened up opportunities for her sister, who went to help with housekeeping and domestic management.

Emma moved with the Holders to a remote spot, St Juliot, in North Cornwall, taking her pony. Close to the age of thirty, her prospects of marriage and children were thin. Then on 7 March 1870, she opened the door of the vicarage to see a young man in front of her. He had a yellowish beard and was wearing a shabby greatcoat. In his pocket she noticed a leaf of blue writing paper, which she thought was probably a work-related document. He was the architect who had come from Dorset, and his name was Thomas Hardy.

CHAPTER 36

Tryphena

Tryphena was never far from Hardy's thoughts. She had begun her training at Stockwell in London. She put up her long dark hair and dressed soberly. Students were told that admission was dependent upon 'neatness and plainness of dress . . . no flower, ornament, or other finery should be worn'.[1] Rules were strict at the training college. The day began at six, with a period of study before prayers and breakfast, followed by six or seven hours of lectures and private study. Lights out was around nine thirty to ten. Each student had a small, sparsely furnished cubicle, divided by a wooden partition and a curtain, which allowed for little privacy.[2] The girls were expected to do the cooking, cleaning and washing. The diet was heavy and dull. Breakfast was bread and butter and coffee. Lunch was meat, bread and vegetables, and supper was bread and cheese, or bread pudding with a glass of milk or beer. And, as always, the students were expected to take care of their moral education, with no blemish upon their conduct. A few years after Tryphena had graduated, a senior teacher wrote down some 'friendly' rules for a new Stockwell student:

1) Never go out alone
2) Don't speak at dinner time

3) Never speak after 10pm

4) Always wear a bonnet on Sundays

5) Never go upstairs without asking

6) If you go for a walk with a young gentleman always leave at the corner

7) Never leave a square inch of dinner on your plate

8) Take a constitutional [walk] daily either between 12 and 1 or 6 and 7.[3]

The school boasted a new gymnasium, and some of the students were given garden plots to encourage healthy exercise. It was a disciplined, severe, and often lonely life. Pleasures such as reading novels or poetry were discouraged – other than the one play or poem required to be learnt by heart in the final year, and this was to encourage better diction and improve pronunciation. Most of the students were recruited from the respectable working class, the daughters of 'labourers, artisans or small tradesmen'. It was unusual for a student to be from a professional background, although there were a few examples of poor, genteel recruits. An article in the *Cornhill* magazine in 1873 reflects the condescending attitude towards the young women who entered the training college: 'Though a visitor may walk through the classroom of a Training School, and be only struck with the general intelligence and lady-like appearance of the Students, there must be a great deal of roughness about many of them when they first enter.'[4]

Girls from genteel backgrounds were discouraged from entering the Training Colleges, not only because their superior social class and polite manners would render their positions 'isolating and painful', but also because the life of a teacher in training was so 'rough and hard', thus more suitable for the daughters of farmers.[5] Mixing the social classes was still deemed to be dangerous. Quite what Tryphena made of this social snobbery can only be imagined.

In her summer holidays, she often went back to Dorset to help look after her widowed father, and to help her sister, Rebecca, with her dress-making business. On the day that Tryphena entered college, Hardy noted the date in his Bible at the head of the book of Joel. He underlined some verses that might have given a clue to his state of mind: 'That which the palmer-worm hath left hath the locust eaten; and that which the locust hath left hath the canker-worm eaten, and that which the canker-worm hath left hath the caterpillar eaten.'

Better news came when Mary was successful in her application for the position of headmistress of the National School in the small village of Piddlehinton, just four miles from home. It wasn't long before her sister Kate joined her as a pupil teacher. This set her on a different path to Mary, and would make it possible for her to apply for a Queen's Scholarship. Payments for tuition in French and music for Kate survive from around this time, and, like Mary, she benefited from being close to home.

Hardy would make good use of the information gleaned from his two sisters, and from Tryphena when he came to writing the character of Sue Bridehead. He was very well aware of the difficulties of their lives, and the sacrifices they made to be economically independent. Perhaps some of the later resentment between his sisters and his wife sprang from the fact that their lives had been very different, and the sisters thought that Emma was spoilt and put on airs. According to Tryphena's daughter, the Hardys regarded Emma as 'a snobbish woman who considered his family peasants'.[6]

But all that was to come later. When Hardy set off for Cornwall – an arduous twelve-hour train journey followed by a horse and trap ride for the final sixteen miles – he was thinking of Tryphena in her college at Stockwell and scribbling a poem on a scrap of blue paper. He was also thinking of Cassie. Hardy set off to

Cornwall by foot in the starlight, at 4 a.m., walking across the heath to the train station. At five o'clock, Cassie Pole was woken by the grandfather clock in Kingston Maurward. Looking out of the window, she saw Hardy walking towards the train station. He had only told her of his expedition the night before he left, when he had mentioned that he would pass by the fields close by to the house.

Later, he would write a poem called 'The Shiver'. Told from the perspective of a deserted lover, it has her waking specially to see her beloved walk away: 'And my lover had told, yesternight of his going— / That at this grey hour he'd be hasting by.' The lover, who is clearly meant for Cassie, watches his figure growing smaller, down to a 'dim dumb speck'. She wishes that he'd stopped by her window and then she feels a wave of fear, 'a shiver / Corpse cold, as he sank toward the town by the river; / And back I went sadly and slowly to my bed.'[7]

Hardy again reveals his capacity to enter sympathetically and imaginatively into the heart of the woman he has let down, but a cold wind blows when he compares her unfavourably with the new object of desire. A transfer of love from the woman whose window he passed on the way to a journey to the woman, a 'sea goddess', who has taken her place. The end of the poem, in the voice of the man, is cruel:

'But I've seen, I have clasped, where the smart ships plough,
    One of far brighter brow.
A sea-goddess. Shiver not. One far rarer
In gifts than I find thee; yea, warmer and fairer:—
I seek her again; and I love you not now.'[8]

CHAPTER 37

Emma Lavinia Gifford

With confusing thoughts of Tryphena Sparks and Catherine Pole, and his novel sent off to Macmillan, Hardy had much on his mind. He later recalled that he did not want to go to Cornwall and had tried to decline the St Juliot job, but was persuaded by Crickmay. When he arrived at the vicarage, exhausted from the long journey, it was dark with a dry breeze blowing. He jotted down a few notes: 'Received by young lady in brown, (Miss Gifford, the rector's sister-in-law).'[1] Nothing more.

Years later, when Hardy found Emma's memoir detailing their first meeting and their courtship, he was moved deeply. For him, he was on a business trip and wanted to get the job done as quickly as possible. For her, she had already imbued the arrival of the 'Architect' (as she called him) with significant meaning and breathless anticipation. The church at St Juliot was in a pitiful and neglected state when Emma and Helen arrived, the tower cracking, the discarded church bells lying on the floor in the north transept, 'their mouths open upwards'.[2] The wooden benches were rotten and ivy hung from the roof timbers. The rector, along with Helen and Emma, had set out to raise the funds to restore the church, and when an architect had finally been appointed, 'the village was alive about it'.[3] All the gossip centred on the arrival of the architect. Emma was among the people most excited. In her memoir, she admits that in such a small, isolated spot, where few strangers came, his arrival was highly anticipated. Her account reads like a romantic novel: the strange and isolated, though wildly beautiful, spot near the sea, the quiet town where people still believed in witchcraft, the lovely young girl, desperate to meet anyone, even a 'school inspector' or a 'dentist'.

Emma wanted her memoir to be read by her husband after her death. She wanted to remind him of all that he had lost when their marriage began to fail. She played up her free spirit and her beauty. She told how she scampered up and down hills on her mare, 'the rain going down my back often and my hair floating in the wind'. She wore a soft brown riding habit, which fell down to her heels, and was thrown gracefully to the left side when she walked or rode her horse. In her habit and brown felt hat, woman and horse were 'one creature'. She recalled the villagers stopping to gaze at her: 'A butterman laid down his basket once to exclaim loudly, for no one except myself dared to ride in such wild fearless fashion.' At other times, she tethered her pony and clambered down the rocks to explore the seal caves. Emma was eager to present herself for posterity as an unfettered and unconventional young woman. And in many respects it was true. The trouble was that she had already fallen in love with the architect before he had arrived. Even before she laid eyes on him, she wrote that nobody could have had 'a more romantic meeting'. Two people from different counties, and hers 'a remote spot, with beautiful sea-coast, and the wild Atlantic Ocean rolling in with its magnificent waves and spray, its white gulls and black choughs and grey puffins, its cliffs and rocks and gorgeous sunsettings sparkling redness in a track widening from the horizon to the shore'.[4] In other words, how could he refrain from falling in love with her?

Little did Emma know how much landscape and geography were intimately entwined in Hardy's emotional life. Before long, he would indeed fall in love with the wild Cornish setting, and then with Emma. But in the initial phase, contrary to the man who so often fell in love at first sight, she seemed unremarkable. In his diary notes she was merely the 'young lady in the brown dress'. The rector's sister-in-law. Then, ELG. He was soon, though 'not immediately', struck by her vitality: 'She was so *living*', he wrote, with a perfect complexion.[5] He was drawn to the corn-coloured hair hanging in long coils. And to her rosy cheeks, which gave her the family nickname 'The Peony'. Emma was not yet the 'sea-goddess' and she was not a conventional beauty; he was too honest to admit otherwise. And he was still grappling with his floundering relationship with Cassie Pole and his much more complex feelings for Tryphena.

At first, he took both sisters to the local slate quarries to look for roof tiles for the church, but it wasn't long before the couple were spending time alone together. In the evening, the ladies sang duets. Emma's good humour was noted in his diary: 'Miss Gifford said that a man asked her for a "drop o' that that isn't gin, please, Miss"', he noted amusingly.[6] Hardy was slowly beginning to notice the young lady in brown.

The following day, he and Emma went to Beeny Cliff. She rode on horseback, which always showed her to advantage. 'The moment she was on a horse she was part of the animal,'[7] he wrote (as he would of his heroine Elfride in *A Pair of Blue Eyes*). Emma was also showing Hardy her fearless side: it takes a rider of extreme confidence to canter along the perilous Beeny Cliff, dangling so high above the crashing Atlantic waves. The sheer drop drew the eye down to the seal caves below. Hardy wrote some of his loveliest lines in his poem 'Beeny Cliff': 'O the opal and the sapphire of that wandering western sea, / And the

woman riding high above with bright hair flapping free – / The
woman whom I loved so, and who loyally loved me.' Hardy set
the poem on a 'clear-sunned March day' – a time for light-
hearted laughter between the young man and the girl on the
horse, their joyful mirth echoed in the 'ceaseless babbling' of
the waves. A sudden cloud brings an 'irised rain' as a rainbow
appears through the sun and clouds, and then the sun bursts
out, irradiating the spring flowers: 'purples prinked the main'.[8]

In his diary, he wrote: 'Went with E.L.G. to Beeny Cliff. She
on horseback . . . On the cliff . . . "The tender grace of a day"
etc. . . . the run down to the edge.' His ellipses are tantalising.
For Emma's benefit, he quoted Tennyson's beautiful poem on
the death of his friend, Arthur Hallam: 'Break, break, break, /
On thy cold gray stones, O Sea! / And I would that my tongue
could utter / The thoughts that arise in me'.[9]

Later, they walked to Boscastle, 'E provokingly reading as she
walked.'[10]

Hardy was due to return to Bockhampton the following day,
and the couple agreed to begin a correspondence. On his final
morning, Emma rose early to see him off, and, if the implication
of his poem 'At the Word "Farewell"' is to be trusted, they kissed
for the first time:

Even then the scale might have been turned
    Against love by a feather,
But crimson one cheek of hers burned
    When we came in together.[11]

Emma was very different from the girls he had previously courted
and jilted. She was well read, funny, and had her own aspirations
to become a writer. She was from a different social class to his

previous lovers, and yet she had a touch of rebellion that he found enchanting. He was to discover that her attraction lay in movement. She was very much a symbol of the wild Cornish settings that had bewitched him, but she also seemed to be a lady. Hardy admitted that after this, his first of many visits, he had probably left his heart in Cornwall.

But all was not as it seemed. Emma was five years older than he thought; her lightness of spirit made her appear younger. Later on, he felt that she was on the shelf and that he had been duped. In her memoir, she claimed that she 'kept myself free until the one intended for me arrived'. This was disingenuous, as she was already involved with the son of a curate, who lived locally. But she had listened when she was told that she would marry a writer, and when she first set eyes on Hardy there was an attraction: 'I was immediately arrested by his homely appearance, as if I had seen him in a dream – his slightly different accent, his soft voice.'[12] Hardy later corrected some of her words. He changed 'homely appearance' to 'familiar appearance', thus creating the impression of souls meeting, as if in another life, a dream. Her second impression was that he looked older than he was. The old Thomas Hardy took umbrage at this, writing testily in pencil: 'he being tired.'[13]

Hardy recorded that 'When I Set Out for Lyonnesse (1870)' referred to his first Cornish visit. Lyonnesse was the romantic name for the ancient kingdom of Cornwall, familiar to Hardy's generation from Arthurian legend and in particular Swinburne's epic poem *Tristram of Lyonesse*. In Hardy's lyric, the poet comes home 'with magic in my eyes'. And in a related poem, 'The Wind's Prophecy', the speaker is blown by the wind away from his present lover to a new lover in the west, away from the girl with 'ebon loops of hair' to a girl who has 'tresses flashing fair'. The poem is full of Cornish imagery: 'gulls glint out like silver flecks', 'the swell cleaves through caves unseen', and 'clots of flying foam' appear.[14] The 'sea goddess' has bewitched him, and there is no going back. At some point Thomas Hardy broke off his engagement with Cassie Pole. He kept the ring.

CHAPTER 38

The Sea Goddess

Who was the girl with the 'ebon loops of hair'? This does not seem to relate to Cassie, who had red hair, but points back to his cousin Phena, though her hair (usually worn down until she left for college) was dark brown. Was it Jane Nicholls, or Martha Sparks? Perhaps Hardy did not even know for sure. Perhaps she was an imagined conglomeration of all his previous lovers. The point remains that for now, he was captivated by blonde Emma with her 'floating hair', reminiscent of the demon lover of Coleridge's 'Kubla Khan'.

With his heart lost in Cornwall, Hardy went to London to try to get his novel published, but feeling desultory and dreamy. Emma filled his mind. He wrote a 'Ditty', subtitled with her initials, about 'the spot / That no spot on earth excels, / Where she dwells!'[1] He kept up a regular correspondence with the 'young lady in brown', and sent her books. Then in August he left London for Cornwall, with some sense of uncertainty. Which was swiftly ameliorated by the sight of Emma in her summer dress.

She seemed to him almost a different person from the one in brown thickly muffled from the wind. She had metamorphosed into a 'young lady in summer blue, which suited her fair complexion far better'. She somehow seemed more blonde, more sunny, the fine weather suiting her looks. The visit was a happy one. He saw for the first time King Arthur's castle at Tintagel. Hardy thought of Emma as a queen of Cornwall, an Isolde, a Valkyrie maiden, with her blonde hair and her strong lithe body. Lingering too long among the ruins, they accidentally found themselves locked in, and escaped imprisonment for the night by waving their handkerchiefs. They visited Boscastle and walked again on Beeny Cliff. Emma sketched Hardy, sitting on a fence, a flag in his hand (the Franco-Prussian war had begun in mid-July).

There were other trips: to Trebarwith Strand and Strangles Beach, where donkeys lined up on the sand. Emma and Hardy explored the coastline, finding coves where the seals lived. They loved walking to Boscastle harbour, with its magnificent views. There had been a heatwave, and sunny, cloudless days stretched out one after another. They talked endlessly about books, and read Tennyson together, and Emma's favourite, Coleridge.

One day 'in the burn of August' the couple went for a picnic in lush green Valency Valley, a wooded area which boasted streams and waterfalls. They had to jump over stones and climb narrow pathways until they reached the sparkling brook. They spread out their picnic, of fruit and wine, sharing a single glass tumbler. Hardy rinsed the tumbler in the stream where it slipped and sank. However hard they tried, they could not dislodge the glass, which was stuck between two boulders. Hardy sketched Emma trying to fish it out. It is a mildly eroticised portrait, emphasising her bottom and bosom as she bends over with her glorious mane-like hair concealing her face.

It was an important moment for them. Emma's description of the incident in her memoir, 'Some Recollections', was reimagined in Hardy's evocative poem 'Under the Waterfall': 'In a drinking-glass; / For down that pass / My lover and I / Walked under a sky / Of blue.' In the poem, whenever the woman plunges her arm into a cold basin of water, she is transformed back into the past. The wine glass is emblematic of their love, as she imagines it still lying, 'By night, by day', there in the stream, under the waterfall: 'No lip has touched it since his and mine / In turns therefrom sipped lovers' wine.'[2]

When Hardy left Cornwall after an idyllic three-week holiday, he had a stash of glorious memories and a promise that book-loving Emma would help him with making a final fair copy of his novel, *Desperate Remedies.* But that summer one of his worst nightmares threatened his happiness. Hardy later composed a baffling poem about the heatwave in the summer of 1870, which would seem to suggest a pregnancy scare between young unmarried lovers. He describes the 'jutting height / Coloured purple, with a margin of blue sea,' which seems to be Beeny Cliff, and a summer so hot and dry that 'even the waves seemed drying'. Two lovers walk, and the woman imparts troubled news, with tension on her face. The poet recalls how for 'weeks and weeks we had loved beneath that blazing blue'.[3]

The woman's news contains both 'wonder and wormwood'. It is information that 'in realms of reason would have joyed our double soul', but 'under order-keeping's rigorous control' it wears 'a torrid tragic light'. The poet recalls 'her words, the spot, the time, / And the thing we found we had to face before the next year's prime.' All of this speaks to pregnancy out of wedlock, so it is tempting to speculate that the free-spirited Emma, who thinks for herself, was also sexually liberated. Nor at this time was she religious: Hardy claimed she was agnostic when they first met. Nevertheless, as with Arabella in *Jude the Obscure*, the woman is mistaken in believing that she was pregnant, though by now the man is 'caught', as Hardy also came to believe about his marriage with Emma.

In October, back home in Bockhampton, he dated and put

Emma's initials against beautiful and erotic passages from The
Song of Solomon. 'Behold, thou art fair, my love; behold, thou
art fair; thou hast dove's eyes within thy locks: thy hair is as a
flock of goats, that appear from mount Gilead.' 'Thy lips are
like a thread of scarlet, and thy speech is comely.' The later
verses are more sexually explicit: 'Thy two breasts are like two
young roes that are twins.' Other references see the poet wishing
to 'feed among the lilies'.[4]

But among his erotic imaginings, he also appeared to be
feeling frustrated and depressed, possibly by thoughts about his
career and his aspirations to be a writer, which appeared to be
continually thwarted. He wrote in his notebook: 'Mother's
notion, & also mine: that a figure stands in our van with arm
uplifted, to know us back from any pleasant prospect we indulge
in as probable.'[5] Macmillan had rejected the novel, praising its
power but being displeased with its overt sensationalism. Their
reader, Morley again, begged the author to 'keep away from
such incidents as violation'.[6] Hardy had included a rape scene
involving one of the main characters, Miss Aldclyffe, which
Morley described as 'a disgusting and outrageous outrage'.[7] Hardy
immediately sent the manuscript to William Tinsley, revealing
his dogged persistence and self-belief. Tinsley offered to publish
it, provided that Hardy put up an advance of seventy-five pounds
and made some alterations.

It seemed to Hardy that Emma was the only person apart
from Horace Moule who encouraged his ambitions to become
a writer. It was she who revised, finished and copied *Desperate
Remedies*, which was sent off to Tinsley in early December. Few
of Emma's letters survive, so it's refreshing to hear her voice in
those that escaped his bonfire. In October, she wrote to him
describing her happiness: 'This dream of my life – no, not dream,
for what is actually going on around me seems a dream rather.'
For the man of doubts in his belief in his ability to become a

successful writer, his insecurity about his lowly origins, his wavering belief in God, Emma appeared to be the answer to his own dreams. In that surviving letter from before their marriage, she wrote a phrase that moved him deeply, and which he would appropriate for one of his novels: 'I take him (the reserved man) as I do the Bible; find out what I can, compare one text with another, & believe the rest in a lump of simple faith.'[8] By early December, he had 'packed off' his revised manuscript.

Soon he was given an early Christmas present with a firm offer from Tinsley to publish *Desperate Remedies*. A few days later, the good news came that the novel was now acceptable. Tinsley's only prudish caveat being that 'the woman who is Mrs Manston's *substitute* need not be put forward quite so prominently as his *mistress*'.[9] Hardy agreed to the change. He was about to become a published author, and he owed much to Emma Gifford.

CHAPTER 39

Cytherea Graye

Hardy sat on a stile at the Kingston Maurward ewe-lease with a copy of the *Spectator* in his hands. Reading the long review of his first published novel, he was seized with bitterness and wished he were dead. The reviewer, mocking his title, described the novel as 'a desperate remedy . . . for an emaciated purse' and excoriated the (anonymous) author for prostituting his powers by 'prying into the way of wickedness'. The reviewer objected to Hardy daring to suppose it possible that a respectable and wealthy spinster could have an illegitimate child. Other reviews were positive. The first review in the *Athenaeum* supposed the author to be a woman, since the novel showed 'close acquaintance with the mysteries of the female toilette', which seemed to the reviewer to be 'entirely accurate'. On the other hand, the review said that parts of the writing were 'so remarkably coarse' that it could not be believed that a female had written it.[1]

From the time of writing his first attempt at a novel, *The Poor Man and His Lady*, Hardy believed that he was gifted with a peculiar knack for presenting convincing female fictional characters. He had plenty of knowledge of lady's maids, from the experience of his mother, his cousin Martha, Eliza Nicholls and

Cassie Pole. Hardy followed to the letter George Meredith's advice to write a more complicated plot, and a more 'sensational' story, so it's hardly surprising to find copious Gothic elements in *Desperate Remedies*: sudden death, illegitimate children, murder and kidnap. Nevertheless, the opening, in which architect Ambrose Graye falls to his death from a scaffolding tower, retains the power to shock. Hardy had joked about architects having fear of heights in his debut in print 'How I Built Myself a House' (is it possible that he too suffered from vertigo?), but in his novel the architect's death is masterfully handled. Five men on scaffolding around a 120-foot-high church spire seem 'little larger than pigeons, and made their tiny movements with a soft, spirit-like silentness'. This is a scene that the architect Hardy probably witnessed many times. But here the scene is being witnessed by Cytherea, the anxious daughter of the architect who is supervising his men:

'I wish he would come down,' she whispered, still gazing at the sky-backed picture. 'It is so dangerous to be absent-minded up there.'

> When she had done murmuring the words her father indecisively laid hold of one of the scaffold-poles, as if to test its strength, then let it go and stepped back. In stepping, his foot slipped. An instant of doubling forward and sideways, and he reeled off into the air, immediately disappearing downwards.[2]

Cytherea is watching from a window of the Town Hall (where she is attending a public reading of Shakespeare), so that the scene looks like 'an illuminated miniature, framed in by the dark margin of the window'. It's almost as if she is looking through the lens of a telescope, just as Hardy had viewed the death of the hanged man on the heath with his father's brass telescope. As if to make the connection clear, subconsciously or not, Hardy writes of what we would now call post-traumatic stress disorder: 'Emotions will attach themselves to scenes that are simultaneous – however foreign in essence these scenes may be – as chemical waters will crystallise on twigs and wires. Even after that time any mental agony brought less vividly to Cytherea's mind the scene from the Town Hall windows than sunlight streaming in shaft-like lines.'[3]

The death of the heroine's father and the illness of her brother force her to take work as a lady's maid. From then on, the plot descends into melodrama. Cytherea is employed by a woman called Miss Aldclyffe, whom she discovers is the very same woman, also called Cytherea, that her father once loved. Miss Aldclyffe forces Cytherea into marriage to her illegitimate son, Aeneas Manston, whose wife has recently perished in a fire. Later, it is discovered that his wife had left the inn before it burned down. Another woman appears, claiming to be Manston's wife, but it transpires that she is an imposter. Manston has in fact killed his wife and used the imposter to escape a charge of murder. He tries to kidnap Cytherea, but is apprehended, imprisoned, and commits suicide in his cell.

So what was all the fuss about its 'coarseness'? Early in the novel, there is an extraordinary bedroom scene between the two Cythereas. The older Cytherea, Miss Aldclyffe, has reprimanded the younger for rising above her station, for her impudence, for not acting like a lady's maid. There is an argument and the young Cytherea retires to bed, having given her notice. Later, there is a knock on her bedroom door. She knows that it is the lady of the house who knocks and begs to come in: 'It was now mistress and maid no longer; woman and woman only.'[4] The women get into bed together, and the older woman asks her maid for a kiss. She gives a perfunctory kiss, which does not satisfy Miss Aldclyffe: 'Why can't you kiss me as I can kiss you?' she laments. Miss Aldclyffe discovers that Cytherea is in love

with a young architect called Edward Springlove and is 'jealous'
and 'gloomy':

> You are not, after all, the innocent I took you for . . . Cytherea
> try to love *me* more than you love him . . . Yes, women are all
> alike. I thought I had at last found an artless woman who had
> not been sullied by a man's lips . . . Find a girl, if you can,
> whose mouth and ears have not been made a regular highway
> of by some man, or another! . . . If men only knew the staleness
> of the freshest of us! That nine times out of ten the 'first love'
> they think they are winning from a woman is but the hulk of
> an old wrecked affection, fitted with new sails and re-used.[5]

Miss Aldclyffe berates herself for being an old fool, 'sipping at
your mouth as if it were honey'. She cannot bear the idea that
Cytherea is sullied, 'a dusty highway' instead of a 'fresh spring
meadow'. This idea of woman as pure, and untouched by another
man, is a theme to which Hardy would return. Even by Gothic
novel standards, the lesbian overtones seem extreme. Miss
Aldclyffe, 'jealous as any man could have been', tells Cytherea
that Edward is false, and that she is nothing more than 'a
temporary link in a long chain of others like you'.[6] But what
seems to have set the critics' tongues a wagging was the old
lady's use of the word 'had'. She tells Cytherea that all women
are susceptible to desire, even those in the villages: 'Leave the
admittedly notorious spots – the drawing-rooms of society – and
look in the villages – leave the villages and search in the schools
– and you can hardly find a girl whose heart has not been *had*.'
To the consternation of his reviewers, Hardy was bringing his
working-class experience to a novel featuring middle-class
women.

There were several working-class women who read the novel
and recognised themselves in the lady's maid, Cytherea. Eliza

Nicholls firmly believed that she was the model for the heroine. Cassie Pole would also recognise herself in the heroine. Perhaps even beautiful Martha Sparks felt herself to be the model. This would be the only Hardy novel in which the heroine is a maidservant, and even then, she is the daughter of an architect in reduced circumstances. But above all, the woman who was reading and writing out the manuscript would have seen that the heroine suddenly has hair that is of 'shining corn-yellow' hanging about her shoulders in loose curls, with eyes of sapphire blue. Emma was also the model for the woman whose true beauty 'lies in motion'.

Most fiction writers write much of themselves in their first novel, and Hardy was no exception. The architect hero, Edward Springlove, wants to rise in his profession, but, more than that, he wants to be a poet. He is deeply romantic. And far better-looking than his creator. If Emma later fussed about Hardy's ordinary looks, she perhaps fell a little bit in love with handsome Edward Springlove. Cytherea's employer warns her lovely maid that men like Springlove fall in love too easily: 'He sees a beautiful face and thinks he will never forget it, but in a few weeks the feeling passes off, and he wonders how he could have cared for anybody so absurdly much.'⁷ Hardy, for all his faults, knew himself very well.

Desperate Remedies is suffused with the sight and sounds of Weymouth, just as the much more accomplished *A Pair of Blue Eyes* would evoke the glorious wild Cornish landscape. The seaside town of 'Budmouth Regis' (Creston in the first edition) is a watering hole where day trippers and tourists walk along the esplanade listening to the town band, take a dip in the sea, and enjoy boat trips around the bay in 'graceful cockle-shell' boats. At night, the harbour sparkles with white, green and red lights, 'in opposition to the shimmering path of the moon's reflection on the other side, which reached away to the horizon till the flecked ripples reduced themselves to sparkles as fine as gold dust'.[8] The heroine first meets Springlove when she takes a steamboat to 'Lulstead Cove' with her brother, just as Hardy took the steamboat to Lulworth Cove with his sister Mary and spotted the mystery woman. The villain, Marston, plans his escape on the steam packet to the Channel Islands. The heroine has her first kiss with Edward Springlove on a small boat on the bay, and the lovers return to their little boat at the end of the novel.

Despite its Gothic elements, and over-the-top plot, there are glimpses of the great writer Hardy was to become. Here is Springlove musing on the transient nature of love:

> How blissful it all is at first. Perhaps, indeed, the only bliss in the course of love which can truly be called Eden-like is that which prevails immediately after doubt has ended and before reflection has set in . . . when on the man's part, the mistress appears to the mind's eye in picturesque, hazy, and fresh morning lights, and soft morning shadows; when, as yet, she is known only as the wearer of one dress, which shares her own person-ality.[9]

The 'Eden-like' state of being in the first flush of love by its very nature cannot last. Sooner or later, the couple will be cast out of paradise. In May, Hardy returned to Cornwall for another extended stay, returning to Dorset in July. He was dejected when he saw copies of *Desperate Remedies* being sold at cut price at the W. H. Smith shop at Exeter station.

Once again, it was Emma who raised his spirits and restored his confidence. During the summer, she had helped him to edit some of the highlights of the three reviews he had received to use as publicity. The more positive response had been to the novel's rustic scenes. Hardy knew that *Desperate Remedies* with its 'wildly, melodramatic situations' went against his natural gift for realism.[10] With Emma's encouragement, he was hard at work on a new novel with a rural setting. This time, his heroine would be a schoolteacher in a country village.

CHAPTER 40

The Maid on the Shore

By August 1871, Hardy had sent his 'pastoral story' to Macmillan and was awaiting a response. That October, he was again in Cornwall. Bad news came that Macmillan wanted to postpone all decisions until the following spring. While in Cornwall, possibly encouraged by Emma, he also wrote to Tinsley about his 'little rural story' – dangling two publishers, as he liked to dangle two women. Tinsley's response was unequivocal. He wanted a new three-volume novel, which was not what Hardy had in mind. Hardy told him that he was in the early stages of a new story, set in Cornwall. This was the first mention of what would become *A Pair of Blue Eyes*.[1]

Earlier in May, Hardy had been shaken to discover that Emma had her own secrets. A jealous and insecure lover, he was determined to discover whether she was truly as innocent as she seemed to be. He had discovered the existence of a rival called William Henry Serjeant, the son of the curate of St Clether's, a parish close to St Juliot. Serjeant had become ill with tuberculosis, which left him housebound. After Emma had made her choice, she visited him for one final time, Hardy waiting outside in a horse and trap. As the dying man looked out of the casement window for one final glance of 'his angel', Hardy put his

arm around Emma in a moment of triumph; it was a cruel and
symbolic act. In his poem about May 1871, 'The Face at the
Casement', he called it a 'deed from hell'. Hardy describes vividly
the 'white face' of the man in the window and the remorse of
the narrator:

> Yes, while he gazed above,
> I put my arm about her
> That he might see, nor doubt her
>   My plighted Love.

> The pale face vanished quick,
> As if blasted, from the casement,
> And my shame and self-abasement
>   Began their prick.

Later, the narrator thinks of the man, now dead: 'O sad Saint
Cleather: / What tears there, bared to weather, / Will cleanse
that stain!' The poem concludes that 'jealousy is cruel, / Cruel
as the grave!'[2]

Hardy was further shaken that October when he left Cornwall
by train at Launceston station, with Emma seeing him off. As
the train was pulling out, he looked out for one final glance of
Emma, but she turned away to greet her friends. The event
inspired his poem 'Love the Monopolist (Young Lover's Reverie)'.
The narrator-poet sees the airy slim form in blue, but she 'turns
round quite / To greet friends gaily.'[3]

At home, he was plunged again into despair. In a fit of frustration, he threw the manuscript of *Under the Greenwood Tree*
into a box with his old poems, and wrote to Emma declaring
that he had 'banished novel-writing for ever'.[4] Again, it was
Emma who gave her full support and advised him to continue
to write. Hardy believed in her woman's 'instinct', her

'preternatural vision' giving assurance that authorship was his 'true vocation'.[5] It was a truly unselfish act on her part, as their marriage would have to be postponed while he earned enough money to support them both. In her memoir, Emma wrote that during the long courtship, Hardy's visits were infrequent, though their correspondence was full. The rarity of his visits 'made them highly delightful to both'. They talked 'much of plots, possible scenes, tales and poetry, and of his own work'.[6]

But she does not speak of her own work. As well as being his muse, his adviser, his secretary, she had literary ambitions of her own. Sometime during the early part of their courtship, Emma began composing a story set in the wild, 'salt-edged' setting of Tintagel.

The heroine, Rosabelle Carlenthen, is betrothed to her handsome though shallow cousin, Claude. His best friend, Alfred During, falls in love with her, but keeps his love a secret. Rosabelle has several admirers, but she is drawn to During, despite his undistinguished physical appearance: 'Mr During's insignificant face and figure and quiet thoughtful manner had an interest for her more matured mind that no merely dashing handsome man like her cousin and some she had been in contact with lately at Truro could have for her again.'[7] During is clearly a figuration of Hardy.

Meanwhile Claude has spotted on the beach a beautiful, wild sand-digger, driving her donkey and wearing a blue dress. Her name is Boadicea Darville, and, later, she elopes to London with Claude. During returns to Tintagel to woo Rosabelle, but is rejected. Meanwhile, Claude's health has broken and his marriage is in a state of collapse, so he returns to Cornwall to restore his health. Now realising that he still loves his cousin, he is shocked to find her confessing her love for his best friend. The story, entitled 'The Maid on the Shore', ends with a dramatic death, and the marriage of Rosabelle and During. It is unclear precisely when Emma finished it; she did not attempt to get it published.

Like her creator, the heroine has 'a fair, round face, and gold-en-brown hair "floating in waves"'.[8] The romantic setting of Tintagel Castle, the bracing, salty Atlantic breezes, the donkeys lining Trebarth Sand, the long walks along the beach and the clifftop, evoke the courtship of Emma and Hardy. But where did she get the idea for a story about two best friends falling in love with the same girl?

The one person that Hardy wanted Emma to meet was Horace Moule. He was the friend whose opinion he most cared about. Just before Hardy's October trip to Cornwall, Moule's assessment of *Desperate Remedies* for the *Saturday Review* had finally come out. It was positive, with some mild criticism, but it meant much to Hardy. As Emma often helped Hardy by making newspaper cuttings of all the reviews, it is highly likely that she was familiar with this, and that Hardy had shared details of their 'unlikely' friendship. Hardy later said that it was a great sadness that he never managed to introduce Emma to Horace. Back home, he again expressed himself determined to abandon all thoughts of a literary life and to make a go of his career as an architect, that being the quickest route to 'an income for marrying on'.[9] And then a chance meeting in the streets of London changed his mind.

Crossing Trafalgar Square, he bumped into Horace. Happy to see his friend, Horace enquired whether Tom 'still kept a hand on the pen'. When Hardy told him that he had given up once and for all, Horace was grieved. Suppose, he asked, anything were to happen to Hardy's eyesight poring over architectural drawings? He would no longer be able to work. But if he dedicated his life to literature, he would still be able to dictate books, articles or poems. Hardy thought this an odd comment to make. Soon after, by a strange coincidence, he began seeing floating specks in his drawing paper and became concerned about his eyesight.[10] He began to wonder if his friend was right. At some point, Hardy told Horace about his understanding with Emma Gifford. Did Horace raise an eyebrow when Hardy told him that she was not a domestic servant, or even a schoolteacher, but a lady?

Not long after the meeting with Horace Moule, Hardy also chanced upon his editor, Tinsley, in the Strand. Hardy was inspecting a poster advertising the Italian Opera, when he felt a heavy hand on his shoulder. It was his editor, who asked if he had another novel for him. Hardy replied that he had a manuscript, but had mislaid it. Tinsley begged him to find the book and send it to him. The story might well have been a fabrication, seeing as they had already been in correspondence about new work. But this is how Hardy remembered the event. It seems more likely that Tinsley asked Hardy to call into the office at Catherine Street and asked him about *Under the Greenwood Tree*. Hardy retrieved his manuscript from Bockhampton, sent it to Tinsley, who made an offer of 30 pounds for the copyright. Hardy accepted, and the book was published in early June.

Under the Greenwood Tree garnered positive reviews, with the common consensus that the novel was original and fresh. The only caveat was criticism of the dialogue of the rural characters, which appeared too grand, too shrewd. Hardy, writing of the people he knew best, was irked.[11] He lived with these people, and had drawn deeply from the well of his background to make them realistic. In his memoir, he described the real-life models for his rural characters, including Mr Penny, the shoemaker, and the tranter. Nevertheless, the positive reviews gave Hardy all the enthusiasm he required to continue writing his Cornwall novel. He was on his way to becoming a respected writer of fiction, and Emma was delighted. But, in mining his own life for *Under the Greenwood Tree*, he had to face his family, who guarded their privacy fiercely, and especially so his mother.

CHAPTER 41

Mrs Dewy & Fancy Day

Jemima Hardy was an avid reader; one of the final images of her shows her in a bath chair with her nose almost literally in a book. Hardy thought his mother had excellent taste and judgement in books, so one wonders what she made of his second published novel, which drew so heavily on his family life in Bockhampton. Hardy could put all the spin he wanted by adding the subtitle 'A Rural Picture of the Dutch School', but Jemima was no fool. Hardy intimated that his mother was displeased with *Under the Greenwood Tree*.

She knew very well that she was the model for the redoubtable matriarch, Mrs Dewy. Her habit of cooking bacon on an open wood fire, sitting by the brown settle, to keep a watchful eye, is Jemima's. Her dress-making skills, too – she surveys critically her husband's dirty, fraying collar: "'And the collar of your coat is a shame to behold – so plastered with dirt, or dust, or grease, or something. Why, wherever could you have got it?'" She disdains 'rascally tailors', in favour of finding her own fabric 'at a bargain' which she has made up 'under my eye' with enough spare fabric in them for 'an honest waistcoat'. Like Jemima, Mrs Dewy is the mother of four children, two girls and two boys: 'the eldest of the series being separated from Dick the firstborn by a nearly equal interval'. She runs a tight ship, stage managing every detail of the children's lives. She respects education and intelligence, remarking of one of her clever sons: 'What wonderful odds and ends that chiel has in his head to be sure . . . I lay a wager that he thinks more about how 'tis inside that barrel than in all the other parts of the world put together.' She is a fountain of wise sayings. When Fancy Day, the heroine, complains about village gossip, she responds kindly, but firmly: '"Well, if you make songs about yourself, my dear, you can't blame other people for singing 'em."'[1]

She bosses her husband around, but their eldest son can see the love between them. At one point, Mr and Mrs Dewy are seen 'standing in an unobtrusive corner in mysterious closeness to each other, a just perceptible current of intelligence passing from each to each'.[2] This is Hardy's loving and profound tribute to his parents. On the other hand, one wonders how Jemima felt reading this sentence: 'Mrs Dewy put her mouth in the form of a smile and put it back again without smiling.' Like Jemima, Mrs Dewy makes constant digs at her husband's inferior family:

'Ay, the Dewys always were such a coarse-skinned family. There's your brother Bob just as bad – as fat as a porpoise – wi' his low, mean, "How'st do, Ann?" whenever he meets me. I'd "How'st do" him indeed! If the sun only shines out a minute, there be you all streaming in the face – I never see! . . . I don't know how ever I cam' into such a family!'

In Mrs Dewy, we see Jemima, the esteemed servant of the big house, who has high hopes for her children, and trusts they will not turn out with vulgar manners and 'work-folk' words. In her family, 'tatties' were called 'pertatoes' and 'mother was so particular and nice with us girls there was no family in the parish that kept themselves up more than we'.[3]

No matter how loving and affectionate a portrayal, Jemima knew that there would be family and village gossip arising from the publication of the novel. Though she loved and supported her son, she made it clear that she would not tolerate the use of private family details in his work. It was fine for him to publish in London, away from the prying eyes of the neighbours. Eight years after his mother's death, Hardy drew attention to the 'realities' of *Under the Greenwood Tree*, and its potential as a blueprint for another book about his childhood: 'But circumstances would have rendered any aim at a deeper, more essential, more transcendent handling unadvisable at the date of the writing.'[4] This suggests a prohibition on the part of his mother. And yet, family recollection gives a different story. One of Jemima's great-nieces recalled that it was she, above all, who encouraged her son to be a writer. That she proudly showed visitors the very tree in the garden under which her talented son wrote *Under the Greenwood Tree*.[5] Admittedly, this account was made many years after Hardy became the most famous English novelist of his generation. But that Jemima was a key factor in his success is surely undisputed. Many years later, Hardy confessed to the autobiographical element of the novel: 'I supposed the impressions which all unconsciously I had been gathering of rural life during my youth in Dorsetshire recurred to me.'[6] It's also true that from henceforth, Hardy would be more subtle in his use of familial autobiographical details.

The publication of *Under the Greenwood Tree* was a turning point for Hardy and Emma. In July, just a few weeks after its publication, Tinsley wrote to Hardy with an exciting proposition. He ran a monthly publication called *Tinsley's Magazine*, and he was looking for a serial story for the September issue. He wondered how far Hardy was progressing with his new three-volume story. Hardy had to work fast, and he negotiated hard.

On 27 July, he agreed to publish a series for the sum of £200. He also did not dispose of the copyright. Before leaving, he gave directions that the book proofs should be delivered to Emma's family home address, near Bodmin. It was time for him to ask her father permission for his daughter's hand in marriage. With money in his pocket, the love of a good woman, and the prospect of abandoning architecture in favour of becoming a novelist, fortune was suddenly turning in his favour.

In the school logbook for the Plymouth Public Free School (Girls Department), a young woman of only twenty years old recorded her arrival as headmistress: 'Miss Amelia Edwards replaced at Xmas by Tryphena Sparks, Cer[tifie]d Mistress.'[7] Tryphena had finished her training at Stockwell. Through determination and hard work, she had achieved a first-class award. It was a bold move to have applied for a senior position at a large urban school. At her interview, the chairman of the board remarked that she was very young. 'Well, sir,' she said, 'that is a thing that time will cure.'[8] She was appointed with a salary of £100 per annum. She was earning far more than any of her sisters, or, indeed, her cousin Mary Hardy.

Mary, less ambitious and more unassertive than her cousin, was content to continue teaching in a country village, close to home. At least she was given a schoolhouse in which to live, and accorded respect by the villagers.[9] Having her sister Kate join her as a pupil teacher did much to assuage her loneliness, as well as helping her professionally. By contrast, Tryphena was responsible for one certified schoolmistress and five pupil teachers. She was expected to run the school, occasionally teach the upper forms, and to monitor and instruct the trainees. It was an arduous life, with little free time for private pleasures, though she joked about 'baiting her hook for young men'.[10] She rose early to teach the pupil teachers from 6.15 until 8 a.m. when school began. The school logbook offers sad testimony to the poor health of many of the young women. But responsibility and arduous work did not deprive Phena of her sense of good humour and natural cheerfulness. Her first school inspection noted that she should 'endeavour to have the lessons conducted a little more quietly'.[11] She dressed gravely but elegantly in grey check or, for special occasions, a black merino. On her feet she wore delicate button boots.

Tryphena was well-liked and respected by her pupils, many of whom appeared to be bright and engaged. On her birthday she was presented with a red and gold leather album, inscribed 'to our dear schoolmistress, Miss Sparks'. Though she often felt lonely, she kept lovebirds in cages. According to her family, she was still wearing Hardy's ring.[12]

In a pocketbook entry for April 1871, Thomas Hardy noted 'a range of hills endways – the near end brilliant in a green dress softening away to blue at the other'. As often in his writings, nature takes the form of clothing: smoke curls a chimney like a feather in a lady's hat and hills wear dresses of blue and green. In that same passage he jotted down the plot for a story about a village girl who becomes a schoolmistress.[13] She would become Fancy Day, the heroine of *Under the Greenwood Tree*. Like Mary, she lives in sparse lodgings above the schoolhouse. She returns to her schoolhouse from home carrying a pile of freshly starched linen, laundered by her mother: a sight that would appear to come directly from Hardy's memory of his sister.

And Fancy owes much to Tryphena Sparks. She is lively and

striking, with 'plentiful knots of dark brown hair' and 'dark eyes – arched by brows of so keen, slender, and soft a curve, that they resembled nothing so much as two slurs in music'.[14] Like Tryphena, she keeps birds in a pretty cage. Fancy herself is described as a 'bright little bird'.[15]

The hero, Dick Dewy, is first attracted to Fancy Day when he is shown her tiny boot, which the shoemaker is mending. The description of the boot is erotic, and Dick feels voyeuristic as he contemplates the object: 'the flexible bend at the instep, the rounded localities of the small nestling toes, scratches from careless scampers now forgotten . . . Dick surveyed it with a delicate feeling that he had no right to do so without first having asked the owner of the foot's permission.'[16] Later, he dances with her at his family's Christmas party, and during supper he touches the verge of her dress with the sole of his boot. Fancy is fancily dressed in a white gauzy gown with blue facings, which makes Dick see that she is 'a flower among vegetables'. He finds her 'touchable – squeezable – even kissable!'[17]

One of her duties as schoolmistress is to play the organ on Sundays in church. Unwittingly she becomes the accomplice of the new vicar, Parson Maybold, and the churchwarden, Farmer Shiner, who wish to disband the old string choir. Dick, who plays in the string choir with his father and grandfather, also discovers that Parson Maybold and Farmer Shiner are love rivals for Fancy's affection. Dick is a tranter, and one of his jobs is to fetch Fancy from her home to bring her back to school. At her home, near Casterbridge, Dick observes bizarre duplicates of furniture and ornaments. The Day family has collected two of everything, one for themselves and another for Fancy's bridal dowry: a pair of kitchen dressers identically completed with cups, dishes and plates, two dumb-waiters, two family bibles, and even two warming pans. There is even a brace of clocks from rival makers: Fancy must choose between the two time-keepers, as later she must choose between Dick Dewy and Maybold.

Dick loves Fancy, but his deepest fear is that she is a coquette and not the innocent girl he wants her to be. He sends her a letter, asking if he stands a fair chance. When they meet, she admits that she does love him. By the end of the ride home, they are engaged, Fancy confessing that she dislikes Shiner, and that it was never her idea to replace the choir. Later, however, Fancy makes another confession: that she had flirted with Shiner and that he has asked her to marry him. She also tells Dick that it is her father's wish for her to marry Shiner, and that he has no idea that she is already promised to Dick. The couple decide that Day must be informed about their engagement, and there is a quarrel over Fancy's dress. She is reluctant to wear the blue gown that Dick loves best, and he is worried that she cares too much about her appearance. He also requests that she wears a matronly bonnet rather than a 'coquettish and flirty' hat.[18] Later, there is another quarrel over her choice of gown. Now Dick has decided that he doesn't want other men to see her in her best blue dress, but Fancy is adamant that she will wear the blue dress.

Eventually the young lovers are reconciled, and Fancy's father gives his blessing to the union. But there is one final, powerful, twist. Maybold, the handsome, cultivated vicar, proposes marriage to Fancy. Carried away by the prospect of marriage to a man of his station, and the promise of a materially comfortable life, she agrees. She does not tell Maybold that she is engaged to Dick. It is only when Dick chances to meet the vicar the following morning that he informs him of their engagement. Maybold writes to Fancy to release her from her promise. She writes back to say that she was wrong to accept his offer, and that she was tempted by 'ambition and vanity'. Maybold urges her to come clean with Dick, sending her a one-line letter: 'Tell him everything: it is best. He will forgive you.'[19]

Fancy and Dick are duly married. But the novel ends with a lie. As they leave the wedding celebrations to begin their life together, Dick tells Fancy that the reason for their happiness is the fact that they have 'full confidence' in one another. 'We'll have no secrets from each other, darling, will we ever? – no secret at all.' She replies evasively: 'None from today.'[20] Hardy leaves Fancy with her entanglements and her indiscretions. Though *Under the Greenwood Tree* has a happy ending, it strikes a cautionary note about the perceived duplicity of women.

Hardy knew that the life of a schoolmistress was demanding and thwarting. He had only to see Mary's situation to know that at times she felt as trapped as Fancy Day's canary in its cage or Phena's lovebirds. Of course, the fictional Fancy is one of the lucky ones. Her beauty and her liveliness bring several suitors and offers of marriage. Many years later, the famous author was asked a question about what kind of a wife Fancy would turn out to be. His answer was simultaneously revealing and obfuscating: 'I don't quite know. We had better draw a veil over her; and yet I have known women of her type turn out all right, some of these early examples of independent schoolmistresses included.'[21] He was becoming adept at 'drawing a veil' over matters he did not want to face, not least his own romantic secrets.

CHAPTER 42

The Five Women

Trimmer's Wharf was a bustling, crowded dock on the River Thames, where paddle-wheeled steamboats of various sizes could be seen 'zig-zagging' between the piers, belching smoke from their funnels. On weekdays, commercial travellers boarded the steamboats, which were used for pleasure trips at the weekends. One fine morning when the English Channel was as 'smooth as a lake', a young couple, deeply in love, boarded the brilliantly painted *Juliet*. All around are life and colour; men in blue jerseys mending equipment with tartwine, porters carrying luggage, the loud music of a steam crane, and the 'sighing sounds from the funnels of passing steamers, getting dead as they grew more distant'. Dashes of sunlight 'like burnished copper' dance into vision, as the steamer glides down the serpentine bends of the Thames.[1]

This account is fictional, appearing in the novel that Hardy was writing 'on the hoof', but it describes with precision the steamer trip he made to Plymouth on 7 August 1872. He boarded the *Avoca*, an Irish Mail steam packet that would take forty hours to reach his destination. It was one of the cheaper ways to travel to the south-west, and it appealed to the writer in him. All the local colour and atmosphere of the journey would be recreated in an important chapter for the book he was writing for *Tinsley's Magazine*. Its working title was 'He had a Smooth Tongue' and the lively heroine who appears 'like a rainbow in a murky sky' is based closely on Emma Gifford.[2]

Hardy's excitement, fuelled by the confidence of his large publishing advance and the prospect of finally achieving his ambition to marry into the Gifford family, was blighted by the pain of ending a long-standing entanglement. This occasion was another reason for taking the boat to Plymouth. Hardy visited his cousin, Phena, and broke the news of his impending marriage to Emma Gifford.

Was she devastated? Perhaps not. According to her family, she was happy to return his ring. She had recently met a young man called Charles Gale, but she had refused his advances because of her relationship with Hardy. Gale told her: 'It isn't much of a ring; besides, it's your cousin.' Gale later told his daughter Eleanor that he 'rubbed this in, stressing to Tryphena her cousinship with Hardy'.[3] Having extricated himself from Phena, Hardy felt excited to make his visit to Kirkland House in Bodmin, the home of Emma's parents, to formally ask for her hand in marriage. The meeting was a disaster. What seems clear is that Emma's father took a dim view of his daughter's suitor. In a later letter, he was said to have referred to Hardy as 'a low-born churl who has presumed to marry into *my* family'.[4] Hardy's second wife reiterated that Mr Gifford was 'very contemptuous of Hardy's social position'.[5] Though there is no direct evidence of a confrontation, Hardy's poem, 'I rose and went to Rou'tor Town' suggests some kind of emotional conflict. Rough Tor was a place close to Bodmin, and the poem speaks, in the voice of a woman, now alone as a result of her lover having been wronged, of 'The evil wrought at Rou'tor Town'.[6] In old age, Hardy was asked about the evil, and he responded 'Slander or something of that sort.'[7]

Intriguingly, the 'slander' might well have pointed not to Hardy's lowly origins but to the rumours that he was engaged to a girl in Plymouth – or to the fact that he had engaged himself too many times before. Hardy told his friend Edmund Gosse that another poem he wrote at this time described a scene between him and Emma before their marriage. He also told his friend Florence Henniker that the poem was 'literally true'. The poem was called 'Near Lanivet, 1872' and describes an ancient, Celtic monument at Reperry Cross, just outside Bodmin.

The incident 'which really happened' was this: weary and depressed after an emotional crisis, Emma, dressed in white, rested herself against the cross, stretching out her arms as if crucified.

> She leant back, being so weary, against its stem,
>   And laid her arms on its own,
> Each open palm stretched out to each end of them,
>   Her sad face sideways thrown.
>
> Her white-clothed form at this dim-lit cease of day
>   Made her look as one crucified
> In my gaze at her from the midst of the dusty way,
>   And hurriedly 'Don't,' I cried.

The couple both feel this was a bad omen, and though Hardy reassures her that there was 'nothing in it', she responds that it's possible to be crucified 'in spirit'. They remain haunted by the accidental vision of Emma's crucifixion:

> And we dragged on and on, while we seemed to see
>   In the running of Time's far glass
> Her crucified, as she had wondered if she might be
>   Some day. – Alas, alas![8]

But this was not the only poem that depicts the emotional crisis in Bodmin. In 'The Chosen' we have the same setting, the same Celtic 'Christ-cross stone', and an argument between lovers. The poet recalls five women he has previously loved, but now their charms have faded: 'And then I thought of the other five, / And of how charms outwear':

> I thought of the first with her eating eyes,
> And I thought of the second with hers, green-gray,
> And I thought of the third, experienced, wise,
> And I thought of the fourth who sang all day.
>
> And I thought of the fifth, whom I'd called a jade.
>   And I thought of them all, tear-fraught;
> And that each had shown her a passable maid,
>   Yet not of the favour sought.

The woman in the poem is confused and angry that her sweetheart has been in love with five significant women:

> 'I feel some curse. O, *five* were there?'
> And wanly she swerved, and went away.
> I followed sick: night numbed the air,
> And dark the mournful moorland lay.[9]

None of this augured well for the future, but both of them were in too deep. Leaving Bodmin, they headed back to St Juliot, and then to Emma's friends in Lanivet. By the end of the month, they visited Emma's favourite uncle at Launceston. It seems clear that the couple were in need of the support of Emma's friends and relations, other than her own immediate family. By August, they had settled back in St Juliot, where Hardy dashed off another instalment of *A Pair of Blue Eyes*. They had survived the crisis.

CHAPTER 43

Elfride Swancourt

The theme of his new novel was sexual jealousy. The plot mirrors Emma's 'The Maid on the Shore', where two best friends fall in love with the same woman. It is Hardy's most autobiographical novel, and he intended it as a loving tribute to the woman he wanted to marry. And it was *intended* also to be tribute to his beloved friend and mentor, Horace. It is an imagining of the fulfilment of Hardy's great desire for his friend to meet the woman who was to be his wife. But an imagining in the form of tragedy: the book ends with the two friends and rivals sharing a train journey with, unknown to them, the coffin of the beloved woman.

In trying to fictionalise his love and admiration for Emma and Horace, he ended up betraying them both, revealing his own sexual, intellectual and class-ridden fears and insecurities into the bargain. Hardy hadn't learnt the lessons from his mother's sense of betrayal when she read the 'warts and all' character of Mrs Dewy. What seems to be especially cruel and disloyal was his allowing Emma to act again as his amanuensis (parts of the manuscript of *Blue Eyes* are in her hand), and expecting Horace to review the novel for the *Saturday Review*, especially as it was the calling card announcing his arrival as a serious novelist: the serialisation in *Tinsley's Magazine* gave it greater coverage, and when it was published in 1873, it was the first of his books to bear his name.

Though Hardy was sometimes open about the fact that the heroine, Elfride Swancourt, was based on Emma, at other times he deflected. Emma's eyes, he insisted, were not blue, but dark grey. This was not the remembrance of others, who commented on Emma's remarkable blue eyes. Perhaps, like the colour of the sea, her eyes changed from grey to blue depending on the colour of her dress; sometimes she wore pale grey and sometimes air blue. Hardy at this point in his recollections was determined to dispel the rumours that the novel was autobiographical. Out of respect for Horace's family, he was also keen to convey the message that his friend was not the model for Mr Knight. But the evidence is very clear.

Stephen Smith, a young architect, comes to Cornwall for the purpose of restoring an old church. He endures a long train journey and takes a trap for the last fourteen miles. When he arrives, his host is laid up with gout, and Smith is entertained by the young mistress of the vicarage. Later, she sings for him, and they take long walks; she on her horse, he walking beside her. They fall in love. Her family oppose the marriage on the grounds that the architect comes from lowly origins. Stephen's best friend is a lead reviewer for the London magazines; he has been an important friend and mentor. Stephen is self-educated. Elfie is jealous of the friendship, believing that she should come first in Stephen's life. Some time later, Knight comes to Cornwall and falls in love with Elfride. While that is a mirroring of the plot line of 'The Maid on the Shore', the architect's courtship manifestly mirrors the real facts of Hardy's relationship with Emma. But there are melodramatic incidents and encounters that have no basis in real life. The introduction of a third lover, Lord Luxellian, is the least convincing part of the narrative.

The most celebrated scene, especially effective in the serialisation, was the original 'cliffhanger': a chapter ends with Knight left clinging to the edge of a precipitous 'Cliff without a Name' (though in Hardy's preface, he explained that it was based on a real cliff – which was Beeny). The incident is in part based on Emma's schooltime memory of hanging on to a clifftop tuft of grass and nearly being blown into the Atlantic far below, in part on a passage in Wordsworth's *Prelude*, and in part on a magazine essay by Leslie Stephen (a keen mountaineer) called 'A Bad Five Minutes in the Alps'.[1] Unique to Hardy – and perhaps indicative of a certain voyeurism – is the manner of Knight's rescue: Elfie removes her underwear and makes it into a rope that saves him. Though one might expect Knight to be concentrating entirely on his effort not to lose his grip and fall to his death, as she approaches his eye is drawn to her 'singularly attenuated' form:

> So preternaturally thin and flexible was Elfride at this moment, that she appeared to bend under the light blows of the rain-shafts, as they struck into her sides and bosom, and splintered into spray on her face. There is nothing like a thorough drenching for reducing the protuberances of clothes, but Elfride's seemed to cling to her like a glove.[2]

The outline of her body – with underwear removed – is revealed beneath her rain-soaked dress, exactly in the manner of the woman who had swung on the gallows.

Hardy drew on not only Emma's physical appearance, her long corn-coloured hair and pink cheeks, but also her unusual character. Elfie's emotions lie 'very near to the surface' and her manner is 'childish and scarcely formed'.[3] Hardy describes her as resembling the Miranda of Shakespeare's *The Tempest* in her unworldliness and innocence. Except she is not as innocent as he would like her to be: he discovers the existence of a previous lover. Like William Serjeant, Elfie's previous lover has consumption. He dies shortly after Elfie rejects him, leading his mother to believe that Elfie has murdered her son. Smith's obsession with his sweetheart's innocence (a theme echoed throughout the novels) is mirrored by Mr Knight's. They both discover she is not Miranda, but a woman with a romantic past. Elfride is indeed innocent, but she dies for her sins, leaving both friends to reconnect and repent their actions.

Hardy would later write that the drama (he adds a *dramatis personae*) was 'an imaginary history of three human hearts'. But he was fooling no one. Emma copied out several of the passages of the manuscript where Stephen Smith's lowly origins are discussed. In the serial version, Stephen's family are more humble than in later versions. His father is a 'journeyman-mason' and his mother is 'a dairymaid'. This was changed to 'a working master-mason' and his mother's people 'well-to-do-yeoman for centuries'.[4] As far as Emma was concerned, humble origins were no impediment to love.

Real-life details were used, such as Elfie's astonishment at Stephen's inability to ride a horse and his strange ways of playing chess and reciting Latin (like Hardy, he is an autodidact). Hardy also quoted directly from Emma's letters. Elfride tells Stephen: 'I suppose I must take you as I do the Bible – find out and understand all I can; and on the strength of that, swallow the rest in a lump, by simple faith.'[5] Emma's references 'to the reserved man' appear almost verbatim later in the book. How Emma truly felt about Hardy's appropriations of her life and work is unclear, but it perhaps helps to explain her insistence, in later years, on the extent of her literary influence on her husband.

And then there is Mr Knight. For all Hardy's protestations to the contrary, he is manifestly based on Horace. According to Stephen, Knight is 'the best and cleverest man in England! Henry Knight is one in a thousand.' He is 'the noblest man in England'.

He is Stephen's 'hero'. When Elfie takes Knight to task for only being a reviewer, rather than like her, a published novelist, Stephen is warm in his friend's defence:

> 'Is he only a reviewer?'
> 'ONLY, Elfie! Why, I can tell you it is a fine thing to be on the staff of the PRESENT. Finer than being a novelist considerably . . . I mean that he is really a literary man of some eminence . . . he writes things of a higher class than reviews . . . his ordinary productions are social and ethical essays.'[6]

When we first meet the legendary Mr Knight, it is in his chambers in London, writing with his pen 'beating up and down like a ship in a storm', the scent of tobacco in the air. Stephen pushes aside a curtain and sees a man 'writing away as if his life depended upon it – which it did'. He is thirty years old, 'with dark brown hair, curly beard, and crisp moustache'. He hides great warmth beneath a demeanour of impassivity. His 'mouth had not quite relinquished rotundity of curve for the firm angularities of middle life; and the eyes, though keen, permeated rather than penetrated: what they had lost of their boy-time brightness by a dozen years of hard reading lending a quietness to their gaze which suited them well.'[7] There could not have been a better physical description of Horace Moule.

When he sees Stephen, Knight takes him to task, asking if he has kept up his Greek. Stephen replies that he has not had time, but that he has 'done one extraordinary thing'. Knight guesses correctly that he has fallen in love and intends to marry, but he is worried about his social inferiority:

> Knight looked ominous as this passed Stephen's lips.
> 'Don't judge me before you have heard more,' cried Stephen anxiously, seeing the change in his friend's countenance.

'I don't judge. Does your mother know about it?'

'Nothing definite.'

'Father?'

'No. But I'll tell you. The young person—'

'Come, that's dreadfully ungallant, But perhaps I understand the frame of mind a little, so go on. Your sweetheart—'

'She is rather higher in the world than I am.'

'As it should be.'[8]

Hardy has captured Horace Moule, living and breathing, in every cadence of his tone, in every flourish of his busy pen. By contrast, the architect Stephen Smith is boyish, pink-cheeked, sexually insecure, and is prone to draw himself in 'with the sensitiveness of a snail'. Even their names symbolically suggest their difference. 'Smith' – the word that signifies the ordinary and the working man, blacksmith, silversmith, locksmith, iron-smith. And Knight, the gentleman, the knight of the round table, the piece in a game of chess.

Elfie is jealous of Stephen's friendship with Knight: 'A pout began to shape itself upon Elfride's soft lips. "You think always of him, and like him better than you do me!" She protests that Knight comes between them because Stephen thinks of his friend 'night and day', and when he thinks of him, Elfie is shut out of his mind. She objects that in the middle of love-making, Stephen breaks into effusions of praise about his friend. She asks who Stephen would save from drowning: 'Mr Clever' or Elfride? When he says he will save both, she is angry: 'You would save him, and let me drown, drown, drown.'[9] In the end, Stephen is 'despairingly' made to confess that he would save his lover and let his friend drown. Which is exactly what Hardy does to Moule. But there is worse to come. Later in the novel, when Knight is made aware that he and his old protégé are love rivals, there is a terrible, harrowing scene between the two men. Hardy prefaces the chapter with an epigram: '*Jealousy is as cruel as the grave.*'[10] Hardy makes Shakespearean references to *The Tempest* and *Hamlet*, but the unspoken play here is *Othello*. Hardy is a master of describing the grip of the green-eyed monster.

Even before Knight is made aware of the truth that Stephen was once secretly engaged to Elfride, Stephen makes ungrateful accusations: 'You were always from the first reserved to me, though I was confidential to you. That was, I suppose, the natural issue of our differing positions in life. And when I, the pupil, became reserved like you, the master, you did not like it.' And it gets worse. Stephen accuses Knight of the 'greatest snub of all – that of taking away his sweetheart'.[11] And when the men meet on a train, in pursuit of Elfride, there is another hostile confrontation:

'Well,' said his friend, 'she was mine before she was yours – you know that! And it seemed a hard thing to find you had got her, and that if it had not been for you, all might have turned out well for me.' Stephen spoke with a swelling heart, and looked out of the window to hide the emotion that would make itself visible upon his face.

'It is absurd,' said Knight in a kinder tone, 'for you to look at the matter in that light. What I tell you is for your good. You naturally do not like to realize the truth – that her liking for you was only a girl's first fancy, which has no root ever.'

'It is not true!' said Stephen passionately. 'It was you put me out. And now you'll be pushing in again between us, and depriving me of my chance again! My right, that's what it is! How ungenerous of you to come anew and try to take her away from me! When you had won her, I did not interfere; and you might, I think, Mr. Knight, do by me as I did by you!'

'Don't "Mr." me; you are as well in the world as I am now.'

'First love is deepest; and that was mine.'

'Who told you that?' said Knight superciliously.

'I had her first love. And it was through me that you and she
parted. I can guess that well enough . . . You have no right to
domineer over me as you do. Just because, when I was a lad, I
was accustomed to look up to you as a master, and you helped
me a little, for which I was grateful to you and have loved you,
you assume too much now, and step in before me. It is cruel
– it is unjust – of you to injure me so!'[12]

Knight showed himself keenly hurt at this.

Knowing everything that Horace had given Hardy, all this
makes for highly uncomfortable reading. Given that Horace
would review the book, and he did, it begs the question of why
Hardy would want to inflict pain on the man he loved. It's
natural that he would want to break away from his mentor and
forge his own path. But had Hardy forgotten his friend's cham-
pioning of working men? The time he had given on lectures for
the Working Men's Institute, reading poetry in his sonorous
voice, and giving them respect and dignity? Hardy's veiled accu-
sation of 'superciliousness', of being 'patronised', was clearly not
shared by the working men who flocked into Horace's lecture
room. And Hardy must have known that reading this heated
exchange between the architect and the reviewer would cut
deeply. Whatever Horace's faults, his intentions towards the
education of the lower classes were entirely honourable, his essays
about social and ethical issues sincere. He believed that every
person should be given a chance, no matter their circumstances
or education. The kindness shown to the violent murderer, Edwin
Preedy, on the last morning before his execution, was genuine,
as was Horace's belief that Preedy possessed natural intelligence
but had been thwarted by life's vicissitudes.

And, of course, Horace never made overtures to Emma, or
indeed even met her, nor put a foot in Cornwall. It was also
true, as Hardy insisted, that some of his own traits were given

to Knight. Knight does not want to kiss the lips of a woman who has already been kissed, and he breaks off the relationship with Elfride when he discovers that she has spent the night with a man. Knight can be priggish, prudish and hypocritical, just as Hardy's jealousy of William Serjeant seems unjust in the face of his own colourful sexual past. Hardy had no reason ever to fear that Horace would be anything but kind and encouraging when he finally met Emma. Horace was no fool, and he no doubt worked out that the love triangle was a subconscious fear, a symbolic reimagining of Hardy's worst nightmare. He was too intelligent and too generous of heart to truly believe that Hardy resented deeply his influence. But a letter he wrote to Hardy about his review of *Blue Eyes* suggests that he perhaps knew he had been made a sacrifice for his friend's art.

Hardy rejected the idea that Horace was a model for Knight. He was outraged when a biography of 1911 drew a parallel between Stephen and Knight and Hardy and Moule. His main objection was the implication that Horace taught him Latin by correspondence, as Knight teaches Stephen. Hardy was adamant that this had never happened. Except that it did. In one of Horace's nine surviving letters to Hardy, carefully wrapped in a seal of white paper, there is a letter answering a query of 1864, when Hardy was working on his Latin:

My dear Tom,
I should say with regard to 'if' & subj that the utmost licence was conceded by usage in English . . . 'Si' in Latin is used with the indic. when certainty or a contingency very nearly approaching cerrty. is indicated by 'si.' Now, the same rule applies in English: and you can often plead the nearness to certainty which obtains in yr. contingent preposition. On the other hand, where yr uncertainty is absolute, I shd. regard the subjunctive as regularly required.[13]

Once again, Hardy was drawing a veil over the matter. It may not have been a formal tutorial arrangement, and money was certainly not handed over for the education that Hardy received from Horace, but he taught him all the same. And nor did Horace ever believe that his friend was not good enough to marry a 'lady'. It was Hardy's own family who felt doubt that miscegenation would work. Horace's reviews of Hardy's three novels were balanced, judicious and generous. If Hardy better understood the manners of the labouring class rather than the aristocracy, as Horace sometimes suggests, it's because he did. In the midst of reviewing *A Pair of Blue Eyes*, Horace scribbled a note from his rooms in Cambridge: 'You understand the *woman* infinitely better than the *lady*.'[14]

CHAPTER 44

The Governess

In the same letter, Horace begged to see Hardy: 'I long to meet you again & must & will meet.' Horace's life had been spiralling out of control. Since leaving his teaching post at Marlborough College, he had gained employment as an assistant Poor Law Inspector, though still reviewing on a part-time basis. His father's interest in sanitation may have helped him secure the Poor Law job at the Local Government Board for East Anglia, but it is difficult to see why the family thought it a good idea. Horace was in an extremely fragile state. His new job, which involved visits to workhouses, including those for young boys, was profoundly depressing. But though the job was difficult and exhausting, it meant that Horace could live in rooms in Queens' College, Cambridge, close to his brother, Charles, who was a fellow at Corpus Christi.

In *Blue Eyes*, Stephen comes to Henry's rooms and notices a great change in his friend: "You out-Hamlet Hamlet in morbidness of mood," he says, with regretful frankness.' Horace's bouts of depression seemed to be getting worse. He was in a vicious cycle, degenerating ever further into alcoholism and opium addiction. His 'recourse to stimulants' led to 'resultant incapacity for work', which was followed by fear of losing employment.[1]

Once again, he had been in the habit of giving people the slip, escaping into the East Anglian countryside in search of an inn, staying drunk for days at a time, until his brother, Frederick, a vicar in the east of England, would find him and bring him back to dry out.

His family, desperate with concern, put him under the care of a new doctor called James Hough. In some of his worse bouts of depression, he had threatened to take his own life and had begun sleeping with a razor blade under his pillow. Horace was also in the midst of an emotional crisis. It would appear that he had confessed his anxieties to Hardy.

A Pair of Blue Eyes was published in May. Hardy dined with Horace in London at the British Hotel on 15 June, and then Horace left for work at the architect's office. On 20 June, Hardy caught the evening train to Cambridge, staying with Horace in his rooms at Queens'. It was his first taste of the university life of which he had once dreamed. The two friends went out for dinner and walked along the river, where there was a 'magnificent evening: sun over "the Backs"'. In the morning, they went to King's Chapel: 'M opened the great West doors to show the interior vista'. They were able to go onto the roof, from 'where we could see Ely Cathedral gleaming in the distant sunlight'.[2]

Hardy's brief notes about the Cambridge visit give no sense of the emotional trauma of the evening. As was his wont, he left his intimate outpourings to his poetry. 'Standing by the Mantelpiece' is subtitled 'H. M. M., 1873'. The scene takes place at a late hour. The candles have burned down and one of them is 'shaping to a shroud'. The 'corpse-candle' motif is a piece of Dorset folklore: if a candle burns one-sidedly, leaving a 'little column of tallow', it is a harbinger of death. In the poem, the speaker touches the candle, thus heralding his own death: 'By touching it the claimant is avowed, / And hence I press it with my finger – so.' The speaker is addressing their beloved, who has called a halt to the affair, having previously 'let warmth grow without discouragement'. But now 'all's lost' and the narrator wants the final word:

> Since you have spoken, and finality
> Closes around, and my last movements loom,
> I say no more: the rest must wait till we
> Are face to face again, yonside the tomb.[3]

The speaker is the voice of Horace Moule. It has been suggested that the poem should be read in homoerotic terms, that Moule made a sexual advance to Hardy and was repudiated.[4] But there is nothing to suggest that this was the case. Whether or not Moule was a closet homosexual is not clear, but there were relationships with women that had caused much anguish. Hardy told his second wife that Moule had had an affair with a 'Mixen Lane' girl of doubtful reputation who became pregnant and was shipped off to Australia, where her son was later hanged. The poem 'She at His Funeral' suggests the possibility that the girl, in her 'gown of garish dye', could have been present as a distant observer of the burial of her 'sweetheart'.[5]

The existence of another mystery woman may shed light on Horace and Hardy's final evening. Sydney Cockerell, Hardy's friend and literary executor, was told by him that Horace had been engaged to an 'un-named lady of title'.[6] Horace's family, by contrast, confirmed an engagement to a governess, who was 'highly cultivated' and of 'sterling character'. Frederick Moule's wife thought the governess a 'splendid person', perhaps capable of solving Horace's difficulties.[7] But there had been a quarrel, leading the governess to break off the engagement. Hardy believed that Horace had been drunk at a dinner, and considered that he had publicly disgraced himself and his lady. The events of 'Standing by the Mantelpiece' would appear to confirm the governess story: that the woman knew about her lover's failings, but there had been a quarrel, leaving the man 'embittered'.

Hardy must have felt his friend's agony on that June night. He was accustomed to the hard drinking and aggressive male behaviour of his own family, but the extreme alcoholism and depression of his educated friend was another matter. Deeply sympathetic as he was to Horace's problems, he was also aware of his friend's greater privilege and opportunities that he had squandered. His feelings were complicated, and perhaps some of the passive-aggressive anger in *Blue Eyes* is better understood in this light. In the morning, Horace saw his friend off at the train station. Of this parting, Hardy later wrote some of his saddest words: 'A never-to-be-forgotten morning. H. M. M. saw me off for London. His last smile.'[8]

Hardy set off for Bath to meet Emma. While there, he spotted a 'commendatory' *Spectator* review of *Blue Eyes* in a newsagent's shop. Its success was 'surpassing his expectations'. Then the influential *Saturday Review* pronounced it to be 'the most artistically constructed of the novels of its time'. In proudly recording this in his self-ghosted autobiography, Hardy did not acknowledge that the review was written by Horace.[9] It was his friend's last gift to him.

On 19 September, returning to Cambridge for a holiday after inspecting two workhouses, Horace visited his doctor to report alarming symptoms. These suggested that he was suffering from an attack of what is now known as agitated depression, a dangerous state for anyone who has previously expressed a wish to kill himself. It is at just this point that a depressed person can overcome his languor and weakness enough to perform the act of self-destruction; he may even seem more energetic and cheerful.

Dr Hough wired Charles Moule, who was not in Cambridge, and engaged a nurse, who was in attendance from the following morning. Moule took the usual drink to combat his symptoms, but it did not help: alcohol is in itself a powerful depressant. He managed to struggle through that day. The next morning Charles arrived and the nurse was sent away. The two men had a long and tiring discussion, during which Horace 'explained his fears'. He had many times previously talked of suicide, but without attempting it. Charles said that his depression had seemed to get better. He had no inkling that suicide was on his brother's mind. But he later told the coroner, that 'there were circumstances to lead to such depression'. At some stage Horace became excited, but this state was followed by exhaustion. He had been 'perfectly sober' when he went to bed at half past seven, saying to his brother: 'I shall lie down now.' He pulled the covers over himself, seized a razor he had secreted beneath his pillow, and cut his throat wide open. Charles, himself exhausted, sat in the next room, trying to distract himself with some writing; it was to him a familiar enough situation. At eight o'clock, he heard a trickling sound. When he rushed into the bedroom, he found his brother bleeding. He rushed to the Porter's Lodge to call for help. The doctor was called. Horace was found lying on his right side, and when he was turned round, Hough saw the laceration across his throat which had severed his windpipe. Before he took his last breath, Horace was able to mutter, 'Love to my mother. Easy to die.'[10]

The coroner's jury brought in a verdict of suicide while temporarily insane – this was usual for people of good family. Dr Hough testified that he had no doubt that the wound was self-inflicted and that for the last thirteen months Horace had been suicidal, but was not in such a state that he should be restrained. He left only two hundred pounds. The family believed that the tragedy of his life was failing his mathematical examination in Cambridge, which had obstructed his career as a classical scholar, leading to the onset of his problems. Charles Moule's son told how his father was so troubled by Horace's suicide, and his failure to prevent it, that he could not talk about his brother. What he did say was that he regarded Horace 'as the most brilliant of an able family'. And Charles said something else. He said that he regarded his influence on Thomas Hardy 'as having been much greater than that of the rest of them'.[11]

The inquest verdict of 'Temporary Insanity' enabled Horace to have a Christian burial in the Fordington churchyard. Tom went to the graveyard on 25 September, the eve of the funeral, and drew a sketch of the mound by the side of the freshly dug grave. He described the moment in a moving poem called 'Before My Friend Arrived', in which he wrote 'Of one who had stilled his walk / And sought oblivion's cave', and ends with the friend long buried in the grave and a looming image of the church tower 'dark on the sky'.[12]

In the copy of Palgrave's *Golden Treasury* that Moule had given him, Hardy wrote the date 'Sept. 25. 73' alongside Shakespeare's sonnet 32: 'But since he died, and poets better prove / Theirs for their style I'll read, his for his love.'[13] Hardy would continue to visit Horace's grave for the rest of his life. He wrote: 'It was a matter of keen regret to him now, and for a long time after, that Moule and the woman to whom Hardy was warmly attached had never set eyes on each other; and that she could never make Moule's acquaintance, or be his friend.'[14]

CHAPTER 45

Helen Paterson

Leslie Stephen, the distinguished author and critic, opened the door of his elegant South Kensington home with one hand outstretched towards his solitary guest, and the other holding back a barking collie dog. The dog's name was Troy. The young man, somewhat taken aback, said: 'That is the name of my wicked soldier-hero.' Stephen answered caustically: 'I don't think my Troy will feel hurt at the coincidence, if yours doesn't.' Hardy rejoined: 'There is also another coincidence. Another Leslie Stephen lives near here, I find.' 'Yes,' he said, 'he's the spurious one.'[1] It was a propitious meeting for the two men.

Leslie Stephen, who would later edit the *Dictionary of National Biography* and become the father of Virginia Woolf, was still married to his first wife, Minny Thackeray, daughter of the great writer whose novels were so beloved by Jemima Hardy. Stephen had taken over the editorship of the *Cornhill Magazine*, founded by William Makepeace Thackeray. Minny's sister, Anne, lived with the couple. Anne was a novelist of some repute. Hardy, having expressed reservations about Leslie Stephen, took an instant liking to him and the feeling never changed.

The next day, Hardy was invited back to lunch to meet Mrs Stephen and her sister. The women, wrapped in shawls to keep out the December chill, chatted about Thackeray, Carlyle, Voltaire, and the Bible. It was a watershed moment for Hardy. Minny and Anne were erudite and lively. Hardy noticed some of her father's humour in Anne. Though she was plain looking, she was noted for her gaiety and vivacity. A polite society where women were competing on equal terms was a new thing for Hardy. He felt himself attracted to Anne Thackeray, though he later insisted that the attraction was more on her part than his. And there was another fascinating woman who came on his radar via the offices of Leslie Stephen. She was an artist, and her name was Helen Paterson. But why was Hardy being courted by one of the most powerful literary men in England?

Back in December of 1872, he had received a fan letter from Stephen, expressing great admiration for *Under the Greenwood Tree*: it was 'long since he had received more pleasure from a new writer'.[2] Stephen asked Hardy for a serial story for the *Cornhill*. Hardy told him that the story he was writing (*A Pair of Blue Eyes*) was promised to Tinsley, but that the next should be at Stephen's disposal. Hardy was thinking of a 'pastoral tale' in which the chief characters would probably be 'a young woman-farmer, a shepherd, and a sergeant of cavalry'.[3] He had already thought of a title, a phrase from Thomas Gray's famous 'Elegy written in a Country Churchyard': *Far from the Madding Crowd*. The men began a correspondence. One of Hardy's queries related to the illustrations for his novel. His main concern was 'a hope that the rustics, although *quaint*, may be made to appear intelligent, and not boorish at all'.[4]

When the novel was prepared for the press, Hardy was shocked to discover that the twelve commissioned illustrations had been drawn by a woman. But it was not until the following late spring that he finally met the 25-year-old Helen Paterson. She was renowned for her skill as a watercolour artist, reputed to research her subjects carefully, with a feel for local colour. At the age of seventeen, she entered the Female School of Art in London. By 1867, she was accepted into the Royal Academy Schools. Three years later, she was hired as one of the founding members (and the only woman) on the *Graphic Magazine* as an illustrator. Helen's work for the *Graphic* was admired by Vincent Van Gogh, who was studying English illustrated journals as a means of developing his own skills as a painter. Two of her watercolour paintings, *The Milkmaid* and *Wait for Me*, were accepted for the Royal Academy Summer Exhibition in 1874. She became the first woman to be admitted to full membership of the Royal Watercolour Society. Helen was also beautiful.

Hardy was immediately attracted and they began a correspondence. He helped her with ideas for her sketches, sending her his own drawings of Dorset farm implements for historical accuracy. They dined at the Pall Mall Cafe. And what of Emma? Her whereabouts during the time Hardy was writing *Far from the Madding Crowd* are shrouded in mystery, though it seems certain that she had left Cornwall in 1873 following a rift with her sister. She then moved to her brother's house in London 'as country cousin'. She was 'bewildered with the size and lengths and distances' of the city, which gave her brother Walter much pleasure.[5] Her mode of transport was the omnibus, 'which seemed a very undignified method of getting about'. Later, she would love London.

But Hardy had begun to have doubts about the relationship. His introduction to Anne Thackeray and Helen Paterson had begun to affect his feelings for Emma Gifford. Emma was educated and from a higher social class than the other working-class women he had loved, but now he was beginning to move in intellectual and artistic circles. And it was a world in which middle-class women were starting to break away from the constraints that bound them to house and home. The first female doctor had qualified in 1866. The first suffragette petition had been presented by J. S. Mill the same year and Girton College, Cambridge, had opened in 1869. Hardy's eyes were being opened.

Under pressure from Leslie Stephen to write his novel as quickly as possible so that the serialisation of *Far from the Madding Crowd* could be published in January 1874, he did much of the writing in Bockhampton. The seclusion of his old home suited him. He wrote at speed, 'sometimes indoors, some-time out'.[6] Finding himself out in the countryside without a scrap of paper, he would be struck with inspiration and would scribble on large dead leaves or pieces of stone or slate that 'came to hand'. He found that 'when he carried a pocket-book his mind was as barren as Sahara'.[7]

Hardy told Stephen that he needed to be on or near the spot that he was writing about. Back under his mother's roof, Hardy felt all the power of her emotional attachment. He once again assisted at his father's cider-making: 'It was the last time he ever took part in a work whose sweet smell and oozings in the crisp autumn air can never be forgotten by those who have had a hand in it.'[8]

After finishing *Madding Crowd* 'at a gallop', he posted the finished manuscript in early August. For the first time, Hardy had not shared his manuscript with Emma. He wanted it to be a surprise. Her first view of *Far from the Madding Crowd* was the *Cornhill* serial with Helen Paterson's illustrations. He claimed that Emma was 'delighted' and that 'her desire of a literary course for Hardy was in fair way of being justified'.[9] But her own words suggest a rather different take. In one of the very few surviving letters to him, she sent some wistful words: 'My work unlike your work of writing, does not occupy my true mind much. Your novel sometimes seems like a child all your own & none of me.'[10]

Helen Paterson's sensitive, intelligent illustrations moved him

deeply, and he began to harbour ideas about a romantic relationship. Many years later, Hardy told one of his closest friends
that she was the best illustrator he ever had, that she was a
'charming young lady' and was the woman he should have
married 'but for a stupid blunder of God Almighty'.[11] A poem
called 'The Opportunity', written 'For H. P.', speaks of a meeting
in May: 'We might have clung close through all, / But we parted
when died that daytime.' The poet believes that if the couple
had thought more deeply 'at that critical date in the Maytime',
then 'One life had been ours, one place, / Perhaps, till our long
cold claytime.'[12] But the moment passes. As so often in both
Hardy's life and his writings, the 'perhaps' does not come to
pass. Nevertheless, he was shocked that in August Helen married
a man almost twice her age, an Irish poet and editor called
William Allingham. A month later, Thomas Hardy married
Emma Lavinia Gifford at St Peter's Elgin Avenue, Paddington.
Their hands were joined by her uncle, the Canon of Worcester.

Many years after the marriage had failed so badly, Hardy
recalled that he should have listened to his mother's advice not
to marry Emma. He did not enter into the details of Jemima's
concerns, but a scene in *A Pair of Blue Eyes* evokes some of the
tensions that had begun to surface. Stephen tells his mother that
Elfie's family are too far above him, and that her family don't
want 'such country lads as I in it'. Wise Mrs Smith sees beyond
the issues of inter-class marriage: 'I don't read the papers for
nothing', she tells her son, 'all men move up a stage by marriage.'
What she fears is that her son has been trapped into marriage
by a 'scheming' woman who is on the shelf: 'Living down in
an out-step place like this, I am sure she ought to be very
thankful that you took notice of her. She'd most likely have died
an old maid if you hadn't turned up.' Hardy would later come
to believe that his mother was right, but now he resented her
interference, and like Stephen Smith in *A Pair of Blue Eyes*,

believed that to marry such a woman would be 'the great blessing of my life, socially and practically'.[13] But there must have been times when he wondered whether a union with the talented and sophisticated Helen Paterson would have been a greater blessing.

CHAPTER 46

Mrs Emma Hardy

'The day we were married,' Emma wrote, 'was a perfect September day – the 17th, 1874 – not brilliant sunshine, but wearing a soft, sunny luminousness; just as it should be.'[1] There were no Hardy family members at the wedding. Jemima had voiced her disapproval of the union, so perhaps that explained her absence, but Mary Hardy's no-show sounded a discordant note. Perhaps like Dorothy Wordsworth, she simply could not bear to witness her beloved brother's marriage ceremony, or perhaps her teaching commitments made a London September wedding impracticable.

The couple spent their first night as man and wife at Brighton. The gentle sunshine of the wedding day had now turned to windy autumnal weather, and the journey to the coast from London was rough. Emma kept a travel diary. With the inclement weather continuing, the next morning the Hardys paid a visit to the aquarium: 'Seals, Turtles. Scuttles. All fish close their eyes while sleeping.' They attended a concert, and visited the Brighton Pavilion, built by George IV: 'Moorish and Indian architecture', Emma noted.[2] From the old pier, they could see Beachy Head in the distance. Emma loved the sea, and sea creatures, and returned to the aquarium in the evening: 'Spider crabs. Mullet have 3 claws & walk as well as swim. Turtles swim as well as walk. Seals' eyes flash extraordinarily as they flounder over in the water. Seal float & swim alternatively.'[3]

A fat baby boy caught her eye on a Sunday promenade: 'Brighton's Sunday is like a Parisian Sunday – All enjoyment & gaiety & bands of music & excursionists.' She was charmed by the goat carriages that transported tourists around the town. Tom bathed in the rough sea, and later the couple attended a dinner in the Concert Hall.[4] The day after the wedding, Hardy somewhat curtly informed his brother Henry, 'I write a line to tell you all at home that the wedding took place yesterday.' Tom told his younger brother that the couple was headed for Normandy and Paris. He made it clear that it was a work trip rather than a honeymoon: 'I am going to Paris for materials for my next story.'[5] Hardy was working on what would become *The Hand of Ethelberta*. The heroine of his new story was a beautiful girl with 'squirrel-coloured hair'. She has transcended her class by marriage to a wealthy man, and spends much of the story trying to hide her lowly origins: her father is a butler, and she has risen from the ranks of the servant class. Her physical attributes and her class origins were those of Cassie Pole. It strikes an odd note that Hardy was thinking of the woman he jilted during his honeymoon with Emma.

The night crossing to Dieppe was rough and stormy. The Hardys took a train to Rouen. Emma was surprised to see a small French boy drinking a quantity of house wine. The newly-marrieds enjoyed a lavish repast: soup, fried sole, veal and peas, medallions of beef with tiny carrots and onions, French beans, delicate pigeons and salad with oil dressing, and then *milles feuilles* for pudding. A plate of cheese and apples and pears concluded the meal.

When they set off for bed, the covers had been turned back, and their nightwear neatly arranged. For Emma, everything seemed a delight and a matter for close observation, even to the chambermaid who interrupted them as they were writing letters, only to apologise and place the chamber pot underneath the washstand. The nightwear on the bed and the chamber pot were stark reminders of the new intimacies that the couple would now share.[6] The next morning they visited the St Ouen Abbey: 'The colouring of the roofs of Chancel & Nave contrasting, French grey & golden buff with dashes of red.' Later, they climbed the hundreds of steps to the central tower of the Rouen Cathedral: 'Island gorgeously coloured – Town violet blue.' Emma loved the 'white spotless' caps of the women and the 'simple, picturesque' jackets over short petticoats. She observed the way the chambermaid 'spins still smiling and chattering out of the room' – a detail that Hardy would borrow for his new novel. The bell striking in the Rouen Cathedral was 'flute-like & deep toned – like a spirit speaking'.[7]

They moved on to Paris, crossing the Seine – 'Long thin trees, winding river' – and looking at the Place de la Concorde by moonlight. Wagon horses wore tinkling bells around their neck. Dinner was soup and vegetables, stewed fish with onions, rabbit, mutton in tomato sauce, beef in gravy followed by baked pears, cheese, grapes and biscuits.[8] At night, the flood of light from the Parisian lamps obscured the stars. By day, Emma watched the Parisians: the men who looked like 'butchers', the children 'sportive & charming in dress & action', and nuns who wore hats 'like bats' wings or cats' ears'. An animal lover, she observed the 'superb' cats.[9]

The Hardys took a train to Versailles, which in late September was a riot of bright green and scarlet foliage. Inside the Galerie des Batailles there was a marble staircase, 'doors gilt round all the panels & bordering in gold.' Emma noted the clock 'set at the hour of death' of King Louis XIV.[10]

Back in Paris, the Hardys visited Notre Dame, and Le Morgue: 'Three bodies – middle one pink – Their clothes hanging above

them. Not offensive but repulsive.'[11] At the Père Lachaise cemetery, they picked an ivy leaf from Balzac's grave. Emma observed
that the working classes 'are very short and small altogether –
pigmies – in fact . . . the old women very *ugly* & dark – *very*
fierce in the poorest streets.' Emma in turn was being gazed
upon, which she found uncomfortable:

> Wherever I go, whoever I pass – at whatever time daytime or
> by night – the people gaze at me as much or more than I at
> them & their beautiful city . . . Am I a *strange-looking* person
> – or merely picturesque in this hat – Women sometimes laugh
> a short laugh as they pass. Men stare – some stand – some look
> back or turn, look over their shoulders – look curiously inquis-
> itive . . . Children gape too.[12]

Quite why Parisians found her a figure of amusement is not
entirely clear. Was it her loose-flowing blonde hair, her out-of-
date hat, or her elaborate manner of dressing? She noted that
while her husband went back to the hotel to fetch a coat, she
was approached by 'three hommes'. Perhaps her confidence and
quirkiness of manner made her stand out among the Parisians.
The male gaze, she noted was given 'admiringly', though she
crossed out this description to replace it with 'tenderly'.[13]

Most poignant was her constant observation of babies and
small children, which suggests she was thinking of what her
own future might hold. The children playing 'wildly' on the
gravel at the Tuileries, boys dressed in loose pinafores sailing
boats, children 'lively on their legs'. Parisian babies seemed 'very
small'. She also admired the women in their snowy white caps
with Valencienne Lace, and the flower shops, 'striking beautiful'.
She was interested in everything and everyone around her.

By contrast, Thomas Hardy left no account of the honeymoon,
other than saying it was his first visit to the Continent.[14]

When they arrived back in London after a rough passage across the Channel, Emma felt deflated: 'Dirty London. Very wet.'[15] With nowhere to live, the Hardys began seeking lodgings, eventually renting rooms at St David's Villa, Hook Road, in Surbiton. It was there, a month later, that Thomas Hardy became famous.

PHASE THE SECOND

The women he made

CHAPTER 47

Bathsheba Everdene

A Pair of Blue Eyes paid tribute to Tom and Emma's romantic courtship among the ruins of Tintagel Castle and the rough seas of North Cornwall. It was Emma's book, and it was suffused with the colour blue. Elfie is 'childish and scarcely formed' but all her beauty lies in her eyes: 'blue as autumn distance', blue as the sea, 'a misty and shady blue'. In her anxious moments her pallor is blue, not white. Rocks are 'blue-black', evening clouds are 'dark blue'. The trees (pine and hollies) are blue. Gravestones are carved from the local dark blue quarrystone. Elfie wears a blue veil when she goes riding, the sailors wear blue jerseys, Lord Luxien's servants wear dark blue livery, and his two small daughters wear blue feathers in their white hats. Stephen's servant mother wears a dress of dark blue 'ground'. There are many descriptions of the blue of the Cornish sea, which turns indigo and grey. The hero from humble origins is told by the local vicar that in fact his ancestry is noble, that he has 'blue blood'. His father's accident at work leaves him with blue and black bruises. Elfie's blueness signifies innocence and purity.

By contrast, *Far from the Madding Crowd* is painted red. Devon cows are 'encased in a warm hide of rich Indian red', as though dipped in dye. The Dorset sky is pure violet with a sun that burns 'rayless, like a red and flameless fire shining over a white hearthstone'. The earth is red. Stars are red. The burning hayricks, saved by Farmer Oak, are 'knots of red worms'. Beech trees are 'rusty red'. Fungi in a swamp have red splotches of 'arterial blood'. The sun is 'blood-red'. Flocks of sheep at the market are 'red' and 'salmon'. The fire in Farmer Oak's shepherd's hut is scarlet. Some of the farm hands are 'crimson' with drink.

Red is the colour of embarrassment's shading into desire. 'Rays of male vision seem to have a tickling effect upon virgin faces in rural districts', Hardy writes at the moment of the first encounter between Gabriel Oak and Bathsheba Everdene. She brushes her face with her hand, 'as if Gabriel had been irritating its pink surface by actual touch'. Oak has already 'looked at her proportions with a long consciousness of pleasure', guessing 'from the contours of her figure in its upper part [that] she must have had a beautiful neck and shoulders', so it is unsurprising that 'it was the man who blushed, the maid not at all'. But when he reveals that he has been peeping at her hatless antics on horseback, 'It was a time to see a woman redden who was not given to reddening as a rule; not a point in the milkmaid but was of the deepest rose-colour. From the Maiden's Blush, through all varieties of the Provence down to the Crimson Tuscany.'[1] On their second encounter, when Oak makes his hasty offer of marriage, Bathsheba appears 'panting like a robin, her face red and moist from her exertions, like a peony petal before the sun dries off the dew'.[2] His proposal is made beside a bush laden with red berries. But, above all, it is Sergeant Troy who is most closely associated with the colour red. It signified danger, sex and death.

Back home in Bockhampton, away from Cornwall and Emma, and back under the dominant influence of his mother and sisters, Hardy wrote the most polished and assured novel of his career so far. He had told Leslie Stephen of the necessity of writing it from home, in order to feel closer to the characters and the landscape. He followed a similar pattern to *Under the Greenwood Tree* in establishing a plot line where a young woman is courted by three suitors, like a story in a ballad.³ In the earlier novel, Fancy Day is wooed by a tranter's son, a rich farmer, and a parson. In *Madding Crowd*, Bathsheba is courted by a shepherd, a rich farmer, and a dashing soldier. Oak's proposal comes before she inherits her uncle's farm, and she refuses him on the grounds that she is too wild and needs someone to 'tame' her. But when she becomes financially independent, she is determined never to marry at all. Like Jane Austen's Emma, she simply doesn't *need* to marry.

Bathsheba is given the distinctive black hair and dark eyes of the Hand/Hardy sisters. Hardy claimed that his beautiful aunt Martha was the model for his heroine, but Bathsheba's striking features, her cherry-red lips, and her fearless spirit were redolent of his cousin Tryphena. The fictional Weatherbury of *Madding Crowd* was based on Puddletown (four or five miles from Casterbridge/Dorchester), where Tryphena lived and taught. And Tryphena's connection to Catherine Hawkins – the famous Dorset female farmer – may have also contributed to Hardy's linking of his cousin to his portrayal of Bathsheba.

For most readers, Bathsheba is the most beloved of Hardy's women with the exception of Tess. Unlike his previous heroines, there is not a jot of sentimentality about her, and she leaps from the pages with her glorious defiance, her courage, her sense of daring, and her insistence at being treated as an equal in a man's world. And, given the strictures of the Victorian era, especially amongst the rural working class, her rebelliousness is refreshing and innovative.

Bathsheba wants to run the farm herself; she does not hesitate to fire the dishonest bailiff. She manages her own accounts and negotiates sales of her produce in the corn market. She even gets her hands dirty with the sheepshearing. From the start, she leaves the farm hands clear about her position: 'Don't any unfair ones among you (if there are any such, but I hope not) suppose that because I'm a woman I don't understand the difference between bad goings-on and good.' Even Gabriel Oak, who loves and admires her, is confounded by the idea that Bathsheba is intending to run the farm herself: 'A woman farmer?' he muses. But she is adamant that she will lead by example: 'I shall be up before you are awake; I shall be afield before you are up; and I shall have breakfasted before you are afield. In short, I shall astonish you all.'[4]

When the shepherd makes his initial proposal, she refuses him on the grounds not only that she doesn't love him, but that she would '*hate* to be thought men's property'. She qualifies this statement by adding: 'Well, what I mean is that I shouldn't mind being a bride at a wedding, if I could be one without having a husband.'[5] Jemima Hardy, working below his window as her son wrote his novel, would surely have approved of Bathsheba's sentiment.

Her comments about not wanting to be men's property recalls the Married Women's Property Act of 1870. Before then the conditions of 'coverture' meant that husband and wife were rendered as one person under the law, and husbands held legal and financial rights over their wives. Coverture meant that once women were married, they lost all control of their property, and were unable to buy, sell or inherit anything they once possessed, or even to sign a legal document. The Act of 1870 allowed women to keep their wages and small investments independently from their husbands. Though its powers were limited, it was the first step in the legal process of financial independence for women.

The legal situation was different for widowed women, such as farmer Catherine Hawkins, who was able to manage her own

Dorset farm. Catherine Hawkins had endured the effects of the bad winter of 1865–6 but had been fortified by the help of a faithful shepherd. Thanks to his expertise, she lost only four ewes and a few lambs. His death left a huge hole, and she worried that she would never find a suitable replacement for him. Some years before, the remarkable Elizabeth Prowse of Northamptonshire was another example of a young widow who took over the management of her late husband's farm after his death. She made significant advancements to their estate of 2,220 acres, improving drainage and experimenting with new crops and agricultural machinery.[6]

The fictional Bathsheba Everdene has no desire to relinquish her new-found independence to Gabriel Oak, nor even to gentleman-farmer William Boldwood, her second suitor. When Boldwood offers marriage, he informs her that he intends to relieve her of her worries around the farmhouse and farm: 'You shall have no cares – be worried by no household affairs, and live quite at ease, Miss Everdene. The dairy superintendence shall be done by a man – I can afford it well – you shall never have so much to look out of doors at haymaking time, or to think of weather in the harvest.'[7] She refuses him. It is only when she meets the dashing Sergeant Troy that her head is turned.

Bathsheba's crimson riding jacket anticipates Troy's scarlet uniform. The scene of their first meeting is erotically charged by the manner in which the gimp (decorative trimming) in her dress is caught in Troy's spurs, and she sees that the man 'to whom she was hooked was brilliant in brass and scarlet'. Later, Troy comes to help with the haymaking 'for pleasure'. He is a 'bright, scarlet spot', suggesting that he comes to the fields in his soldier's uniform.[8]

Then he comes again to her rescue when she is hiving the bees. Troy, cross-dressed in her hat, veil and gloves, dares to emasculate himself, tossing his helmet into a bush. After the manoeuvre is completed, he asks to be released from the confines of her bee-keeping garb: 'Would you be good enough to untie me and let me out? I am nearly stifled inside this silk cage.'⁹ This disarming scene is merely foreplay. He is preparing for his seduction by sword, though it is Bathsheba who boldly asks to see his technique. There he is all male.

In one of the most erotic scenes in Victorian fiction, Hardy sets up the atmosphere of 'The Hollow Amid the Ferns'. The brake fern are 'plump and diaphanous' and they caress Bathsheba's gown with their 'soft, feathery arms' as she enters the hollow to meet Troy. She is 'literally panting and trembling'. Troy tells her that he heard her gown rustling through the ferns before he saw her – a subconscious reference to the erotic rustle of Julia Martin's silk ruffles. Once Troy begins his display of chivalry and swords-manship, Bathsheba is appalled and transfixed. The sword 'is a living thing' which cuts and darts and thrusts. It is part of his arm. Using her as his 'antagonist', he flicks the sword first to her side, then to her hip, before moving to her right side. She feels that his sword has 'passed through her body'. Bathsheba excitedly asks Troy if his sword is sharp. He tells her that she must stand perfectly still so that he can 'perform'. It is all 'electricity' and light. The 'sword arm' is spread in 'a scarlet haze' and it whistles, hisses and rushes as it circles dangerously around her body: 'In short, she was enclosed in a firmament of light, and of sharp hisses, resembling a sky-full of meteors close at hand.'

Just when he appears to have slowed down and then come to a stop, he begins again, this time shearing off a lock of her hair. A caterpillar has crept onto the front of her gown. Troy spears the caterpillar with the tip of his sword. Lest we be in any doubt of the phallic imagery, Hardy spells it out: 'She saw the point glisten towards her bosom, and seemingly enter it.' Afterwards, Bathsheba, discovering that Troy has lied about the bluntness of his sword, realises that her life has been in danger. In an allusion to Pope's *The Rape of the Lock*, Troy steals her lock of hair, twisting it around his finger. Later, he will metaphorically twist her around his finger. And his final action is another stolen embrace:

That minute's interval had brought the blood beating into her face, set her stinging as if aflame to the very hollows of her feet, and enlarged emotion to a compass which quite swamped thought. It had brought upon her a stroke resulting, as did that of Moses in Horeb, in a liquid stream – here a stream of tears. She felt like one who has sinned a great sin.[10]

The circumstance had been the gentle dip of Troy's mouth downwards upon her own. He had kissed her.

Hardy encountered some problems with Leslie Stephen while sending off chapters for serialisation. Stephen, acutely aware of moralising Victorian England, and perhaps conscious of his own Evangelical upbringing, knew that eyebrows would be raised by some of Hardy's plot lines. Sergeant Troy's illicit sexual relationship with the servant girl Fanny Robin was a potential problem. He wrote to Hardy to say that the 'seduction of Fanny Robin must be treated in a gingerly fashion', though admitting that his reservations were due to an 'excessive prudery of which I am ashamed'.[11] There was another detail that Stephen found troubling. Fanny is pregnant by Troy, and dies a sordid death in a workhouse, giving birth to a stillborn child. Stephen was alarmed, questioning Hardy as to 'whether the baby is necessary at all'. Was there any need for Bathsheba to find the dead baby in the coffin? Stephen got his way for the *Cornhill* serialisation, but the baby was restored on publication of the novel.

Nevertheless, a striking description of the dead baby, lying by its dead mother's side, was omitted in the printed editions. In the original manuscript Bathsheba, who has forced open Fanny's coffin, sees a baby whose 'cheeks and the plump back of its fists' reminded Bathsheba of the 'soft convexity of mushrooms on a dewy morning'.[12] The vivid metaphor roots the novel in its rural context. And there were many others. A toad crossing Gabriel Oak's path is 'soft, leathery and distended like a boxing glove'. And a 'huge, brown, garden-slug' who has come in for shelter has left a 'thin glistening streak' like varnish. Farmer Oak takes the note like the good shepherd that he is: 'He knew what this direct message from the Great Mother meant . . . It was Nature's second way of hinting to him that he was to prepare for foul weather.'[13]

It was in part the effectiveness of the details of rustic life that led a reviewer in the *Spectator* to suggest that the anonymous author of the first episode of the book's serialisation was George Eliot. Hardy was flattered and annoyed by the comparison. Though he did not think that George Eliot was a 'born storyteller', he greatly admired her as a 'great thinker – one of the greatest living'. Nevertheless, he complained that she had 'never touched the life of the fields'. His models, he said, for 'real country humour' were Shakespeare and Fielding, not Eliot.[14] The speculation in literary London that *Madding Crowd* was written by a woman was reported to Hardy by Anne Thackeray. When she was asked to identify the author, she coyly replied: '*It* lives in the country, and I could not very well introduce you to *it* in the town.'[15] The literary-minded Ann Procter, wife of a prolific writer of the Romantic age who used the pseudonym Barry Cornwall, was introduced to Hardy by Leslie Stephen. She became another London friend and ally, who greatly amused and charmed Hardy with her literary anecdotes of 'past celebrities'. She wrote to him about his novel: 'You would be gratified to know what a shock the Marriage of Bathsheba was. I resembled Mr Boldwood – and to deceive such an old novel-reader as myself is a triumph.'[16]

Cunning Ann Procter had hit the nail on the head. Bathsheba's shock marriage to Sergeant Troy, and its ugly aftermath, is a startling plot twist. Like Boldwood, the reader is alarmed to discover Bathsheba inviting Troy to her bedroom. Not knowing that they have been secretly married in Bath, Boldwood bribes Troy to do the right thing by promising to wed Bathsheba, horrified that she has gone so far in her sexual desire for Troy: 'She must love you indeed to sell soul and body to you so utterly as she has done. Wretched woman – deluded woman – you are, Bathsheba!'[17]

Boldwood is wrong; the couple are married. But even more shocking in its ruthless brilliancy is the scene when it becomes clear that the marriage is a hopeless failure, that Troy is very quickly disillusioned and indifferent to his lovely bride. Hardy has forewarned the reader: 'When a strong woman recklessly throws away her strength she is worse than a weak woman who has never had any strength to throw away.' The disintegration of the marriage and the incompatibility of Troy and Bathsheba are rendered with deadly precision as Troy is forced to ask his wife for money for Fanny Robin and their unborn child.

'The money is not wanted for racing debts at all,' he said.

'What is it for?' she asked. 'You worry me a great deal by these mysterious responsibilities, Frank.'

Troy hesitated. He did not now love her enough to allow himself to be carried too far by her ways. Yet it was necessary to be civil. 'You wrong me by such a suspicious manner,' he said. 'Such strait-waistcoating as you treat me to is not becoming in you at so early a date.'

'I think that I have a right to grumble a little if I pay,' she said, with features between a smile and a pout.

'Exactly; and, the former being done, suppose we proceed to the latter. Bathsheba, fun is all very well, but don't go too far, or you may have cause to regret something.'

She reddened. 'I do that already,' she said, quickly.

'What do you regret?'

'That my romance has come to an end.'

'All romances end at marriage.'[18]

So much is conveyed in dialogue extraordinary in its emotional and economic directness. She is *spiritually* independent, which is what makes the scene with Troy so distressing.

Directly after he has gone, Bathsheba bursts into great sobs, 'dry-eyed sobs, which cut as they came, without any softening by tears'. But she is determined to 'repress all evidences of feeling':

She was conquered; but she would never own it as long as she lived. Her pride was indeed brought low by despairing discoveries of her spoliation by marriage with a less pure nature than her own. She chafed to and fro in rebelliousness, like a caged leopard; her whole soul was in arms, and the blood fired her face. Until she had met Troy, Bathsheba had been proud of her position as a woman; it had been a glory to her to know that her lips had been touched by no man's on earth – that her waist had never been encircled by a lover's arm. She hated herself now. In those earlier days she had always nourished a secret contempt for girls who were the slaves of the first good-looking young fellow who should choose to salute them. She had never taken kindly to the idea of marriage in the abstract as did the majority of women she saw about her. In the turmoil of her anxiety for her lover she had agreed to marry him; but the perception that had accompanied her happiest hours on this account was rather that of self-sacrifice than of promotion and honour. Although she scarcely knew the divinity's name, Diana was the goddess whom

Bathsheba instinctively adored. That she had never, by look, word, or sign, encouraged a man to approach her – that she had felt herself sufficient to herself, and had in the independence of her girlish heart fancied there was a certain degradation in renouncing the simplicity of a maiden existence to become the humbler half of an indifferent matrimonial whole – were facts now bitterly remembered.[19]

And worse is to come when she is faced with Troy's continued passion for his dead mistress, which he uses to taunt his wife:

'This woman is more to me, dead as she is, than ever you were, or are, or can be. If Satan had not tempted me with that face of yours, and those cursed coquetries, I should have married her. I never had another thought till you came in my way. Would to God that I had; but it is all too late!' He turned to Fanny then. 'But never mind, darling,' he said; 'in the sight of Heaven you are my very, very wife!'

At these words there arose from Bathsheba's lips a long, low cry of measureless despair and indignation, such a wail of anguish as had never before been heard within those old-inhabited walls . . .

'If she's – that, – what – am I?' she added, as a continuation of the same cry, and sobbing pitifully: and the rarity with her of such abandonment only made the condition more dire.

'You are nothing to me – nothing,' said Troy, heartlessly. 'A ceremony before a priest doesn't make a marriage. I am not morally yours.'[20]

––––

Hardy revealed that Troy's sword-exercise scene was taken from real life. He describes the men and boys who 'peeped through chinks or over walls into the barrack-yard returned with accounts of its being the most flashing affair conceivable; accoutrements and weapons glistening like stars – here, there, around – yet all by rule and compass'.[21] Gabriel Oak is seen peeping 'through the loophole' of his hut to watch Bathsheba – the same ventilation hole that he forgets to open and leads to his suffocation and rescue by Bathsheba. Troy peeps through a slit of his dressing-room tent to see his wife sitting in the audience of his circus act. The voyeuristic motif of the peeping Tom recalls Hardy's guilt when he peered through the family telescope to witness a public execution, and his subsequent remorse.

And there is another memory that haunts the novel. Boldwood's incipient madness and obsessive desire for Bathsheba recall the spectre of Horace Moule, driven to madness and suicide by the failure of his doomed love affair. Parson Maybold in *Under the Greenwood Tree* – an early version of Boldwood – loses his love to a rival, even though she has agreed to his proposal of marriage. Maybold releases Fancy from her promise and keeps her secret. But in the character of Boldwood, we witness an essentially noble and tragic figure, whose romantic obsession drives him over the edge of reason, while seeming outwardly to retain his composure. The way that his equilibrium has been shaken by Bathsheba's Valentine is rendered faithfully enough, but it is only after his murder of Troy and his suicide attempt that the extent of his 'mental derangement' is revealed. The onset of his 'excited and unusual moods' is located to the Greenhill Fair (where Hardy was visiting at the time Moule slit his own throat), where Troy is performing his Dick Turpin show. As Boldwood lies in the county gaol awaiting his death sentence, a startling discovery is made at his home:

In a locked closet was now discovered an extraordinary collection of articles. There were several sets of ladies' dresses in the piece, of sundry expensive materials; silks and satins, poplins and velvets, all of colours which from Bathsheba's style of dress might have been judged to be her favourites. There were two muffs, sable and ermine. Above all there was a case of jewellery, containing four heavy gold bracelets and several lockets and rings, all of fine quality and manufacture. These things had been bought in Bath and other towns from time to time, and brought home by stealth. They were all carefully packed in paper, and each package was labelled 'Bathsheba Boldwood', a date being subjoined six years in advance in every instance.[22]

Boldwood's state of mind 'crazed with love and care' becomes the stuff of public house gossip, as do the details of his trial and public execution. As with the Dorchester trial that would obsess Hardy, the defence of insanity is raised and a case is made to the Home Secretary and a petition signed by the Casterbridge people. The execution date is set and the public await a last-minute reprieve. In the meantime, Gabriel Oak makes his last visit to Boldwood, on the day before his execution, and sees the gallows being erected: 'Over the chimneys he could see the upper part of the gaol entrance, rich and glowing in the afternoon sun, and some moving figures were there. They were carpenters lifting a post into a vertical position within the parapet. He withdrew his eyes quickly, and hastened on.' At the eleventh hour, Boldwood is reprieved and sentenced to life imprisonment. Gabriel is relieved, but, somewhat surprisingly, believes 'in his conscience that he ought to die'. Nor does Oak, who is also the conscience of the novel, believe that Boldwood is deranged.

Though *Far from the Madding Crowd* was the novel that launched Hardy's career as a major figure on the Victorian literary scene, it had its detractors. Henry James found the novel lacking in 'magic', and described Bathsheba as 'vague', 'coarse' and 'artificial'. She is, he opined, 'a young lady of the inconsequential, wilful, mettlesome type which has lately become so much the fashion for heroines'.[23] James' harsh criticism belies the extent to which Hardy was the pioneer of a new kind of heroine, one whose inner life and marital despair are brilliantly expressed. A few years later, in *The Portrait of a Lady* Henry James would himself enter imaginatively into the consciousness of a unique heroine – Isabel Archer – whose marriage is a catastrophe. It is very difficult to imagine how James could have achieved this without Hardy's example. For both Isabel and Bathsheba, marriage (with the wrong man) becomes a spiritual prison, changing them irrevocably. Bathsheba suffers. After her marriage and its chilling aftermath, she is no longer the 'romping girl' but a woman whose despair is all in her 'miserable' eyes. The difference between Bathsheba Everdene and Isabel Archer is that Hardy's heroine is permitted to leave and find another love. But Henry James was not at this moment ready to admit to Hardy's genius. The only believable things in the novel, he said, were 'the sheep and the dogs'.

CHAPTER 48

Ethelberta Petherwin

'It is difficult for a woman to define her feelings in language which is chiefly made by men to express theirs', Bathsheba tells Boldwood. This sounds like the language of Hardy's London ladies, or of Emma. Jemima's speech was the Dorset vernacular, more muscular and down-to-earth. Hardy was fortunate to be surrounded by strong-minded women, even when he didn't agree with their views. One of William Boldwood's problems, and the reason he misunderstands women, is that he lacks female company and advice: 'No mother existed to absorb his devotion, no sister for his tenderness, no idle ties for sense.'[1] *Far from the Madding Crowd* was written at home, among Hardy's own people, alert to mother and sisters, but henceforth he would write as a married man.

On his marriage licence, he described himself boldly as 'Author'. His identity as the author of London's most talked about book had been revealed in the *Spectator* of 7 February 1874. He was set on his path, and he was about to become much in demand as a writer. Living in the suburb of Surbiton, he claimed, kept him initially from realising 'the full extent of the interest that had been excited among the reading public', but he and Emma were aware of the many 'London ladies' who they spotted carrying copies of the novel on their travels to and from the capital.[2] And then the letters came flooding in. One of them was from Julia Martin. How could she ever have imagined that her 'dear Tommy' was now the author of the most popular contemporary book? Though she was now 'quite an elderly lady', her signature at the bottom of the letter sent 'revived throbs of tender feeling in him': it was here that he recalled his thrill at the rustle of her silks as she bent over him as a child. Hardy replied to her letter, but did not call on her. 'Their eyes never met again . . . nor their lips from the time she had held him in her arms.'[3]

The novelist and travel writer Katherine Macquoid wrote to Hardy on the subject of Bathsheba. Macquoid's novel, *Patty*, had depicted a heroine, the daughter of a gardener, who inherits a large fortune and is assimilated into the middle classes by marriage to a gentleman. Patty is certainly not typical of the virtuous mid-Victorian heroine of fiction, but virtuous she is. Macquoid queried Hardy's decision to portray a flawed woman of an 'ordinary type' as his heroine. He took the time to write a full and considered letter: 'I myself, I must confess, have no great liking for the perfect woman of fiction, but this may be for purely artistic reasons.'[4] Macquoid responded quickly, assuring Hardy of her admiration for Bathsheba: 'I feel now too late that it was ungrateful to find fault with Bathsheba who must have cost you infinite time & labour to create – She is almost true to herself but then her nature is such that of a true woman – because she is centred on self.' Macquoid felt that Hardy had misunderstood her critique: 'You have not understood me – I quite agree that the ordinary type of woman shd not be idealised in a novel.'[5]

Hardy was keenly interested in Macquoid's views, and the couple arranged to meet in person. He took no offence; the main point was that Bathsheba was being talked about, discussed as a new kind of heroine. In January 1875, *The Times* got to the nub of the matter, praising Hardy for being concerned with the lower classes: 'There is not a lady or gentleman in the book . . . they are all working people, and ever so much more interesting than the idle lords and ladies.'[6]

Hardy was already thinking of his next heroine. *Cornhill Magazine* was pestering him for another story. He had begun a 'woodland story', but now decided to put it aside in order to make 'a plunge in a new and untried direction'. Henry James' criticism had stung, and he decided against 'writing forever about sheep farming, as the reading public was apparently expecting him to do'.[7] *The Hand of Ethelberta: A Comedy in Chapters* was the title of the new tale. Hardy had hesitations, worried that he was being rushed into print too soon, but he had bills to pay.

And he had a wife to support. The reviewer John Hutton wrote to Hardy to congratulate him on the success of his latest novel: 'How your wife must glory and triumph in your genius – Tell her we sympathise in her glory.'[8] The couple moved from Surbiton to an address in central London close to his old stamping ground of Westbourne Grove: to glean copy for *Ethelberta* he needed to be nearer 'society'. A round of 'museum, theatre and concert-going with some dining-out' ensued.[9] Hardy confessed to Anne Thackeray that he disliked the social scene. He was surprised that she ticked him off: a novelist ought to be interested in such things, she admonished. Emma, by contrast, thoroughly enjoyed all that London had to offer. But she had reason to be concerned by her husband's new novel, in which the heroine was to be based upon an old love. Ethelberta was to be a rich widow, with a mysterious past. Hardy wanted to explore 'some London scenes occurring in her chequered career, which I want to do as vigorously as possible – having already visited Rouen and Paris with the same object, other adventures of hers taking place there'.[10] He dipped into Emma's honeymoon

journal for details of Rouen. And soon there was a meeting with
the Hardy in-laws. In July, the Hardys left London for a three-day
stay in Bournemouth. From there, they were bound for Swanage,
close to Bockhampton, for an extended stay in order for Hardy
to finish the book. Emma's journal entry was curt: 'Monday
July 12. Left London for Bournemouth'.[11]

By this time, Emma had met Jemima, although no reference
to the visit exists. Emma wrote to Jemima suggesting a further
meeting in Bournemouth, which Jemima turned down, asking
Kate to send a letter on her behalf:

> My dear Emma,
> Mother is much obliged to you for your kind invitation but she
> is so very busy just now that she cannot possibly come. She
> would like to have come as she says she wants to see you again.
>
>   Mother says you are not to get into the sea or go boating at
> Bth [Bournemouth] because she is afraid that you will both be
> drowned or come to some untimely end. You would be much
> safer she says on Rainbarrows or Cowstairs.[12]

There is a little tartness here. Hardy's act of marrying a 'lady'
was quickly becoming a subject of family gossip. A deeply sad
poem written in Bournemouth suggests that the marriage was
already in trouble. 'We Sat at the Window' describes a couple
watching the rain pouring down outside their room. In contrast
to the noisy weather, the couple are silent. They are getting on
each other's nerves. And they are no longer soulmates. As often,
Hardy gave place and date in a subtitle: 'Bournemouth, 1875':

> We sat at the window looking out,
> And the rain came down like silken strings
> That Swithin's day. Each gutter and spout
> Babbled unchecked in the busy way

            Of witless things:
Nothing to read, nothing to see
Seemed in that room for her and me
            On Swithin's day.

We were irked by the scene, by our own selves; yes,
For I did not know, nor did she infer
How much there was to read and guess
By her in me, and to see and crown
            By me in her.
Wasted were two souls in their prime,
And great was the waste, that July time
When the rain came down.[13]

From Bournemouth, they boarded the steamer for the coastal town of Swanage, near Purbeck, a place Hardy would always associate with Eliza Nicholls. They took rooms in West End cottage from Captain Joseph Masters, master mariner, who would find his way into the pages of Hardy's new novel, as Captain Flowers. The detached house stood on a hill overlooking the sea. Hardy used the cottage and the outlook for Ethelberta's lodgings in 'Knollsea', a seaside village 'lying snug within two headlands as between a finger and a thumb'.

In September, Mary and Kate came for a two-week visit with the newly-weds. By now, Mary had left her Piddlehinton School and taken up a new role as Headmistress of the Bell Street School in Dorchester. It was a larger establishment, bringing her more responsibility. Kate had been a pupil teacher at Piddlehinton alongside her sister, and now joined her at Bell Street to complete her five years' training, before applying to Salisbury training college. Mary came equipped with her

sketch book, and completed several sketches of Swanage. The
party took a boat trip to the Isle of Wight. Emma recorded
mundane observations in her diary: 'Weather exceedingly fine
and a very warm sun all day . . . We then passed through the
Needles. All eyes gaze. Sea rough . . . the island most beautiful
now.' She felt that the island seemed to be cut off from the
world. Ryde was livelier, with a 'splendid pier' and a 'thoroughly
good band'.[14]

Everyone was on best behaviour. Though Emma would later
accuse the Hardy women of making trouble from the very start
of the marriage, there was as yet no clear evidence of a family
rift. The visit ended with a breakfast picnic at Corfe Castle.
Emma's diary records no details about Kate and Mary, other
than noting down their presence on the expeditions. But one
entry perhaps points to hidden tensions:

> Dismal conversation is very disagreeable.
>   Why?
>   Because one is not accustomed to the words as they flow &
> it is not easy to make sense of them.[15]

Emma's Corfe diary was more evocative and detailed than her
Isle of Wight entries, and there might have been more than a
little relief that this was the final morning with the Hardy sisters.
They drove to Corfe by housecart: 'A sweet-smelling clear
morning Sun shining carelessly and lazily.' They climbed up to
the castle, and sipped tea, before scrambling down the castle
slope. She noted: 'Mary and Katie took their way to Wareham
along a hot road, & we parted on King Edward's bridge, watched
them out of sight.' Corfe Castle had been 'a splendid day'. On
the way home, there were 'plenty of jokes'. Riding 'home on
the top of the bus' she noticed hedges 'flowing over into the
wide-sided roads, growing freely into the fields behind. Nut trees

reaching a good way up to them, the yellow ox eyes almost halfway up to the nut trees.'[16]

Emma was also writing her novella 'The Maid on the Shore'. Tom was under pressure to finish *The Hand of Ethelberta* as soon as possible, so his absence gave her plenty of time to concentrate on her own fiction. Emma's friend, Miss D'Arville, wrote to her: 'You are I dare say both very busy with your new work, which I hope to read when published.'[17] No doubt, this kind encouragement gave Emma a sense that she was on her way to becoming a published writer, like her husband. Her prose was pedestrian, but there were flashes of interest, such as her description of an infant boy who 'opened the gate for her swinging all his strength to keep its width open'.[18] Other passages, though, struck an alarming and confused note:

> The moon rose red gold out of the sea dropping as she trod the sky her gemmed scarf band unrolled her pearl robe which shook its gems on the dull blue waters, which lay in length & breadth across till it touched our shore. A white sail was coming into it but yet lay off the shaded blue waves. Two figures sudden rose tall well-formed & graceful youth directly in the shining light broader the band spread itself & higher the moon passed up her way.[19]

Hardy and his family would come to believe that Emma had a family history of insanity, which had been concealed from him until after the marriage had taken place. He also feared that Emma had lied about her age, and that she was beyond child-bearing years. There was no sign of a pregnancy, which no doubt contributed to the increasing unhappiness of both, especially Emma, who loved children and whose journals frequently mentioned babies and toddlers. Two months later, Hardy made a poignant diary entry: 'I sit under a tree, and feel alone'. It was only seeing the insects around him that made him feel part of something.[20]

And then there was the novel he was writing, which conjured the ghost of his old love, Cassie Pole, with her 'squirrel-coloured hair'. Ethelberta is a rich young widow, who was trained as a schoolteacher before becoming governess to an aristocratic family. Her beauty and brains attract the attention of the son of the household. They marry, and he dies shortly after their honeymoon. Ethelberta is taken up by her mother-in-law, Lady Petherwin, who sends her to a boarding school in Bonn to complete her education. On her return, Ethelberta is enjoined by Lady Petherwin to become her companion on the condition that she never tells the secret of her past. Ethelberta agrees to this demand. But when Lady Petherwin dies, she disinherits Ethelberta, although allowing her to live in their London home for a period of years.

Ethelberta is also a published poet and a professional storyteller. She attracts three well-born lovers, who offer marriage but are unaware of her past. The hero of the story is Christopher Julian, whom Ethelberta jilted. They are still in love and he also knows her secret: that she is the daughter of a butler from the West Country, with many siblings to look after and support. Ethelberta, known as 'Berta' to her lower-class family, is forced to reject Christopher, in order to marry well and provide for her large family. An added complication is that Berta's sister, Picotee, a pupil teacher, is in love with Christopher.

Hardy knew that his new work was not in the same league as *Far from the Madding Crowd*. He intended it to be a 'light' comedy or a satire on social class and manners, but its episodic nature was not suited to his talents for realism and verisimilitude. However, the novel is fascinating for its autobiographical allusions and its pioneering attempt to reveal the manners of the servant class. In his 1895 preface, Hardy argued, reasonably, that

the novel was ahead of its time, 'wherein servants were as important as, or more important than, their masters; wherein the
drawing-room was sketched in many cases from the point of
view of the servants' hall'.[21] From the opening lines, Hardy's
tone took aim at the upper classes: 'By her look and carriage
she appeared to belong to that gentle order of society which has
no worldly sorrow except when its jewellery gets stolen.'[22]

Berta herself, a thinly veiled version of Hardy, has transcended
her lowly origins through a good education and social aspiration.
As an aspiring writer, she struggles to make ends meet, and
marries out of her social class. Like Hardy, Berta is displaced.
Her family condemn her for marrying above herself, but they
also expect her financial support. Her ambition and 'enterprise'
are a source of irritation to those around her, and her marriage
to an aristocratic fool alienates her from the family she loves.
Strong and resourceful, her rise to the top leads to feelings of
isolation: 'by getting on too much you are sneered at by your
new acquaintance, who don't know the skill of your rise, and
you are parted from and forgot by the old ones who do.'[23]

The hero, Christopher Julian, also has similar traits to Hardy.
He is a musician, devoted to his aptly named sister, Faith, to
whom he confides his deepest secrets. Like Mary Hardy, the
sister gives sound advice: 'and [he] listened to hear her opinion,
having proved its value frequently; passive assent was her usual
praise'. No matter how much Christopher loves Berta, his sister
remains a constant: 'However, love her or love her not, I can
keep a corner of my heart for you, Faith.'[24]

Like Hardy, the hero's countenance does not reflect his inner
thoughts and feelings: 'He looked sad when he felt almost serene,
and only serene when he felt quite cheerful. It is a habit people
acquire who have had repressing experiences.'[25] Berta sends
Christopher a volume of her poems, which includes an autobiographical love-lament called 'Cancelled Words'. Christopher

is convinced that the poem is about him. One wonders if Hardy
was concerned that Cassie Pole – the red-haired daughter of a
butler-father – might have felt a similar sensation. One scene
draws closely on real life. Berta is invited to a supper party, in
which her father serves the company in his role of butler. This
recalls the dinner party to which Hardy was invited when Cassie's
father refused to serve the man who had jilted his daughter.

The most original parts of the novel depict the lives of those
'downstairs'. When Berta moves into her salubrious London
home, she brings her sisters and brothers as her servants,
including cook and housekeeper. They are all sworn to secrecy,
pretending that their mistress is a stranger. Berta loves her
siblings, but is frustrated and embarrassed by their countrified
manners, their lack of ambition and their rustic dialect. She
tries to confide in her elder sister, Gwendoline, the cook, but
all her efforts fall on stony ground: 'The wretched homeliness
of Gwendoline's mind seemed at this particular juncture to be
absolutely intolerable, and Ethelberta was suddenly convinced
that to involve Gwendoline in any such discussion would simply
be increasing her own burden, and adding worse confusion to
her sister's already confused existence.' Berta is made wretched
by the class divide that education and wealth have brought
about: 'It was that old sense of disloyalty to her class and kin
by feeling as she felt now which caused the pain, and there was
no escaping it.'[26]

There is something desperately painful and noble about Berta's
proud brothers, who are happy to paint her house, refusing to
take payment:

'Ah, that's all very well,' said Sol, with an unbelieving smile; 'but
if we bain't company for you out of doors, you bain't company
for we within – not that I find fault with ye or mind it, and
shan't take anything for painting your house, nor will Dan

neither, any more for that – no, not a penny; in fact, we are glad to do it for 'ee. At the same time, you keep to your class, and we'll keep to ours.'[27]

When Berta decides, partly out of a desire to help her family and partly from social ambition, to marry an elderly aristocrat, straight-talking brother Sol scolds her for betraying her social class and her family values for a 'coronet':

'Don't be harsh, Sol. A coronet covers a multitude of sins.'
  'A coronet: good Lord – and you my sister! Look at my hand.' Sol extended his hand. 'Look how my thumb stands out at the root, as if it were out of joint, and that hard place inside there. Did you ever see anything so ugly as that hand – a misshaped monster, isn't he? That comes from the jackplane, and my pushing against it day after day and year after year. If I were found drowned or buried, dressed or undressed, in fustian or in broadcloth, folk would look at my hand and say, "That man's a carpenter." Well now, how can a man, branded with work as I be, be brother to a viscountess without something being wrong? Of course there's something wrong in it, or he wouldn't have married you – something which won't be righted without terrible suffering.'
  'No, no,' said she. 'You are mistaken. There is no such wonderful quality in a title in these days. What I really am is second wife to a quiet old country nobleman, who has given up society. What more commonplace? My life will be as simple, even more simple, than it was before.'
  'Berta, you have worked to false lines. A creeping up among the useless lumber of our nation that'll be the first to burn if there comes a flare. I never see such a deserter of your own lot as you be! But you were always like it, Berta, and I am ashamed of ye.'[28]

Berta may well be a 'deserter' of her own lot, but it's her enterprise, sacrifice and ingenuity that rescues her family from poverty
and homelessness. She sacrifices her true love, Christopher,
because she knows that her sister is in love with him. Berta is
the one who has transcended her class, and in doing so she will
always be responsible for her parents and siblings. The novel
ends with Picotee, now engaged to Christopher: 'Berta will never
let us come to want . . . She always gives me what is necessary.'[29]

Hardy himself always gave what was necessary. To his mother,
his sisters, and his wife. He also took what he needed. Mary
gave her blind faith, her loyalty and her reassurance. His mother
was his constant. Emma was the person who believed in his
powers as a writer. He also took snippets from her journals – for
example, a lovely description of the French maid who spins and
the houses from the Fleche, which look like mosaic. One wonders
what Mary made of Hardy's description of sister Faith as the
youngest of old maids. It strikes a cold note.

On the other hand, Christopher's loyal, truth-telling sister is
bold enough to tell her brother: 'If I had to describe you I
should say you were a child in your impulses and an old man
in your reflections.'[30] Hardy was playing a complicated game
with his women. The hero, who falls in love with one sister and
marries another recalls the love triangle with Eliza and Jane
Bright Nicholls. The girl with 'squirrel-coloured hair', daughter
of a butler, recalls Cassie Pole. But the message that his family
received, and which no doubt Emma received loud and clear,
was that family was all. His hero tells his faithful sister Faith:
'The only feeling that has any dignity or permanence or worth
is family affection between close blood-relations.'[31]

Nevertheless, the schism that was already beginning to open
between wife and family was a source of conflict and pain for
all concerned. Emma's affectations and middle-class refinement
hardly helped matters. She had entered into a large, extended

family of Hands and Hardys, where money was tight and morals were loose. Hardy's cousin, Ellen Hand, had given birth to an illegitimate baby. Mary's best schoolfriend, Annie Lanham, also pregnant with Nathaniel Sparks' child, had a shotgun wedding, and joined the Hardy family. Mary was happy that Annie was married to her cousin, but it was another reminder that she was a young old maid, with few prospects of marriage and a home and establishment of her own. Mary was still emotionally dependent on her elder brother, which could not have been easy for a new wife feeling her way in this family where the roots of kinship ran deep.

By now, Emma was well aware of the social class that she had married into, and that her mother-in-law had once been a servant. She also had to suffer alienation from her own family. Quite what she thought of Hardy's insistence on showing life downstairs in his latest novel is not known. Nor how much assistance she gave as amanuensis, since no manuscript of *The Hand of Ethelberta* survives. Nevertheless, given Emma's love of animals, and especially horses, she must have felt discomposed by a deeply disturbing scene in which the heroine visits the ancestral home of one of her suitors only to discover that part of the land has been turned into a knacker's yard. Berta sees that an enclosure has been built at the front of the house, but what lies inside is horrifying: 'It consisted of numerous horses in the last stage of decrepitude, the animals being such mere skeletons that at first Ethelberta hardly recognized them to be horses at all; they seemed rather to be specimens of some attenuated heraldic animal, scarcely thick enough through the body to throw a shadow: or enlarged castings of the fire-dog of past times.' But worse is yet to come. In an adjoining enclosure there is a horse cemetery. Berta peeps through a crevice of a high fence and sees a shocking sight: 'Horses' skulls, ribs, quarters, legs, and other joints were hung thereon, the whole forming a huge open-air larder emitting not too sweet a smell.'[32] The scream of hounds from a nearby kennel reveals that the horses are being starved and killed for dog food. The gentleman who is responsible for this outrage is given the name Neigh, a joke in extremely poor taste.

While he was still living in Swanage, Hardy had his first poem published in the *Gentleman's Magazine*. It was a comic ballad entitled 'The Bride-Night Fire'. A young maid called Barbree is married off to an old drunken tranter, who accidentally sets his house on fire on his wedding night. Barbree escapes half-naked and runs to the orchard where she is seen by her old sweetheart, who lends her his male clothes and hides her in his attic. In the original, the heroine has 'cold little buzzoms' which was changed for publication to 'a cold little figure'.[33] Whether or not the reading public was ready for horsemeat in a novel, they certainly couldn't be exposed to cold bosoms.

In the spring of 1876, the Hardys left Swanage for Yeovil in Somerset. They took lodgings, where Hardy corrected the final proofs for *Ethelberta*. It was the last novel he would publish with Leslie Stephen. The book was well received, better than Hardy expected. One reviewer wrote a private letter to Hardy commending the heroine: 'Show me the lady in the flesh, and I vow on my honour as a bachelor to become a humble addition to her devoted train.'[34] It was a testament to the way that Hardy's heroines achieved a realism that affected his readers. One dissenting voice complained about the 'impossible' scene of the heroine sitting at the dinner party at which her father was present as butler. Hardy took exception to this criticism of a situation he had himself experienced.[35]

With the book complete, the Hardys took off for another continental holiday, this time to Holland and the Rhine. Emma kept a travel diary of notes, observations and sketches. She observed babies, clogs painted white, park lamps swinging in the trees, and groups of little children at The Hague. After two years of marriage, there was no sign of a Hardy baby. Emma was now thirty-six, the prospect of motherhood slipping away.

They quarrelled in Cologne – Hardy 'angry about the brandy flask'.[36] Heidelberg was happier for Emma: she loved the old town and in the Castle on the Königstuhl she was impressed by a remarkable picture of the head of Mary Queen of Scots, 'after she had been on the block'.[37] Hardy was gloomier: on the top of the tower, looking down on the Rhine, he observed a 'tragic' mist, which 'glared like a riband of blood, as if it serpentined through the atmosphere above the earth's surface'.[38]

In Strasbourg, Emma was poorly. Hardy claimed it was 'excessive walking' that made her sick, but a 'thick brown mysterious fluid' soon set her right.[39] They returned, via Brussels, visited the field of Waterloo, and saw the house where Victor Hugo wrote the ending of Les Misérables. There had been a long walk to the station and Emma was exhausted. Still tired the following morning after 'the Waterloo day' Emma was rebuked by her husband: 'I am still greatly fatigued, & Tom is cross about it.'[40] In a huff, he left his wife alone because there was a picture gallery he wished to see. She rallied to visit the Cathedral, where a wedding was taking place; the bride resplendent in white satin. The priest, she noted 'is spangling with jewels'.[41] The wedding ceremony was a sad reminder of the fact that Emma's own marriage was in trouble.

In Antwerp they visited a picture gallery. Emma had a wonderful knack of describing the religious paintings. A fine triptych of the crucifixion caught her eye, 'Agonised thief has torn his foot from the nail', another of the 'Adoration of the Magi' in which the artist drew Mary as 'fleshy & earthly beautiful & smiles much'. Another of Jesus after the crucifixion: 'Christ's limbs much distorted & the handling of the body is very tender & loving by the women.'[42] A picture of Doubting

Thomas was startlingly realistic: 'The hand with red hole very natural, so are apostles' faces.'[43]

Emma, a natural traveller and lover of culture, was depressed by the prospect of returning: 'Going back to England where we have no home & no chosen country.'[44] By June, they were back in Yeovil. Hardy seemed shocked when his 'relatives' (probably his sharp-tongued mother) told him 'he and his wife appeared to be wandering about like two tramps'.[45] But it was a rebuke that he took to heart. He determined to find a house where they could live a settled life, allowing him to concentrate on his next novel.

The native had returned to Dorset, within fifteen miles of his mother in Bockhampton. Jemima's psychological grip on her son was as strong as ever, but Emma was no shrinking violet and she was not going to allow herself to be bullied by her mother-in-law. There was an argument about a chipped teacup, a seemingly trivial incident that came to symbolise a fissure that had opened up between the two women and that would never be resolved.

Given the family and marital tensions, it was perhaps not surprising that for his next novel, the immensely powerful *Return of the Native*, Hardy would take for the main character an inanimate object: Egdon Heath.

CHAPTER 49

Eustacia Vye

By a stroke of good fortune, a pretty cottage called Riverside Villa became available in the market town of Sturminster Newton in the Vale of Blackmoor. Sturminster was also the home of the Dorset dialect poet William Barnes, who had written often of the vale and its inhabitants. Two years earlier, Barnes had sent Hardy a copy of his *Poems about Rural Life in Common English* with a kind note of good wishes for his writing. Riverside Villa, nestling above the River Stour and its water-meadows, was a haven for the Hardys. For the first time in their married life they put down roots, and they hurriedly bought a hundred pounds' worth of furniture from a shop in Bristol. The house was small, according to Hardy, but 'probably that in which they spent their happiest days'.[1]

They acquired a rowing boat and watched the eels and fish swimming beneath the surface of the Stour. They would gather meadowsweet and water lilies with 'long ropey stems'. One evening when they were boating on the river, they disturbed a flock of swallows roosting in the bushes. The sun was setting and Hardy noted 'a cloud in the sky like a huge quill-pen'.[2] This was rural peace. And yet there was a sense of some intangible absence: one late autumn evening he copied a remark of Emma's into his notebook: 'A gentle day, when something seems gone from the garden & you cannot tell what.'[3]

Hardy had begun keeping a notebook in the spring of 1876, with his wife's active assistance. It was different to the working notebooks that he had been keeping for many years, indicative of a more reflective, creative method of note-taking. There are extracts from books, newspapers and reviews that he found striking or interesting. By April 1876, Emma had provided him with over 200 entries. He then took over the notes himself, though she continued to help in a more sporadic way. Some of the quotations and excerpts from classical history and literature, history of art, essays and articles, would appear in *The Return of the Native*. Husband and wife were working together as a team, smoothing over the hairline cracks that had occurred in the first year of marriage. Emma felt valued and needed, and they had a common purpose: to help make Thomas Hardy one of the greatest writers of his time. That Hardy was thinking along these lines is suggested in the notebooks: 'The world often feels certain works of genius to be great, without knowing why; hence it may be that particular poets and novelists may have had the wrong quality in them noticed and applauded as that which makes them great.'[4] Emma believed (not unreasonably) that her supportive role was intrinsic to her husband's literary success, and she still cherished an ambition to be an author in her own right.

Domestic happiness inspired 'a poetical time'. In the auto-biography, Hardy mentions 'Overlooking the River Stour' and 'On Sturminster Foot-Bridge'.[5] On the banks of the river are swallows who fly 'in the curves of an eight / Above the river-gleam.'[6] Sunlight is reflected on the water and a moorhen darts from the bank. Kingcups, small yellow marsh flowers, nestle on the green mead, bathed in golden sunlight. But in these poems, and in others he wrote at this blissful time, there is a significant sense of loss and regret at his failure to grasp the happiness that still seems to elude him. Furthermore, there are hints at something far darker that had become apparent to him in his marriage with Emma. Something he was loath to unravel, and which he pushed to one side.

At Christmas, they were invited to spend the festival with Jemima and Thomas at Bockhampton. Christmas was always a special festival for the Hardys, as is apparent from the warmth of descriptions in *Under the Greenwood Tree*. If ever Emma were to see her husband's family at their best, it was during the festive season. The visit was a disaster, and the relationship between Jemima and Emma never fully recovered. Hardy's father, kind and genial as always, told stories of his own childhood at Christmas time. Though the exact nature of the quarrel is unknown, matters between the two women came to a head. Jemima, always possessive of her eldest son, seems to have resented her daughter-in-law's family pride, her belief that she was in a higher social class than the Hardys. But Jemima was also a woman of fierce pride. For her part, Emma would come to feel that the Hardy women were against her from the start, never giving her a fair chance.

Hardy would later recall his mother's volatility in middle age, the way she could fly from a gentle mood to raging anger in a blink of an eye. Always a fiery character, Jemima was possibly suffering from the menopause, mood swings, irritability and rages being the most common emotional symptoms. Surrounded as Jemima was by (working-class) women who seemed to get pregnant at the drop of a hat, it was difficult for her to understand Emma's inability to produce a child. Similarly, it was painful for Emma, who desperately wanted a baby, to feel like a failure in the eyes of her mother-in-law.

Despite (or because of?) the unpleasantness arising from the Christmas visit, Hardy decided to put at the heart of his next novel a mother and son relationship strained irrevocably by the son's marriage to a strong and vivacious woman. He also returned to Riverside Villa with a renewed stock of superstitious legend and Dorset folklore, which would find its way into his new novel. That Christmas, his father had told folk stories of the hobby horse, often used in winter entertainments. Dating back to medieval times, it involved a horse-like frame wrapped around the entertainer's legs, allowing the person to run about the room. The wooden horsehead with huge painted eyes was sinister in appearance. Hardy's father remembered a servant 'terrified death-white at the sight of it running about'.[7]

Walks on the heath that Christmas reminded him of its wild splendour and the connection he imagined it held to 'the King of Wessex, Lear'.[8] The novel would begin with the heath, and he would give it an ancient-sounding name. But a queen, not a king, would reign over Egdon Heath.

Her name is Eustacia Vye, and when we first see her she is lighting a bonfire on 5 November. Building bonfires is not only a custom associated with Guy Fawkes, Hardy reminds us, but stretches further back to the 'Festival fires to Thor and Woden . . . the lineal descendants from jumbled Druidical rites and Saxon ceremonies than the invention of popular feeling about Gunpowder Plot.' The lighting of fire is 'the instinctive and resistant act of man' and 'indicates a spontaneous, Promethean rebelliousness against that fiat that this recurrent season shall bring foul times, cold darkness, misery and death. Black chaos comes, and the fettered gods of the earth say, Let there be light.'[9] With this darkly powerful and extraordinary vision, Hardy propels the reader into a universe entirely different from any he had previously explored in his rural tales. He was beginning to unleash the full force of his imagination. No one would mistake Thomas Hardy for George Eliot in *The Return of the Native*.

Eustacia's bonfire is one of many that line the Wessex

countryside, but hers burns more brightly and fiercely. Her fire has a secret meaning, which connects her to a different primordial instinct than the one of warding against winter cold and darkness: she is sending a message to her former lover, Damon Wildeve. Eustacia has learnt that Wildeve jilted his bride, Thomasin Yeobright, at the altar. She is wrong; a technical legality in the marriage licence has merely delayed the marriage. But when Wildeve receives the fire signal, he cannot help himself from responding to Eustacia's prior claim, her beauty, her 'hot little bosom'. There is still time to extricate himself from a safe marriage to a 'pleasing, innocent' woman and return to Eustacia. In contrast to his previous heroines, Hardy takes his time describing Eustacia's diabolical beauty in a chapter dedicated to her Cleopatra-like charm, entitled 'Queen of the Night'. She has 'pagan eyes full of nocturnal mysteries'. She is half Sappho and half Mrs Siddons – the latter's most celebrated role being Lady Macbeth. Eustacia compares herself with the 'witch of Endor' summoning her Samuel.

Her hair is as black as that of a sorceress, 'a whole winter did not contain darkness enough to form its shadow', and her nerves, we are told, 'extended into those tresses, and her temper could always be softened by stroking them down'. Other girls wear coloured ribbons in their hair, but she wears a band of black velvet which sets off her exotic beauty. Her mouth is made to kiss. In physical beauty she recalls Phena Sparks. The darkness that seems to surround her is connected to the heath, which is her 'Hades, and since coming there she had imbibed much of what was dark in its tone'. Hardy also hints at a depressive disorder: she is given to 'sudden fits of gloom'. Part of her trouble is environmental: she hails from the seaside town of Budmouth (her father is from Corfu), meaning that she longs for the sea. And her only escape from the darkness that surrounds her is love: 'To be loved to madness – such was her great desire. Love was to her the one cordial which could drive away the eating loneliness of her days. And she seemed to long for the abstraction called passionate love more than for any particular lover.' Wildeve, she confesses, is only a passing attraction until she can find a 'greater man'.[10] Like Hardy, she carries her grandfather's telescope onto the heath for 'spying' purposes. But Eustacia only sees what she wants to see, and what pertains to herself.

She doesn't see that there is another character who is closely observing all the players in this drama, the reddleman, Diggory Venn. He is as 'lurid red' as his van, in which he drives around the country delivering red ochre for marking sheep. The vermilion chalk has seeped into his clothes, his boots, his skin and his hair: 'He was not temporarily overlaid with the colour; it permeated him.' When Venn appears at the bonfire festivities, the locals associate him with the devil or the 'red ghost' of folklore. Children are frightened of him and are warned by Wessex mothers to be good or else the 'reddleman is coming for you'. He is a 'Mephistophelian visitant' associated with the country traditions before the arrival of the railways. There is something of the 'Ancient Mariner' in Venn, but he is no devil. He has come to the rescue of Thomasin Yeobright, the woman who has been delayed in her marriage to Wildeve, and whom Venn loves and protects. Thomasin is the second of the 'Three Women' (the title of the first part of the novel). The third woman is Mrs Yeobright, the mother of the hero, Clym, who has returned from Paris for the nuptials of his cousin, Thomasin.

In Mrs Yeobright, Hardy poured out all his complicated feelings regarding the mother with whom he was so emotionally fused. Mrs Yeobright has all the plain-speaking good sense of Jemima Hardy, is highly respected by the locals, and lives in 'an old, irregular thatched house' that borders the heath. She is a curate's daughter, and 'ladylike', but she married a man 'as rough as a hedge' and lived with him in his humble cottage, with floors that they sand themselves and where they drink mead in the kitchen before the fire.[11] Like Jemima, Mrs Yeobright holds grudges. If the relationship between Emma and Jemima soured over a chipped teacup, then the fictional Mrs Yeobright's propensity to cut someone off for life over an 'accidental' offence makes perfect sense. When her beloved only son falls in love with Eustacia, she is horrified. Eustacia (in love with the idea of being in love with Clym before she has met him) makes her first bold and calculated move. She appears cross-dressed as a mummer in the play that is being performed at Mrs Yeobright's Christmas party in order that she can have a good look at Clym. Intrigued, Clym pursues Eustacia, despite her reputation among the locals that she is a witch. When Eustacia is stabbed in the arm by a local woman during a Sunday service in church, Clym is moved to compassion. Though he calls her a 'half-witch' he is entranced by her intelligence and beauty. But the courtship strains his primary relationship, that between mother and son.

Knowing Hardy's closeness to his mother, her disdain for the institution of marriage and her dislike of Emma, the rift between Mrs Yeobright and her son makes for painful reading. Hardy's power here is to simultaneously be inside both mother and son as they battle one another. For Mrs Yeobright, her son is 'a part of her' and 'their discourses were as if carried on between the right and the left hands of the same body'. For Clym, his mother is his 'best friend', the person whose wisdom and judgement he most values. Clym marvels at his mother's 'singular insight into life, considering that she had never mixed with it'. Her gift is like that of the blind poet, Blacklock, 'who could describe visual objects with accuracy'. Hardy's allusions to blindness foreshadow Clym's Oedipal loss of sight later in the novel. But he uses the metaphor to make clear that in the battle of the sexes it is the female race that have sharper cognition: 'In the social sphere these gifted ones are mostly women; they can watch a world which they never saw, and estimate forces of which they have only heard. We call it intuition.'[12]

It is not simply then that Mrs Yeobright is jealously possessive of Clym, but more that she knows that he is making a life-changing mistake by choosing the wrong wife. She is also shrewd enough to know that Clym's return to the heath to become a schoolteacher to the poor and uneducated is quixotic and foolhardy. Clym's social and intellectual displacement means that he can never return to his people: 'After all the trouble that has been taken to give you a start, and when there is nothing to do but to keep straight on towards affluence, you say you will be a poor man's schoolmaster. Your fancies will be your ruin, Clym.'

As in *A Pair of Blue Eyes*, there is a dramatic scene between the plain-speaking, no-nonsense mother and the romantic, worldly son over his choice of wife. It was a topic that Hardy could not get enough of, something he needed to expiate in his work:

'You are blinded, Clym,' she said warmly. 'It was a bad day for you when you first set eyes on her. And your scheme is merely a castle in the air built on purpose to justify this folly which has seized you, and to salve your conscience on the irrational situation you are in.'

'Mother, that's not true,' he firmly answered.

'Can you maintain that I sit and tell untruths, when all I wish to do is to save you from sorrow? For shame, Clym! But it is all through that woman – a hussy!'

Clym reddened like fire and rose. He placed his hand upon his mother's shoulder and said, in a tone which hung strangely between entreaty and command, 'I won't hear it. I may be led to answer you in a way which we shall both regret.'[13]

Hardy takes the familial conflict a step further when Eustacia, now married to Clym, is confronted by her estranged mother-in-law. There is a blazing row, with each woman giving 'heat for heat', leading to complete and final estrangement between mother and daughter-in-law. Clym's moral blindness in believing Eustacia to be a pagan goddess instead of a flesh-and-blood woman who is simply not suited to him is played out in his loss of eyesight through extreme studying (an echo of the temporary vision loss that Hardy suffered during his own extreme programme of self-study). The marriage fails rapidly, with the realisation of both partners that they married for the wrong reasons, each feeling disappointed and trapped. Clym stumbles half-blind through the heath, cutting furze, singing songs in French and incurring his wife's contempt. Eustacia tells Clym that he was wrong to return to his 'native place'.

The pace gathers when Mrs Yeobright swallows her pride, and calls on her son at his lowly cottage on the heath. Because Clym is fast asleep by the hearth, he does not hear the knocking on the door. Mrs Yeobright, who glimpses Eustacia at an upstairs window, wrongly believes that the couple have turned her away: 'Shut out! She must have set him against me. Can there be beautiful bodies without hearts inside? I think so. I would not have done it against a neighbour's cat on such a fiery day as this!'[14] The echoes of *King Lear* are clear: a parent turned out onto the bleak heath.[15]

Mrs Yeobright, suffering the intense heat of a summer's day, collapses on the heath. Her suffering is recounted in heart-breaking, agonising detail. She is accompanied only by little Jonny Nunsuch, in a role akin to Lear's fool. He narrates her final moments: the trembling and shaking of her extremities, her face 'white and wet', her shortness of breath 'like a lamb when you drive him till he's nearly done for'.[16] But Hardy could not quite bring himself to allow Mrs Yeobright to die without a reconciliation with her son. Clym awakes from a dream about his mother and setting off for her home finds her on the heath. Though half-blind, he carries her in his arms to safety to a hovel where he discovers that she has been bitten by a snake. The only remedy is to apply snake oil, and an adder is duly captured and killed, but it is not enough to save her.

The revelation of Mrs Yeobright's final words that she was 'a broken-hearted woman, cast off by her son' plunges Clym into despair, guilt and madness. His 'ravings' about his mother, his fiery pupils, and his longing for death, recall Horace Moule's final hours and suicidal despair. For more than a week, he is 'out of his senses'. Over and over he berates himself for his neglect and ill treatment of the mother he loved.

> 'Why didn't she come to my house? I would have taken her in and showed her how I loved her in spite of all. But she never came; and I didn't go to her, and she died on the heath like an animal kicked out, nobody to help her till it was too late. If you could have seen her, Thomasin, as I saw her – a poor dying woman, lying in the dark upon the bare ground, moaning, nobody near, believing she was utterly deserted by all the world, it would have moved you to anguish, it would have moved a brute. And this poor woman my mother!'[17]

Clym, like Shakespeare's Edgar in *Lear*, believes that the worst is over, but he is wrong. His discovery that not only was his mother turned away from his door in the heat of the day, but also that Eustacia was in the house with her former lover, Wildeve, drives him to murderous rage. He accuses Eustacia of killing his mother, grabs her violently and threatens to kill her. The scene between husband and wife echoes Shakespeare's *Othello* with Eustacia in her white nightdress and Clym repeatedly calling her 'madam', as though she is a prostitute:

'What are you going to do?' she said in a low voice, regarding him with a proud smile. 'You will not alarm me by holding on so; but it would be a pity to tear my sleeve.'

Instead of letting go he drew her closer to him. 'Tell me the particulars of – my mother's death,' he said in a hard, panting whisper; 'or – I'll – I'll—'

'Clym,' she answered slowly, 'do you think you dare do anything to me that I dare not bear? But before you strike me listen. You will get nothing from me by a blow, even though it should kill me, as it probably will. But perhaps you do not wish me to speak – killing may be all you mean?'

'Kill you! Do you expect it?'

'I do.'

'Why?'

'No less degree of rage against me will match your previous grief for her.'

'Phew – I shall not kill you,' he said contemptuously, as if under a sudden change of purpose. 'I did think of it; but – I shall not. That would be making a martyr of you, and sending you to where she is; and I would keep you away from her till the universe come to an end, if I could.'[18]

But Clym comes to believe that he *has* killed his wife when she is drowned in the weir while trying to escape the heath and flee to Budmouth with Wildeve. Though Hardy does not specify whether or not Eustacia dies by design or accident, Clym takes responsibility for her death. He learns that she previously contemplated suicide and thought of shooting herself with her grandfather's pistols, blaming herself for the death of her mother-in-law. Clym is left with the conviction that he has 'driven two women to their deaths'.

Clym shuts himself away, until he finds a vocation as an itinerant preacher and lecturer. Though he considers himself a murderer, and longs for God to punish him with death, he cannot take his own life. He is last seen preaching on the heath to the local men and women, on 'morally unimpeachable subjects'. He lectures everywhere to the everyday man and woman, 'from the steps and porticoes of town halls, from market-crosses, from conduits, on esplanades and on wharves, from the parapets of bridges, in barns and outhouses, and all other such places in the neighbouring Wessex towns and villages'.[19] The madness/suicide theme and the itinerant lecturer teaching the working-class people: these are evocations of the memory of a beloved friend. The ghost of Horace Moule still haunted Thomas Hardy.

Queen Victoria's Jubilee, 28 June 1877, was celebrated with games and maypole dancing on the village green at Sturminster Newton. Hardy observed the 'pretty girls, just before a dance, stand in inviting positions on the grass'. He watched them whirling round the maypole and laughing with their girlfriends who stood on the side waiting for a partner.[20] Hardy would use a similar incident in *The Return of the Native*, where Eustacia goes maypole dancing and reignites her affair with Wildeve.

The Jubilee was a happy day, but there was an incident the following night. Their maidservant, Jane, had been given the day off to go to Bournemouth with her young man. She returned at ten in the evening, but seemed 'oppressed'. At half past twelve, when Jane thought that her employers were asleep, she crept downstairs and went out of the door. Hardy was awake, watching through the back bedroom window. He saw Jane and her young man coming out of the outhouse. Jane was wearing her night-gown with a shawl around her shoulders. He noted her 'slight white figure in the moonlight' and her man's 'dark and gigantic' form.[21] They came to the back door and before Hardy had a chance to consider what to do, Emma ran downstairs and ordered Jane to bed. The man disappeared.

Hardy examined the back door bolts and discovered that they had been oiled. The man had been a regular visitor at night when the Hardys had been asleep. There was a scene. Jane was quiet all day until she gave them the slip and jumped out of the dining-room window. Horrified, the couple went to Jane's father's cottage. 'Found them poorer than I expected', Hardy noted.[22] Jane's father was haymaking, but one of the children fetched him. When he arrived back, he 'read bad news' in Hardy's face. Jane had not returned home. She had eloped to the town of Stalbridge with her lover, dressed in her best clothes. Tom and Emma pursued her there, but the young man, Jamie, was haymaking, and refused to be seen. Jane did not return, and then in August, they discovered that she was pregnant.

The affair upset Hardy and his wife far more than might be expected, since it was not unusual for a servant girl to suddenly find herself with a baby on the way, out of wedlock – this was precisely what had happened to Hardy's mother. The explanation may be that they were projecting their own bitterness at being childless themselves. It would appear from a comment Hardy made at this time that Emma had a late period, but it was a false alarm: 'The sudden disappointment of a hope leaves a scar which the ultimate fulfilment of that hope never entirely removes.' To clarify this thought he wrote: 'We hear that Jane, our late servant, is soon to have a baby. Yet never a sign of one is there for us.'[23]

By March of the following year, they decided to return to London. Hardy wrote: 'End of the Sturminster Newton idyll' – he later added 'Our happiest time.'[24] He had sold the serial rights to his novel to *Belgravia Magazine* in the previous autumn. Hardy knew that he had reached great heights with *The Return*

of the Native. But its theme of the returning native who inadvertently causes the deaths of his embattled wife and mother
begs a question: what did his own wife and mother think of his
latest novel? Emma and Jemima remained silent. Nor did the
breach between them heal. In trying to explain the rift between
her and Mrs Yeobright, Eustacia explains: 'Sometimes more
bitterness is sown in five minutes than can be got rid of in a
whole life.' Hardy told one of his friends, Sydney Cockerell,
that Mrs Yeobright was based on his mother. Her anger and the
force of her intractable personality is fully revealed when Clym
marries a woman she dislikes: 'Sons must be blind if they will.
Why is it that a woman can see from a distance what a man
cannot see close? Clym must do as he will – he is nothing more
to me. And this is maternity – to give one's best years and best
love to ensure the fate of being despised!'[25]

Hardy had also let loose many of the strange superstitions of
his childhood. Before Eustacia's drowning, a local woman, Susan
Nunsuch, moulds a wax voodoo doll in her image. She gives it
a red ribbon and black sandals, and sticks pins into its head, its
body, even its feet. Susan believes that Eustacia is a sorceress
who has cast a 'malign spell' on her young son, who is now
running a high fever. Only Eustacia's death will free her child,
so Susan busies herself with this 'ghastly invention of superstition,
calculated to bring powerlessness, atrophy, and annihilation on
any human being against whom it was directed. It was a practice well known on Egdon at that date, and one that is not quite
extinct at the present day.'[26] The novel was a return to the
folklore and the superstitions which had filled his Dorset childhood.

Eustacia prophesies that Clym's return to his native home will
have bad consequences. Like Hardy, Clym is displaced and feels
that he does not fit in with either his own people or the Parisians
among whom he has moved. Yet he is inexorably drawn back

to the heath of his boyhood. Eustacia despises the heath, but for Clym it is a magical place, full of amber butterflies, emerald-green grasshoppers, blue and yellow snakes, purple bells and golden furze. He cut his teeth on the nursery of the heath. His 'toys' were 'the flint knives and arrow-heads' which he found there: 'He was permeated with its scenes, with its substance, and with its odours. He might be said to be its product.'[27]

So it was a matter of great curiosity that Hardy was turning his back on his home and the heath and returning to the bright lights of London. He believed that London was bad for his health, mental and physical, and so it would prove to be. But he felt that 'the practical side of his vocation of novelist demanded that he should have his head-quarters in or near London'.[28] Furthermore, Emma was fond of city life, and perhaps Hardy thought it prudent to keep his wife and his mother at a safe distance from each other.

There might also have been another reason for Hardy to take his wife back to resume their London life. In *The Return of the Native* he had come closer than ever before to exploring the impact of Horace Moule's depression, mania and suicide. His witnessing of this trauma fed into his imagining of Eustacia's black moods and suicidal thoughts, and then Clym's week of madness and ravings, his eyes 'lit by a hot light, as if the fire in their pupils were burning up their substance'.[29] Years of witnessing Horace Moule's mood swings, his binge-drinking, his deep depressions, had made Hardy sensitive to mental illness. Now, to add to this, he thought he was beginning to see signs of strangeness in his wife.

Another in the group of poems about the supposedly idyllic residence at Sturminster is called 'The Musical Box'. It begins with the 'fair colour of the time' seeming to be 'lifelong'. The poet walks by Sturminster Mill, 'where broad / stream-lilies throng'. His love is waiting for him wearing a white muslin dress and listening to the tinkling of a music box. He suspects that there is a spirit in the music box. It tells him to make the most of his happiness because it will not last, but 'I did not hear, / I did not see.'[30] Something is not right, but he can't yet put his finger on it.

On arriving in London, the Hardys took a three-year lease on a terraced house in Tooting, close to Wandsworth Common. In dramatic fashion, Hardy claimed 'it was in this house that their troubles began'.[31] It was a cold and damp house at the end of the row, with a tiny garden and a north-east aspect. They were to endure some harsh winters, when the rain and snow would pour in through the badly-hung front door.

Nevertheless, it was an exciting time filled with friends old and new. There were art galleries to visit and the London theatre, where Hardy saw Henry Irving in *Richard III*. He and his friends (Emma was not present) went to Irving's dressing room after the performance and 'found him naked to the waist: – champagne in tumblers'.[32] On June 18th, Hardy was elected to the elite Savile Club. Many of the gatherings were men only, so it is of little surprise that Emma felt left out. Old Mrs Procter, now widowed, whom Hardy admired greatly, wrote to him to congratulate him on *The Return of the Native*, which was published in November: 'Poor Eustacia. I so fully understand her longing for the Beautiful.' She also wrote drily of 'stupid' Thomasin and her happiness with Diggory Venn: 'Beauty fades, and intelligence and wit grow irritating; but your dear Dulness is always the same.'[33] Mrs Procter understood. She also understood and was kind to Emma. She liked her, which Hardy reported was unusual as Mrs Procter had a reputation for not liking women.[34] But the wedge between husband and wife was thickening.

On the last day of 1878, Hardy's father wrote to him to say that Jemima was unwell and that they should come and visit.

Shortly afterwards, an 'incident' took place at Tooting, where the couple seemed to believe 'there had passed away a glory from the earth'.[35] Hardy, without explaining the incident, directed his readers to the poem 'A January Night (1879)', in which the death of an unknown neighbour stands in for his foreboding of some catastrophe closer to home:

> The rain smites more and more,
> The east wind snarls and sneezes;
> Through the joints of the quivering door
>   The water wheezes.
>
> The tip of each ivy-shoot
> Writhes on its neighbour's face;
> There is some hid dread afoot
>   That we cannot trace.
>
> Is it the spirit astray
> Of the man at the house below
> Whose coffin they took in to-day?
>   We do not know.[36]

CHAPTER 50

Paula Power

Hardy duly returned to Dorset alone to visit his sick mother. His father told his usual tales of whipping and public hangings, telling his son that in his day executions took place at about one o'clock, as the custom was to wait until the mail coach came with news of whether or not there was a reprieve.

This time it was Jemima's health that had a reprieve. She made a good recovery and Hardy returned to the city. But something had undoubtedly changed. He found himself attracted to an actress called Helen Mathews. He wrote in his notebook a description of her face: 'A profile not too Greek for an English fireside, yet Greek enough for an artist's eye: arch, saucy kind of countenance, dark eyes, brows & hair, the last low on the forehead.'[1] His eye was starting to rove; there were chance encounters with beautiful, random women. A train journey to Tooting saw him entranced by a 'statuesque girl' with perfect features, her face 'not unlike that of a nymph'.[2] During this time, Hardy dashed off his one and only historical novel, *The Trumpet-Major*, set in Weymouth during the Napoleonic Wars. The novel was a success, but Hardy's health was beginning to fail. He turned his attention to what was to be his most autobiographical book. It was called *A Laodicean*.

Emma was to play a large part in getting it written, making possible a lucrative serialisation in America in *Harper's New Monthly Magazine*.

Even though Hardy had expressed concern for Emma's mental fragility, it was in fact he who was suffering from morbid fears and anxiety. One night in May, he was beset with 'eerie feeling' – he was haunted by the image of a 'monster whose body had four million heads and eight million eyes'.[3] When the Hardys went to France for a summer holiday, he insisted on swimming in the sea off Normandy, and staying in too long. He blamed 'these frequent immersion' for starting a long illness which would last until the following winter. His feelings of paranoia increased in Le Havre, where he 'fancied that the landlord's look was sinister'. Their room was painted 'a bloody red' and their curtains were made of heavy dark velvet. When the chambermaid came in, she 'sighed continually' and 'spoke in a foreboding voice'.[4] Terrified, Hardy and Emma suspected they were to be robbed of their cash. They discovered a secret door behind the bed, leading to a passageway and then an outer door, so they barricaded themselves in with their luggage. They kept an oil lamp burning, but soon fell asleep. In the morning 'nothing had happened' and they awoke to bright sunshine. But then in Honfleur, the figure of Christ on a wayside Calvary 'seemed to writhe and cry in the twilight'.

Back home, he felt no better. The Hardys made a visit to Cambridge, the place where he had seen Horace Moule for the last time before his suicide. At a service in King's Chapel, the sputtering and guttering of the wax candles formed 'the most fantastic shapes I ever saw – and while the wicks burnt down these weird shapes changed form'. Inevitably, these wax shrouds reminded him of his final moments with Moule. Hardy's health continued to decline: 'After the first day or two he felt an indescribable physical weariness, which was really the beginning of the long illness he was to endure.'⁵ The doctor was called and diagnosed internal bleeding. Emma sent for a more skilful doctor, who sent Hardy to bed, diagnosed inflammation of the bladder – a condition that recurred for the rest of his life. An operation was mooted, but yet another doctor, a famous surgeon, decided against the operation in favour of continued bed rest.

Convinced that he was going to die, Hardy freely mined his own life for the serialisation contracted by *Harper*. Emma proved herself to be as resourceful, compassionate and supportive as ever. She willingly took on the role of amanuensis. Too exhausted to lift a pen, Hardy dictated the novel from his sickbed. As he acknowledged, she 'worked bravely both at writing and nursing'.⁶ She was indefatigable. Hardy's new heroine was a woman called Paula Power.

———

George Somerset is an architect in church restoration, who is employed by Paula Power to restore the medieval castle she has inherited. It once belonged to the ancient De Stancy family, but was bought by her industrialist father when the De Stancys fell on hard times. Paula is kind, intelligent and resourceful. Unlike Eustacia Vye, who is a pagan queen, Paula is a 'modern' heroine; even her looks are 'ultra-modern'. She has erected a makeshift gymnasium in her grounds so she can exercise in her 'boy's costume' and has also installed an electric telegraph line in the castle so that she can receive the latest news from London. Somerset, who has a 'heart susceptible to beauty of all kinds, – in women, in art, and in animate nature', falls in love with Paula, despite the fact that she represents the new era. Somerset not only dislikes the modern world, he 'felt a violent reaction' towards modernism, eclecticism, new aristocracies, everything, in short, that Paula represented:

'You represent science rather than art, perhaps.'

'How?' [Paula] asked, glancing up under her hat.

'I mean,' replied Somerset, 'that you represent the march of mind – the steamship, and the railway, and the thoughts that shake mankind.'[7]

In fact, though Paula is nicknamed 'Miss Steam-Power', she thinks of herself as 'romantic and historical' and is in love with the ancient Greeks. Her plan is to build a Greek colonnade and establish a pottery on Hellenic principles. Her love of physical exercise (athletics) is based on Greek principles, as is her belief in female education:

'As you may have heard, she holds advanced views on social and other matters; and in those on the higher education of women she is very strong, talking a good deal about the physical training of the Greeks, whom she adores, or did. Every philosopher and man of science who ventilates his theories in the monthly reviews has a devout listener in her; and this subject of the physical development of her sex has had its turn with other things in her mind. . . .'[8]

Her gymnasium is 'in imitation of those at the new colleges for women' (Tryphena's London training college had such a building for physical exercise), and it is there that a plan is hatched to force a meeting between the heroine and the handsome Captain De Stancy, whose family once owned the castle. In a strange, voyeuristic scene, the captain peeps through a hole in the wooden structure to observe Paula exercising, 'the white manilla ropes clung about the performer like snakes':

Paula, in a pink flannel costume, was bending, wheeling and undulating in the air like a gold-fish in its globe, sometimes ascending by her arms nearly to the lantern, then lowering

herself till she swung level with the floor. Her aunt Mrs
Goodman, and Charlotte De Stancy, were sitting on camp-stools
at one end, watching her gyrations, Paula occasionally addressing
them with such an expression as – 'Now, Aunt, look at me –
and you, Charlotte – is not that shocking to your weak nerves,'
when some adroit feat would be repeated, which, however,
seemed to give much more pleasure to Paula herself in
performing it than to Mrs. Goodman in looking on, the latter
sometimes saying, 'O, it is terrific – do not run such a risk
again!'[9]

Captain De Stancy falls in love with Paula, becoming a rival
suitor to George Somerset. Following a convoluted plot in
which falsified telegraphs and faked photographs are used to
discredit the architect, Paula and Somerset are united. But the
castle is burned to the ground by Captain De Stancy's illegitimate son, who orchestrated the plot against the architect. The
married couple vow to build a new home from the ashes of
the castle, and 'show the modern spirit forevermore'.[10] But Paula
ends the novel wishing that Somerset was a De Stancy, and
that the castle had not burned to the ground. She is forever
torn between the pull of modernity and the claims of romantic
medievalism.

The novel lacks the emotional and psychological power of *The
Return of the Native*. The plot is unconvincing and awkward; at
one point Paula, learning of the conspiracy against Somerset,
chases him to France. Of course, Hardy was writing for serialisation and so the twisty plot was crucial. But he was ahead of
his time in showing how modern inventions such as photography
and the telegraph can be distorted, manipulated and misused.
The architect is photographed to give the false impression that
he is in a drunken state; the telegraph is discovered to be an
unreliable force when Paula wrongly believes that Somerset is

sending incriminating telegrams. Many Victorians believed that food (and even people) could be sent by telegram. Somerset, like Hardy, has an ambivalent view about this new-fangled form of communication: 'Such short messages were in themselves poor substitutes for letters, but their speed and easy frequency were good qualities which the letters did not possess.'[11] Nevertheless, not only can telegraphs be faked, they can also be delayed. They are not infallible and can fall into the wrong hands.

Likewise, characters in the novel often misread one another and engage in performative exhibitions where their true motives are concealed or revealed. In a private theatrical performance of *Love's Labour's Lost* the audience are confused as to whether Paula and Captain De Stancy are playing their parts or expressing their real emotions towards one another (was Hardy alluding to the courtship of Lady Susan and the actor William O'Brien conducted through private theatricals?). When Paula 'performs' her gyrations in the gymnasium in her pink costume, she is aware that she is giving a show of her athleticism to her aunt and to Charlotte, even though she does not know that Captain De Stancy is peeping at her through the concealed hole. He observes the two women who are also observing the heroine.

Hardy gave *A Laodicean* the subtitle 'A Story of Today'. Paula is a thoroughly modern heroine. Her refusal to be baptised in the local church – like the Laodiceans of the Bible, she is luke-warm in her faith – suggests her spirit and independence. She believes not only in the importance of education for women, but also in physical exercise. There is more than a hint of a Sapphic relationship between Paula and her best friend, Charlotte (a recapitulation of the risqué element of *Desperate Remedies*). Her admiration for all things Greek may have influenced Paula more than she knows. Her relationship with Charlotte is more like that of 'lovers than maid and maid'. Paula's love of modern technology is ultimately a destructive force, and leads to the destruction of a beautiful medieval castle, which can never be replaced. Hardy himself is torn (Laodicean-like) between the wonders of modern technology and the glories of the past.

CHAPTER 51

Lady Constantine

January of 1881, as Hardy lay on his sickbed, was unbearably cold. There was driving snow, so 'fine and fast' that the individual snowflakes could not be seen.[1] The snow crept into their Tooting home, covering Emma's house plants that withered on the windowsills. The downstairs indoor passage was 'sole-deep' showing the imprint of Emma's shoes as she went to and fro nursing her husband and trying to keep warm. Hardy heard the news that George Eliot had died. He was often irritated by the fact that several critics had mistaken him for Eliot, but now her death stirred thoughts of realism in fiction: 'Style: Consider the Wordsworthian dictum (the more perfectly the natural object is reproduced, the more truly poetic the picture). This reproduction is achieved by seeing into the *heart of a thing* (as rain, wind for instance) and is realism.'[2]

He noticed that being bed-ridden for so long had left his feet as white and 'shapely as a Greek statue'. He observed other changes: 'keys get rusty; watch dim, boots mildewed; hat and clothes old-fashioned; umbrella eaten out with rust.' There was an added poignant note: 'children seen through the window, are grown taller'.[3] His pain was so acute (perhaps kidney stones) that he remained convinced that he was going to die. His poem

'A Wasted Illness' suggests the extent of his physical suffering: 'Through vaults of pain, / Enribbed and wrought with groins of ghastliness, / I passed, and garish spectres moved my brain / To dire distress.' Later in the poem, 'I saw a door extend – / The door to Death.' The word 'groins', a combination of groans and groin, is masterful.[4]

For the time being, relations between Emma and the Hardy sisters remained warm. Mary and Kate were deeply grateful for Emma's ministries to their sick brother, on whom the whole family so depended. At the end of January, Mary wrote to Emma: 'I was very glad to hear from you but the iron has again entered into my Soul regarding Toms [sic] illness.' Iron in the soul was a metaphor often used by the Hardy women. Mary's letter shows the extent of the family's suffering during that freezing winter, when they feared for their brother's life. 'Our enemies, *winter and rough weather*', she wrote, were responsible for lack of food for the Bockhampton folk. Jemima, Thomas and Henry were forced to live 'wholly on potatoes'. The baker was unable to get to the village. Mary told Emma not to worry, as 'Henry is young and strong and they killed a pig quite recently.'[5] The snow was so deep and heavy, Mary said, that it recalled Granny Hardy's tale of walking to church on the top of snow-buried hedges.

Mary's letter makes painful reading, alluding to the miseries of the Hardy sisters in the lives chosen for them by their mother. Kate had entered the Salisbury Training College a few years before in 1877. Like Mary, she was subjected to strict discipline and hardships. Rules were most strictly enforced in the dormitory, where the girls rose at six for prayers, opened the windows, whatever the weather, and were not allowed to enter any other dorm without permission. Food hampers from home were prohibited. The young women often went cold and hungry. Reading novels was strictly forbidden, only books of devotion were permitted. Kate, who loved beautiful clothes, resented the plain, dowdy uniforms they were forced to wear. Like her sister, she wore the absurd white cap that made the young women look like housemaids. Parasols were forbidden in favour of the serviceable umbrella. The only compensations were musical evenings or the occasional outing, such as a picnic at Stonehenge.

Even though she had won a Queen's Scholarship, Kate was academically weaker than her sister, and her reports, including her performance in the practice school, were marked either 'fair' or 'pretty fair'. She was, however, musical, like her brother, and achieved 'very fair' in her report on that subject.[6] Kate was unfortunate, also, that Mary's beloved superintendent, Mrs Duncan, had retired, and new laws had come into place that exacerbated the hardships for the students. One of the main changes was to the college funding, which was now 'Payment by Results', decreasing the college income and leading to extra household duties for the students. By nature more outgoing and livelier than her sister, Kate suffered badly at college. She resented the stern discipline, the onerous duties, and the dreadful food. One of the people she came to rely upon was her sister-in-law. Emma's encouraging letters, with their news of beloved brother Tom, offered a lifeline.

After leaving college, Kate was appointed schoolmistress at a village school in Sandford Orcas, near Sherborne. The school had 85 students, and Kate's salary was £55 per year. In the log book she wrote: 'I took charge of this school on Monday. Found some of the children in a very backward state. The attendance for the week was small considering the number of children on the register.'[7]

During the winter of 1881, the sisters' respective schools were closed down because of the snow and the cold. Mary told Emma that her younger sister suffered badly: 'Poor Katie was reduced, a few days ago, to a few onion jams and potatoes – a little coal and no candle.' In their loneliness, they longed for the prospect of a visit to London: 'I should very much like to come and see you again. All this dull weather Katie has been quite lonely & so have I. I wish we could have been with you – if you would have liked us.'[8]

Despite the pleas of the Hardy sisters, no invitation was forthcoming. Hardy was in no state to receive visitors, and Emma had her hands full. But she did extend an invitation to Hardy's first cousin, Mary Hand: to come and live with them as a domestic servant. Mary Hand's father William (Jemima's oldest brother) had recently died. What Hardy felt about having his first cousin in the role of his maidservant cannot be known, but Mary Hand wrote Emma a grateful letter: 'I feel I owe you a great deal for your kind consideration when my poor Father died.'[9] As soon as Hardy recovered, a move out of London was deemed necessary, and the couple began to look for a house to rent in Dorset, no doubt to be nearer to his family. Towards the end of June 1881, they moved into a house called Lanherne, in Wimborne in east Dorset. Hardy wrote to another cousin, John Antell, telling him that they had returned to the country because he needed clear air.

In many respects he was right. Dorset *was* necessary for his health, mentally and physically. From this point on, Dorset would become his permanent home. And it would become Emma's, whether or not she wished it to be.

————

That May, the Australian astronomer John Tebbut was scanning the western sky, when he spotted a hazy object just below the constellation 'Columbia'. He rushed to get his telescope, which confirmed the head of a comet, and he contacted the Government Observatories. By late June, the Great Comet with its bright tail was visible in the night sky of the northern hemisphere. On their first night in the Wimborne House, Hardy and Emma watched it from the conservatory. It gave him an idea for his next novel, which was to be serialised in the *Atlantic Monthly*.

The next morning they discovered that the garden was full of old-fashioned flowers in full bloom: white and blue Canterbury Bells, Sweet Williams. And there was an abundance of fruit: 'strawberries and cherries that are ripe, currants and gooseberries that are almost ripe, peaches that are green, and apples that are deliciously immature'.[10] It was the perfect place to recuperate. Soon after their arrival, Kate came to visit and they hired a wagonette to visit Badbury Rings, a large Iron Age fort. For all her loneliness, she was making the best of her new life in the classroom. A monitor had been appointed to assist her with her duties and a recent visit from Her Majesty's Inspectors (always a frightening experience for Kate and Mary) suggested that she was making very satisfactory progress.

Kate had written to Emma that spring, describing the lovely weather. During recess, she gazed from the window at the children 'like cats sitting in the sun watching birds and pretending to be asleep'. She had been greatly looking forward to her visit to Wimborne: 'I shall eat such a lot', she wrote, 'and talk a great deal so I should be rather troublesome.' She begged them to 'make a fuss about my coming. I hope you've got some cake.'[11]

On the journey to Badbury Rings, the group passed Charborough House, with its extensive parkland and its famous folly, Charborough Tower, located on a hill south-east of the great house. The tower would be at the centre of the novel Hardy had been mulling over since his observation of the comet. It is shown in the book's frontispiece.

Some years before, he had contemplated a novel in which a tower is the meeting place for an erotic liaison. In his notebook, he wrote a possible plot line: 'The honest Earl is accidentally shut up in a tower – the Hardy monument, say – with a blacksmith's daughter. Goes to parson next day & says he feels it his duty to marry her. Does so. Finds her not so good as she seemed.'[12] Now he revived the idea, though reversing the genders; the aristocrat would be a woman and she would fall in love with a poor man. The old theme of 'the poor man and his lady' was rarely far from his thoughts.

On the ride to Badbury Rings, the driver regaled Hardy with stories about the two big houses, Kingston Lacy and Charborough House. He told him the scandalous story of the heiress of Charborough, who married a much younger man; 'not in her first bloom', she was 'won over' by the handsome young lieutenant. Hardy scribbled down the details in his notebook, and added the astronomy theme. In November, he applied to the Astronomer Royal at Greenwich to ask permission to view the observatory. He was asked if the visit was connected to scientific research, and Hardy drew up a 'scientific letter', the gist of which was to ask whether it would be possible for him to adapt an old tower, built in a plantation in the West of England. In his preface to the Wessex edition of *Two on a Tower*, he explained his theme: 'This slightly-built romance was the outcome of a wish to set the emotional history of two infinitesimal lives against the stupendous background of the stellar universe, and to impart to readers the sentiment that of these contrasting magnitudes the smaller might be the greater to them as men.'

From the outset, the tower is described with strong phallic overtones. Its column rises above the treetops from a bush of pine-trees, 'unimpeded, clean, and flushed with the sunlight'.[13] The heroine is a married woman, Lady Constantine, whose impotent husband, Sir Blount, unable to produce an heir, has escaped to hunt lions in Africa, leaving her alone and unprotected, and expecting that she will live like a 'cloistered nun'. She decides to enter the tower, requesting that her driver should set her down on the path so that she can have a 'close inspection':

'The column now showed itself as a much more important erection than it had appeared from the road.' Suffering from 'an almost killing *ennui*', she finds herself 'falling into confidential intercourse' with the young man. When she first sees the astronomer in her tower observing the night sky, she asks him: 'Have you entirely taken possession of this column?' He replies 'Entirely.' Swithin's oversized telescope becomes a symbol of their desire. Lady Constantine, attracted to the boy's beauty, his fair hair and 'early-Christian face' is drawn irresistibly to the tower.[14]

> 'You said you would show me the heavens if I could come on a starlight night. I have come.'
>
> Swithin, as a preliminary, swept round the telescope to Jupiter, and exhibited to her the glory of that orb. Then he directed the instrument to the less bright shape of Saturn.[15]

Later, he accidentally smashes the new eight-inch lens that he has bought for his telescope. Lady Constantine takes it upon herself to buy him another more 'powerful instrument'. But Swithin is still not satisfied and requests an even larger instrument to be affixed to the masonry of the tower. She agrees, but the boy is worried about her husband's reaction: 'what would Sir Blount say, if he came home and saw the goings on?' At which, 'Lady Constantine turned aside to hide a sudden displacement of blood from her cheek. "Ah – my husband!" she whispered.'[16]

Lady Constantine is aware that the beautiful youth has aroused her sensual desires: 'that which is called the Eve in us will out sometimes'.[17] Unable to resist Swithin, she marries him in secret, but she later learns that her marriage is invalid. They separate, and he travels abroad. After he has gone, she learns that she is pregnant. To save her reputation she marries the Bishop of Melchester and passes off her baby son as the bishop's own. The bishop dies, and Swithin returns to find her in the tower, but time has wreaked its revenge. She is old, and no longer beautiful. Though Lady Constantine wants to be a liberated woman, she is confined by the stultifying morals of Victorian society. There is no happy ending for the lady and her young lover.

The novel was poorly received. Hardy professed to be shocked when the critics accused him of being 'improper' and immoral. But what did he expect when he chose for his theme a love affair between a young man and a much older woman who finds herself pregnant by him and traps an unsuspecting bishop into marriage to save her reputation? Critics felt that he was not only attacking the morals of the day, but also the established church.

The harrowing scene in the tower, where Swithin is confronted with a middle-aged matron whose bloom has faded is suggestive of Hardy's shock at his visit to Julia Martin. And in his preface, he confirmed that the tower was based on *two* follies in the west of England: not only Charborough Tower, but also Clavell, the site of his liaison with Eliza Nicholls. Without realising that he was doing so, Hardy was giving false hope to Eliza. She read the novel, and believed that she still held a place in his affections. Though she knew that he had married, she kept tabs on him and held out the hope that they would one day be reunited.

CHAPTER 52

Elizabeth-Jane Henchard

After Kate left Wimborne, she wrote an affectionate letter to Emma and Tom beginning 'My dearest dears'. She had almost missed her train connection, but had managed to get home safely. In September, Emma sent her a warm cloak as a birthday present. Kate seemed much more cheerful. She was planning to leave her position in Sandford Orcas and return to Dorchester to join her sister at the Bell Street School, where Mary was headmistress. In 1881, Mary had written a sad letter to Emma about her poor social life, complaining that people only showed interest in her as the sister of a famous local author: 'But what can I do? Nobody asks me to dinner or treats me like a lady.' Mary was discovering that her position of headmistress conferred respectability, but not status. Meanwhile, she and Kate watched on from the sidelines as Tom took Emma on a tour of Scotland, Windermere and Chester. There was more travel when they went to Liverpool to see a dramatisation of *Far from the Madding Crowd*, though Hardy was disappointed with Marion Terry, the actress who played Bathsheba – she was a far less accomplished performer than her sister Ellen.

In the autumn of 1882, Tom took Emma to Paris for a holiday.

They rented an apartment on the Left Bank to keep away from the English and American tourists, and wandered the city, visited Versailles, and studied the paintings at the Louvre. They enjoyed 'practising housekeeping in the Parisian bourgeois manner', buying their own groceries and dining at local restaurants.[1] The excursions to Scotland and Paris may well have been a sop for Emma, as Hardy had concocted a plan. He had discussed with his family (without Emma present) his intention to design and build a house in Dorset. For some time, he had been looking for a plot of land. Early in 1882, he wrote to the Earl of Ilchester's agent about the possibility of a site on Stinsford Hill, close to his family home.

In the meantime, they left Wimborne and rented a house in the centre of Dorchester. By October, Hardy negotiated with the Duchy of Cornwall for a plot of land in Fordington Field, near the Wareham road, beside an old toll gate. Hardy designed and paid for the house, and his brother Henry would be the builder. Hardy seems to have calmed Emma's fears of being close to his family by promising that they would spend 'several months of each spring and summer' in London, regarding the new house as their 'country quarters'.[2]

The sights and scenes of Dorchester would inspire his next novel. Hardy, always sensitive to criticism, had been cast down by the lukewarm reviews of *Two on a Tower*. However, a long (anonymous) review essay of all of his novels appeared in the *Westminster Review*. This was a turning point. The review began by describing Hardy as the 'head of the English novelists'. The reviewer sensibly noted that the reason that he was often mistaken for George Eliot was due to the feminine style and features of the writing. He argued that the best writing in English fiction was by women such as Jane Austen, George Eliot and Charlotte Brontë, because of the way they used the 'art of psychology' in their writings (for this reason, he perceived Dickens and

Thackeray as failures). Hardy's greatness, the reviewer argued, is revealed in his gallery of women, the 'Undines of the earth' who have 'no like anywhere'. Hardy's women, he explains, are 'young, healthy creatures, instinct-led'. They fight against circumstances that are stacked against them. They are never 'very bad' women, but have an 'instinctive purity' and 'instinctive self-respect'. It was a review essay of great insight and depth which went to the heart of Hardy's art, concluding that his women, or rather his way of *regarding* women, was incredibly difficult to define because it was 'new'.[3]

This was exactly what Hardy needed to hear. He discovered that the writer was the notorious 'sexual expert' Havelock Ellis, and he wrote him a warm letter of thanks. He told Ellis that he thought his paper 'remarkable' and 'appreciative'. The reviewer had truly understood what he was trying to achieve with his fictional women. Novelists, Hardy wrote, lack the capacity to stand outside their work – they are always inside them like the 'man inside the hobby-horse at a Christmas Masque'.[4] Ellis had described *The Return of the Native* as 'the life-history of a woman in all its revelations'.

Somewhat paradoxically, given this praise of his women, Hardy would try a different tactic for his new novel: it would take for its theme the rise and fall of 'a man of character' – a magnificent, dark, damaged figure. The setting of the novel germinating in his head was Dorchester, renamed as Casterbridge, where he and Emma were now living. Proximity to the place where he had gone to school, trained as an architect and fallen in love several times, fired his imagination. As a young man he had attended Horace Moule's lectures to the working men's club in the town hall. He had heard his mesmerising uncle John Antell's stories of a Dorchester apprenticeship, tales rendered fiercer and exhilarating by his uncle's propensity for hard liquor. He had imagined the young woman farmer, Bathsheba Everdene, selling her goods in the corn exchange in *Far from the Madding Crowd.*

The corn exchange in Hardy's fictional Casterbridge, like Dorchester, sat in the centre of the Roman square at the junction of High East Street, South Street, High West Street and North Square. It would provide the background for the tragedy of Michael Henchard. In his preface, Hardy asked his readers to 'bear in mind that, in the days recalled by the tale, the home Corn Trade, on which so much of the action turns, had an importance that can hardly be realised by those accustomed to the sixpenny loaf of the present date'. The full title of the new novel was *The Life and Death of the Mayor of Casterbridge: A Story of a Man of Character.*

The Hardys' rented home was Shire-Hall Place, the old headmaster's house of the Dorset County School, close to the courthouse and County Hall. Dark and narrow, it looked out into Gaol Lane, and Hardy described it as 'a most queer, rambling old house, such as would rejoice your heart, built on ever so many levels at ever so many periods'. Hardy had befriended the writer Edmund Gosse, who was one of the first visitors to Shire-Hall Place. Gosse was not impressed by Emma, whom he described as middle-aged, garrulous and not handsome – though he added that 'She means to be very kind'.[5]

In 1884, a year after his arrival, Hardy was appointed a justice of the peace for the Borough of Dorchester, taking his seat in early September. He sat in court on almost forty occasions from then until 1912, playing the part, in his own words, of 'Justice Silence'. In an interview with *The World* two years after his appointment he spoke of the 'sterner facts of existence' that are 'apt to be lost in the dream-world of books'.[6] The experience would give him inspiration for the novel that was fermenting in his brain: Henchard would also be a magistrate. In addition, Hardy began working his way through the files of the local newspaper, *The Dorset County Chronicle*, taking down notes of notable incidents and ideas. One of these concerned a Somerset man who had sold his wife. Hard as it is to comprehend now, wife sales were by no means unusual in poor communities: men paraded their wives around the auction room with a halter around their neck, arms or waist. Such sales were seen as a practical means of ending an unsatisfactory marriage when divorce was impossible for all but the wealthiest people. The practice continued into the early twentieth century.

Most novels end with marriage and a happy resolution, but Hardy begins his with the shocking scene of a man who sells his wife and daughter in a fit of drunken temper. Henchard, his wife and small daughter take refreshments at a country fair. Henchard requests that his 'furmity' (a kind of porridge made of grain) be laced with strong liquor. By the fourth bowl, his mood has changed from jovial to 'quarrelsome', and what starts out as a joke becomes a reality. Henchard reasons to the crowd in the tent who have gathered to watch that if a horse can be sold off, why not a wife? Henchard's wife Susan, also tired of her bad bargain in the marriage stakes, begins to warm to the idea:

> 'Will anybody buy her?' said the man.
>
> 'I wish somebody would,' said she firmly. 'Her present owner is not at all to her liking!'

Yet it's a shock to both when an offer is made, and Susan and her small daughter are sold to a sailor for five guineas. She goes willingly, and her last act is to take off her wedding ring, which she throws at Henchard, and says her final words:

> 'Mike,' she said, 'I've lived with thee a couple of years, and had nothing but temper! Now I'm no more to 'ee; I'll try my luck elsewhere. 'Twill be better for me and Elizabeth-Jane, both. So good-bye!'[7]

The following morning, sober, and horrified by his actions, Henchard makes a vow never to touch alcohol for twenty-one years. Despite all his efforts, his wife and daughter cannot be found, and so begins Henchard's rise to success and wealth. Eighteen years later, the widowed Susan and her daughter, Elizabeth-Jane, return to Wessex to find Henchard, and discover his reincarnation as the Mayor of Casterbridge. And this is where the story truly begins.

Michael Henchard is a colossus of a man. His own worst enemy, he is by turns taciturn, overbearing, honest, straight-talking, and eager to make amends for his fatal mistake. He is a king amongst men. The word 'powerful' is often used to describe him. His hulking physical presence towers over the narrative as much as the terrible secret that governs his life. When Susan first sees him, in the role of Mayor, she is amazed by the transformation:

> Facing the window, in the chair of dignity, sat a man about forty years of age; of heavy frame, large features, and commanding voice; his general build being rather coarse than compact. He had a rich complexion, which verged on swarthiness, a flashing black eye, and dark, bushy brows and hair.[8]

Henchard roars like a bull one moment and is gentle as a dove the next. His weakness, and the chink in his armour, is his affection for the young Scottish man of science, Farfrae, who is new man in opposition to Henchard's old ways, David to his King Saul. Like David, Farfrae woos Henchard through singing, but, when he rises to become more popular than Henchard, he is cast out. As Henchard declines, and loses everything he cares about, Farfrae rises to inexorable heights. Hardy makes the comparison clear in the scene where Henchard begins to drink again and requests the musicians to sing David's 109th Psalm:

> "Od seize your sauce – I tell ye to sing the Hundred-and-Ninth to Wiltshire, and sing it you shall!' roared Henchard. 'Not a single one of all the droning crew of ye goes out of this room till that Psalm is sung!' He slipped off the table, seized the poker, and going to the door placed his back against it. 'Now then, go ahead, if you don't wish to have your cust pates broke!'

As with King Saul, the music calms him and brings him to tears:

> 'Thank ye, thank ye,' said Henchard in a softened voice, his eyes growing downcast, and his manner that of a man much moved by the strains. 'Don't you blame David,' he went on in low tones, shaking his head without raising his eyes. 'He knew what he was about when he wrote that! . . . If I could afford it, be hanged if I wouldn't keep a church choir at my own expense to play and sing to me at these low, dark times of my life. But the bitter thing is, that when I was rich I didn't need what I could have, and now I be poor I can't have what I need!'⁹

What Henchard comes to realise, too late, is his paternal love for Elizabeth-Jane. One of the most interesting of Hardy's heroines, she is the polar opposite of his former 'Undines of the earth'. Hardy knew that no character could come close to Henchard for sheer force of personality. He does not even try to create one. Instead, he fashioned a heroine who is the epitome of self-sacrifice, denial, humility and resignation. Such is Elizabeth-Jane's lack of self-esteem that she barely flickers when her sweetheart (Farfrae) rejects her for another woman. Henchard is angered by his daughter's passivity and self-effacement, but comes to love her for her own sake. She is Cordelia to his Lear, and his lonely death on the heath (with only his fool, Abel Whittle, for company) completes the Shakespearean theme.

———

Elizabeth-Jane is like no other Hardy heroine. She is a timid 'field mouse' who suffers from thwarted promise. Hardy tells us that 'light-heartedness' does not come easy to her. Blighted by her early circumstances, she is anxious to improve herself by a programme of self-education, 'mastering facts with painful laboriousness'. She is the picture of 'patient fortitude'. She is also 'broken in spirit'. But Hardy himself is confused by his own Henchard-like irritation at her self-imprisonment: 'Her craving for correctness of procedure was, indeed, almost vicious.' Not daring to believe that she is loveable, he writes of his heroine: 'Thus she lived on, a dumb, deep-feeling, great-eyed creature, construed by not a single contiguous being.'[10]

Worse is the state of her heart, which he describes as 'sober and repressed'. When she dares to dream of love, she reprimands herself: 'No, no Elizabeth-Jane, such dreams are not for you.' And when she learns that she has lost her sweetheart, she is to be seen 'corking up the turmoil of her feeling with grand control'.[11] At times, though, Hardy presents her morbidity and her repression as positive attributes:

Perhaps, too, her grey, thoughtful eyes revealed an arch gaiety sometimes; but this was infrequent; the sort of wisdom which looked from their pupils did not readily keep company with these lighter moods. Like all people who have known rough times, light-heartedness seemed to her too irrational and inconsequent to be indulged in except as a reckless dram now and then; for she had been too early habituated to anxious reasoning

to drop the habit suddenly. She felt none of those ups and downs
of spirit which beset so many people without cause; never – to
paraphrase a recent poet – never a gloom in Elizabeth-Jane's soul
but she well knew how it came there.[12]

Even when Elizabeth-Jane gets her happy ending, she is hardly
elated. She learns the 'secret' of 'making limited opportunities
endurable'.[13]

Was Hardy tactless in naming his heroine after the two
Nicholls women; the one he fell in love with (Elizabeth) before
transferring his affections to her younger, prettier sister (Jane)?
One of the great themes of *The Mayor of Casterbridge* is the
dilemma between honouring your first love and the arbitrary
switching to another. Henchard is in love with Lucetta, but
he is duty-bound to make amends for his terrible crime to
Susan, and so he rejects Lucetta. Farfrae courts Elizabeth-Jane,
but rejects her when he meets Lucetta. When Lucetta asks
Elizabeth-Jane for advice about whether she should choose the
first lover (to whom she feels bound) or the second lover (to
whom she feels a strong sexual attraction) she admits that 'it
wants a Pope to settle that'.[14]

Once again, Hardy was (unbeknownst to him) giving false
hope to Elizabeth Nicholls in the naming of his heroine and
his seeming remorse for switching his affections from sister to
sister. She was watching and waiting from the sidelines. And
then there was his beloved sister, Mary, the silent witness to his
affair with Elizabeth and Jane. Living so close to his favourite
sister, now headmistress of the elementary school in Dorchester,
had brought her struggles to the forefront of his mind. Mary
was resigned to her fate, but she resented it bitterly. Lonely,
insecure, 'sober and repressed of heart', she was the living epitome
of Elizabeth-Jane. Little wonder that Thomas Hardy said that
the only book he wrote that made him weep in the writing was

The Mayor of Casterbridge. Hardy's final words are not for his wretched, flawed hero, but for Elizabeth-Jane (and for Mary), as she learns to be stoical, to endure and to take 'happiness' as an 'occasional episode in a general drama of pain'.[15]

Thomas Rowlandson, *Selling a Wife*

CHAPTER 53

Marty South

Michael Henchard, the most wealthy and powerful man in Casterbridge, is brought down by a street woman urinating outside the walls of the church. She is the 'furmity woman' who goes on to make the shocking revelation to the council that the Mayor once sold his wife and daughter. Hardy loved plot twists, seemingly trivial but highly significant events and reversals of fortune of this kind. His work as a Dorchester magistrate put him in touch with all facets of human nature, and he made the most of every opportunity, writing in his diary: 'Rural low life may reveal coarseness of considerable leaven, but that libidinousness which makes the scum of the cities so noxious is not usually there.'[1]

His own social background, in which violence, debauchery and drunkenness were not uncommon, meant that very little was shocking to him as far as his council work was concerned. The inhabitants of Mixen Lane (the 'back slum' of Casterbridge) are a far remove from the kindly, romanticised country folk of previous novels. The public shaming of Henchard and Lucetta during the 'Skimmity ride', an ancient folk custom in which two effigies (representing the adulterous couple) are paraded around the town to a jeering audience, shows the rural folk in a disturbing light. They are a simmering mob who threaten to riot, indirectly causing the death of Lucetta.

Around the time he was immersing himself in the insalubrious incidents of the lower echelons of Dorchester, Hardy was being 'taken up' by ladies of the aristocracy. In March 1885, he was invited to visit Lady Portsmouth at Eggesford House, a country seat in Devon. Emma was ill and so Hardy went alone. He received a warm welcome from Lady Portsmouth and her daughters, and they would become lifelong friends. A great admirer of Hardy's novels, her ladyship begged him to make use of her library and to use her home as a writing retreat. She said that she would not let anyone disturb his labours, but in the event Hardy spent most of the time enjoying the lively company. Lady Portsmouth had invited her niece, Lady Winifred Herbert, and they formed a merry house party. Hardy walked in the park with Lord Portsmouth: 'He is a farmer-like man with a broad Devon accent. He showed me a bridge over which bastards were thrown and drowned, even down to quite recent times.'[2]

Lady Dorothea, Lady Camilla, Lady Margaret and Lady Rosamund, the daughters of the family, made a great fuss of Hardy. They told him tales of how their cousin, Auberon Herbert, impersonated a groom in order to make love to a woman he admired, and Lady Camilla made a remark about 'love' that he noted down: 'A woman is never so near being in love with a man she does not love as immediately he has left her after she has refused him.' Lady Portsmouth confided in Hardy, telling him 'she never knew real anxiety till she had a family of daughters'.[3] She asked Hardy to come and live in Devon, promising him that she would find a house for him. Hardy knew that Emma would jump at the chance to live back in 'her native country', but he knew that he could not leave Dorset.

The theme of wife-selling in his novel might suggest a kind of wishful thinking on his part, but, on the contrary, his letters home to Emma were full of warmth and affection. She is 'My dearest Em' and 'my dear Emmie'. He told her that Lady Portsmouth had instructed her lovely daughters to 'take care of me'. They 'were very attentive & interested in what I tell them'.[4] They had sent their best wishes to Emma and invited her to Eggesford another time. Soon after, Hardy met them again in London. He was invited to a party given by Lady Portsmouth's sister-in-law, Lady Carnarvon. Once again, Emma was left behind, but Tom sent her a chatty letter, describing the party and all the fine ladies. There was Lady Winifred in 'divine blue' with a ruff around her neck (slightly crumpled); Lady Margaret in a low cut, black lace gown, with 'a necklace of brilliants & black ornaments', and wearing gloves of salmon and buff.[5]

Once Emma joined him, there were more 'crushes' and Hardy was much lionised. He enjoyed the intellectual attractions of the women he met in polite society, though he needed Emma's reassurance on matters of etiquette. He met his admired Ann Procter and the society hostess Mrs Jeune. Lady Galway invited the Hardys to her crushes, where he met the Dowager Viscountess and gossiped about General Gordon's death.[6] He was living a life far removed from that of Bockhampton, and of his mother and sisters. Emma loved their London life, was highly sociable, and seems to have been well-liked. Hardy, shy and less sociable, remained ambivalent, writing in his diary: 'the roar of London! What is it composed of? Hurry, speech, laughter, moans, cries of little children. The people in this tragedy laugh, sing, smoke, toss off wines, etc, make love to girls in drawing rooms . . . and yet are playing the parts in the tragedy just the same.' He was uncomfortable with London's extremes of wealth and poverty, and his own sense of displacement was evident: 'Some wear jewels and feathers, some wear rags. All are caged birds; the only difference lies in the size of the cage.'[7]

Hardy could endure a few months in London, but he longed

for Dorset. This time, he and Emma were returning to live in their newly built country home, Max Gate. After all these years, and nearly a decade of marriage, they were finally to have a home of their own. Emma had waited long enough to be mistress of an impressive house – except that from the very start it had the Hardy family fingerprints all over it, from the architectural design to the builders, and down to the very red bricks marked with T. H. & Co.

Built in Queen Anne style (Hardy fashionably deemed it a 'villa'), Max Gate resembled a Victorian schoolhouse. Set in over an acre, it was wild and windy, and one of the first tasks Hardy undertook before they moved in was the planting of hundreds of trees to serve as windbreaks and provide much-coveted privacy. He created a kitchen garden for Emma with an apple orchard planted with trees from Bockhampton. The garden had views to the south and south-east across Fordington Field, to the monument of Admiral Hardy and the Downs beyond. From the top windows, one could see Stinsford Church, Kingston Maurward House and the heath and woodlands surrounding the Bockhampton cottage. The house was also close to the railway, which meant easy access for friends (and later fans, a source of great irritation). Whether or not Max Gate was considered an ugly house by his society friends, or, even worse, middle-class, it was an extraordinary achievement for a self-made man. The Hardys employed two servants, a gardener and a cook. Their first visitors were fellow writer Robert Louis Stevenson and his wife, Fanny.

The Stevensons invited themselves to Max Gate. Robert wrote: 'I could have got an introduction, but my acquaintance with your mind is already of old date.' Given the short notice and Hardy's kindness in entertaining the pushy guests, it was ungracious of Fanny to leave a cruel account of Emma. She described her as '*very* plain, quite underbred and most tedious'. She much preferred Hardy, finding in him 'something so modest, gentle and appealing', despite his being 'small, *very* pale, and scholarly looking, and at first sight most painfully shy'. She felt an 'instinctive tenderness' for Hardy having to suffer such a wife, 'ugly is no word for it!' To another friend, she wrote: 'What very strange marriages literary men seem to make.'[8] That she herself had married a literary man seems to have been an irony she passed over.

Fanny Stevenson's catty comments about Emma were echoed by many literary men and women as Hardy became more and more famous. She was often ridiculed, marginalised and made to feel unimportant. Hardy was not always easy to live with; that November he suffered a severe bout of depression, feeling 'as if enveloped in a leaden cloud'. Several days later he suffered from a 'sick headache'.[9] Under pressure from *Macmillan's Magazine* for a new serialisation, he returned to a novel he had set aside several years ago. It was his 'woodland story' and it drew heavily upon his mother's childhood. Once again, he turned to Emma for help, and she made a fair copy of the manuscript, copying out pages and pages in her neat handwriting.[10]

———

'Well, Mrs. Fitzpiers has her remedy.'

'How – what – a remedy?' said Melbury.

'Under the new law, sir. A new court was established last year, and under the new statute, twenty and twenty-one Vic., cap. eighty-five, unmarrying is as easy as marrying. No more Acts of Parliament necessary; no longer one law for the rich and another for the poor.'[11]

The new divorce laws of 1857 lie at the heart of *The Woodlanders*, rendering obsolete the barbaric practice of wife-selling explored by Hardy in his previous novel. But Hardy revealed the inequity of the new law, which seemed to protect powerful men more than vulnerable women.

The novel's setting is a village called Hintock, based on his mother's village, Melbury Osmond. The heroine, Grace Melbury, daughter of a timber merchant, has been sent to boarding school, where she has received a superior education for a woman of her social class. When she returns to Little Hintock, a hamlet outside of Great Hintock, she feels displaced and far removed from her fellow villagers. Though Grace has been promised to a local apple farmer, Giles Winterbourne, she is pressured to make a 'good' marriage, so she rejects Giles for a professional man, a doctor. Edgar Fitzpiers is handsome, cultivated and scientific. He has ambitions far beyond the confines of a rustic practice. Though he falls in love with Grace, he expects her to reject her humble background and move away from her home. Beneath Dr Fitzpiers' smooth manner lies a corrupted soul. He seduces a local woman, and lies about their relationship; then, shortly after his marriage to Grace, he embarks on a sexual affair with the lady of the manor house. Dr Fitzpiers abandons his faithful wife and runs away to the Continent with his lover. Grace returns to her childhood sweetheart, Giles Winterbourne, but the relationship is chaste, as Giles cares deeply about Grace's reputation.

A breakthrough occurs with the advent of a lawyer, who tells Grace's father that he can help Grace to obtain a divorce, leaving her free to marry Giles. The new law allowed legal separation by either the husband or wife on the grounds of adultery, abandonment or cruelty. However, the courts decided that Dr Fitzpiers' conduct has not been sufficiently heinous and Grace does not obtain the divorce that she so desperately seeks. When her husband returns from abroad to reconcile with Grace, she runs away to Giles' cottage in the woods. In order to protect her reputation, and despite being ill from typhoid fever, Giles sleeps outside in the woods. He dies. Grace returns to her husband, knowing that he has not changed his ways, and will continue to philander and cheat.

In Grace Melbury, Hardy poured out his own feelings of class displacement. Her education alienates her from her own people, and yet her husband is ashamed of her lowly origins. Dr Fitzpiers despises the common folk, refuses to mix with them socially, considering himself to be superior. Grace is torn between the people she loves and the husband she admires and respects. But when her husband abandons her for the glamorous and sexy Mrs Charmond, she realises that her heart truly belongs to Giles, who is a spirit of the woodlands. Quiet, good, a man of very few words, Giles is a dead ringer for Hardy's father. To make the reference explicit, Hardy makes Giles a cider-maker, recreating the memories of time spent with his father in the apple orchards of Bockhampton. The woman who is truly worthy of Giles is Marty South. She is in love with Giles, though she knows that he does not return her love and will always remain committed to Grace.

We first see Marty working hard at crafting spar gads for thatched roofs. Her 'rough man's work' is brutal, and poorly paid. She is so poor that she sells the only thing she possesses of any beauty: her long, luxuriant hair. Like so many of the Hardy women (his mother, his aunts and cousins), she supplements the low income of the household by her cottage work. The palms of her hands are red and blistering from the spars, and yet she works uncomplainingly: 'Nothing but a cast of the die of destiny had decided that the girl should handle the tool; and the fingers which clasped the heavy ash haft might have skilfully guided the pencil or swept the string, had they only been set to do it in good time.'[12] Marty is not gifted with beauty, but she is brave and resolute. She is deserving of Giles but knows she does not possess the physical attraction to draw him in, so her love is hopeless and unrequited. She says very little, but she observes the action around her, unwittingly playing a part in Mrs Charmond's seduction of Grace's husband.

Mrs Charmond, a former actress, and lady of the manor, is a fading beauty who buys Marty's lustrous mane and affixes it to her own thinning hair. Used to playing a part on stage, she finds Dr Fitzpiers an easy target for coquetry and seduction. His attraction fades when he discovers that her beautiful hair is fake. One of Hardy and Emma's friends, Rebekah Owen (we will be meeting her again), believed that Mrs Charmond was partially based on Emma. The character makes a speech about how she finds herself full of ideas, but is unable to write down her thoughts on 'cold, smooth paper'.[13] In her copy of *The Woodlanders*, the friend wrote: 'Exactly. E. L. H.'[14] Emma, who transcribed so much of the novel, could not have failed to notice the comparison with her own striking mane of hair, one of the features which so attracted Hardy to her during their courtship. If Emma felt the symbolism of the revelation of Mrs Charmond's fakeness, she did not comment. Nor did she comment on Grace Melbury's social displacement, so much like her husband's, and which caused him much suffering.

Hardy had mixed feelings about his heroine, Grace Melbury. Rebekah Owen recalled him saying that Grace did not interest him much, and that she 'provoked him'.[15] He wanted Grace to show self-abandonment and passion and run off with Giles, but he somehow could not make it happen. She was too 'commonplace and strait-laced'. In speaking of Marty, Hardy agreed that she was a noble woman, but only because she did not 'get Giles'.[16] If she had got him, she would have been different. Hardy's remarks were significant for the way in which his female characters were real to him, and sometimes acted in ways contrary to what he wished. Not one of the three women in *The Woodlanders* gets a happy ending. Mrs Charmond tells her doctor-lover: 'Women are always carried about like corks upon the waves of masculine desires.'[17] Hardy was at pains to tell admirers of the novel that Grace meets her retribution by returning to her husband and his bad ways. Hardy condemns Marty to a life of loneliness and pain. Her only comfort is tending Giles' grave. The novel ends:

> 'Now, my own, own love,' she whispered, 'you are mine, and on'y mine; for she has forgot 'ee at last, although for her you died. But I – whenever I get up I'll think of 'ee, and whenever I lie down I'll think of 'ee. Whenever I plant the young larches I'll think that none can plant as you planted; and whenever I split a gad, and whenever I turn the cider-wring, I'll say none could do it like you. If ever I forget your name, let me forget home and Heaven! – But no, no, my love, I never can forget 'ee; for you was a *good* man, and did good things!'[18]

Marty is another silent witness of the type of woman Hardy deeply admired. Plain, lacking in self-worth, but loyal, she knows that Giles has sacrificed his life for love. And although Giles is cold in the ground, she takes comfort in the fact that she no longer has a rival. There will be no husband, no warm home and children for Marty. She is condemned to a life of poverty and loneliness. 'Solitary and silent', she wears the 'marks of poverty and toil'.[19]

Take the 't' out of her name, and she becomes Mary.

CHAPTER 54

Tess Durbeyfield

Thomas Hardy, wearing a fur-edged coat, was walking through the streets of Rome when he was attacked by a group of robbers. They saw he was carrying a small painting in his hands, and, thinking he was alone and defenceless, made a grab for his purse. Except he wasn't alone. His wife Emma, walking on the opposite side, anticipated the ambush, and shouted out to her husband. She followed up with a rush on their attackers, before they disappeared, according to Hardy, 'as if by magic'. A few days before, she had attacked a persistent 'shoe-black' by beating him with her umbrella until it broke.[1] Though Emma was naturally courageous, the attempted robbery had left her shaken: 'The attack by confederate thieves dreadful fright to me'.[2] Nevertheless, she summoned her courage and carried on, writing her impressions of the tour of Italy in her diary. They visited Pisa, Florence, Rome, and eventually Venice. She wrote of the gaily coloured dresses and headscarves of the lower-class women, and 'Italian suavity'. As was her wont, she noticed and made friends with small children and cats. She bought a necktie for her brother-in-law Henry Hardy and enjoyed a gondola ride on the Grand Canal.

But the tour was not without its difficulties. Emma, a

horse-lover, was upset to find their Florentine driver driving a horse weak with fatigue. She remonstrated with the driver, fully expecting to be shouted at in the manner of a London cabbie, but the Italian was charming, and 'delighted to have any interest taken in his horse'.[3] After a luxurious meal on a train, she recorded that 'Tom [was] very vexed, Dyspeptic, before and worse now.'[4] On the way back to Paris, Tom got into a confrontation with a male passenger, the father of three unruly children. Emma sympathised with the father, and when they left the train, the gentleman apologised '& seemed really sorry – no doubt out of gratitude for my taking his part & pitying his trying situation with the children'.[5]

They arrived back in London in late April to excellent reviews of *The Woodlanders,* though the publishers had received a letter of complaint about the immorality of the theme of 'conjugal infidelity'. The writer was shocked by the 'coarse flirtations' and finished by adding that it was not a story fit 'to be put into the hands of pure-minded English girls'. The 'pure-minded' phrase stuck with Hardy and was to be used in the novel that had germinated in his mind for years.

Back in London, the Hardys were thrown into a whirlwind of parties and crushes. His list of the many aristocratic ladies he met this season reads like a paragraph in the court register or Burke's Peerage. There was the fashionable Mrs Mary Jeune, Lady Carnarvon, Lady Winifred Byng, Lady Camilla Wallop, Lady Rosamund, Lady Pollock, and more. He finally met Lady Catherine Milnes Gaskell: 'the prettiest of all Lady Portsmouth's daughters. Round luminous inquiring eyes.'[6] He went to lunch with Lady Stanley, where he met Lady Airlie.

The more he was drawn to the aristocratic women who treated him like a pet, the less he leaned on his wife for support. A story later circulated (though is not proven) that Emma complained about the London ladies who 'spoilt' her husband.

'They are the poison. I am the antidote' is what she was rumoured to have said.[7]

After tea with Lady Portsmouth, he was struck once again by her aristocratic mien: 'Looked more like a model countess than ever I have seen her do before, her black brocaded silk fitting her well and suiting her eminently . . . she is one of the few, very few, women of her own rank for whom I would make a sacrifice: a woman of talent, part of whose talent consists in concealing that she has any.'[8] Soon after this meeting, he began writing his short story 'The First Countess of Wessex'. Throughout that year, he confined himself to writing short stories, a collection of which would make up his *Wessex Tales* published in 1888.

When back in Dorset, he remained deeply enmeshed with his mother, seeing her at the family cottage every Sunday. Emma was becoming more and more estranged from the family. In January, they had heard troubling news about her brother, Richard. He had suffered some kind of breakdown and tried to commit suicide. One of his symptoms was delusions; he believed he was verminous, dirty, and unfit to live. He was unmarried, and it was left to Emma's mother and sister to have him committed to the Cornwall County Asylum; he was subsequently transferred to Bethlem Hospital in London, and then to the Warneford hospital in Oxford. Hardy began to believe that there was inherited mental instability in his wife's family. This view would come to be shared with his mother and his sisters.

Few seemed to sympathise with Emma. The Hardy family found her uppity and felt she looked down on them, whereas people such as Fanny Stevenson considered her manners vulgar. Even some of her relatives preferred Tom to Emma. Mrs Jeune's two children by her first marriage, Dorothy and Madeleine, adored 'Uncle Tom', but, as one of them declared, 'We all hated' Emma.[9] Hardy's propensity to become infatuated with young women seemed to increase the older he became, and, as he lost himself in the writing of *Tess of the D'Urbervilles*, Emma felt even more isolated.

He was always able to fall in love with a beautiful woman at a single glance. When he was in his forties, he spotted an attractive maid milking her cows on her grandfather's dairy in Dorset, near the Kingston Maurward estate. The Way family had taken up residence in a part of Kingston Maurward House, where Hardy's mother had worked as a servant, and where he had once known Julia Martin. The milkmaid was eighteen years old, and her name was Augusta May. Later, Hardy would tell her daughters that she inspired his portrayal of Tess.

On another occasion, he would explain that 'Girls resembling the three dairymaids in *Tess* used to get me to write their love letters for them when I was a little boy' and that 'unconsciously I absorbed a good deal of their mode of life and speech', enabling him to reproduce it in the novel.[10] The dairy scenes at Talbothays are among the most evocative that he ever wrote. The girls sing old ballads to calm their cows: as a countryman, Hardy knew that this was a way to ensure free-flowing milk.

Years before, Hardy had made a note of a story recounted by a 'very old' country woman called Mrs Cross. She told of a girl she had known who had been betrayed and deserted by her lover. The girl kept her baby 'by her own exertions, and lived bravely and throve'. After a time, the man returned and wanted to marry her, but she refused, and he went into the workhouse. Hardy was greatly struck by the young woman's conduct in not caring to be 'made respectable'. He wanted to know the name of the girl, but Mrs Cross refused: 'Oh, never mind their names: they be dead and rotted now.' Hardy continued to obsess about the story: 'The eminently modern idea embodied in this example

– of a woman's not becoming necessarily the chattel and slave of her seducer' impressed him 'as being one of the first glimmers of women's enfranchisement'. He wrote that he would make 'use of it in succeeding years in more than one case in his fiction and verse'.[11]

He had already tried out the idea of an innocent swept up by a worldly man in his novella, 'The Romantic Adventures of a Milkmaid'. Feeling the pressure from his editors, he returned to this theme of the milkmaid heroine. On one of his Sundays at Bockhampton, his mother told him a story about a local woman called Nanny Priddle who refused to take on her husband's name on marriage 'because she was too proud'.[12] For all of her married life, she was known by her own surname and not her husband's. Once again, Hardy was impressed by these working women's 'glimmers of enfranchisement'. And Jemima's tale about surnames was important for *Tess*. Hers would take on great significance, and, ultimately, be the cause of her downfall. His epigraph for the book, from *Measure for Measure,* makes this clear: 'Poor wounded name! My bosom as a bed / Shall lodge thee.'

Hardy would take up the idea of a once illustrious family that has fallen on hard times. He had been thinking about his 'own' descent from the Le Hardys. In September 1888, he made a pilgrimage to Woolcombe House in the Vale of Blackmoor, once the seat of a branch of the ancient family: 'The decline and fall of the Hardys much in evidence.' He recalled his mother pointing out a senior member of the Hardy family – a tall, thin man, who had a lot of children. 'So we go down, down, down', he noted in his journal.[13] He even considered calling his new novel *Tess of the Hardys* but felt this was too personal. He would finally set on the name of D'Urberville, a derivative of a genuine ancient family called Turberville. He was inspired by the stained-glass Turberville window in the church at Bere Regis, referenced towards the end of the novel.

On Christmas Eve, he wrote a letter to the female author Eliza Lynn Linton, disclosing his 'leading idea of a long story planned some time ago'.[14] He told the newspaper syndicate Tillotson's (to whom the serial was promised) that he had begun the new novel by February of 1889. By mid-July, it was called 'The Body and Soul of Sue', but it was not until August that he settled down 'daily' to writing his 'new story'. A journal note discloses: 'When a married woman who has a lover kills her husband, she does not really want to kill the husband. She wants to kill the situation.'[15] On 4 August he wrote that he had a new title, 'Too Late, Beloved', and set out the plot: 'The heroine of the narrative is a young country girl, a milkmaid, who is, however, a lineal descendent of one of the oldest country families in the kingdom.' Hardy made clear that 'her position is based on fact'.[16]

In the preface to the second edition of 1892, Hardy expanded on his intention to write about 'the shaded side of a well-known catastrophe' – in other words, pregnancy out of wedlock. It was a subject he had been tackling since *Desperate Remedies*, most recently in *Two on a Tower*. Lady Constantine is protected by her wealth and status, and is able to trap the unwitting bishop into a hasty marriage, which legitimises the baby she is carrying. Now Hardy took for his subject a lowly milkmaid, who is seduced and impregnated by a predatory man that she mistakenly believes is her cousin.

Unlike Lady Constantine, his new, as yet unnamed, heroine would have no wealth or protection for herself or her bastard baby. But Hardy was intrigued by the idea that many a rural labouring-class visage bore the outline of an aristocratic heritage. Soon after his novel was published, he told a journalist that he intended it to be an 'absolute fact' that this was the case with his heroine. He explained that there were many such cases in Dorset: 'You will trace noble lineage in many a face, and there is a certain conscious pride about some of these people which differentiates them at once from middle-class cockneyism or provincialism.' He added that 'the rather free and easy mode of life adopted by the squires of the last century has contributed to the ancient lineage and to the fine features of many of the labouring classes in this neighbourhood'.[17]

Hardy had numerous examples within his family circles of pregnancy out of wedlock; his grandmother, his mother, several aunts, his maidservant, his sister's best friend had all found themselves trapped by the consequences of unprotected sex. Biographers have searched for the real-life model for his most famous heroine: was she his grandmother, Mary Hand, or his maidservant Jane Philipps?[18] But this is to misinterpret his motives: Tess was all of the seduced country women he knew, and none of them. Perhaps the closest mirroring of her early circumstances was the story of the nameless Dorset woman who proudly refused to marry her seducer or make herself 'respectable' by the standards of Victorian society. If Mrs Cross had given Hardy his theme, the problem was how to make his tainted heroine 'pure'.

Her beauty he was sure of, and it would be her burden and her downfall. And it wasn't only the milkmaid, Augusta May, who was the physical model for Tess. Three days before his forty-ninth birthday, Hardy glimpsed a girl in an omnibus: 'one of those faces of marvellous beauty which are seen casually in the streets but never among one's friends . . . where do these women come from? Who marries them? Who knows them?' At the Royal Academy, he ruminated on feminine beauty: the 'red flesh shades' of Romney; 'In a Botticelli, the soul is outside the body . . . in a Rubens the flesh is without, and the soul (possibly) within.' He began to be fixated on physical beauty, making notes about the society women he met at London parties: 'Lady Coleridge could honestly claim to be a beauty . . . Really fine eyes.'[19] But Lady Rothschild did not make the cut: 'an amply-membered, pleasant woman, unfashionable dressed in brown silk. She and I talked a good deal – about wit, the nude in art.' The 'pretty woman of the party' was Amelie Rives, a 'fair, pink, golden-haired creature, but not quite ethereal enough, suggesting a flesh-surface too palpably.'[20] His fixation on the physical beauty as well as the interior life of young women accounts for that draft title 'The Body and Soul of Sue'.

And then there was Agatha, wife of a sculptor named Hamo Thornycroft who would later model Hardy's head: 'Of all the people I have met this summer, the lady whose mouth recalls more fully than any other beauty's the Elizabethan metaphor: "Her lips are roses full of snow" is Mrs HT.'[21] Hardy would use this exact description to describe Tess's mouth. Edmund Gosse recalled Hardy's later words about Agatha Thornycroft: 'I have been cheered up by seeing the most beautiful woman in England . . . her on whom I wrote *Tess*.'[22]

But, then again, he saw the image of his heroine in every beautiful and sensuous woman he encountered. He would later claim that he once met the real Tess driving a horse and cart on the outskirts of Egdon Heath. She was swearing at her horse and lashing it to go faster.[23] 'She coloured up very much when she saw me, but – as a novelist – I fell in love with her at once and adopted her as my heroine.'[24] He informed several journalists that he only saw this girl the once, but late in life he told the actress playing the part in his dramatisation of the novel that he saw the 'original' Tess a second time, but 'she was totally different'.[25] As so often, the second glimpse was a reality check.

There was, however, one woman he could not yet bring himself to mention in relation to Tess – the one whose memory was indelibly marked on his imagination, but deeply repressed.

As always, in writing *Tess* Hardy drew on people he knew. He said that Angel Clare's Evangelical father was based on Horace Moule's father, and there are aspects of Angel that owe much to Horace. But whereas his previous heroines were partly based on the women he loved, Tess was not. Though his descriptions of her physical appearance were sparked by such beauties as Augusta May the milkmaid, her character was entirely the product of his imagination. Despite this, she was more real to him than any woman he had yet created on the page.

Stories of the seduction and downfall of young women of the servant class were as common as dirt in the rural, working-class communities of his kinfolk. Hardy's essential dilemma was how to make a seduced maid pure of body and soul. His subtitle, 'A Pure Woman', was one that he knew would offend his critics. How could he put the blame squarely and firmly on the men who let her down? First, her feckless father, whose delusions of grandeur and insistence on his noble ancestry put her in the path of her seducer. Then the seducer himself, who takes carelessly what thousands of aristocratic men had taken from innocent maids, simply because they could. And the worst betrayal of all, that of the ironically named 'Angel' Clare, who accuses his wife of the same 'crime' that he himself has committed. A litany of people hurt and exploit Tess. 'At last *one* pays the penalty', Hardy wrote in a poem called 'The Coquette – and After', 'The woman – women always do!'[26] Phase the Fifth of *Tess* is duly entitled: 'The Woman Pays'.

Deceptively simple in plot, the novel is deeply complex. It presents morally ambiguous questions about ancestry, nobility, purity, shame and guilt, but it never loses sight of the innocent girl who is at the centre of the storm. Angel Clare describes himself as a 'cork on the waves' of his own moral dissipation when he is in London with a prostitute, but it is Tess who is truly the cork. Her mother, Joan, a brilliant depiction of a woman hardened and coarsened by poverty and a huge brood of children, knows that her daughter's extraordinary beauty is her only currency. She fully expects Alec to seduce Tess (why should she be any different to any other peasant girl put in the way of a wealthy man?), but she hopes that her daughter has the good sense to bargain hard. When Tess returns home, sullied and pregnant with Alec's baby, Joan is horrified to learn that she has let Alec get away. He has gone to London and the only promise he has made is to look after his bastard financially, and to make Tess his mistress; an offer she refuses, not only because it degrades her, but because she doesn't love him. She cannot sell herself, or her baby, for money.

Because she is pure of heart, Tess considers herself married to Alec in an ethical sense. When she finally agrees to marry Angel, she feels morally bound to confess her past, and to quell the nagging doubts that she, in fact, belongs to Alec. When Angel abandons his lawful wife (without consummating the marriage), she reverts back to thinking that she is Alec's wife. Then when Angel returns to claim his lawful wife, she tells him that Alec has won her back. She is the cork tossed between them. Pantomime villain that he is, Alec is symptomatic of his sex and wealth. Even when Tess returns to him, to save her family from penury, he is abusive, taunting her and calling her insulting names. Yet it is the good Angel, hypocritical and sanctimonious, who is the real villain of the piece.

Hardy takes his time describing Tess's beauty. He has to, because the price of it is unwanted male interest. Her beauty puts her at high risk: 'But 'tis always the comeliest! The plain ones be as safe as churches.' One of the main features of beauty is her hair: 'a thick cable of twisted dark hair hanging straight down her back to her waist'.[27] Her face is not 'ethereal' but has 'real vitality, real warmth, real incarnation'. Angel regards her beauty with the eyes of an artist:

Her mouth he had seen nothing to equal on the face of the earth. To a young man with the least fire in him that little upward lift in the middle of her red top lip was distracting, infatuating, maddening. He had never before seen a woman's lips and teeth which forced upon his mind with such persistent iteration the old Elizabethan simile of roses filled with snow.[28]

Even her breath 'tasted of the butter and eggs and milk and honey on which she mainly lived'.[29] Though Angel's mother has not seen Tess, her son's description of her physical attributes makes her seem real: 'I can see her quite distinctly. You said the other day that she was fine in figure; roundly built; had deep red lips like Cupid's bow; dark eyelashes and brows, an immense rope of hair like a ship's cable; and large eyes violety-bluey-blackish.'[30]

Hardy also draws attention to her full bosom, which makes her appear older than her years:

She had an attribute which amounted to a disadvantage just now; and it was this that caused Alec D'Urberville's eyes to rivet themselves upon her. It was a luxuriance of aspect, a fulness of growth, which made her appear more of a woman than she really was. She had inherited the feature from her mother without the quality it denoted. It had troubled her mind occasionally, till her companions had said that it was a fault which time would cure.[31]

The place where she finds herself in Phase the Third is a topographical manifestation of her brand of luscious beauty: 'Amid the oozing fatness and warm ferments of the Froom Vale, at a season when the rush of juices could almost be heard below the hiss of fertilization, it was impossible that the most fanciful love should not grow passionate. The ready bosoms existing there were impregnated by their surroundings.'[32] Then on her desperate journey to Flintcomb-Ash, after she has been abandoned by Angel, she reaches 'the irregular chalk table-land or plateau, bosomed with semi-globular tumuli – as if Cybele the Many-breasted were supinely extended there – which stretched between the valley of her birth and the valley of her love'.[33] It is on that journey that she swaddles her face in rags to hide her beauty and nips off her fine dark brows with scissors. Looking ugly is necessary for her own protection.

Alec's first words to Tess are 'Well, my big Beauty, what can I do for you?'[34] Reviewers took exception to this explicit reference to her large breasts: 'the story gains nothing by the reader being let into the secret of the physical attributes which especially fascinated him in Tess. Most people can fill in blanks for themselves, without its being necessary to put the dots on the i's so very plainly; but Mr Hardy leaves little unsaid.'[35] Stung, Mr Hardy removed the word 'big' from the second edition published a few months later. But the initial encounter remains highly eroticised, as Alec feeds Tess a juicy strawberry:

He conducted her about the lawns, and flower beds, and conservatories; and thence to the fruit-garden, where he asked her if she liked strawberries.

'Yes,' said Tess, 'when they come.'

'They are already here.' D'Urberville began gathering specimens of the fruit for her, handing them back to her as he stooped; and, presently, selecting a specially fine product of the 'British Queen' variety, he stood up and held it by the stem to her mouth.

'No – no!' she said quickly, putting her fingers between his hand and her lips. 'I would rather take it in my own hand.'

'Nonsense!' he insisted; and in a slight distress she parted her lips and took it in.[36]

Hardy knew his English strawberries. The 'British Queen' was bred in 1841 by Joseph Myatt of Kent. It was the first large-fruited hybrid, the most famous English strawberry, with its deep red skin and white firm flesh, its flavour rich, exquisite and deep.

Though Tess is forced by Alec to eat the berry, feeling 'a slight distress', she is granted an element of volition. She parts her lips and takes it in. The scene foreshadows the question of Tess's complicity in her undoing: is she raped or seduced?

Tess is confused when she is offered a strawberry so early in the season. In yet another revision of the novel, in 1895, Hardy explained its ripeness by adding a phrase: Alec takes her to the fruit-garden 'and green-houses'. Greenhouse strawberries were force-fed, so they ripened all year round: the suggestion of force-feeding tilts the interpretation towards rape.

Hardy's adaptation of *Tess* for the Hardy Players is more ambiguous. There, the seduction takes place off-stage, so Hardy incorporates the vital strawberry scene, shifting its location to Tess's cottage. Alec arrives with a basket of early strawberries:

ALEC: Well, never mind. Try one, dear. (HE takes a strawberry from the basket and holds it by the stem to her mouth. TESS covers her mouth.)

TESS: No, no. I would rather take it in my own hand.

ALEC: Nonsense! (HE persists; SHE retreats till she is against wall; laughs distressfully, and takes it with her lips as offered.)

ALEC: There's a darling.

TESS: Don't call me darling. I don't like it!

ALEC: But you will like it some day.[37]

The stage direction skilfully combines force (retreat against the wall, distress) and complicity (a laugh, albeit a distressful one, but not a scream, as she takes what is offered between her lips). She doesn't like it, but Alec's question remains: will she like it some day? Does she succumb to Alec more than once? How long is she his mistress? In the several versions of the novel – manuscript, serialisation, successive editions – Hardy deliberately muddies the water. Tess is savvy enough to know the game that her parents are playing when they send her to Alec's manor house. They know the script well. But when she returns, pregnant and abandoned, Tess tells her mother that she was sexually naive: 'How could I be expected to know? I was a child when I left this house four months ago. Why didn't you tell me there was danger in men-folk? Why didn't you warn me?'[38]

In the serialisation, the deflowering itself is softened for the benefit of morally upright female readers by a 'mock marriage' undertaken by Alec and Tess. In the various editions of the full novel, the scene varies. In the 1891 version, Alec drugs Tess: 'He went to the horse, took a druggist's bottle from a parcel on the saddle, and after some trouble in opening it held it to her mouth unawares.' There can be no complicity here. But in the 1912 version, Hardy removed this section, replacing it with: 'He pulled off a light overcoat that he had worn and put it round her tenderly.' A careful reading of all the texts, including the play, suggests that Tess is 'dazed' or 'dazzled' by Alec. She is 'temporarily blinded by his ardent manners'.[39]

What remains clear is that Tess stays with Alec for almost four months following the initial seduction, and leaves when she discovers she is pregnant. When speaking of *Tess*, Hardy would repeatedly use the phrase 'seduction' rather than rape, but the description of her innocence, with tears brushing her eyelids, in sleep, leaves little doubt of who is to blame. For Hardy, the *who* is manifest, but the *why* is inexplicable, as he makes clear in the concluding passage of Phase the First, after which Tess will be 'Maiden No More':

> Why it was that upon this beautiful feminine tissue, sensitive as gossamer, and practically blank as snow as yet, there should have been traced such a coarse pattern as it was doomed to receive; why so often the coarse appropriates the finer thus, many thousand years of analytical philosophy have failed to explain to our sense of order.[40]

It is because there is no answer to this question that Hardy has lost all faith in 'the President of the Immortals'.

There is a spirited exchange between Alec and Tess when she leaves to return home in disgrace. She tells him, 'I didn't understand your meaning till it was too late.' He replies cruelly: 'That's what every woman says.' She is robust in her defence of women: '"How can you dare to use such words!" she cried, turning impetuously upon him, her eyes flashing as the latent spirit (of which he was to see more some day) awoke in her. "My God! I could knock you out of the gig! Did it never strike your mind that what every woman says some women may feel?"'[41] Nevertheless, she blames herself for the seduction ('my weakness'), and when she confesses to Angel on the night of their honeymoon, she feels deep shame. But she also reveals that she is not a victim, and that her sin is no worse than his own: 'O, Angel – I am almost glad – because now *you* can forgive *me*!'[42]

When she discovers that this is not how Angel views male and female purity, she challenges the sexual double standard:

'"Forgive me as you are forgiven! *I* forgive *you*, Angel . . . But you do not forgive me?"' When Angel tries to describe his feelings of being sexually repelled by Tess, he gives the lame excuse that he has loved 'another woman in your shape'. She knows the truth: that he can only love her as a virgin. What she requires is that he loves her for her true self, 'my very self'. She is 'a guilty woman in the guise of an innocent one'. Her beautiful mouth, one of her loveliest features, has become a 'round little hole'. When Tess tells Angel that she will 'obey him' like a 'wretched slave', he becomes as cruel as Alec: 'You are very good. But it strikes me that there is a want of harmony between your present mood of self-sacrifice and your past mood of self-preservation.' Her pleas that she was just a child when she was seduced permits Angel to admit that she is 'more sinned against than sinning'.[43]

It is the 'idea' of the woman he loves that he has lost, not the woman herself. Tess explains that many peasant husbands make such discoveries about their wives and have 'got over it'. But Angel blames her bad D'Urberville seed: 'Decrepit families imply decrepit wills, decrepit conduct. Heaven, why did you give me a handle for despising you more by informing me of your descent! Here was I thinking you a new-sprung child of nature; there were you, the belated seedling of an effete aristocracy!'[44] It is only after he returns from Brazil, weakened by illness and loneliness, that he truly discovers his wrongdoing and his wrong-thinking.

Hardy's dramatisation in five acts is a fascinating text, because it clarifies some of the moral ambiguities that dog the novel. Though Angel's 'more sinned against' phrase is a quotation from *King Lear*, the play suggests that – as with Clym and Eustacia in *The Return of the Native* – the deeper Shakespearean comparison is with the male rage of the 'brothel scene' in *Othello*. Angel insinuates that Tess is no different to the 'ten thousand cases' of London whores: 'Every woman on the streets of London has precisely the same story to tell.'[45] His obsession with female purity resembles that of Othello.

The theatrical adaptation includes a powerful scene in which Joan Durbeyfield chastises Angel for his heartlessness:

ANGEL: Mrs. Durbeyfield? (*JOAN nods, still holding TESS's letter.*) I came just now – but I thought you were engaged and I've waited . . . We've never met before I think.

JOAN: I don't think we have.

ANGEL: I am Tess's husband – just come home from Brazil. – Where is my Tess? I want to see her at once.

JOAN: Do you, sir? (*Puts away letter.*)

ANGEL: Will you please inform me, Mrs Durbeyfield?

JOAN: Lord! You ought to know better than I where she is. It is more your business than mine. She's your wife.[46]

There is another telling moment in the play when Angel is reunited with Tess and begs her forgiveness. She informs him that he is too late, and that she has become Alec's mistress. In the novel, Angel confesses that it is his fault, but in the play he acknowledges that the blame lies with both men: 'ANGEL (*after a silence in which he turns aside*): Ah . . . It is my fault – mine only – and his.' Alec is less forgiving, telling Tess: 'If you hadn't been willing to sell yourself, you wouldn't have been here, you little humbug.'[47] In both novel and play, it is Alec's cruel taunting that drives Tess to stab the man who has been responsible for her misery.

The play ends on Stonehenge, as Tess prepares herself to be taken away by the authorities, thankful for her final moments with Angel, and ready for death. In the novel, there is one further chapter, in which Tess's execution takes place off-stage. Having witnessed the execution of a woman who had killed her husband in similar circumstances, Hardy felt unable to recreate the scene. Angel, sitting on the hill outside the prison, sees only the triangular black flag being hoisted to signify her death. Probably unconsciously, Hardy was recollecting another youthful memory: his reading of *Windsor Castle* by William Harrison Ainsworth, the historical novelist he so loved. That novel also ends with a view from a distance. From the vantage point of a high hill, King Henry VIII and Herne the Hunter see only the flag blowing in the wind over the castle, giving 'The Signal' of the execution of Queen Anne Boleyn.

The Signal.

PHASE THE THIRD

The women he loved and
the women he lost

CHAPTER 55

Tryphena

Hardy began the new year of 1890 with a depressing note in his journal: 'I have been looking for God 50 years, and I think if he had existed, I should have discovered him.'[1] Emma's increasing interest in religion was driving an even deeper wedge between the couple. Then in early March he was struck by a heavy blow. The writing of Tess, the beautiful girl with the coil of thick dark hair, who aspired to be a schoolteacher, had brought back memories of his cousin, Tryphena. On a train to London, Hardy began to write a poem about his lost love, 'Not a line of her writing have I.' It was, he wrote, 'a curious instance of sympathetic telepathy. The woman whom I was thinking of – cousin – was dying at the time, and I quite in ignorance of it.'[2]

Hardy had lost touch with Tryphena since his marriage to Emma. Her school was in a poor part of Plymouth; it was overcrowded and ill-equipped. In her logbook, Miss Sparks noted that the children 'have not enough room to work well . . . and it is now too cold for out-of-door classes'. Her pupil teacher performed badly, and she had problems with parents and grandparents. A woman lied about one of her grandchildren being free from typhoid, but Tryphena refused to let the child back to school without a note from the doctor. School attendance was erratic, and children were kept home on washing days: 'Kept to mind the baby' was one of the frequent excuses.[3] It was a lonely life, even though she had begun 'walking out' with a man called Charles Gale. The Sparks family decided to act. The eldest sister, Rebecca, was recently married, but the couple parted immediately after the wedding, so that the bride could go to live with her sister. She took her wedding knives and forks with her. It was a strange story (that would find its way into *Tess*), but the Sparks believed that Rebecca was 'doing her duty'. Her duty was not to herself but to her family and her 'dear sister'. There was no 'falling out' with Mr Payne, Rebecca's husband, but she could not let 'prized Tryphena' go on living without someone to look after her needs. Mrs Payne was accordingly employed by the school as a sewing mistress.

Given the promising start to her career, becoming a headmistress at such a young age, Tryphena's story ended badly. Her daughter Nellie would later recount the circumstances. By 1877, she had become engaged to a man called Charles Gale. She left the school (with Rebecca) to set up home in Topsham, near Exeter. For her wedding day, she wore a white frilled muslin dress and white satin shoes, her dark coil of hair swept back with a long lace veil. Charles owned a pub called 'The Steam Packet' and a 'fashionable' hotel in Fore Street. Next door was the family home, divided into two self-contained parts; his mother and sister in one, and his wife and her sister Rebecca in the other. The Gale family considered the Sparks as socially inferior, and Mrs Gale barely spoke a word to her daughter-in-law for five years. Her husband's sister, Sarah, set out to make her life unhappy. On one occasion, as Tryphena was carrying hot coals from room to room, Sarah slammed every door in her face. Neither Mrs Gale nor Sarah would call Tryphena by her Christian name. Later, with the advent of children, relations improved. Tryphena took great pleasure in her children. The

Gales grew strawberries in their greenhouse to sell out of season. Six large strawberries were harvested to be sold for a shilling each, but Tryphena's eldest daughter, unable to resist the lush strawberries, took a small bite from the bottom of each strawberry before placing it back on the plate. The Gales were furious, but Tryphena thought it an ingenious way for her daughter to hide her tracks.

Charles Gale was a difficult man. He once berated his wife for mopping up a splash of water when she had maids to clean for her, and, to make his point clear, poured a bucket of cinders over the floor, leaving Tryphena in tears. He took up with a local prostitute and was seen driving her in the family pony trap. Tryphena went to meet them on the Topsham–Exeter road, where 'Mrs Sullivan' was turned out and Mrs Gale driven home by her husband, 'much vexed'.[4]

When Rebecca died suddenly in 1885, Tryphena was distraught. A year later, she gave birth to her fourth child, a boy, but soon after she suffered a serious rupture by lifting a pail of water from the duck pond. She never fully recovered from her accident. She died in 1890 at the house in Fore Street.

Charles Gale refused to allow Hardy to come to Tryphena's funeral, but four months after her death, he and his brother Henry visited her grave to lay down a wreath. The Hardy brothers called in at Fore Street. Tryphena's daughter remembered that her father stayed in the pantry to avoid Hardy and told Nellie that she should 'entertain' Tom. Nellie told Tom that she had read *Far from the Madding Crowd*. He said nothing, but only smiled. As the men were leaving, Henry kissed her and told her that she looked exactly like her mother. Hardy remained silent, but Nellie intuited Tom was upset by the striking resemblance: 'of course he was hurt'. Nellie never saw Tom or Henry again, but the memory of their visit was vivid: 'My father was coldly polite and Tom was formal as well. I knew there was friction there. You couldn't shove one man down another's throat. I said to my father afterwards: "You served him a dirty trick, you know."'[5]

Two days before Tryphena's death, Hardy had been invited to a crush at Mrs Jeune's house. By then, he knew that his cousin was dying. At the party he saw the beautiful Rosamund Watson, whom he had met a year before in 1889. She was a poet, who wrote under the pseudonym Graham R. Tomson. She had sent Hardy an inscribed copy of her collection of verses, *The Bird Bride*, and they had begun a correspondence. Hardy had grown infatuated with her, and at the party he noted her 'great eyes in a corner of the rooms, as if washed up by the surging crowd'. She was 'The most beautiful woman present' – though not without competition in the form of the Duchess of Teck in 'black velvet with long sleeves and a few diamonds' and her daughter, a 'pretty young woman in skim-milk-blue muslin', not to mention Lady Burdett Coutts beneath a headdress of a 'castellated facade of diamonds'.[6] But Tryphena was still on his mind: his thoughts returned to the naturally beautiful country girls of his youth. In his journal he wrote a phrase that would find its way into *Tess*: 'But these women! If put into rough wrappers in a turnip-field, where would their beauty be?'[7]

CHAPTER 56

The New Women

The 1890s heralded the age of the 'New Woman'.[1] Who was she? She came from the middle or upper class, and was educated, career-minded, independent, ambitious and sexually liberated. New laws gave her the freedom to divorce, and remarry if she cared to, without losing her social respectability. Her mode of transport was the bicycle. There were 'New Women' plays, such as Ibsen's *A Doll's House*, Henry Arthur Jones's *The Case of Rebellious Susan* and George Bernard Shaw's *Mrs Warren's Profession*. Max Beerbohm joked that the New Woman sprang fully formed from Ibsen's brain.

Among the many New Women writers and artists were South African born Olive Schreiner; Violet Paget, who published as Vernon Lee and had an intimate relationship with poet Mary Frances Robinson; the cosmopolitan Mary Dunne (pseudonym George Egerton); Anglo-Irish Sarah Grand (born Frances Clarke), who brought the phenomenon of the 'New Woman' to prominence in a series of printed exchanges with the prolific romantic novelist Ouida; and Ella Hepworth Dixon, whose novels written under the pseudonym Margaret Wynman had titles such as *My Flirtations* and *The Story of a Modern Woman*. They pushed the limits of a male-dominated society and showed female characters who exercised control over their own lives. They wrote about marital discord, divorce, and female sexuality. George Egerton wrote about the lives of working-class women. These writers of the 1880s and 1890s were often condemned and derided in the press as literary degenerates.

The New Women were the forerunners of the suffragettes. Emma and Thomas Hardy became deeply interested in women's suffrage. Later, when the movement took off, Emma would march in the suffragette demonstrations. Hardy was supportive of the New Women writers and became a mentor to several aspiring literary women. Later, he would even propose that a woman should become Poet Laureate.[2] Emma, who had always regarded herself as Hardy's literary helpmeet and muse, became deeply insecure about the women who wrote to her husband for literary advice and lionised him at society parties.

In 1879, the Hardys met Frances Mabel Robinson (sister of the poet Mary Frances Robinson) at a garden party given by the publisher Macmillan. She was a poet, novelist and translator who wrote under the name W. S. Gregg. Educated at the Slade School of Art, she became widely regarded as a leading author, publishing six novels during the 1880s and 1890s, provocative in their handling of female status, illegitimacy and seduction. One of them was called *A Woman of the World*, a phrase that could well have been applied to Mabel herself.

A few years later, soon after they moved into Max Gate, they invited her to stay. She had a 'delightful' week, revelling in the song of the larks on the downs and exploring the Roman remains and clerical gardens of Dorchester. She thought the Hardys were '*very* kind'. Hardy showed her his 'beautiful manuscripts' and after dinner Emma lit a bright fire. Hardy read aloud from his latest novel (probably *The Woodlanders*). He read badly, she thought – and every now and then he would be 'suddenly overwhelmed with a sense of the inadequacy of his words'. 'No, no,' he would say, 'Its not at all what I thought!' She felt that Hardy kept dipping into the work 'in the vain hope of touching his own heart'. She seemed puzzled by the Hardy marriage, as increasingly others would discover, and Mrs Hardy she found 'had not the intellectual value nor the tact it would have needed to hold the heart of her husband against all the world . . . Her thoughts hopped off like a bird on a bough.' Mabel was moved to feelings of compassion for Emma: 'I found it hard that no one took her literary accomplishments seriously.' Rather, 'as I saw her she was a perfectly normal woman without much brain power but who wanted to be a poet or a novelist'. She was, however, 'a nice, loveable, inconsequential little lady of whom one grew very fond'.[3]

Robinson met the Hardys frequently at parties during their springtime London season. Whenever Hardy was given praise from others in the room, Emma wrote down their words in a little notebook to read to Hardy when he felt despondent about his work. Mabel (who died in 1956 at the age of ninety-eight) recalled this as an example of Emma's devotion to Hardy. But she also observed the souring of the relationship: 'Then came great success and the adulation of women, some lovely and rich, others just lovely. Others influential. Hardy became the fashion.'[4]

He became the fashion in these circles because of *Tess*. The arrangement with Tillotson's for serialisation fell apart when the publisher read the proofs of the early chapter and discovered their scandalous nature. Hardy refused to make the changes that were asked for. He explored various other options. It seemed to the editor of *Macmillan's Magazine* that Tess's mother was complicit in her daughter becoming Alec's mistress and that even Angel Clare had a 'purely sensuous' admiration for her. He noted that the word 'succulent' was frequently applied to the Frome Valley and suggested that 'the general impression left on me by reading your story . . . is one of rather too much succulence'.[5] That, he granted, made the novel 'entirely modern' – which is to say, the kind of thing that could have been written by Ibsen or one of the New Women. In 1891, the serialisation appeared in the *Graphic*, shortly followed by *Harper's Bazaar* in the United States (which paid very well). The full novel was published in three volumes that December, and swiftly went through several bestselling editions.

The critical reception was mixed: for the *Pall Mall Gazette*, it was the finest English novel in a generation, whereas the *Quarterly Review* was shocked by the emphasis on Tess's 'sensual qualifications': the novel offered 'a coarse and disagreeable story in a coarse and disagreeable manner'. As for the subtitle's provocative description of Tess, the fallen woman, as 'A Pure Woman', this 'put a strain upon the English language'.[6] For the New Woman, on the other hand, Hardy's sympathy for Tess made him into a powerful ally. So, for example, just a few months after the publication of *Tess*, he paid a call on Mrs Mary St Leger Harrison, daughter of the novelist Charles Kingsley. Under the pseudonym Lucas Malet, she wrote novels about unhappy marriages – something of which she had personal experience. Hardy described her as 'A striking woman: full, slightly voluptuous mouth, red lips, black hair and eyes; and most likeable'.[7] She gave him a copy of her latest bestseller, *The Wages of Sin*, a sexually explicit New Woman novel that in certain respects foreshadows *Jude the Obscure*.[8] They struck up a lively correspondence.

The Hardys' annual visits to London for the season brought them into contact not only with women writers such as Mabel Robinson and 'Lucas Malet', but also with fashionable and aristocratic women with whom Emma was often unfairly compared. As she grew older, she appeared to become more eccentric. She gained weight, dressed in an over-elaborate fashion, and her once glorious golden hair 'faded drab'. Worse, Hardy began to 'see Emma as others saw her – rather plain, very coun-trified and scatter-brained'. As Mabel Robinson intuited: 'May-be the admiration of many accomplished women of the world turned his head a bit.'[9]

The novelist Gertrude Atherton saw Emma at a social gath-ering: she watched as Hardy walked by with 'an excessively plain, dowdy, high-stomached woman with her hair drawn back in a tight little knot, and a severe cast of countenance'. Her companion explained that the woman was Mrs Hardy, and added, 'Now you may understand the pessimistic nature of the poor devil's work.'[10] Emma had at least believed that she had pretensions of being of a higher social class than her husband and related to an archdeacon (a connection much mocked by Hardy's friends), but now he was being lauded by the aristocratic ladies of London who paid her scant respect and looked at her husband with pitying eyes. His collection of short stories, *A Group of Noble Dames*, had been published some months before *Tess*: now Hardy was encircled by his own group of noble dames, all wanting to be friends with 'the Author of *Tess*'.[11] There was Lady Jeune, Lady Dorothy Neville, Lady Hilda Broderick, Lady Salisbury, Lady Wimborne, Lady Metcalf, Lady Malmesbury, and even a princess. Lady Hilda Broderick told Hardy that she had wept bitterly over the fate of Tess. This made him, he wrote, feel like a criminal.[12] He also recorded that the Duchess of Abercorn's dinner guests had been 'almost fighting across her dinner party over Tess's character'. Her guests were divided over whether she was the 'little harlot' who deserved hanging or the 'poor wronged innocent'. At another party, he was seated between 'a pair of beauties', one with 'violet eyes' was 'the more seductive' and 'warm-blooded', the other 'more vivacious'.[13]

Emma began to be forced into the background, as Hardy compartmentalised his life. As his fame and finances grew, he spent more time and money on his family. He took his brother

Henry to Paris, visiting the Moulin Rouge, where they watched the cancan dancers, and he bought his sisters a house in Dorchester close to their school.

It was extremely difficult for Emma to witness her husband's growing fame, and to feel that she was being pushed away. She had fair-copied much of *Tess*, and given her husband excellent suggestions; for example, it was her idea that Tess should be wearing the Clare family jewels on the night she makes her confession to Angel. It was Emma who wrote to the editor of the *Spectator*, whose reviewer had complained about Tess's use of the word 'whorage'. Emma explained that the word simply implied a 'company of slatternly, bickering and generally unpleasant women' rather than 'the coarse idea of its root-meaning'.[14] She was also aware of the changing names and titles of Tess, as it evolved from *The Body and Soul of Sue* to *Too Late, Beloved!* to *Tess of the D'Urbervilles: A Pure Woman Faithfully Presented by Thomas Hardy in Three Volumes*. Her letters, her journals and an article she published in the *Daily Chronicle* (1891) on the education of the young, do not give an impression of a 'scatter-brain' or someone who was lacking in 'intellectual value'. And yet still she was criticised, and much of the condemnation focused on her appearance and behaviour.

Meanwhile, Hardy was flirting with outrageously beautiful women such as the poet 'Graham R. Tomson'. She had sent photographs of herself, requested by Hardy, though he suggested 'neither of them does justice to the original'. On a rainy day he wrote to her suggestively about how 'lovers walk two & two just the same, under umbrellas – or rather under one umbrella (which makes all the difference.)'[15] Two years later, she sent him 'a charming pair of volumes' (of her poetry), and he admired the author's photograph: 'the view of yourself sitting in the shadows of your garden is not the least charming feature in them'.[16]

Hurt and betrayed, Emma began to write down her anguished feelings in diaries that deeply condemned her husband, his family, and their failed marriage. Hardy insisted for posterity that it was Emma who wrote down all the aristocratic names of fine ladies in these diaries, which he later destroyed. He wanted to present to the world that details of 'the world of fashion' interested his wife Emma, but which he himself 'did not think worth recording'. He was still conflicted by social class. In respect of the London parties he wrote: 'Society, *collectively*, has neither seen what any ordinary person can see, read what every ordinary person can see, read what every ordinary person has read, nor thought what every ordinary person has thought.'[17] His noble dames were not to be compared with the beautiful peasant girl in the turnip fields. And then he met Florence Henniker.

"*Tess flung herself down upon the undergrowth of rustling spear-grass as upon a bed.*"

"TESS OF THE D'URBERVILLES"
By THOMAS HARDY,

AUTHOR OF "FAR FROM THE MADDING CROWD," "THE MAYOR OF CASTERBRIDGE," &c., &c.

ILLUSTRATED BY PROFESSOR HUBERT HERKOMER, R.A., AND HIS PUPILS, MESSRS. WEHRSCHMIDT, JOHNSON, AND SYDALL

CHAPTER 57

Florence Henniker

Florence Henniker was named for the woman her father had deeply fallen in love with but failed to win over: Florence Nightingale, who became godmother to her namesake. Born in 1855, and raised in luxury, Florence's father was Richard Monckton Milnes, the first Baron Houghton. Educated at Cambridge, he was a poet and a politician with a strong interest in social justice and the emancipation of women. He was a pious and religious man, and a keen collector of erotica, which he later bequeathed to the British Library. Alongside the first biography of Keats, he penned a pornographic poem on the subject of flagellation, *The Rodiad*. He was a mentor for many famous writers, such as Tennyson, Emmerson and Swinburne, and a firm believer in the rights of women – he was great friends with, amongst others, Elizabeth Gaskell.

Hardy had met Florence's father in London and admired him, not least for his defence of P. B. Shelley. When Hardy met Florence in Dublin in May 1893, he became infatuated. Their intense relationship posed the first serious threat to his marriage with Emma. Florence was striking and cultivated. She played the zither. She had dark chestnut hair, a slender carriage and grey-blue eyes that appealed to Hardy. She was a published author in her own right. She was always exquisitely dressed, weaving flowers into her hair. Emma, dressed in muslin and blue ribbons, looked overdressed and absurd. Though Florence was happily married, she formed an intense connection with Hardy, and was flattered by his interest and attention. He wrote down his first impressions: 'a charming, *intuitive* woman apparently'.[1] Their friendship would last until her death. It's possible that she was the woman in his journal entry who wept over Tess: 'I feel very guilty this morning. A lady I much respect writes that she wept so much over the last volume of "Tess" that her husband or brother said with vexation he would leave her to read it by herself.' Upset, he hinted at his capacity for heartlessness: 'I have apologised. Truly, whatever romance-writers feel about being *greater*, they may feel that they are *crueller* than they know.'[2]

Hardy, who soon read Florence's novels, appeared to confuse her liberated fictional creations with the author. Her novels explored the limitations of heterosexual relationships, suggesting that the patriarchy is maintained through the formation of strong bonds between men. Women have to find their own independence, outside of marriage. Mary Gifford, the heroine of her second novel, *Bid Me Goodbye,* rejects four suitors, and, at the end of the novel, remains single and liberated. In print and in person, Florence was known for her pessimism towards the institution of marriage, despite her own happy union. Her nephew recorded her 'insisting on the unhappiness of many marriages'. Perhaps this aspect of her character made her even more appealing to Hardy. Her literary salon in London was filled with eminent writers and poets. Her friend Justin McCarthy described her as London's 'gifted and charming hostess . . . who if she had lived in Paris at a former time, would have been famous as the presiding genius of a *salon* where wit and humour, literature and art, science and statesmanship found congenial welcome.' She was an 'authoress of rare gifts, a writer of delightful stories' with a 'rich poetic endowment'.[3]

Hardy's father had died the year before he met Mrs Henniker, and the absence of his loving and constant presence had deeply affected him and left him feeling vulnerable. His father, for all his gentleness and easy-going temperament, had kept Jemima's acerbity in check. Relationships between the Hardy women and Emma began to deteriorate. In what he saw as a symbolic gesture, Hardy was driving home from Dorchester a few months after his father's death when he saw flames licking around Stinsford House. Hardy leapt from the carriage and ran to help, carrying out books and furniture. He felt the 'bruising of tender memories' as he recalled the close association between Stinsford and his parents' courtship, as well as the vault his grandfather had built for the bodies of Lady Susan and William O'Brien. By coincidence, his sister Mary was in the churchyard and Hardy met her there as she was laying flowers on her father's grave. Always obsessed with the theme of the poor man and the lady, he had finally, in Mrs Henniker, found his Lady Susan.

The Hardys were now wealthy enough to lease an entire house for the London season, which was in 70 Hamilton Terrace, Maida Vale, close to the church in Elgin Avenue where they had married nineteen years before. Hardy had wasted no time in writing to Florence soon after their first meeting, telling her 'I must desire to go somewhere with you.' Florence, whose father so greatly admired Hardy, was flattered by his interest. He promised to teach her about church architecture: 'I want you to be able to walk into a church and pronounce upon its date at a glance; and you are apt scholar enough to soon arrive at that degree of knowledge. Oral instruction in actual buildings is, of course, a much more rapid and effectual method than from books, and you must not think it will be any trouble to me.'[4] Emma was not invited along.

He also took on the role of literary mentor: 'Indeed I fancy you write your MSS. a little too rapidly: though "Sir George", which I have just finished, is a far more promising book than I guessed it was going to be when I began it, and I should like ten minutes conversation with you concerning it when you come to London.' They were together at a small party of four (not including Emma) who went to the theatre to see Ibsen's *The Master Builder* (he had seen *Hedda Gabler* and *Rosmersholm* earlier that week). Hardy made some kind of move towards Florence, which was swiftly repudiated. He soon promised to 'redress by any possible means the one-sidedness I spoke of, of which I am still keenly conscious'.[5] He added: 'I sincerely hope to number you all my life among the most valued of my friends.' It's probable that Florence kept him at bay by emphasising their spiritual compatibility. He wrote: 'Well – perhaps you are right about the story of the two people spiritually united – as far as the man is concerned.'[6]

In the meantime, he read her novel, *Foiled,* and offered honest praise: 'It is really a clever book – quite above what I had been led to expect from the reviews. I don't like some of the men in it – though they are truly drawn: and speaking generally I may say that as a transcript from human nature it ranks far above some novels that have received much more praise.' He also confirmed that she had become his chief female sounding board, a role hitherto taken by his wife: 'If ever I were to consult any woman on a point in my own novels I should let that woman be yourself – my belief in your insight and your sympathies being strong, and increasing.'[7]

Hardy was not above trying to make Florence jealous of his relationships with other New Women authors, such as Pearl Craigie aka John Oliver Hobbes: 'she is very pretty'. Another letter described a party in which a woman flirted with him and showed off her cleavage:

After the theatre we went on to the Academy crush – where, of course, we met a great many vain people we knew. One amusing thing occurred to me. A well-known woman in society, who is one of those despicable creatures a flirt, said to me when I was talking to her: "Don't look at me so!" I said, "Why? – because you feel I can see *too much of you*?" (she was excessively *décolletée*). "Good heavens!" said she. "I am not coming to pieces, am I?" and clutching her bodice she was quite overcome. When next I met her she said bitterly: "You have spoilt my evening: and it was too cruel of you!" However I don't think it was, for she deserved it.[8]

Around this period of longing and frustration, he wrote a journal entry: 'I often think that women, even those who consider themselves experienced in sexual strategy, do not know how to manage an *honest* man.'[9] He continued to tell himself that his motives were pure, but his behaviour towards Florence (and Emma) suggested the very opposite.

Florence gave Hardy some of her verse translations from French and Spanish, which she copied into his literary notebook. This was an act of intimacy. Emma had previously copied out quotations for Hardy, and, as we have seen, helped to make fair copies of his novels. Not only was his wife being pushed out of his life, but she was being replaced by Florence in the one place he had always relied upon Emma's help. It was now Florence who was his 'dear fellow-scribbler'. Perhaps, too, the emotional intensity of the verses gave him false hope:

We were together, – her eyes were wet
But her pride was strong, & no tears would fall;
And *I* would not tell her that I loved her yet,
And yearned to forgive her all!
So, now that our loves are for ever apart,

She thinks – 'Oh! had I but wept that day!'
And *I* ask in vain of my lonely heart –
'Ah!, why did I turn away?'

Hardy was full of praise: 'What beautiful translations those are!
I like the two verses from the Spanish best. You are a real woman
of letters: and must be invited to the next Mansion House dinner
to literature.' He added a barb at the 'many ladies' who bailed
from the Mansion House dinner, because their husbands were
not invited: 'So much for their independence'.[10]

The couple began to exchange books, in which they both
wrote their annotations. Hardy gave Florence a copy of Browning,
drawing a line alongside the lines: 'We loved. Sir – used to meet:
/ How sad and bad and mad it was – / But then, how it was
sweet!' There was banter exchanged on the battle-of-the-sexes
debates of the time. A collection of short stories by the 'New
Woman' George Egerton (Mary Chavelita Clairmonte, née
Dunne) was also exchanged. It was in this book, *Keynotes* (1894),
that Hardy read of how men should not be surprised that 'a
refined physically fragile woman will mate with a brute, a mere
male animal with primitive passions – and love him' because
there is equally an 'eternal wildness, the untamed primitive
savage temperament that lurks in the mildest, best woman'.
Hardy wrote in the margin of his copy: 'This is fairly stated is
decidedly the *ugly* side of woman's nature.' Against another
passage that pricks the bubble of man's romantic idealisation of
woman, Hardy scribbled '*ergo: real* woman is abhorrent to man?
Hence the failure of matrimony?'[11]

His romance with Florence energised him: 'I sleep hardly at
all, and seem not to require any.' He was trying to persuade her
to meet him at Lady Jeune's dinner, threatening her that his
attentions should not be taken for granted: 'I would give Ada
Rehan, Miss Milman, Lady G. Little, her sister, Mrs S. Wortley,

or any other of that ilk, lessons in architecture at astonishingly low fees, to fill up the time.'[12] Hardy was sending her some of his early books, including *A Laodicean*. He explained that he had written it during a serious illness, which had prevented him from meeting Florence's father. The thought that he might have known her earlier in his life made him feel 'morbid'. He ended the letter on a wistful tone: 'You seem quite like an old friend to me, and I only hope that Time will bear out the seeming. Indeed, but for an adverse stroke of fate, you would be – a friend of 13 years standing.'

Frustrated, he wrote an important letter on 16 July 1893. Florence had sent him an anthology of ballads, which included some verses written by Rosamund Watson/Tomson, but she had refused his invitation to be his guest at Lady Jeune's dinner. She had enquired about Hardy's new novel, but he replied that he was more inclined to 'fly off to foreign scenes or plunge into wild dissipation'. He told her that he could 'fill your place at table with some new female acquaintance' but that 'she will certainly not remove my disappointment at your absence'. Florence and Hardy had been reading Shelley's *Epipsychidion*, and Hardy wanted her to read Swinburne's erotic *Poems and Ballads*. Florence's father, alongside Arthur Hallam, representatives of the Cambridge Union, had debated at the Oxford Union that Shelley was superior to Byron. With thoughts of Shelley's concept of free love, he berated Florence for her conventionality:

I had a regret in reading it at thinking that one who is pre-eminently the child of the Shelleyan tradition – whom one would have expected to be an ardent disciple of his school and views – should have allowed herself to be enfeebled to a belief in ritualistic ecclesiasticism. My impression is that you do not know your own views. You feel the need of emotional expression of some sort, and being surrounded by the conventional society form of such expression you have mechanically adopted it. Is this the daughter of the man who went from Cambridge to Oxford on the now historic errand!

His passion aroused, he angrily told her that from now on he would think of her as a sister: 'I will follow Tennyson's advice in future, ("Leave thou thy sister . . .") and trust to imagination only for an enfranchised woman.' There was more than a veiled threat in Hardy's warning about another female poet and 'enfranchised woman' (Rosamund Watson/Tomson) he had admired, before cutting her off in the belief that he was being used: 'Her desire, however, was to use your correspondent as a means of gratifying her vanity by exhibiting him as her admirer, the discovery of which promptly ended the friendship, with considerable disgust on his side.'[13]

With only his side of the correspondence extant, it is impossible to know how Florence reacted to Hardy's insistent and persistent threats. He had wanted more from his mentoring than the two women were willing to give, despite their being 'enfranchised', which he seemed to imply meant being sexually liberated. That Rosamund and Florence valued his friendship, his literary mentoring and his company, was clearly not quite enough for him. Florence did not want to lose his friendship, but nor did she want to enter into an extra-marital affair with him. She defended herself on the charge of her 'unfaithfulness to the Shelley cult' and invited him to lunch. In a calmer mood, and grateful for the chance of seeing her again, he modified his charge:

P.S. What I meant about your unfaithfulness to the Shelley cult referred not to any lack of poetic emotion, but to your view of things: e.g., you are quite out of harmony with this line of his in Epipsychidion:

'The sightless tyrants of our fate.'
which beautifully expresses one's consciousness of blind circumstances beating upon one, without any feeling, for or against.[14]

Following the meeting with Florence, he wrote again. This time
round, in order to enhance his desirability, he dangled a 'pretty
actress' who was about to call upon him, before chastising her
one more time: 'I cannot help wishing you were free from certain
retrograde superstitions: and I believe you will be some day, and
none the less happy for the emancipation.'[15] The Hardys were
leaving London for Max Gate for the summer, but Hardy took
a roundabout route alone in order to stay with the Jeunes and
grab a few precious hours with Florence. He had concocted a
plan. Florence's interest in the topography of *Tess* gave him the
idea of an intimate visit to Winchester, Tess's final destination.
For the first time in twenty years, he made an entry into his
prayer book of the date of the visit: 8 August 1893. The pilgrimage
would inspire some of his finest poems, and it would also signal
the dashing of any hopes Hardy entertained of a full-blown
sexual relationship with Florence.

————

They met at Eastleigh railway station en route to Winchester.
There was a scene in the railway carriage, where, once again,
Florence made her feelings clear that she wanted only friendship. In his poem 'The Month's Calendar' Hardy wrote: 'You
let me see / There was good cause / Why You could not be /
Aught ever to me.' They carried on to Winchester, where they
headed to the George Inn. Once there, they were mistaken
for lovers by the staff: 'Veiled smiles bespoke their thought /
Of what we were.' They were left alone in a room, 'as love's
own pair / Yet never the love-light shone / Between us there.'

They are, in his imagination, lovers who 'had all resigned / For love's dear end.' Another poem about the incident, 'At an Inn', blames 'the laws of men' for separating the lovers. Hoping for a kiss, the poet-narrator is unhappy that it doesn't come: 'The kiss their zeal foretold, / And now deemed come, / Came not: within his hold.'[16] Another Mrs Henniker poem, 'A Thunderstorm in Town', confirms that they never exchanged a single kiss, though Hardy told a friend that when they visited Winchester Cathedral there was an intense emotional moment when they clasped hands beside the high altar. The couple also walked to West Hill, to the very place where Angel and Liza-Lu watch the black flag rise above the prison to signal that Tess has been executed.

If Hardy is to be believed, the pilgrimage to Winchester was highly charged emotionally. After the trip, he wrote a passionate letter (now lost), criticising Florence's conventional views. Then he wrote another letter: 'You allude to the letter of Aug 3. If I shd never write to you again as in that letter you must remember that it was written *before* you expressed your views – "morbid" indeed! *petty* rather – in the railway carriage when we met at Eastleigh. But I am always your friend.'[17] It is to Florence's credit that she managed to keep Hardy's friendship and patronage without alienating him. That autumn, she sent him a present of a silver inkstand, engraved T. H. from F. H., a symbolic gift that celebrated them both as writers. He kept it on his desk for the rest of his life. She sent him 'beautiful large' portrait photographs to add to his ever-growing collection of lovely literary women. Knowing him perhaps better than he knew himself, she intuited that unattainable, unrequited love inspired his work.

Over the next few months, there was some distance between them. Hardy was 'a trifle chilled' to hear Florence had read some of his 'effusive' letters aloud:

Feeling that something was influencing you adversely, &
destroying the charm of your letters & personality, I lost confidence in you somewhat. I know, of course, that there is nothing
in my epistles which it matters in the least about all the world
knowing, but I have always a feeling that such publicity destroys
the pleasure of a friendly correspondence.[18]

He still resented that her behaviour was not as free-thinking or
'modern' as her novels: 'If you mean to make the world listen
to you, you must say now what they will all be thinking &
saying five & twenty years hence: & if you do that you must
offend your conventional friends.' But there was still deep admiration for her as a writer: when Florence accused him of having
'contempt' for her story 'Desire', he replied, 'you know I *never*
can have that for *anything* you do'.[19]

That autumn they collaborated on a short story, which was
called 'The Spectre of the Real' – its theme a clandestine romance
between a 'noble lady' and a poor officer. Again, Florence accused
Hardy of being 'unkind', for which he was sorry. He assured
her that 'Never could I give *you* pain.'[20] But he was also writing
in secret another story, which he knew would have special
meaning for Florence. A month after the Winchester trip, he
sent off the manuscript of 'An Imaginative Woman', in which
he explored his longing for Florence. It would be one of several
works that would have as its theme an unsatisfactory marriage.
Hardy knew that, as a writer, he was capable of cruelty, and he
knew that Florence was sensitive and hated to upset him, but
he could not help himself.

The heroine, Ella Marchmill, is companionably married to
her husband, a gun-maker. Though they are in 'age well-balanced,
in personal appearance fairly matched, and in domestic requirements comfortable', they differ in temper and temperament.
Ella is a poet who writes under the pseudonym John Ivy. She

is described as elegant: 'an impressionable, palpitating creature' of 'delicate and ethereal emotions'. One of the poets she most admires is a man called Robert Trewe. The Marchmills rent rooms in a seaside town, and Ella takes for her own boudoir the one that belongs to the young man from whom they are sub-letting. Ella discovers that she is in the room of the very poet she admires. That Hardy was representing himself in Robert Trewe (True) is evidenced by the description of him as 'a pessimist in so far as that character applies to a man who looks at the worst contingencies as well as the best in the human condition'. Ella falls in love with the poet for his words, and then falls in love with his photograph. Becoming obsessed, she dresses in his clothes, kisses his image, and sleeps in his bed. There is an erotic moment when, half undressed, she contemplates Trewe's image, only to be interrupted by the unexpected arrival of her husband. He kisses her and tells her 'I wanted to be with you, tonight', but she refuses. Ella writes a letter to Trewe in her guise as John Ivy, and hopes to meet him, but she is thwarted in her desires. Trewe kills himself, leaving a suicide note in which he explains his yearning for a woman he has never met: 'I have long dreamed of such an attainable creature, as you know; and she, this undiscoverable, elusive one, inspired my last volume: the imaginary woman alone.' The supreme irony is that they are both searching for a soulmate, but they never meet, and they both end up dead.

It is inconceivable that Florence Henniker would not have recognised herself in the portrait of Ella, or, indeed, Hardy as the mysterious, shy and sensitive poet. In the original manuscript Hardy gives his poet-hero the name 'Crewe', that of Florence's mother. Hardy inserted intimate details that Florence would recognise, such as poetical fragments drawn on the wall, 'ideas in the rough, like Shelley's scraps'. Trewe's 'mournful ballad' is called 'Severed Lives', remarkably similar to Hardy's

'In Death Divided' and 'The Division', poems associated with Florence. Another link is provided by the setting: Solensea, which is clearly Southsea, where she lived. Her dull husband, who is a gun-maker (as Florence was married to a soldier), is associated with 'the destruction of life'.

Despite Ella's attractiveness and her aspirations to be a poet, the portrait is a cruel one, with many barbs intended solely for Florence. Ella writes 'feeble' poetry in order 'to find a congenial channel in which to let flow her painfully embayed emotions, whose former limpidity and sparkle seemed departing in the stagnation caused by the routine of a practical household'. She imitates the great poet Trewe, but her 'inability to touch his level would send her into fits of despondency'. Nobody reads her poetry and nobody reviews her work. Like Florence, Ella is in her thirties, and is entering the 'tract of life' when her looks will fade and she will keep the 'blinds down' when receiving a male visitor to obscure the signs of ageing. In an especially unkind sentence, Hardy took a jibe at both Florence and her husband. Ella feels a strong connection to the poet: 'She knew his thoughts and feelings as well as she knew her own; they were, in fact, the self-same thoughts and feelings as hers, which her husband distinctly lacked; perhaps luckily for himself; considering that he had to provide for family expenses.' Ella is punished because she does not have the guts to be unconventional and call in person on the poet.

But the cruellest jibe of all was Hardy's writing of the story in the jejune style of Florence Henniker's own novels. Every line spoken by Ella is written from the perspective and manner of a 'timid', 'immature' and 'juvenile' author:

'O, if he had only known of me – known of me – me! . . . O, if I had only once met him – only once; and put my hand upon his hot forehead – kissed him – let him know how I loved him – that I would have suffered shame and scorn, would have lived and died, for him! Perhaps it would have saved his dear life! . . . But no – it was not allowed! God is a jealous God; and that happiness was not for him and me!'

Ella dies in childbirth, and her husband remains convinced that his wife was unfaithful with the poet in a lodging house 'the second week of August'. By using the very date of his own failed tryst with Florence in Winchester, he dealt the final blow. Though given to the husband, the last words of the story summed up Hardy's impotent humiliation and fury: 'Get away, you poor little brat! You are nothing to me!'[21]

Hardy had exacted his revenge.

CHAPTER 58

Susanna Florence Mary Bridehead

'I don't mind if Tom publishes how badly we were used,' Kate Hardy wrote in reference to the miserable existence she and her sister endured at teacher training college.[1] This was back in the early 1880s, when she and Emma were still on friendly terms, and suggests that Hardy had long been contemplating a book about a schoolteacher heroine, which drew on the experiences of his sisters in Salisbury. As he would note in the preface to the book that he eventually wrote, it was the death of that other beloved schoolmistress, Tryphena Sparks, that inspired him to return to the theme: 'The scheme was jotted down in 1890, from notes made in 1887 and onward, some of the circumstances being suggested by the death of a woman in the former year.'[2] From August 1893 (the time of the Winchester expedition), Hardy had begun writing the novel 'at full length'. In October, he had written to Florence Henniker: 'What name shall I give to the heroine of my coming long story when I get at it?'[3] In the event, he named her Susanna Florence Mary Bridehead.

The death of his father, the year before, had propelled him back into the lives of his mother and sisters. As the eldest son, and with no children of his own, he was the nominal head of the Hardy family. His diary entries of the time record tales told by his mother of his father as a young church musician. He was moved when she told him that she felt she didn't belong to the Bockhampton cottage: 'My Mother says she looks at the furniture and feels she is nothing to it. All those belongings to it, and the place, are gone, and it is left in her hands, a stranger. (She has, however, lived there these fifty-three years!).' Hardy, too, was feeling his age: 'I look in the glass. Am conscious of the humiliating sorriness of my earthly tabernacle, and of the sad fact that the best of parents could do no better for me.'[4]

In October, he visited his grandmother's village of Great Fawley. The following spring, he took a trip to Oxford, during the university's festive season of Encaenia, 'with the Christ-church and other college balls, garden parties, and suchlike bright functions'. He did not make himself known as the famous author of *Tess of the D'Urbervilles*: his object was 'to view the proceedings entirely as a stranger'.[5] For the purposes of research, he wanted to remain Hardy the Obscure. Back in 1888, he had written a note: 'A short story of a man – "who could not go to Oxford" – His struggles and ultimate failure. Suicide. There is something [in this] the world ought to be shown, and I am the one to show it to them.' His hero, Jude, had been forming in his mind for most of his adult life, ever since his brilliant, alcoholic uncle, John Antell, had given him Latin lessons at the back of his boot store. The man who did not go to Oxford was protesting too much when, in his journal entry about the germination of the novel, he wrote: 'I was not altogether hindered going, at least to Cambridge, and could have gone up easily at five-and-twenty.'[6] But he had not had the privilege of going up to one of the ancient universities; even in his fame, he still considered himself an outsider. And a visit to a university town inevitably stirred one of his most painful memories: Cambridge and his last sight of Horace before his suicide.

His heroine, Sue, had been conceived as a country school-mistress in the vein of cousin Tryphena and sister Mary. Now Sue took on not only Florence's name, but also some of her 'intellectual' characteristics. That Emma became aware of how she had lost her husband's affections during this time is evident in a letter she wrote many years later, in which she suggested that around the age of fifty was the time when 'a man's feelings too often take a new course altogether. Eastern ideas of matrimony secretly pervade his thoughts, & he wearies of the most perfect and suitable wife chosen in his earlier life.'[7]

It was indeed in his early fifties that Hardy became infatuated with the aristocratic and literary ladies of London and became especially interested in the new divorce laws that made it possible for men and women to escape unhappy unions. Shortly after his fifty-third birthday, still in love with Florence, he called on his friend Lady Londonderry, 'a beautiful woman still . . . and very glad to see me, which beautiful women are not always'. They were joined by the Duchess of Manchester and Lady Jeune: 'All four of us talked of the marriage-laws . . . of the difficulties of separation, of terminable marriages where there are children, and of the nervous strain of living with a man when you know he can throw you over at any moment.' More divorce talk occurred at a country house weekend at Wenlock Abbey, where Hardy heard an 'amusing story' told by the host. A recently divorced man had celebrated his freedom by throwing a 'congratulatory dinner' and the mayor made a speech beginning 'On this auspicious occasion'.[8]

One of the unexpected results of the publication of *Tess* had been a flurry of 'strange letters' that Hardy had received from admirers of the book: 'some from husbands whose experiences had borne a resemblance to that of Angel Clare, though more, many more, from wives with a past like that of Tess; but who had *not* told their husbands . . . some of these were educated women of good position.' Hardy had been troubled by the fact that many of the women had begged to meet him. Hardy was unsure and asked advice from Mary Jeune's husband, 'who had had abundant experience of the like things in the Divorce Court where he presided'. Sir Francis Jeune told Hardy that he had received similar requests from troubled women, but deemed it prudent to refuse. Hardy took his advice, 'though he sometimes sadly thought that they came from sincere women in trouble'.⁹

In *Jude the Obscure*, Hardy would tackle the 'marriage question' (divorce and 'living in sin'), causing outrage from the critics and many of his friends. Emma, too, would be horrified by his 'attack on marriage', and felt that Hardy was sending her a very clear message about their own unhappy union. For Emma, the detestable *Jude* signified the end of her marriage, and the beginning of 'Keeping separate'. Emma's relationship with Mary and Kate also began to suffer. 'Interference from others is greatly to be feared', she wrote, 'members of either family too often are the cause of estrangement. A woman does not object to being ruled by her husband, so much as she does by a relative at his back.'¹⁰

In 1891, Hardy visited Tryphena's training college in Stockwell. He noted down the custom whereby each new student was assigned a college 'mother' to look after her, though 'Sometimes the pair gets fond of each other; at other times not.'¹¹ He now saw himself in an analogous quasi-parental role: buying a house for his sisters was one way of assuaging any sibling guilt about his wealth and status. He also became closer to his brother. In the autumn of 1893, Henry and Thomas began working together to build a substantial house two miles east of Max Gate. Called Talbothays, it would eventually be a home for both Henry and the two sisters. The brothers also took on the renovation of St Peter's church in West Knighton, close to Henry's building yard, a project which overlapped with the writing of *Jude*, which has a stone mason as a hero.

Relations with Florence had improved. She had worried that Hardy had turned against her:

> Of course I shall *never* dislike you, unless you do what you cannot do – turn out to be a totally different woman from what I know you to be. I won't have you say that there is little good in you. One great gain from that *last* meeting is that it revived in my consciousness certain nice & dear features in your character which I had half forgotten, through their being of that ethereal intangible sort which letters cannot convey. If you have only *one* good quality, a good *heart*, you are good enough for me. Believe me, my dear friend.[12]

A few weeks later he told her that his novel was slowly progressing: 'I am creeping on a little with the long story, & am beginning to get interested in my heroine as she takes shape & reality: though she is very nebulous at present.'[13] To his friend the author Edmund Gosse, he would describe Sue as 'a type of woman which has always had an attraction for me – but the difficulty of drawing the type has kept me from attempting it until now'.[14] Paula Power in *A Laodicean* was the closest he had come.

Earlier, following the Winchester debacle, Hardy had assured Florence that his unrequited love had dissipated: 'You may be thankful to hear that the *one-sidedness* I used to remind you of is disappearing from the situation. But you will always be among the most valued of my friends, as I hope always to remain one at least of the rank & file of yours'. In the same letter, he thanked her again for the present of the inkstand and promised her that 'the next big story shall be written from its contents.'[15] Even the ink with which he wrote *Jude* was permeated with thoughts of Florence.

Over and over again, Hardy would express outrage that *Jude the Obscure* was taken as an attack on the institution of marriage. He told Gosse, who had given the novel a bad review, that 'It is concerned first with the labours of a poor student to get a University degree, & secondly with the tragic issues of two bad marriages, owing in the main to a doom or curse of hereditary temperament peculiar to the family of the parties'.[16] For Hardy, the twin themes of education and marriage were inextricably linked, so perhaps it was an error of judgement to give the novel an epigraph (from the Old Testament book of Esdras) that only hinted at the latter: '*Yea, many there be that have run out of their wits for women, and become servants for their sakes. Many also have perished, have erred, and sinned, for women . . . O ye men, how can it be but women should be strong, seeing they do thus?*'

As with *Tess* Hardy ran through various possible thematic titles – 'Hearts Insurgent', 'The Simpletons', 'The Recalcitrants' – before making the wise choice of naming the novel from its lead character. Jude is a working-class boy, self-taught, who longs to go to Christminster (Oxford). He is trapped into an unsatisfactory marriage by a peasant woman called Arabella. Bored with her husband and his dreams, Arabella abandons Jude and emigrates to Australia, where she enters into a bigamous marriage. Jude falls in love with a photograph of his first cousin, Sue, before going to live in Christminster to be close to her. Sue decides to train as a teacher and studies at Melchester Training College. She is rusticated from college for spending the night with Jude. Despite her damaged reputation, she marries Jude's schoolmaster and mentor, Phillotson. The marriage is a failure, as Sue is sexually repulsed by her husband. She sleeps in a spider-strewn closet to escape his advances and jumps out of a window to flee from her conjugal duties. Sue leaves her husband to live with Jude. Jude divorces Arabella, but agrees to raise their child. Sue divorces Phillotson. Jude and Sue have children out of wedlock. Jude's son murders his half-siblings and kills himself; Sue has a miscarriage with her third child. She recants her free life and returns to her husband, and Jude returns to Arabella. Given this plot, Hardy's claim that the novel was not about 'the marriage question' is more than disingenuous.

Almost from the opening pages, the sensitive, book-loving orphan boy, Jude, is told by his great-aunt, Drusilla Fawley, that the institution of marriage is not for him: 'Jude, my child, don't you ever marry. 'Tisn't for the Fawleys to take that step any more.' Later, Jude discovers that his own parents had parted, his mother drowning herself when he was just a baby. Following his own imprudent marriage to Arabella, his great-aunt (Jemima-like) reiterates that the family were not made for marriage: 'The Fawleys were not made for wedlock: it never seemed to sit well upon us. There's sommat in our blood that won't take kindly to the notion of being bound to do what we do readily enough if not bound. That's why you ought to have hearkened to me, and not ha' married.'[17]

Hardy poured much of himself into the portrayal of Jude. He is a lover of animals and nature, bookish and solitary, different from the other country boys, unable to harm any living creature. He walks on tiptoe to avoid stepping on the lowliest of the low, the earthworms. He feeds the birds that he is supposed to be repelling when employed as a living scarecrow. He feels more affinity for starving birds than for his fellow creatures: 'A magic thread of fellow-feeling united his own life with theirs. Puny and sorry as those lives were, they much resembled his own.' Like his creator, 'he could scarcely bear to see trees cut down or lopped, from a fancy that it hurt them; and late pruning, when the sap was up and the tree bled profusely, had been a positive grief to him in his infancy'.[18] He is self-taught, learning Latin and Greek from battered second-hand grammars. Like Hardy, Jude's 'private study' comes chiefly from Horace, Virgil and Caesar in cheap Delphin copies, 'roughened with stone dust'.[19]

In a paragraph repeated almost word for word in Hardy's autobiography, Jude lies in the sun and thinks about his desire to stay forever a boy:

> He pulled his straw hat over his face and peered through the interstices of the plaiting at the white brightness, vaguely reflecting. Growing up brought responsibilities, he found. Events did not rhyme quite as he had thought. Nature's logic was too horrid for him to care for. That mercy towards one set of creatures was cruelty towards another sickened his sense of harmony. As you got older and felt yourself to be at the centre of your time, and not at a point in its circumference, as you had felt when you were little, you were seized with a sort of shuddering, he perceived. All around you there seemed to be something glaring, garish, rattling, and the noises and glares hit upon the little cell called your life, and shook it, and warped it.

If he could only prevent himself growing up! He did not want to be a man.[20]

Longing for the 'heavenly Jerusalem' of Christminster/Oxford, Jude sees its domes and spires in the distance, and knows that it is the place for him: it is a 'city of light', 'a place that teachers of men spring from and go to' and 'a castle, manned by scholarship and religion'. Above all, 'the tree of knowledge grows there'.[21] It's a typical Hardy joke (much disliked by his critics) that Jude's Eve is the vulgar and common Arabella, who attracts his attention by throwing a pig's penis at his face, hitting him on the ear. Trained as a stone mason, he aspires to be a son of Christminster, and it is while he is reciting his dreams aloud that he is hit by Arabella's pizzle.

Arabella represents the working-class life he is trying to escape. She is gloriously crude and forthright. She has 'a round and prominent bosom, full lips, perfect teeth, and the rich complexion of a Cochin hen's egg. She was a complete and substantial female animal – no more, no less.' Jude is drawn to her sexually and knows that she is not innocent: 'It had been no vestal who chose *that* missile for opening her attack on him.' Thus, she is able to trap him into marriage by pretending she is pregnant: 'he's to be had by any woman who can get him to care for her a bit, if she likes to set herself to catch him the right way.'²² When Arabella confesses to a friend that she has entrapped Jude, her friend tells her to expect physical punishment: 'He'll give it to 'ee on Saturday nights!'

Jude discovers Arabella's treachery, but senses that the institution of marriage has bound him to her for ever. They have their first row: Arabella tells him, coldly: 'Every woman has a right to do such as that. The risk is hers.' He responds: 'I quite deny it, Bella. She might if no lifelong penalty attached to it for the man, or, in his default, for herself; if the weakness of the moment could end with the moment, or even with the year.' There is a physical tussle over his beloved books, which Arabella tosses to their floor and covers in grease. Jude is left with the knowledge that his hasty marriage has ruined his prospects, and that there is no real companionship or intellectual or spiritual union: 'Their lives were ruined, he thought; ruined by the fundamental error of their matrimonial union: that of having based a permanent contract on a temporary feeling which had no necessary connection with affinities that alone render a lifelong comradeship tolerable.'²³ And yet he is partially released from his bond when, ironically, Arabella is the one who escapes to a new life.

Of course, Arabella *has* to be painted in the worst possible light in order to provide a contrast to Sue. As Arabella is buxom and fair, Sue is slender and girlish: 'She was light and slight, of the type dubbed elegant. That was about all he had seen. There was nothing statuesque in her; all was nervous motion. She was mobile, living, yet a painter might not have called her handsome or beautiful. But the much that she was surprised him.' She is the most intellectual of Hardy's heroines, the most free-spirited and passionate. Where Arabella is all lusty cheerfulness, Sue is all trembling feeling. Hardy confided to a friend called Edward Clodd that Florence Henniker was his most 'immediate' model for Sue. But there was one important exception. Sue, with her disdain for the institution of marriage and for organised religion, was the 'enfranchised woman' of his imagination that he wanted Florence to be, and which she steadfastly refused to embrace in life, despite flirting with it in her novels. Though the initial idea for the novel was the man who could not go to Oxford, Hardy's feelings for Florence led him to enter deeply into the creation of Sue, as can be judged from a letter to Florence: 'Curiously enough I am more interested in this Sue story than in any I have written.'[24]

Like Hardy, Jude wants and deserves to go to Oxford/ Christminster. Yet even before he is rejected by the master of Bibliol (Balliol) College, Jude has already realised that his dreams are built on fantasies and are an 'iridescent soap-bubble'. He knows that it is the 'curious and cunning glamour' of the university that has enchanted him:

> To get there and live there, to move among the churches and halls and become imbued with the *genius loci*, had seemed to his dreaming youth, as the spot shaped its charms to him from its halo on the horizon, the obvious and ideal thing to do. 'Let me only get there,' he had said with the fatuousness

of Crusoe over his big boat, 'and the rest is but a matter of time and energy.'

Feeling dejected and an imposter, it is he who decides, before the rejection letter arrives, that he could never belong there: 'Those buildings and their associations and privileges were not for him. From the looming roof of the great library, into which he hardly ever had time to enter, his gaze travelled on to the varied spires, halls, gables, streets, chapels, gardens, quadrangles, which composed the ensemble of this unrivalled panorama.'[25]

It therefore comes as a breath of fresh air when Sue scornfully tells Jude that she despises the university and all its associations: 'I have no respect for Christminster whatever, except, in a qualified degree, on its intellectual side . . . And intellect at Christminster is new wine in old bottles. The medievalism of Christminster must go, be sloughed off, or Christminster itself will have to go.' When Jude disagrees, she persists. While the dons are locked in befuddled scholasticism, the students have their places on the grounds of wealth and status, not ability:

'It is an ignorant place, except as to the townspeople, artizans, drunkards, and paupers,' she said, perverse still at his differing from her. '*They* see life as it is, of course; but few of the people in the colleges do. You prove it in your own person. You are one of the very men Christminster was intended for when the colleges were founded; a man with a passion for learning, but no money, or opportunities, or friends. But you were elbowed off the pavement by the millionaires' sons.'[26]

Like the emancipated woman that she is, Sue is equally forthright about the marriage ceremony, in which a woman is 'given away' by another man:

'I have been looking at the marriage service in the prayer-book, and it seems to me very humiliating that a giver-away should be required at all. According to the ceremony as there printed, my bridegroom chooses me of his own will and pleasure; but I don't choose him. Somebody *gives* me to him, like a she-ass or she-goat, or any other domestic animal.'[27]

And she scorns the sexual hypocrisy of the age:

'As to our going on together as we were going, in a sort of friendly way, the people round us would have made it unable to continue. Their views of the relations of man and woman are limited . . . Their philosophy only recognizes relations based on animal desire. The wide field of strong attachment where desire plays, at least, only a secondary part, is ignored by them – the part of – who is it? – Venus Urania.'[28]

When Sue seeks release from her stultifying marriage, she expresses the views of the heart and soul, not of convention: 'Why can't we agree to free each other? We made the compact, and surely we can cancel it – not legally of course; but we can morally, especially as no new interests, in the shape of children, have arisen to be looked after. Then we might be friends, and meet without pain to either.' Even when she divorces Phillotson and lives 'in sin' with Jude, she refuses to make the union legal or to enter into what she perceives is a 'sordid conditions of a business contract'. Jude agrees that marriage is not for them: 'The intention of the contract is good, and right for many, no doubt; but in our case it may defeat its own ends because we are the queer sort of people we are – folk in whom domestic ties of a forced kind snuff out cordiality and spontaneousness.'[29] It is society which demands the sacrifice of Sue and Jude, forced out of town because of their lawless union, and ending with the appalling sacrifice of their innocent children. Sue returns to Phillotson, recants her views, and finds religion. But worst of all, as Hardy makes clear, she is returning to the marital bed of the man she loathes.

The presentation of Sue's sexuality is one of the reasons why the critics dubbed the book, *Jude the Obscene*. Because she is in love with Jude, she believes that having sex with her husband is 'adultery'. She is the least outwardly 'sexy' of Hardy's heroines. Even Jude perceives her as an ethereal being: 'you spirit, you disembodied creature, you dear, sweet, tantalizing phantom – hardly flesh at all; so that when I put my arms round you I almost expect them to pass through you as through air!' Hardy makes it clear, however, that it is her husband who is the object of her sexual disgust. Because she is honest, she tries to be explicit about her 'eccentric' and 'super-sensitive' nature. She confides in Jude her 'physical objection – a fastidiousness, or whatever it may be called' towards her husband. Later, she calls it 'torture to me to – live with him as a husband'. Sue rejects the notion that she is 'cold-natured – sexless . . . But I won't have it! Some of the most passionately erotic poets have been the most self-contained in their daily lives.'[30]

It is significant, though, that Sue asks Jude to recite the poetry of Shelley: 'Say those pretty lines, then, from Shelley's "Epipsychidion" as if they meant me!" she solicited, slanting up closer to him as they stood.' Phillotson convinces himself that Sue and Jude's relationship is spiritually 'Shelleyan' rather than corporeal. Shelley was the poet of Hardy and Florence Henniker, and the inference is clear. In what seems like a Hardy wish-fulfilment, Jude makes an impassioned plea – from a married man to a married woman: ' You are dear, free Sue Bridehead, only you don't know it! Wifedom has not yet squashed up and digested you in its vast maw as an atom which has no further individuality.' There are moments when Hardy appears to be writing (from her inkstand) only to Florence Henniker: "'O Susanna Florence Mary!" he said as he worked. "You don't know what marriage means!'"[31] It is not hard to see why Emma hated the book so much, and why she believed it was the final nail in the coffin of their marriage.

––––

Often it appears that Hardy is writing about two different heroines: the 'Florence' Sue, who is 'so ethereal a creature that her spirit could be seen trembling through her limbs', and the 'Tryphena' Sue who escapes through a window at night and is rusticated from college for immoral conduct. When Jude visits his cousin at Melchester College, she is dressed in a murray-coloured school uniform with a little lace collar, she is 'the bright-eyed vivacious girl with the broad forehead and pile of dark hair above it; the girl with the kindling glance, daringly soft at times – something like that of the girls he had seen in engravings from paintings of the Spanish school'.[32]

Sue becomes a pupil teacher at Mr Phillotson's school in Oxford, and, like Tryphena and Kate, wins a Queen's Scholarship. Hardy used details from Tryphena's Stockwell training college and combined them with Mary and Kate's experience in Salisbury, in order to flesh out the life of the Victorian school-mistress. Melchester College is set in a Cathedral Close. Drawing on his knowledge of Salisbury Training College, Hardy described it as a 'nunnery' housing a 'very mixed community, which included the daughters of mechanics, curates, surgeons, shop-keepers, farmers, dairy-men, soldiers, sailors, and villagers'. The girls are 'inmates'. Late into the night the students peer out of the mullioned windows at the vast west front of the cathedral opposite, and the spire rising behind it. Following evening prayer, the girls are confined to their cubicles, 'their tender feminine faces upturned to the flaring gas-jets which at intervals stretched down the long dormitories'. Hardy's pity for their hardship shows that he was bitterly aware of the price his own sisters had paid for their mother's ambition: 'They formed a pretty, suggestive, pathetic sight, of whose pathos and beauty they were themselves unconscious, and would not discover till, amid the storms and strains of after-years, with their injustice, loneliness, child-bearing, and bereavement, their minds would revert to this experience as to something which had been allowed to slip past them insufficiently regarded.'[33]

Sue has the 'air of a woman clipped and pruned by severe discipline, an under-brightness shining through from the depths which that discipline had not yet been able to reach'. She 'hated the place she was in'. Like Hardy's sisters, she is lonely and miserable, 'utterly friendless'. She is also undernourished. When Jude tells Sue that he would like to buy her a little present, she asks him to feed her. She explains to Jude that the girls are kept 'on very short allowances in the college, and a dinner, tea, and supper all in one was the present she most desired in the world'. Jude takes her to a local inn. As she eats, she 'tells him about the school as it was at that date, and the rough living, and the mixed character of her fellow students, gathered together from all parts of the diocese, and how she had to get up and work by gas-light in the early morning, with all the bitterness of a young person to whom restraint was new.' Jude suggests that they go and sit in the cathedral, but Sue rejects his offer:

'Cathedral? Yes. Though I think I'd rather sit in the railway station,' she answered, a remnant of vexation still in her voice. 'That's the centre of the town life now. The cathedral has had its day!'

"How modern you are!'

'So would you be if you had lived so much in the Middle

Ages as I have done these last few years! The cathedral was a
very good place four or five centuries ago; but it is played out
now . . . I am not modern, either. I am more ancient than
medievalism, if you only knew.'[34]

Jude's visit to the training college marks the beginning of Sue's
downfall. Jude takes lodgings in the Close Gate and is hired to
restore the cathedral. On Sue's day off, he takes her on an outing
to Wardour Castle: 'There duly came the charm of calling at the
college door for her; her emergence in a nunlike simplicity of
costume that was rather enforced than desired.' Disaster strikes
when they miss the last train and Sue fails to arrive for supper and
evening prayers. In the morning, Sue's little cot is still empty.
Furthermore, she has been spotted at the railway station with Jude.
Nobody believes that he is her cousin: he is assumed to be her
lover. The other students are forbidden to speak to her without
permission. She is given a severe reprimand from the principal and
punished with a week of solitary confinement. Escaping through
a window, she wades into the river and is presumed drowned: 'The
mind of the matron was horrified – not so much at the possible
death of Sue as at the possible half-column detailing that event in
all the newspapers, which, added to the scandal of the year before,
would give the college an unenviable notoriety for many months
to come.'[35]

Sue appears at Jude's room, wet through, and he dresses her
in his clothes. Sue confesses to a past relationship with a brilliant
Oxford/Christminster student, who lent her books and caused
her to lose her religious faith. She tells Jude that her scholar
friend was the 'most irreligious man I ever knew, and the most
moral'. Shortly afterwards, he went to London and became a
'leader writer of the great London dailies'.[36] The scholar dies
soon after, and Sue worries that it was of a broken heart. Horace
Moule was never far from Hardy's thoughts.

When Sue is dressed in Jude's clothes, he is struck by their family resemblance. At times, they resemble brother and sister, 'almost the two parts of a single whole'. Phillotson remarks: 'They remind me of – what are their names – Laon and Cythna' – that is to say, the incestuous siblings of Shelley's poem.[37] Hardy told an interviewer (Ibsen's translator, William Archer) of a relation whose thoughts would so 'jump with' his own that 'after a long silence, both of us, in the same breath, would speak of some person or thing apparently quite absent from the thoughts of either five minutes before'.[38] It is usually assumed that he was thinking of his mother, but this belies the deep connection he had with his sister Mary. In a deleted passage in the original manuscript, Jude looks at Sue sleeping and is struck by her likeness: 'the rough material called himself done into another sex – idealized, softened, & purified'.[39]

However, the strong family likeness in cousins who are in love also reflects Tryphena, the woman whose death, Hardy claimed, inspired Sue. In his poignant poem 'Thoughts of Phena; at news of her death', he paid tribute to the girl with laughter in her eyes and 'dreams upbrimming with light' – his cousin of 'sweet ways' and many 'gifts and compassions'. She is his 'lost prize', and yet the poem comes full circle from lamenting the fact that the poet has 'no line of her writing, nor a thread of her hair' to the realisation that he does not need a relic because he has the memory of his love 'fined in my brain'.[40]

CHAPTER 59

Agnes Grove

Hardy told his second wife that Emma died 'some twenty years' before her actual death.[1] What did he mean? During the last two decades of her life, she became a keen suffragette and an animal rights activist, and she discovered a love for the new craze for cycling. She established a close bond with her brother's children, Lilian and Gordon, who were regular visitors at Max Gate, and enjoyed her London 'At Home' gatherings. Her Gifford niece and nephew, given her childlessness, were the nearest thing to family. During the years of her marriage, Emma had seldom visited her hometown of Plymouth. She returned for her father's funeral in 1890, where she had been shocked by the changes to her beloved home city, and damages to the family vault by alterations to the church where they lay. Hardy wrote about her visit to Plymouth in the poem 'Lonely Days', which imagines the 'sad lady' returning home alone with 'none there to share it, no one to tell'. In her memoir, she wrote about the visit and her return to the Max Gate 'prison'.[2]

Perhaps what Hardy meant was that his marriage died in 1892, just before he met Florence Henniker. Yet, as his letters attest, he was still affectionate and kind to his wife; she was 'My dear Em' or 'My dearest Em'. There were holidays together, and always the presence of their beloved pets who became surrogate children. In the summer of 1894, the Hardys planned extensions to Max Gate: a new kitchen and scullery, and a larger study at the front of the house on the first floor. The financial security brought by the publication of *Tess* (and the new American copyright legislation laws of 1891)[3] also meant that they could afford a better London residence during the season. In the spring of 1895, Hardy went to London to secure lodgings. His letters to Emma suggest just how far he had come. The boy from Bockhampton was now fussing about china, servants, flats furnished or unfurnished, location – should it be close to Hyde Park, to his club (the Athenaeum), or to the Army and Navy department store where Emma shopped? In the end, he secured a flat in Ashley Gardens, near Victoria station. Though Emma had wanted lodgings 'with attendance' (staff), it proved to be impossible: 'They don't leave their servants behind, so you must bring a parlour maid.' One wonders if Hardy thought about his mother and aunts, and their time spent in London as maid-servants. Hardy made sure to give travel instructions to his wife: 'It wd save trouble, I shd think, if you & the servants come by the same train – but not same class.'[4]

Hardy was sensitive to the fact that London was a lifeline for Emma. His letters to her were peppered with references to polite society. But he was the class-torn man. Nowhere was this schism more pronounced than in his view of women. The year before, he had made a visit to the Countess of Yarmouth, 'a woman very rich and very pretty', and had been amazed when she confessed to him that she was 'snubbed' by polite society. Hardy reassured her that it was a figment of her imagination and made her the subject of his poem 'The Pink Frock'. The Countess, who took a great liking to him, invited him back to an evening party. When he arrived, he found her in 'a state of nerves', lest a sudden downpour of rain should ruin her gathering and cause her party to flop. Mystified by her sensitivity to her social status, he took a bus home, sitting alone on the open top deck with his umbrella sheltering him from the rain. He was soon joined by a prostitute, who asked for the shelter of his umbrella. She held tight to his arm and showered him with kisses. He left the bus at South Kensington and watched the bus bearing her away: 'An affectionate nature wasted on the streets! It was a strange contrast to the scene I had just left.'[5]

He was often confounded by the women he met in London. Having attended the first anniversary meeting of the Women Writers' Club, he was surprised to find himself in a group of 'fashionably dressed youngish ladies instead of struggling dowdy females'.[6] A visit to a music hall made him observe that 'dancing girls are nearly all skeletons . . . they should be penned and fattened for a month to round out their beauty'.[7] He was moved by a visit to a London lunatic asylum, where he found himself in the female wing listening to the mad women's 'stories of seduction' and a 'Jewess who sang to us'. There was a particular young woman who evoked his pity when 'with her eyes brimming with reproach', she said to the doctor, 'when are you going to let me out of this?' He was less interested in 'the ladies who thought themselves queens – less touching cases, as they were quite happy'. He made a journal note of his visit: 'All the women seemed prematurely dried, faded, *fletries.*'[8]

The one woman who remained fresh and vibrant was Florence Henniker. He fretted about her health, continued to mentor and support her writing, and told her that he wished he could take her to the real-life 'scenes of the Jude story'.[9]

The only way Hardy could get over his heartbreak was by falling in love again. In September, he and his wife were invited to the stately Rushmore House on the border of Wiltshire and Dorset. Colonel Pitt Rivers, who had recently inherited the estate, had created the Larmer Tree Gardens as free pleasure grounds for 'public enlightenment and entertainment'. Like a mini-Vauxhall, there were flower gardens, sculptures, a bowling green, a golf course, and lawn tennis courts. Eight picnic areas were enclosed by cherry laurels and supplied with thatched buildings for inclement weather. The Colonel built a 'Singing Theatre' for plays and poetry readings. During the summer months, a band played on Sundays. Thousands of Vauxhall-lights illuminated the gardens where there were open-air dances.

On 4 September there was an annual sports day, with dancing in the evening. The Hardys were special guests. The press recorded the 'dancing of hundreds of couples under these lights and the mellow radiance of the full moon'.[10] Hardy was asked to lead off the country dancing with the Colonel's beautiful daughter, Agnes. Perhaps recalling the opening of *The Return of the Native*, he recorded that this was 'the last occasion on which he ever trod a measure . . . on the greensward'. He was bewitched not only by the gardens, 'quite the prettiest sight I ever saw in my life', but also by Agnes. After her death, in 1926, Hardy wrote the poem 'Concerning Agnes', celebrating the first time he danced with 'that fair woman . . . As in the Prime / Of August, when the wide-faced moon looked through / The boughs at the faery lamps of the Larmer Avenue.'[11] If he is to be believed, they sat together in the shade after the dance, holding hands. She became another of Hardy's literary pupils, filling the gap left by Florence Henniker.

———

Hardy wasted no time in writing to Florence to inform her of his Rushmore visit and hinting that he had finally found a replacement muse: 'the most romantic time I have had since I visited you at Dublin'.[12] Agnes Grove had sent, for his perusal and advice, a response she had drafted to a provocative article by the Bishop of Albany in New York entitled 'Why Women do not want the Ballot'.[13] Hardy encouraged her 'spirited' piece, but also gave good advice, and offered his assistance in editing and modifying. He told Agnes how much he had enjoyed her company and hoped for more of it. He had promised to send her a copy of *Jude the Obscure* and asked her to keep an open mind about it: 'You are, I know, sufficiently broad of view to estimate without bias a tragedy of very unconventional lives.'[14] Agnes wrote back with a prompt thank-you and took his critique of her writing with good grace. She liked *Jude* and Hardy was gratified: 'Don't let it depress you, even though it is a tragedy: or I shall not forgive myself for having written it.'[15]

He was bracing himself for the *Jude* storm, which duly came. Much of the criticism, according to Hardy, seemed to be centred on Arabella's assault by pig's penis, which was considered the height of vulgarity. Hardy remained defiant: 'The throwing of the pizzle, at the supreme moment of his young dream, is to sharply initiate . . . the contrast between the ideal life a man wished to lead, & the squalid real life he was fated to lead.'[16] To Florence Henniker, he claimed, not entirely convincingly, that he was 'rather indifferent' to the public reception of *Jude*, denying that the novel was a 'sort of manifesto on the marriage question'. He tried to explain, using his mother and sister's oft-used phrase: 'The tragedy is really addressed to those into whose *souls the iron of adversity has deeply entered* at some time of their lives, & can hardly be congenial to self-indulgent persons of ease & affluence.'[17]

Hardy wrote a journal note a week following publication: 'The Reviews begin to howl at Jude.'[18] The reviewer who coined the term 'Jude the Obscene' described the novel as full of 'dirt, drivel, and damnation'.[19] Another reviewer adapted the title into *Hardy the Degenerate*.[20] For Hardy, this 'onslaught started by the vituperative section of the press' was comparable to that which greeted his admired Swinburne's *Poems and Ballads*, which had led to reviewers dubbing him Swine-borne. Somewhat to his surprise, Swinburne himself wrote him a sympathetic if somewhat double-edged letter: 'The tragedy – if I may venture an opinion – is equally beautiful and terrible in its pathos . . . But (if I may say so) how cruel you are.'[21]

What he wasn't prepared for was the extent of his own wife's hostility. Emma's nephew, Gordon Gifford, who was living with the Hardys at this time, wrote that his aunt, 'a very ardent Churchwoman and believer in the virtues and qualities of women in general, strongly objected to this book'. Gifford, perhaps getting to the heart of the matter, added that this was the first of Hardy's novels 'in which she had not assisted by her counsel, copious notes for reference and mutual discussions'.[22] Emma coined the word 'Jude-*ites*' to describe those in praise of the novel.[23] Rumours of her seeking to burn the manuscript are not verifiable. Nevertheless, a reliable source, Alfred Sutro, corroborated the story of Emma's extreme antipathy: when he praised the novel, Emma retorted that it was the first novel Hardy had published without letting her read the manuscript. She claimed that if she had been consulted it would *not* have been published. Emma reported that the book had not gone down well locally. Sutro was saddened to see Hardy reduced to silence by this, looking gloomily down at his dinner plate.[24]

Later, the family doctor said that Emma was 'very clever' and that he 'suspected her of writing the famous novels'. She told him that Hardy 'always submitted them to her', giving the impression that she 'revised them pretty freely'. But when it came to *Jude*, she told Hardy that 'she would never have anything more to do with any book he wrote'.[25]

Her nephew's description of Emma as an 'ardent Churchwoman' was another reason for the ever-widening gap between husband and wife. Sue's moral recantation at the end of the novel and her return to religion is a spiritual death for the heroine, but perhaps Hardy had believed naively that it would be a sop to Emma and other religious minds: 'I felt that by the heroine's recantation of all her views, at the end of the story, & becoming a penance-seeking Christian, I was almost too High-Churchy', he wrote to Lady Jeune.[26]

In the meantime, Hardy had been continuing to help Agnes Grove with her journalism. He used his influence to write to the editor of the *North American Review* in the hope that her reply to the bishop on the subject of the women's ballot would be published. When her article was rejected, Hardy was all support and encouragement: 'But you must not be out of heart about it. The refusal has obviously nothing to do with the merits or demerits of the article.' He suggested that she should draft an article based on *Jude*, perhaps on the subject of Sue's words to little Father Time: 'Some remarks of yours about Sue's talk with the child in "Jude" suggested to me that an article might be written entitled "What should children be told?" – working it out under the different headings of "on human nature", "on temptations", "on money", "on physiology", &c. It would probably attract attention.'[27]

Hardy had been mollified by the fact that his female friends and admirers (other than his wife) did not feel the same moral outrage for *Jude* as his male admirers. His best friend, Edmund Gosse, had told him to his face that the novel was the most indecent ever written. Hardy noted grimly that a young German lady of his acquaintance was unconscious 'of any impropriety in the book: indeed the only people who faint & blush over it are fast men at clubs, so far as I see'.[28] Ellen Terry, Mrs Craigie, and 'George Egerton' were among those who saw the true merit of *Jude the Obscure*, the latter praising the psychologically penetrating treatment of Sue, a woman of 'a temperament less rare than the ordinary male observer supposes . . . the most intuitively drawn of all your wonderful women. I love her, because she lives – and I say again, thank you, for her.'[29] With all this female support, the pain of Emma's hatred of the book cut deep. The marriage never recovered from this point on. As 1895 drew to a close, Hardy confessed to his friend George Douglas: 'I feel that a bad marriage is one of the direst things on earth, & one of the cruellest things.'[30]

Emma was beginning to carve her own path. Mary Haweis, an author, artist and suffragette, had written to her with an invitation to join the National Society for Women's Suffrage. She was delighted to accept and to learn more about the Society. She was interested in the social reformer and women's rights activist, Laura Ormiston Chant, who was on a crusade to clean up the streets of London. Ormiston Chant was known for her campaigns against music-halls as temptations to vice, focusing not only on the immorality of the theatres, but on the prostitutes who paraded its environs. In typical shrewd fashion, Emma Hardy refused to blame the prostitutes for the problem: 'if only she [Ormiston Chant] would organize a crusade to clear the young men from the streets – to attack them rather than the women – how she would do it!'[31]

Mary Haweis had hoped that Mr Hardy himself would be interested in the Suffrage Cause, but Emma made it clear that her husband was not to be depended upon: 'His interest in the Suffrage Cause is nil, in spite of "Tess" & his opinions on the woman question not in her favour.' And then she delivered one of her sharpest, most damning remarks about her famous husband, which contained all her rage, frustration and pain: 'He understands only the women he *invents* – the others not at all.'[32]

CHAPTER 60

Emma

Only a handful of Emma's letters survive. The majority were destroyed by Hardy and his second wife, but one important missive was saved by Mary Hardy. It was given to the family solicitor for safekeeping as evidence that Emma was certainly vitriolic and perhaps mentally unstable. She had been unwell, with what was probably shingles. While recuperating by the sea in Worthing, she wrote a furious letter to her sister-in-law, addressing it coldly to 'Miss Hardy'. There had been a row between the women, in which Mary had accused Emma of being unkind to her brother. She also accused Emma of being mad, a charge that was vehemently denied. Emma, for once, abandoned her customary politeness and launched into a blistering attack: 'Miss Hardy – I dare you, or any one to spread evil reports of me – such as that I have been unkind to your brother (which you actually said to my face) or that I have "errors" in my mind, (which you have actually said to me,) and I hear you repeat to others.' Emma did not hesitate to blame the sorry state of her marriage on Mary: 'Your brother has been outrageously unkind to me – which is *entirely your* fault.'

Emma believed that her marriage never stood a chance because of Mary: 'ever since I have been his wife you have done all you can to make divisions between us; also, you have set the family against me.' She accused the Hardys of 'frequent low insults'. Emma had been (not unreasonably given her family history) deeply upset by Mary's accusations of mental instability: 'I defy you ever to say such a thing of me or for you, or any one, to say that I have done anything that can be called unreasonable, or wrong, or mad, or *even unkind!* And it is a wicked, spiteful & most malicious habit of yours.' Despite all of Emma's assistance with her husband's career, Mary had accused Emma of being 'no help' to Hardy: 'That statement, false & injurious, as it is, you have constantly repeated without warrant or knowledge of the matter.' In a rare moment of calm in the course of writing the letter, she tried to make her sister-in-law view things from her perspective: 'How would you like to have your life made difficult for you by anyone saying, for instance, that you are a very unsuitable person to have the instruction of young people?'

Quite what started the fight is unclear. For years hostilities had been simmering on both sides, stoked by Emma's vulnerabilities, and Mary's loneliness and unhappiness. Mary had been forced to watch her beloved brother grow increasingly miserable, feeling trapped in what had become a loveless marriage, and yet knowing that he would never abandon his wife. But perhaps some of her own rage and frustration at her spinster existence, the refusal of Dorchester people to treat her like 'a lady', the difficulties of being the sister of the most famous English novelist, were also responsible for her ire. Certainly, Emma believed that Mary felt injured and inferior to her brother: 'You have ever been my causeless enemy – causeless, except that I stand in the way of your evil ambition to be on the same level with your brother by trampling on me.' Emma, perhaps not unreasonably, thought that Mary's blind devotion had hindered Tom: 'If you did not know & pander to his many weaknesses, & have secured him on your side by your crafty ways, you could not have done me the irreparable mischief you have. And doubtless you are elated that you have spoilt my life as you love power of any kind, but you have spoilt your brother's & your own punishment must inevitably follow.'

By now, Emma's rage was fuelled, and she knew that she had nothing to lose. Perhaps it was her only opportunity to fully express her hurt at the rejection she felt at the hands of the Hardy women: 'You are a witch-like creature & quite equal to any amount of evil-wishing & speaking – I can imagine you, & your mother & sister on your native heath raising a storm on Walpurgis night. You have done irreparable harm but now your power is at an end.'[1]

It is important to remember that Emma was unwell and in pain when she wrote this missive. It is difficult to imagine that she really believed that her mother-in-law and daughters were the three witches/weird sisters casting a spell on the night (Walpurgis Eve) when bonfires were lit to ward off evil spirits. At the same time, Emma had probably had her bellyful of Hardy's fascination with folklore and his mother's tales of superstition, all of which she felt were deeply pagan and an offence to Christianity. Emma knew that Mary would spill the beans: 'Doubtless you will send this on to your brother but it will not affect me, if you do as he will know from me that I have written to you thus.' She offered forgiveness ('If you will acknowledge your evil pride & spite & change your ways'), though she felt she could never trust Mary.

As ever, Hardy fell silent on the rift. He was caught between strong female personalities, and he took the line of least resistance. In trying to hurt nobody in his family, he ended up hurting everybody.

Emma made a fine sight in her cycling outfit, which matched
her green bicycle nicknamed the Grasshopper. She was at the
forefront of the latest mode of transport, which gave women an
unprecedented degree of freedom, allowed them to escape the
confines of the home and to exercise in the fresh air. The Lady
Cyclists' Association was founded in 1892 by Lilias Campbell,
who believed that the bicycle signalled emancipation. Its invention was 'the greatest boon that has come to women for many
a long day'. The Association organised rides, tours and social
gatherings, provided a handbook of locations, and places to stay,
and published a journal, *The Lady Cyclist*. Hardy noted that
Emma, 'not being a good walker' (due to her lameness) found
her bicycle invaluable.[2] He made plans to join in with the craze,
telling Emma that he had spotted 'the loveliest "Byke" for myself
– wd suit me admirably – "The Rover Cob". It is £20! I can't
tell if I ought to have it.'[3]

She took the Grasshopper on a holiday to Malvern, Worcester,
Warwick, and Stratford-upon-Avon. Hardy, who had been in
regular correspondence with Agnes Grove, wrote to tell her of
his travels: 'We have been idling about Shakespeare's country
– my wife on "The Grasshopper" (her green bicycle), & I on
foot at present. To day we go on to Coventry, & thence to the
coast – to cross over, as I suppose, weather permitting.'[4] In
Dover, Emma was knocked off and laid up for a few weeks with
a sore shoulder. More mishaps occurred in Belgium, where the
Grasshopper had 'several adventures in its transit from place to
place, always getting lost, and miraculously turned up again
when they were just enjoying the relief of finding themselves
free of it'.[5] Their eight-week holiday had been a success, judging
by the letters Hardy sent to Florence Henniker describing 'an
agreeable & instructive time'. Emma had asked Tom to learn
to cycle 'to keep her company'.[6] Hardy found it 'arduous' at
first, but soon became a convert. Their shared passion for cycling

drew them closer, as he noted in his diary: 'Bicycling was now in full spirit with the Hardys – and indeed with everybody – and many were the places they visited by that means.'[7]

By 1897, Kate and Mary had retired from school teaching, which enabled them to spend more time in Bockhampton with their mother. Kate had remained on cordial terms with her brother and sister-in-law, and when the Hardys were in London or abroad, she took on the role of sorting their correspondence and sending it on to them. In Switzerland, he wrote to her with instructions on sending his letters, adding, wistfully, 'I should like to bring you here some day.'[8] Soon after, to avoid more building work on Max Gate, Emma and Tom took a holiday to Salisbury. Being there was a reminder of his sisters, and their unhappy experience at the training college. He wrote to Kate, asking if she could 'run up for the day' and stay for lunch and tea: 'I would meet you, & you could have a good long day. The weather is so fine that it wd be worth while.' He told Kate that the King's House was empty for the holidays 'so you wd have no unpleasant reminders'.[9] Hardy had heard a story about the late Cathedral organist, who 'went out of his mind' because he couldn't play the new organ. He asked Kate to tell Mary about the mad organist, remembering her own difficulty playing the school organ. Hardy had walked alone into the Close by moonlight; bats were flying around, and it was peaceful.

Kate continued to act as Hardy's secretary and looked after Max Gate in his absence. Hardy wrote to 'Dear Kitty' fussing over his servant, Sarah Ann: 'please ask if [she] wants anything – if she has enough coals, potatoes, Etc.' Kate had also purchased a bicycle (perhaps a present from him), and he shared an amusing story from his London lodgings.

The young people seem to cycle about the streets here more than ever. I asked an omnibus conductor if the young women (who ride recklessly into the midst of the traffic) did not meet with accidents. He said 'Oh, nao; their sex pertects them. We dare not drive over them, wotever they do; & they do jist wot they likes. 'Tis their sex, yer see; & its wot I coll takin' a mean adventage. No man dares to go where they go.'[10]

Emma had suffered another cycling accident. She had been thrown off her bicycle by a heap of stones in the road and sprained her ankle. With her usual courage, she was soon back on the saddle. Despite the holidays, cycling excursions and theatre trips, all was not as well as it seemed. The Hardys were moving towards separate lives. Emma took refuge in her social and religious movements, while Hardy retreated into his new study determined to forgo novel-writing (though he was preparing his serialised novel, *The Well-Beloved*, for publication, and had edited the revised texts of the Wessex novels). The 1896–7 chapter of his memoir was entitled 'Tess, Jude, and the End of Prose'. He made a note: 'Poetry. Perhaps I can express more fully in verse ideas and emotions which run counter to the inert crystallised opinion – hard as a rock – which the vast body of men have vested interests in supporting.'[11]

Emma reported that her husband was now in his 'fourth' Max Gate study. Her irritation and frustration at being the wife of a famous author was as strong as ever. 'It strikes me', she wrote to a correspondent, 'that I ought to have an Author's wives *day* occasionally . . . One thing I abhor in Authors. It is their blank materialism . . . I get irritated at their pride of intellect – & as I get older I am more interested in ameliorations & schemes for banishing the thickening clouds of evil advancing.' She had heard that another author 'with a kind of Shelley face' was in his second marriage. Musing on what the second wife looked like, she supposed she was like Mary Godwin (Shelley's second wife), who was 'a little of the minx kind to fly into his arms as she did whilst Harriet was still out of the depths of water'.[12] Harriet Shelley had killed herself by drowning on hearing about her husband's affair with Mary Godwin. Soon enough, Emma would contend with another of the 'minx kind' who would seek to usurp the place of the first wife.

Back in the summer of 1892, two well-to-do American sisters arrived at Max Gate, on a mission. One of the peculiar by-products of Hardy's fame was the legions of 'fans' who increasingly appeared at Max Gate expecting to meet and chat with the author of *Tess*. Rebekah Owen, the daughter of a Madison Square banker, had dragged her older sister Catherine across the Atlantic to keep her company. Rebekah had become enamoured with the writer of *Tess of the D'Urbervilles*, and they were determined to make his acquaintance. Having spent a great deal of time and ingenuity on acquiring an introduction, the sisters met their idol and formed a friendship with the Hardys (they eventually moved to England). Initially, Hardy was flattered by their attention, finding Rebekah 'an intelligent observer'. The Hardys arranged a tour of Woolbridge Manor in Dorset, once home to the Turbervilles and the model for Wellbridge House in *Tess*, where the heroine and Angel spend their wedding night. The Owen sisters were told the story of how Hardy managed to obtain admittance to the house in order to see the 'two horrible life-sized portraits' that were described in the novel. It was Emma who had thought of this ruse.[13] At Bindon Abbey, across from Woolbridge, Rebekah lay down in the stone coffin where Angel had lain Tess in the sleepwalking scene. Later, the group walked around Dorchester in the footsteps of the Mayor of Casterbridge, including a stop at the Ten Hatches Weir, where Henchard had contemplated suicide.

Hardy soon grew bored and handed the ladies over to Emma. On an expedition to Swanage, the setting of *The Hand of Ethelberta*, the Misses Owen were told that Emma disliked the novel: 'too much about servants in it'.[14] Rebekah also noted Emma's aspirations to be a writer: 'she felt a crowd of fancies thronging in her brain, but she couldn't find the energy to put these impressions systematically down on paper.'[15] Another pilgrimage was made, this time to Waterston Manor, the model for Bathsheba's farmhouse. Emma told the sisters that the lovely farmer's daughter resembled their idea of Bathsheba so much that she sent the daughter a copy of *Far from the Madding Crowd*. At Wareham, they stopped in at the post office, where they met a descendant of the ancient Turberville family, a young man called George Tollerfield, who was teasingly called 'Tess' by his friends. Emma's passion and interest for almost every character, every place in Hardy's novels, is striking, and sheds a light on her disappointment when he shut her out of *Jude*. For Rebekah, it was 'the most wonderful two months she had ever lived'.[16] Hardy, in the meanwhile, refused Miss Owen's request for a pilgrimage to the tombs of the Turbervilles in the church of Bere Regis, and wrote to Florence Henniker that he wished he could go there with her instead. He did, however, enjoy Miss Owen's presents; she sent trees, flowers, and other gifts over the years of her devotion to her literary hero.

Most of Emma's surviving letters are written to Rebekah Owen, who faithfully preserved the correspondence. Emma confided in her 'New York correspondent' even though Owen was a 'Jude-ite'. She told Rebekah about her 'prolonged attack of rheumatism & neuralgia' and her problems with house-keeping: 'Our new maid has the footfall of an earthquake! And daily crashes the china – *placidly*! But she is sweet-tempered & sweet to look at.'[17] Her boy servant, she wrote, 'gapes at the visitors, & hardly gets them in, or out, of the house'. She later shared her frustration with her husband, and her feeling of being ignored: 'T.H. has always so much to say by voice, & pen, that letter-writing is my only resource for having all the say to myself, & not hearing his eloquence dumbly.'[18]

Emma threw herself into her causes. She held an 'Anti-Vivisection' meeting in her drawing room and continued her interest in women's suffrage. She persisted with her writing, which included the secret diary about Hardy and her unhappy marriage. But she was to be dealt another blow. If Emma felt that her husband had betrayed her in the writing of *Jude*, she was to feel mortified when he published his first volume of poetry. In February of 1897, he wrote a diary entry: 'Title: "Wessex Poems: With Sketches of their Scenes by the Author."' He claimed he had been getting together the poems since 1865.[19] The author's own illustrations were an ingenious idea, which brought the collection to life. During the winter of 1897–8, Hardy had returned to East Lulworth (as part of his assistance with the Society for the Protection of Ancient Buildings), close to Clavell Tower, where he had courted Eliza Nicholls, and which formed one of the sketches for the 'She to Him' sonnets.

Despite his protestations in the preface, the poems were deeply personal, and they both knew it. There were more than twenty love poems in the collection of fifty-nine (dated from the 1860s to the 1890s), but only the one brief 'Ditty', written back in 1870, was dedicated to Emma. Eliza, Tryphena, and Florence were among the women (his 'little fancies') honoured in the collection. 'Ditty' itself could barely be described as flattering. It feels as if it honours that spot where they met more than the woman herself. The poet-narrator writes of lapsing to what he was in days gone by, then adds parenthetically,

(Such can not be, but because
    Some loves die
Let me feign it)

The woman he knows 'by rote' is now 'Spread a strange and withering change, / Like a drying of the wells / Where she dwells'. The poet muses on the others he 'might have kissed' or 'missed', 'Had I never wandered near her.' A final cruel twist is 'the thought that she is nought.'[20] After Emma's death, he (guiltily?) revised 'Some loves die' to 'Some forget'.[21]

Understandably, Emma was distraught. She also became convinced that she was the subject of the poem 'The Ivy-Wife', written in the voice of a woman who suffocates her men. The ivy seeks to entwine herself around high trees – a beech, a plane, and an ash, to be 'as high as he'. But the beech drips poison, she loses her grip on the plane tree, and the ash tree is felled, bringing her crashing to the ground. The tree receives her love, but her 'soft green claw' only serves to cramp and bind him tighter: 'Such was my love: ha-ha! / By this I gained his strength and height / Without rivalry.'[22] It is not difficult to see why she believed the poem was a derogatory swipe at her rivalry, her insistence on their literary 'partnership', her clinginess, and her penchant for social climbing. She confided in Betty Owen her dislike of *Wessex Poems*, telling her that she was reading a friend's poetry collection: 'Much of *this* poetry is good . . . Of recent poetry perhaps you admire "The Ivy Wife". Of course my wonder is great at any admiration for it, & SOME others *in the same* collection.'[23]

She confided her distress to Alfred Pretor, a Cambridge don and minor novelist, with whom she had formed a new friendship. Pretor had dedicated a book of animal short stories 'to Mrs Hardy, who suggested and encouraged the publication of these tales'. He wrote back a comforting letter: 'T. has said again

& again to me little casual things that are absolute proofs that all his reminiscences are little fancies evoked from the days of his youth & absolutely without bearing on the real happiness of life.'[24] But Emma was not comforted. Her humiliation was profound. She wrote again, expressing her husband's ingratitude, and the help she had given him throughout his literary career. Pretor urged her to take comfort in being Hardy's helpmeet. To Rebekah Owen, she vented her feelings freely, woman to woman: 'He should be the last man to disparage marriage! I have been a devoted wife for at least twenty years or more – but the last four or five alas! Fancy it is our silver wedding this year! The *thorn* is in my side still.'[25]

Hardy's cruelty seems extreme. But his feelings for Emma were far more complex than she assumed. That he felt his own sense of rejection is evident from 'The Dead Man Walking' (also written in 1896), in which he describes the slow death of his soul, first 'iced' by his ambition, then the death of Horace, 'When passed my friend, my kinsfolk, / Through the Last Door, / And left me standing bleakly, I died yet more.' But the final blow is rendered by his wife: 'And when my Love's heart kindled / In hate of me, / Wherefore I knew not, died I / One more degree.'[26]

Following the publication of *Wessex Poems* in December 1898, Emma moved into the two recently built attic rooms at Max Gate. It is tempting to think that she was banished like Bertha Mason, Mr Rochester's first wife in *Jane Eyre*. Reports of Emma's insanity from friends and family also complete the picture of the mad wife in the attic. The truth was that it was her own idea to escape into her retreat: 'I sleep in an *Attic*', she wrote to Betty Owen. 'My boudoir is my sweet refuge & solace – not

a sound scarcely penetrates hither. I see the sun, & stars &
moon rise & the birds come to my bird table when a hurricane
has not sent it flying.'²⁷ She thought of her pair of rooms as a
'little apartment where not a sound – even the dinner bell –
scarcely reaches me'.²⁸ Here she could write, paint, and sew. In
early 1899, she was working on a portrait of her nephew Gordon
Gifford, who was living with them: 'I have succeeded in taking
the portrait of a handsome young nephew – if I continue I must
do young, beautiful, care-line free faces.'²⁹

Emma was surprised when the new wife of Kenneth Grahame
(author of *The Wind in The Willows*) wrote to ask her for marital
advice. She responded somewhat sharply: 'It is really too "early
days" with you to be benefited by advice by one who has just
come to the twenty-fifth year of matrimony . . . You are *both*,
at present in a "Benedict" state. (Women can be anything in
these days).' She told the newly-wed authorial spouse of her
jaded view of men: 'I can scarcely think that love proper, and
enduring, is in the nature of men – as a rule – perhaps there is
no woman "whom custom will not stale."' Men are like children:
they give 'but little in return for our devotion and affection'.

She told Elspeth that 'keeping separate a good deal is a wise
plan in crises', as was 'being both free'. But her anger and
bitterness got the better of her: '*expecting little* neither gratitude,
nor attentions, love, nor *justice, nor anything* you may set your
heart on. Love interest – adoration, & all that kind of thing is
usually a *failure – complete* – some one comes by & all upsets
your pail of milk in the end.' Very soon, the Hardys were to
meet a young woman who would upset Emma's pail of milk,
though she did not at first suspect it. Emma was still feeling
the injustice of being married to a famous author: 'If he belongs
to the public in any way, years of devotion count for nothing.
Influence can seldom be retained as years go by . . . it is really
a pity to have any ideals in the first place.'³⁰

Now that Hardy had given up novels in favour of poetry, he had no need for her help in fair-copying, so she felt that she had wasted time and energy, neglecting her own needs. Any woman married to an author should avoid making the same mistake: 'Do not help – him – so much as to extinguish your own life – but go on with further pursuits.'[31]

She wrote letters to the papers, protesting against cruelty to animals – a tiger being whipped before the public, the horror of bullfighting letter – signing them 'PROTEST' or 'An old-fashioned Englishwoman'.[32] Emma and Hardy's love of birds and cats was one of their points of common interest. She fed breadcrumbs with raspberry jam to the birds, who ate out of her hand. There were solitary bicycle rides: 'I went out for a ten-minute bicycle canter over the mud', she reported to the lady from Madison Square, who was now living in Coniston in the Lake District: *My* beloved country is Devon', she wrote, 'my beloved people, the gentle good-hearted Devonians – without guile any of them, & altogether lovely.' The energetic Emma could cycle fifty miles a day with ease. She also became immersed in gardening. 'We are engineering the lower lawn', she wrote chattily to Betty Owen, 'it will be a fine croquet or tennis lawn next summer. I have a swing there too, & the trees grow all round it, quite nicely at last.'[33]

The outbreak of the Boer War in the autumn of 1899 was the talk of the Max Gate household. Emma had her own forthright views: 'The battles will be on a huge scale, that's certain – & a terrible ending it will all have', she wrote. 'But the Boers fight for homes & liberties – we fight for the Transvaal funds, diamonds, & gold!' She was unafraid to show her independent spirit: 'Why should not Africa be free, as is America?' The Hardys came together to 'rush at the papers by day, & send to the Dorchester for telegrams'. As she remarked to Betty Owen, 'Well, we gabble all day long about this war.' Though Emma admitted that they had 'no near relatives or friends at the front', the Hardys worried about the impact on the horses on the battlefields. Hardy and Emma both belonged to the London Anti-Vivisection Society. Vivisection remained one of Emma's chief causes: 'It makes me ill to think of the Vivisection tortures. Coleridge the animals' greatest champion is a hero to me.'[34]

Where Emma's response to the war was strongly political, Hardy's was more emotional. On reading that one of the casualties was a regimental drummer who was a native of a village near Dorchester, he wrote his magnificent elegy 'Drummer Hodge', which with its image of a dead countryman in some corner of a foreign field anticipates Rupert Brooke's 'The Soldier', written in the next and even more terrible war: 'They throw in Drummer Hodge, to rest / Uncoffined – just as found / . . . Yet portion of that unknown plain / Will Hodge for ever be'.[35]

———

As Emma grew older, she became more and more religious. She had ticked off Hardy's great friend Edward Clodd for his book *Pioneers of Evolution*: 'It is to be remembered that whatever Darwin arrived at, he never yet distinctly denied the existence of a Supreme Thought or word.'[36] In his diary, Clodd wrote: 'Letter from Mrs Thomas Hardy about the Pioneers: a curious mixture of sentiment & ignorance.'[37] She felt that the world was 'very wicked' and that young people were growing wild: 'Catechisms are not learnt as they used to be. Honesty seems an elementary virtue.' In 1901, she wrote a letter to the editor of the *Daily Chronicle* about the importance of educating the young: 'The knowledge acquired in schools is *not* making for happiness for all, but far otherwise . . . Regard attentively the position of infancy. Almost always the plastic minds and hearts are in ignorant hands.' With the right kind of education, resources, compassion for others, society would be improved and happiness would be obtained: 'All should try to become makers of happiness.' And, as ever, her focus was on women: 'Women's perplexities and trials would vanish. They it is who would, who must, be the first instructors, paid, or unpaid.' The words spilled out of her uncontrollably, partly because she felt that at home her voice was not heard: 'it seems scarcely allowable for *me* to say what I like or do not like'.[38]

Despite her appeal for the importance of good teachers, and acknowledging their importance with the education of the poor, she continued on poor terms with the former schoolteachers in her husband's family. In her letter to Elspeth Grahame she had spoken about the dangers of family interference. In a sad letter to Betty Owen, she also confessed her dislike for Dorset: 'I care little enough for Dorchester, & wish I were back in dear Devon – the people are rougher and more evil-speaking in this country – in fact Devon is *nearly* perfect in every way.' She told Betty that she believed in the Chinese superstition 'that *places* affect one's happiness & success'.[39]

Hardy had continued supporting his two literary protégés, Florence Henniker and Agnes Grove; the latter visited Max Gate twice in early 1900. Emma, perhaps in competition with these ladies as well as her husband, submitted one of her own poems, 'Spring Song', to the *Sphere*, where it was published on 14 April:

Why does April weep?
And why does April smile?
And why we look both sad and sweet
A-wondering all the while.

The narrator of the poem wonders if the return of summer will encourage the 'sun's heart glow / To ours in a steady flow / Of joy and sure delight / Of new deeds, and thought of might?'[40]

A year later, another of her poems, 'The Gardener's Ruse', was published in the *Academy*. Here, rose trees are planted with an onion to feed its roots. Emma explores the incongruous image of the plain onion enabling the flowers to thrive and grow and give off their glorious scent:

Down far in the earth, hidden its worth,
The Onion, coarse and meek,
Sought the roots of the flowers to give scent to its posies,
And brilliance in colour – A Freak![41]

Was the implication that she was the force behind the scenes who enabled her husband to dazzle in the literary world?

When Emma left Max Gate for a prolonged absence to take care of her dying sister, her niece, Lilian, came to keep the house. She and Hardy had long cycle rides, and he enjoyed her company. He sent chatty letters to Emma, with details about the cats, Tip and Croppy, who fought a lot. There was also news of a local man who was given five years' penal servitude for 'nearly' killing his wife. But he fretted about the effect on her health of nursing her sister: 'I am dreadfully afraid you will break down; & cannot tell why you shd have so much to do. Lilian is longing for you to come back – less, I tell her, from a wish to see you than from a desire to escape her penal servitude here.'[42] Emma came home for a brief spell, before returning to sort out her sister's probate. Hardy fussed again: '"Take it stiddy" as they say here', he wrote.[43]

When she was away, Betty Owen came alone and was intrigued to find Lilian Gifford as mistress of the house: 'Niece is as fat as butter and the image of a China doll, with bushy frizzy dark hair, round red cheeks between which the tiny nose is scarcely visible.'[44] By now, Betty seemed to have turned against Emma. She noted: 'Max Gate proved to be a very different place with Madame away.'[45] Tom, Lilian and Betty took bicycle rides together, Betty much admired in her pink waistcoat with matching hat and coat. Betty asked Hardy if he would take her to see the original 'Mixen Lane', preferably by nightfall. She was delighted to have Hardy to herself. They arranged a bicycle ride for the following day, but Lilian had sent the alarm to Emma, who hurried back to Max Gate. 'No action of Emma Lavinia's ever surprises me', Betty noted, 'I haven't a doubt it is niece's letters telling of my being here which has brought Madam home.'[46] Betty repeated malicious local rumours about Emma, that 'She leads him a Hell of a life' and that she was 'half-cracked'.

As the century came to an end,[47] Emma wrote to Betty, complaining of her confusion at the 'new poetry', especially W. B. Yeats's mystical dramatic poem, 'The Shadow Waters' (she mistakenly calls it 'The Shadowy Land'). 'What does it mean? That no woman's love is worth offering to a man who is a god? . . . Supposing women had always held the reins of this world would it not have been – by now, getting near the goal of happiness? This is a *man's world*.'[48]

Hardy's ode to the turn of the century, 'The Darkling Thrush', was published by the *Graphic* on 29 December 1900 with the title 'By the Century's Deathbed'. It caught his own mood to perfection: his peculiar mix of pessimism (the landscape is a 'corpse', the sky is a 'crypt' and the wind a funeral lament) and love of nature – the song of a common bird ('an aged thrush, frail, gaunt, and small') restores 'Some blessed Hope whereof he knew / And I was unaware.'[49] 'Pessimism. Was there ever any great poetry which was not pessimistic?' he had written gloomily in his notebook the previous year.[50] And yet there are glimmers of hope even in his darkling poetry, like the light that streams through the 'sun-comprehending glass' of the high church windows of Philip Larkin, the poet he influenced more than any other.[51]

The poem was reprinted, with the date changed to 31 December, in Hardy's second verse collection, published the following year: *Poems of the Past and of the Present*. Once again, it included love poems to other women, which Emma, not amused, described as 'personal – moans, & fancies'. She felt that their marriage troubles would be improved if his 'later writings were of a more faithful, truth & helpful kind'. She confided again in Betty Owen: 'Written to *please* others! Or himself – but not ME, far otherwise.'[52]

CHAPTER 61

Jemima

Hardy did not include one of his best and most moving poems in his early collections. Written in 1896, 'Wessex Heights' was deeply personal, detailing his depression and feelings of displacement. His second wife said 'it wrung her heart' and made her 'miserable to think that he had ever suffered so much'.[1] It was written, she said, a little while after the publication of *Jude the Obscure*, 'when he was so cruelly treated'. The poet stands alone, from the hills, surveying the views of his Wessex countryside, but feeling alienated and misunderstood: 'nobody thinks as I.' In the towns and the lowlands, he is criticised and sneered at by his own people: 'They hang about at places, and they say harsh heavy things.' He feels 'tracked' and haunted by ghosts of the past. 'Down there I seem to be false to myself, my simple self that was.' In the words of the critic Tom Paulin, no stranger to clinical depression: 'the enormous iambic couplets create a terrifying monotony . . . the poem sounds what it is – a speech delivered by someone in a state of such acute depression that he has almost totally lost his own will.'[2]

Hardy's second wife explained that the four women mentioned in the poem were 'actual women. One was dead & three living

when it was written.' Biographers have argued over the identi-
fication of three of the women:

> There's a ghost at Yell'ham Bottom chiding loud at the fall of
>   the night,
> There's a ghost in Froom-side Vale, thin-lipped and vague, in
>   a shroud of white,
> There is one in the railway train whenever I do not want it
>   near,
> I see its profile against the pane, saying what I would not
>   hear.[3]

Only one significant woman in his life was dead at this point,
Tryphena Sparks, but the ghosts of Eliza Nicholls, Emma,
Jemima and Mary also seem to be invoked. A quote from
Corinthians ('Her who suffereth long and is kind; accepts what
he is too weak to mend') and a mention of the 'tall-spired town'
(Salisbury) seems to point to Mary. The only woman strongly
identified in the poem is Florence Henniker: 'As for one fair,
rare woman, I am now but a thought of hers.' Hardy writes
that 'time cures hearts of tenderness, and now I can let her go'.

Jemima may well be the 'figure against the moon' on 'the
great grey Plain' earlier in 'Wessex Heights'. She is certainly
present in his masterly three-part sequence, 'In Tenebris'. The
third part of this intense evocation of despair and thoughts of
death explores a series of personal incidents from his childhood,
where he describes clearing the winter snow from the crocus
border and an incident in the evening on the heath with his
mother:

> She who upheld me and I, in the midmost of Egdon together
> Confident I in her watching and ward through the blackening
>   heather,

Deeming her matchless in might and with measureless scope
endued.[4]

In her old age, she was indeed 'matchless in might': Hardy
recalled his mother walking the distance from Bockhampton to
Max Gate at the age of seventy-seven 'in slippery wintry weather'.
When Hardy and Emma asked with alarm why she had ventured
out, she replied coolly: 'To enjoy the beauties of Nature of
course: why shouldn't I?'[5]

Now that Jemima was in her late eighties, Hardy was thinking
of his own mortality and of the past. His maternal and paternal
grandmothers were much on his mind. 'Autumn in King's
Hintock Park' and 'Her Late Husband' were written about
Betty Hand; the latter is a poignant poem about her husband's
wish to be married alongside his mistress. 'One We Knew' was
about his paternal grandmother, Mary Hardy, and her tales of
France in the era of the revolution. Looking back to the era of
his grandparents, he was embarking on his verse-drama about
the Napoleonic Wars, *The Dynasts*. By a bizarre coincidence,
Emma's mentally ill brother, long-term patient at Oxford's
Warneford Asylum, was collecting material for his own poetic
treatment of the Battle of Waterloo. Richard Gifford, suffering
from delusions, was convinced that his epic poem would bring
him great success and lead to his discharge.

As his mother neared the end of her life, Hardy was in poor
health himself. The journalist Henry Nevinson left a pen portrait
of him at this time: 'Face a peculiar grey-white like an invalid's
or one soon to die . . . and much wrinkled – sad wrinkles,
thoughtful and pathetic, but none of power or rage or active
courage . . . Head nearly bald in top but fringed with thin and
soft hair.'[6] He was suffering from arthritis and beginning to
show signs of deafness. Emma was also in poor health. Her
relationship with the wider family remained fraught: 'I have

suffered much, & greatly from the ignorant interference of others (of the peasant class).' She continued to feel that her husband exacted revenge by being one of those authors who undertook 'stabbings with their pen'.[7]

Knowing that he had not long with his mother, Tom spent as much time as he could at Bockhampton. Jemima was also visited by her Sparks relatives. James and Nathaniel Sparks (the sons of her nephew, Nathaniel) cycled from Bristol. Mary Hardy wrote to James, asking him to come to Wollaston Road 'as Mother is too old to receive anyone at Bockhampton and her house is small'. Mary explained that she was usually at Bockhampton looking after Jemima, along with Kate and Cousin Polly. Henry, too, was living with his mother, to ensure that her final years were spent in comfort. Jemima had retained her forthright manner; old age had not mellowed her strength of character. She maintained her hostility to her daughter-in-law. Nathaniel Sparks recounted her harsh words about Emma: 'A thing of a 'ooman . . . She were wrong for I.'[8]

Other visitors spoke of the lively talk in the cottage: 'the 90 year old Mrs Hardy, in its salt and savour, made the ordinary party talk very insipid indeed', noted the writer Evangeline Smith.[9] The family doctor, Fred Fisher, remembered stories told around the hearth: 'They could all tell stories, and did, in the large, low-ceilinged downstairs room . . . It had been a family custom dating far back, and many a wild winter evening did they pass away so occupied and without any light save that from the big wood fire.'[10] Fisher said the family 'criticised one another's efforts very freely'. The impression left is that of warmth; not only from the big fireplace but from the teasing conviviality often found in large, working-class families. Though Hardy was famous and celebrated, his family kept his feet on the ground. Fisher was particularly taken with Jemima: 'Her cleverness I soon realised,' he wrote, 'Undoubtedly she was the fount of her son's genius.' She told the doctor that her favourite book was Dante's *Commedia*.[11]

Now confined to a bath chair, and increasingly deaf, she insisted on being pushed to the side of the Puddletown road to witness a crowd of Hardy supporters, who had come to visit Wessex. They saw the old lady waving a handkerchief to show her appreciation. This was one of the rare occasions when we see her in the act of showing her pride in her son. Mary wrote to James and Nathaniel's father, a year later, to give an update on Jemima's failing health: 'Henry jogs on, not troubling much about what is going to happen next. Katie and Polly do what they can to make the best of their quiet life here for on account of Mother's age and illness they don't go out much.' Mary confirmed that 'she is as outspoken as ever'.[12]

A late photograph shows her reclining in her bath chair, her nose quite literally in a book. Hardy wrote to Arthur Moule that she was 'unchanged mentally, & speaks of & recollects you & yours the same as ever'.[13] Henry Moule died in March 1904, leaving Jemima distraught. Hardy reported her distress:

> She has known him more than 60 years – longer, I suppose, than any living person outside his family. She is now lying on a sickbed, from which I fear, she may never rise, & has been so much distressed at yr brother's death that we are compelled to change the subject as soon as we can. She used always to say to him, when they compared ages – 'You are a mere boy to me.' – & yet, you see, he has gone first.

Jemima sent a wreath from Bockhampton, 'made on the premises of the old fashioned flowers up there (which he had often admired)'. In her last days, she spoke of Reverend Moule, 'in her feeble voice', recalling him 'as a fine, noble-looking young man'.[14]

In another rare glimpse of Jemima's pride in her famous son,

Hardy wrote that she 'took a keen interest in the fortunes of "The Dynasts"' – the first part had been published in January 1904. He saw her two days before she died, but she failed to understand what he was saying to her. Jemima Hardy died on Easter Sunday, 3 April. Hardy wrote to his friend Edward Clodd that although she was old and infirm, she still seemed young: 'I shall miss her in many ways – her powers in humorous remark, for instance, which were immediate. It took me hours to be able to think & express what she had at the tip of her tongue.' Jemima approved of Clodd, as he had once invited Hardy to Aldeburgh for a change of air. Hardy confided that his mother had always regarded her Tom as a 'rather delicate "boy"'. He acknowledged that her death had left a hole: 'The gap you speak of is wide, & not to be filled. I suppose if one had a family of children one would be less sensible of it.'[15]

His poem 'After the Last Breath' captures the bittersweet moments of the death of 'a well-beloved' who is 'prisoner in the cell / Of Time no more.'

> There's no more to be done, or feared, or hoped;
> None now need watch, speak low, and list, and tire;
> No irksome crease outsmoothed, no pillow sloped
> Does she require.[16]

When the press asked for a photograph of Jemima to go along-side an obituary, Hardy sent a copy of his sister's splendid oil portrait of her. He thought it the best of all portraits, showing 'a face of dignity and judgement'.[17]

CHAPTER 62

Florence Emily Dugdale

Jemima's death did not ease tensions between husband and wife. Emma's behaviour was criticised by family and friends, partly because she was a strong personality, and partly because she felt sorely abused and was unafraid to give rein to her feelings. Hardy's tendency to stay silent – like his father before him, also married to a 'woman of character' (to use his own words) – made matters worse. The more Emma complained and lashed out, the more he withdrew. By nature, Hardy was a gentle person. Many people described his 'modest, quiet, smiling simplicity' – simplicity here meaning his lack of guile or pretension.[1] That he was a genius, 'a name to be written in gold, to be placed next to Shakespeare's', was also how many people saw him, hyperbolic as that might sound.[2] The hero-worship was a source of embarrassment to Hardy and deep resentment in his wife. She clung to her social pretensions as armour; her middle-class upbringing, her status as the archdeacon's niece, and her (increasingly shaky) position of muse to the great author. In times of strain, when the couple had visitors, she often showed her worst side.

George Gissing (himself a terrible snob) was one of her cruellest critics. He stayed with the couple in 1895, a time of great strain between the couple: 'The drawback was Mrs Thomas – an extremely silly & discontented woman, to whom, no doubt, is attributable to a strange restlessness & want of calm in Hardy himself.'[3] Gissing objected to Hardy's 'deplorable inclination' to talk about 'fashionable society', and 'Lords & dignitaries. This, I think, is greatly due to his wife's influence.' In Gissing's view, Hardy was 'Born a peasant' and 'retains much of the peasant's views of life'.[4] Gissing saw how the class differences were a source of unhappiness between the couple: 'Most unfortunately he has a very foolish wife – a woman of higher birth than his own, who looks down upon him, & is utterly discontented. They have no children, & they travel about a good deal. But not to much purpose. I admire Hardy's best work very highly, but in the man I feel disappointed.'

Gissing, like so many others, blamed Emma for Hardy's discontent: 'A strange unsettlement appears in him; – probably the result of his long association with such a paltry woman. Essentially, he is good, gentle & poetically minded.'[5] A kinder, more measured view came from Bertha Newcombe, an artist, who visited the Hardys in March 1900, and reported her sympathy for Emma to Edmund Gosse's wife: 'struggling against her woes. She asserts herself as much as possible and is a great bore, but at the same time is so kind and goodhearted.' Emma had presented Bertha with a photograph of herself as a young girl. The picture 'was very attractive' and moving: 'one cannot help realising what she must have been to her husband'. Emma repeated the story of how she had met the 'ill-grown, under-sized young architect' in Cornwall, discovered his genius and encouraged him to write: 'I don't wonder that she resents being slighted by everyone, now that her ugly duckling has grown into such a charming swan.'

Bertha Newcombe echoed the sentiments of so many of Hardy's friends and relations: 'It is so silly of her though isn't it not to rejoice in the privilege of being wife to so great a man?'[6] Another family friend, Christine Wood Homer, the daughter of a wealthy landowner near Puddleton, met Hardy when she was a schoolgirl, and recalled his kindness towards young people. She also remembered his sense of humour and cheerfulness, and how much he liked local gossip and a good joke. Though Christine had heard that the couple were unhappy, and that Hardy 'suffered much from the behaviour of his wife', she liked Emma and thought of her as 'like a little child'. In private she called her 'Lady Emma'. Christine recalled that Hardy would look at his wife 'in rather a quizzical but kindly way when she said something particularly childish. She was an increasing embarrassment to her husband.' Christine also lamented the fact that Emma 'had the fixed idea that she was the superior of her husband in birth, education, talent and manners. She could not, and never did recognise his greatness.'[7] Yet Emma was the very first person who believed in his talent and his capacity for greatness; it had been she who encouraged him to give up his respectable job and take the risk of becoming a freelance author. It was only in the later years, when she felt passed over, that her resentments took hold. Her childlessness, when she so loved children, had been a great disappointment, and her loneliness and bitterness had increased over the years. Her own attempts at verse, now that Hardy had committed himself to poetry, were perhaps written not so much as competition (she was not foolish enough to believe she had her husband's extraordinary poetic gifts), but rather in the hope of finding some renewed common ground.

She remembered a time when she and her husband had been so intimately entwined that he would ask her to correct him on the 'names and incidents' of his novels, which he had forgotten, knowing that she would put him right.[8] When she was his 'first reader and kind critic', when he had relied upon her to make fair copies of his novels, discuss details, and defend him from negative press. If she were a laughing stock amongst his family and friends, she could at least hold on to the idea of them as a poor but happy couple before Hardy was one of the most famous men in England. For an article about Hardy, to be published in an American magazine, the journalist asked for some details about Mrs Hardy. Emma refused to send a photograph of herself, but a pen portrait was delivered: 'In appearance Mrs Hardy is striking: her hair is dark and slightly tinged with grey; her eyes are also dark. She is dignified and very graceful, and looks as though she might be the wife of some ecclesiastical dignitary.'[9]

George Douglas, who met Emma in 1891, could appreciate the vivacity which had first captivated Hardy; she had 'belonged essentially to the class of woman, gifted with spirit and the power for deciding for herself, which had attracted Hardy in early manhood. She had the makings of Bathsheba, with restricted opportunities.'[10] Douglas, who had time to observe the marriage, and had heard the rumours of the couple's unsuitability, had his own opinion. He had seen how Hardy was always keen to 'take her with him' in his pursuits, 'whether it was a question of reading books together cycling or sight-seeing or of associating her with his literary labours'.[11]

Douglas understood the difficulties of Hardy's 'mental isolation' and the strain it had put on the marriage: 'Absorption in creative work puts a sore strain on human ties.' Douglas saw the care that Emma gave to her husband and felt that if Emma did not appreciate his genius, then neither did Hardy, who belittled his own achievements. Perhaps showing greater understanding of the marriage than most, he concluded: 'Each had sacrificed something to the other, but their attachment was strong enough for each to be resigned to that sacrifice.'[12]

And then along came another Florence. She was twenty-six years old. She initiated the relationship with Thomas Hardy by writing him a letter, and asking if she could call on him at Max Gate.

By now, he was used to the kind of attention that his celebrity brought, but, kind as he was, he wrote back. Florence had assured him that although she had experience as a journalist, she was not intending to write about him. In common with Hardy's sisters, she had trained as an elementary school teacher, first as a pupil teacher. Though she had passed her exam for the Queen's Scholarship, she was turned down on medical grounds. She began teaching at a boys' school in the London suburb of Enfield, where her father was headmaster, while training at a college in central London for her Acting Teacher's certificate. Florence's health was delicate, and she found the boys difficult to teach. She had begun to dabble in journalism, contributing articles and stories to the *Enfield Observer*. She had also contributed articles to the *Globe* and *Daily Mail*. She would later report that she disliked journalism: 'the most degrading work anybody could take up'.[13] Her ambition was to be a writer of children's stories.

Florence would later claim that she met Hardy for the first time with Florence Henniker, though it is by no means certain that she was telling the truth. What is certain is that Hardy felt an instant attraction to this dark, slender and willowy young woman with huge soulful eyes. She was timid and shy, and she aroused his protective instincts. After their first meeting at Max Gate (Emma stayed upstairs), Hardy escorted Florence to the door, and into the front garden, where she observed the sweet smell of the privet, still in flower. Hardy had not noticed this detail before and felt moved. It was a moment of connection and emotion that they would always remember, and that Hardy would commemorate in his poem 'After the Visit'. Following his wife's death, he added a dedication to Florence. It begins,

'Come again to the place / Where your presence was as a leaf that skims . . . Come again, with the feet / That were light on the green as a thistledown ball.' The young woman's presence heightens the sensations of the older man, intensifying his consciousness of the 'faint scent of the bordering flowers'. If the poem is to be believed, Florence fixed him with her 'large luminous living eyes' (her best feature) and asked him questions 'of what Life was / And why we were there.' She also enquired about the 'strange laws / That which mattered most could not be.'[14]

It wasn't long before Florence returned to Max Gate, sending a present: 'I must thank you for the box of sweet flowers that you send me', he wrote. 'They are at this moment in water at the table, & look little the worse for their journey: I did not think you stayed too long, & hope you will come again some other time.'[15] Hardy asked Florence if she would be interested in doing some research for him at the British Library for his final part of *The Dynasts*. He sent two signed photographs of himself. Florence would later say that Hardy probably invented the tasks, knowing the pleasure she took in helping him.[16]

She and her four sisters were expected to earn their own living. Her parents were from working-class backgrounds, and had risen into the lower middle classes through sheer hard work. Her mother was the daughter of a butcher, and her father was born in the rough working-class area of Portsea in Hampshire. He had qualified as an elementary school teacher at St John's College in Battersea. Two of Florence's sisters became schoolteachers, and one was a nurse. Teaching noisy boys was taxing; the classes were between forty and fifty, and Florence had a quiet voice, which made it hard to be heard, and difficult to discipline. The school's logbooks record Florence's frequent absences through illness. Eventually, she gave up teaching and tried to make a living by her pen.

Given what Hardy had witnessed with his two sisters, and

the toll it had taken on them, he fretted about Florence's health, and did his utmost to help her with her writing career. When she was asked to contribute to a series called *Tales for the Children*, he advised her to negotiate for a larger fee: 'I hope you have not agreed to write that 21,000 words of Children's stories for £8. The *lowest* you should agree to is 21 guineas – a guinea a thousand words.' In March 1907, he wrote her a gently chiding letter: 'I am sorry to hear that you have had such a severe cold – why were you so careless as not to change when damp! I daresay it has been even worse than you say.' If necessary, she should go easy on the research he had asked her to undertake: she was 'not to & search in the B. Museum for me if you are not *quite* well'.[17]

Florence Dugdale's first children's book, published in 1907, was *Old Time Tales*. The stories had titles such as 'Clytie: The Story of the Sunflower', 'Echo and Narcissus' and 'The Golden Fleece'. It was followed by her second collection, *Country Life*, beautifully illustrated with coloured plates.

She also had a temporary job as companion and nurse to the wife of the brilliant Irish surgeon, Sir William Thornley Stoker, brother of the author of *Dracula*. Emily Stewart Stoker suffered from severe mental illness, and Florence was employed during the Christmas of 1906–7 to take care of her in Ely House, their mansion home in Dublin. Stoker, as well as being a celebrated neurosurgeon, served for a time on the Board of Governors of the Richmond Lunatic Asylum in Dublin, where he was closely involved in patient care. Emily's symptoms were indicative of schizophrenia (then known as dementia praecox) and her mental illness has been seen as an important influence on Bram Stoker's creation of Dracula's devoted but deranged servant R. M. Renfield.[18] Renfield is 'morbidly excitable', delusional and has periods of gloom ending in 'some fixed idea'. He also believes that eating live animals will increase his life force. He has olfactory and auditory hallucinations, and suffers from grandiose delusions – all common signifiers of schizophrenia. Baronet Stoker commented on and edited his brother's *Dracula* manuscript, giving him his expertise on mental illness.

The impact of his wife's mental illness was well documented by the Irish poet and doctor, Oliver St John Gogarty, who lived across the road from Ely House. He wrote in his memoirs about a disastrous dinner party given by Stoker. Halfway through the dinner, they were interrupted by the arrival of an elderly nude woman, who cried 'I like a little intelligent conversation' and ran around the room followed by two attendants who covered her up and bundled her out of the room. Sir William was mortified and asked his guests never to mention the incident, nor speak of what they saw.[19]

Florence's devotion to the couple – 'my dear lost friends in Dublin' – was rewarded by their present of an expensive typewriter for the budding author. She always spoke kindly of the Stokers, and, despite her own nervous disposition, coped well with her temporary duties. When Lady Stoker died in 1910, Sir William told Florence what a 'crushing blow' it was to him, bringing 'stress and & anxiety' as he felt compelled to sell the contents of his home and found himself neglecting his patients.[20] At the time, Hardy and Emma were mourning the death of a cat, which left Florence cold: 'I cannot write & sympathise very deeply with T.H. upon the death of "Kitsey", although he writes, poor man, to ask: "Was there ever so sad a life as mine?"'[21]

Hardy began to send Florence inscribed books, including *Wessex Poems* and Edward FitzGerald's *The Rubaiyat of Omar Khayyam*. He asked her to join him in a research trip at the South Kensington Museum: 'I will look for you in the architectural gallery at 4 – say by the Trajan column.'[22] He was determined to help her career, and wrote to his own publisher, Maurice Macmillan, requesting his assistance. It is an important letter, as it gives a reading of how Hardy viewed Florence at this time:

> She has been accustomed to teach in her father's school at Enfield for some years & is, in fact, certificated as a competent mistress. But a delicacy of voice, strong literary tastes, & a natural gift for writing, suggest to her that she might do better in editing class books, &c, than in using them – in which opinion I quite agree, for she has a thorough knowledge of the nature & requirements of children & is capable of doing more important work than the drudgery of teaching. I speak from experience of Miss Dugdale's assiduity & trustworthiness, as she has carried out some researches for me in the British Museum Library, to my great satisfaction. She will tell you what she has already done in the way of journalism & the writing of children's books; & I may mention that she is skilled in shorthand & in the use of the typewriter.[23]

In the event that his publisher might get the wrong idea (why should he?), Hardy added a little white lie: 'she comes of an old Dorset family that I know well.' He had helped other literary women such as Agnes Grove and Florence Henniker to succeed in their professional writing. But there was an important difference with Florence Dugdale. She did not have the wealth, social status or the confidence of the New Women. Her insecurities and vulnerabilities made Hardy feel protective in the way he felt protective about his sisters. But it was also clear that his interest in Florence was not entirely avuncular.

And what of Emma at this time? Hardy told a friend that his wife no longer socialised or came out in the evenings. She was busy with her own poems, and she took great pleasure in judging a competition in the *Tatler* to find the three prettiest children in Britain. She took the opportunity to send photographs of her 'remarkable-looking Cats', Snowdove and Comfy, in the hope that *Tatler* would publish them. Shortly afterwards, Snowdove escaped onto the railway track and was killed: '*Cut-in-two* on the railway which runs at the back – & where we have lost several dear Pussies in a horrible manner.' The cats were her children, and she begged the editor of *Tatler* to commemorate Snowdove: 'His body lies in our little cemetery here – Will you let him appear? Or not? Being now dead.' The 'lovely children' in the *Tatler* had brought her joy and sadness: 'What a pity they should change by time and the world's buffeting as we all have.'[24]

Emma was also saddened by Agnes Grove's 'dirge-tale' – a ten-page allegory written in memory of her youngest son, Terence, who died in a drowning accident. Emma wrote: '*I* have read your lovely little dirge-tale with my woman's heart, twice over. Perhaps, never having had a babe I do not quite comprehend the grief, yet I believe I do too. How many sweet poems have been written about a child's loss. I think I know them all.' Emma was moved by Grove's description of Terence 'kissing your eye-*covers*'. She tried to explain: 'I do love children greatly, *even* poor people's lacking breeding etc. They all know me in the parish here.' Agnes had been poorly, and Emma sent her wishes for a speedy recovery and the hope that it was not consumption. There was an odd moment in her letter when Emma made an ill-bred reference to the large bosom of the woman who had once been one of her husband's 'little fancies'. She told Agnes that as a girl she herself was thought to be consumptive, 'but the doctor said, with *my width* and *shape* of chest it was quite impossible, so I recovered, & how much more must it be so with *your* physique'.[25] Such comments did not endear Emma to her husband's friends, and it was an awkward thrust in a letter that had been full of genuine warmth and sorrow. But it also hints at Emma's fragility. Agnes Grove, however, was not the rival to be worrying about: she had no idea of the true feelings of her husband for the delicate young woman with 'luminous eyes' and a budding career as a children's author.

CHAPTER 63

Emma & Florence

On a bitterly cold and rainy day in early February 1907, between three and four thousand women converged by the statue of Achilles, near Hyde Park Corner. They were of all ages and classes. There were aristocratic women and professional women; doctors, schoolmistresses, artists. There were working women from the North and the provinces; bobbin winders, clay pipe makers, power loom weavers and shirt makers. They had assembled, with their banners, to march to the Strand in support of women's suffrage. It was the largest public demonstration to date in the campaign for the vote, and it became famous as the 'Mud March' due to the incessant rain, which left the women bespattered and drenched. They formed a line that stretched to Rotten Row. A brass band led the way. Lady Frances Balfour, Millicent Fawcett and Lady Jane Strachey headed the procession, followed by thousands of women wearing red and white rosettes, and waving red and white banners. Some women carried bouquets of red and white flowers. There were carriages and motor cars, which carried flags bearing the letters WS. Men lined the streets to stare and heckle, but one of the women observed that most of them were respectful, 'not much joking at our expense, and no roughness'.[1]

One of the women marching in the rain was Emma Hardy. She had been in uncertain health; she had experienced a serious fainting fit the previous May. She had been gardening, and then suddenly collapsed, writing in her diary: 'My heart seemed to stop; I fell, and after a while a servant came to me.'[2] She was now in her late sixties, so her marching in such adverse weather is testimony to her strong will and determination.

A month later she contributed, alongside Millicent Fawcett, to a 'symposium' published in *The Woman at Home* magazine. She also wrote an extensive piece on the rights of women that was published in the *Nation* in May 1908. In this, she argued that 'law and force' should be superseded by 'a more advanced and complex machinery of the State', which would be better served by 'the gentle, resourceful feminine mind, so used, as it is, to such measure in home life'. She also argued that 'both sexes must progress together, emerging from barbarism at the same era to perfection'. Her impassioned letter proclaimed that 'The time is ripe, women are capable, and their demands of momentous interest and *importance*.' Women's voices should be heard: 'Silently, humble to abjectness, she is to wait for the men's decision of what concerns her and the children vitally.' She added, speaking from the first-hand experience of her marriage, that 'Women have been sacrificed for ages to men.' She believed that male 'tyranny' was bound up with a fear of the 'real capabilities of women, who are abashed and crushed by their treatment'. Male praise, furthermore, 'has seldom been for a good woman except safely on a tombstone'.[3]

Emma attended another major rally on 21 June 1908, where the new suffragette colours – purple, white and green – were seen for the first time in public. Emmeline Pankhurst led the procession. Women were asked to wear white dresses and adorn them with accessories, such as sashes, scarves and brooches in the new colours. Men who were in support wore ties in the same colours. Sylvia Pankhurst proudly quoted a report from the *Standard* newspaper: 'From first to last it was a great meeting, daringly conceived, splendidly stage-managed, and successfully carried out. Hyde Park has probably never seen a greater crowd of people.'[4]

Hardy, too, was sympathetic to the cause. Millicent Fawcett asked him to contribute to a projected pamphlet. He replied that he 'had long been in favour of woman-suffrage'. The female vote would 'break up the present pernicious conventions in respect of manner, customs, religion, illegitimacy, the stereotyped household . . . the [identity of the] father of a woman's child (that it is anybody's business but the woman's own).' Fawcett thanked him but felt that she did not feel it was appropriate to use some of his more radical ideas: 'John Bull is not ripe for it as present.'[5]

Courageous as she was, Emma told Betty Owen that her 'strength & SIGHT are fast failing'. In a previous letter she had told her friend of her fear of old age and loneliness: 'In thinking about illness and getting over the after-weakness: that is a dread for the coming years with me, & I have no really *sweet* attentive relatives to sympathize.' According to Betty, Emma had asked Lilian Gifford to leave the house, fearing that she was getting too close to Hardy. She had also made what sounds like another jibe at Hardy's sisters, when Betty had asked a question about witches: 'Well you know they always live on *Heaths*, or Moors or desolate plains or Mountains – but have no mediaeval ways or any broomsticks etc, but are *modern* evil-*wishers* as the name means . . . There are, as a matter of fact, many malicious defamers *here* in, ah even, in "Casterbridge."' Hardy was away in London, and Emma was left alone to take care of the house and enjoy the spring flowers, but her bitterness remained: 'My Eminent partner will have a softening of brain if he goes on as he does.'[6]

Hardy was doing everything he could to get Florence Dugdale

journalist work, writing to the books editor of the *Daily Mail* on her behalf. Her 'growing practice in journalism & discriminating judgment in literature would render her, I think, of use in one or other department of the paper. She is a certificated school teacher, & might, in my opinion, do good work in reviewing books for the young. She has already written a few things for the Daily Mail, but has not, I think, been sufficiently discovered by the Editors.'7

In September 1907, Hardy sent a story of hers called 'The Apotheosis of the Minx' to the editor of the *Cornhill*. The editor clearly saw Hardy's mark on it, so he agreed to publish. Hardy reiterated the false claim: 'Her family is an old Dorset one from near here which I have known of all my life.'8 The story drew on Florence's experiences as a schoolteacher of boys. They whisper and play tricks, and are bored by the (male) protagonist's teaching of Shelley: 'With all the energy left him he endeavoured to make the schoolboys feel that here a poet had poured forth his soul for their delight, but even the few pairs of eyes that were fixed on him remained dull and uncomprehending.' The hero has a love of poetry 'over-keen for an elementary school teacher' and is too delicate to control the boys. He is a projection of Florence's struggles in the 'unhealthy atmosphere' of a London schoolroom. The boys, who are beaten with a cane, are not only shiftless and bored, they wear 'rough dirty clothes' and 'hobnailed boots' and have 'unintelligent bovine faces'. The 'contemptuous grins' with which they greet his attempts to awake in them 'some sense of honour and beauty' are 'a nightmare under which he laboured daily'. The schoolmaster is in love with a vulgar working-class girl, Etty, who eventually throws him over to marry the son of a grocer. It is only after her death in childbirth that the schoolmaster begins to idealise her: 'Out of the memory of the commonplace and narrow he step by step created an ideal image, which became more and more real, obscuring all her faults, annihilating all her sordidness, and winning his worship.' In reality 'this divine creature' was 'no more like Etty Clark, as she had existed in the flesh, than the glow-worm by night is like the glow-worm by day'.[9] The most curious aspect of this mediocre story was the way in which it anticipated Hardy's worship of Emma after her death.

Biographers have suggested that Hardy's handprint is evident in the story. But it is hard to imagine that he would write such a hackneyed tale – other than the insertion of some Hardyesque phrases, such as this: 'as he awoke from these alluring phantasms the sordid rigidity of his life hemmed him round like a prison.' The dialogue of the working-class Londoners seems to be all Dugdale's own, with none of the 'romantical' poetry of Hardy's own rustics. 'Look here! I've had enough of this . . . of mooning along here like a pair of ninnies' is a typical example.

Hardy was also supportive of his old favourite, Agnes Grove, who that year published a book on etiquette, *The Social Fetich*, which she had dedicated fulsomely to him 'in grateful recognition of timely aid and counsel, and in memory of old and enduring friendship'.[10] This was a mark of his generosity to women writers and the affection in which he was held, but it left Emma feeling disgruntled. Hardy wrote to Agnes with words of thanks: 'I have never ceased to bless the day on which we met at Rushmore, do you remember? – now receding so far into the past – & that dance on the green at the Larmer Tree by moonlight. But though at this point I have a strong temptation to grow "romantical" (delightful old form of the word, which the old people formerly used down here) I am not going to, being long past all such sentiments.'[11]

Florence Henniker's latest novel was also duly admired, though he disliked the ending: 'Of course *I* should not have kept her respectable, & made a nice, decorous, dull woman of her at the end, but shd have let her go to the d— for the man, my theory being that an exceptional career alone justifies a history (i.e. novel) being written about a person. But gentle F.H. naturally had not the heart to do that.' Hardy was growing too close to Florence Dugdale to be objective about *her* writing. He began to spend more time in London, without Emma, whose health was still poor. He booked himself into a small hotel near Russell Square, rather than renting a house or apartment. His letters home suggest that he did not want his wife to come to London: 'Your card has come, & though I should like to see you in London I feel, to tell the truth, rather anxious about your venturing up here. The hotel is so very noisy just now, & the heat so great, that I fear you will be prostrated.'[12]

They were rarely together that summer of 1908, and in September, to avoid the alterations being made to her 'boudoir', Emma escaped to Dover. On an impulse, she crossed to Calais to her beloved France. Hardy began slowly to introduce Florence Dugdale to his friends, describing her as 'my young friend'. The following year, Clodd invited the Hardys to Aldeburgh, but Hardy wrote to say that it was difficult to accept due to Emma's reluctance to reciprocate: 'The only scruple I have about it lies in my domestic circumstances which, between ourselves, make it embarrassing for me to return hospitalities received, so that I hesitate nowadays to accept many.'[13] It wasn't long before Clodd took the hint, and invited Hardy to bring Florence instead, incurring his gratitude: 'Your kindly opinion of my young friend & assistant pleases me much (& her, too, whom I told of it). I have known her for several years, & am very anxious about her health & welfare; & am determined to get her away to the seaside if I can, or she will break down quite.' The 'young friend and assistant' was being brought into the fold. Hardy wrote: 'Your timely hint that I might bring her to Aldeburgh is really charming. After a few days there I could send or bring her to Weymouth.'[14] That July, Hardy invited Florence to the opening night of the operatic version of *Tess*, but, at the last minute, Emma decided to attend. Clodd agreed to chaperone Florence and cover for his friend.

At Aldeburgh, Clodd photographed them on the shore together. They are sitting very close to each other, Hardy gazing at her, with a bathing hut behind them.

Several poems associated with Florence Dugdale explore the pains and pleasures of their secret meetings. In 'To Meet, or Otherwise' the poet questions his desire to meet 'the girl of my dreams', but remembers that when they are both dead, nobody will care about their relationship: 'Yet I will see thee, maiden dear, / And make the most I can / Of what remains to us.' But he is also mindful of 'things terrene' that 'Groan in their bondage'. The lovers in the poem are tortured by their circumstances, and grope for a 'path or plan' deciding 'By briefest meeting something sure is won.' The poet/narrator reflects that what has happened between them cannot be unseen or 'undo the done'.[15]

His poem 'On the Departure Platform' explores the pain and pleasure of leaving one's beloved at the train station: 'We kissed at the barrier; and passing through / She left me, and moment by moment got / Smaller and smaller.' Finally she is 'but a spot; / A wee spot of muslin fluff.' The poet is left bereft: 'And she who was more than my life to me / Had vanished quite.'[16] Yet, despite being in love with Florence, he remained something of a peeping Tom: whenever he was on the top deck of an omnibus he would be incapable of 'concentration on inner things' because of the distraction of young women in 'fluffy blouses'.[17]

Florence was non-negotiable for Hardy. She was his 'Heartmate' – though he worried about being in Max Gate without her:

'But she will never see this gate, or bough' he wrote in the poem, 'The Difference'.[18] Following their week together in Aldeburgh in August 1809, they arranged an October tour of Chichester Cathedral, home of the famous Arundel Tomb. Hardy then introduced Florence to his brother, Henry, and the three of them undertook a cathedral tour around the North of England. Florence would always love Henry Hardy, later describing him as the living epitome of Giles Winterbourne in *The Woodlanders*. She would also come to be devoted to Mary and Kate.

In the spring of the new year, there was another visit to Aldeburgh, and a pilgrimage to Swinburne's grave in the Isle of Wight. In London, Hardy introduced Florence as a 'young cousin' to his friend, Lady Gregory. By now, Florence had given up teaching, and was doing more of the journalism she disliked. She published an article about Hardy to mark his seventieth birthday. The problem was how to introduce her to Emma in a way that did not arouse her suspicion and jealousy. It was a clever plan: to hide in plain view. At first, Florence befriended Emma in the women's club The Lyceum, of which they were both members. It was a short step to an invitation to one of Emma's 'At Homes' at their rented flat in Blomfield Terrace. Florence was making herself indispensable to Emma. She poured the tea and kept an eye on the flat when Emma was away. Her letters to Emma at this time were kind and full of respect: 'I cannot find words to thank you sufficiently for all your goodness to me', she wrote, 'if there is anything you wish me to do for you, it will be a great joy.' She sympathised with Emma about her poor health and her worry about her husband: 'the anxiety as to how he is cannot be good for you', she chided gently.[19] Emma had longed for a kind caretaker, and she now believed that she had found her in Florence.

By the summer, Florence had acquired her invitation to Max Gate. Somewhat unexpectedly, Florence warmed to Emma. She began to act as Mrs Hardy's companion and secretary. Armed with her typewriter, she set to work on the older woman's stories and letters. She began a typed copy of the old novella *The Maid on the Shore*. 'The more I see [of it], the more I like it', she confirmed. Though it tells the story of a love triangle not unlike that of Hardy's love triangle in his own Cornish novel, *A Pair of Blue Eyes*, Emma had, seemingly, no idea about the love triangle in her own home – Florence would call it the 'Max Gate menage'. Florence told Emma that her novella needed many corrections, such as the 'costumes' which would now seem 'ridiculous' twenty-one years after it had originally been written. Emma's description of the heroine, 'a robe of yellow velvet, golden coins hanging over her brow, & dusky hair floating over her shoulders', seemed particularly irksome to Florence.[20] Did she realise that the girl with golden floating hair was based on the young Emma Gifford? It's hard to imagine that she did not.

Florence was also typing up some of Emma's religious prose, which she hoped to publish. Increasingly frail, and now seventy, Emma had become more pious, and vehemently anti-Catholic. She resigned from the London Society for Women's Suffrage in 1909, because of the violent turn the movement had taken – their stone throwing and attempting to assassinate the prime minister – and instead was pouring all her energy into her 'campaign' to prevent Catholic infiltration into the Anglican church. To Emma's horror, Betty Owen had converted to Catholicism. 'I cannot comprehend', she wrote to Betty, 'how the world of 1900 can turn to Roman Catholicism for Christianity, & accept such a *travesty* of Christ's life, teaching, & death.'[21]

Florence further sought to ingratiate herself into Emma's good books by seeming to share in her anti-Catholic campaign as well as continually telling her how much she was enjoying *The Maid on the Shore*: 'I was again impressed by the vivid & picturesque descriptions of Cornish scenery.' She told Emma that she believed an even greater success would be Emma's new novel, 'The Inspirer'.[22] As its title suggests, its theme was a wife who was the main inspiration and muse for her writer husband. During these final years of her life, Emma became increasingly obsessed with the idea of herself as Hardy's one true muse. In the meantime, Florence began typing Emma's memoir and shopping for her, buying pink candleshades in Selfridges on her behalf.

Emma had written a sad letter to her friend, Alda Hoare, telling her that she had always expected to live in London, with only occasional visits to the countryside. She felt deeply unhappy in Dorset. It was 'Authorship' that had caused all her troubles, she believed, because of its 'undesirable proximity'. She was long used to her husband devoting himself to writing in his study for hours on end, but she still remembered a time when he had shared his work, when she had made fair copies of his novels, and they had discussed the characters as though they were real people. But now Hardy had forbidden Emma to enter his study, closing her out of his new world of poetry. Hardy was back in London and Emma had stolen into his forbidden room: 'I am ensconcing myself in the Study in *his* big chair foraging,' she told Lady Hoare, 'he keeps me *out* usually – as *never* formally'. She finished her letter: 'I have my private opinion of men in general & of him in particular.' Though her husband had 'grand brains', she thought him lacking in 'judgement of ordinary matters'. His lack of common sense unfitted him for the role of borough Justice of the Peace (magistrate) that he had taken on in Dorchester: 'utterly useless & dangerous as magistrates! & such offices'.[23]

Emma took comfort in her novel about the wife who inspired her husband's work. She had approached Hardy's American publisher about 'The Inspirer', who had unsurprisingly rejected it. Florence was her chief advocate: 'There are other – and better

– publishers for your purpose. We must make *that* a success, for it will be a big thing.'[24] Florence was playing a double game. She could not have believed that Hardy would have encouraged a novel clearly based on Emma as muse to a great author, and she knew Hardy's intense fear of publicity. Of course, it was important to keep Emma on side, but maybe some sensible words of constructive criticism would have been more befitting.

And what of Mary and Kate? How much they were implicit in the secret relationship is not entirely clear, but they had invited Florence to Hardy's birthplace, and were very taken with this gentle, shy woman. Florence wrote a postcard to Kate in October 1910: 'This is Enfield. It is not so pretty as Dorchester – & of course not nearly so sweet as Bockhampton – but still it might be worse . . . Hope I shall soon see you all again.'[25]

To Hardy's friend, Edward Clodd, who knew and seemingly approved of their relationship, Florence wasn't above mocking Hardy: 'Mr T H. has been in the depths of despair at the death of a pet cat', she wrote, quoting his hyperbolically anguished outburst at Kitsey's death: 'Providence has dealt me an entirely gratuitous & unlooked for blow.' She told Clodd that she was going back to Max Gate for a week or two. Hardy was delighted. He kept up the fiction, even to Clodd, that she was his 'secretary' or his 'little cousin' and told him 'Miss D – my handyman, as I call her – appeared yesterday with her typewriter, & we are going to be amazingly industrious – in intention, at least, though fine days tempt one out of doors.'[26]

That November, the Dorchester Debating and Dramatic Society (later renamed the Hardy Players) were performing an adaptation of *Under the Greenwood Tree* in London. They all went along, Emma and Hardy's siblings awkwardly together for the first time in years, while Florence sat next to Clodd. Soon afterwards, Hardy orchestrated a meeting between the two Florences: 'Miss Dugdale mentioned to me that she had been with you. It was a great enjoyment for her. *Nobody* but you does kind things like that, & I am sincerely grateful to you. I am so glad you like her: she quite loves you – indeed you have no idea what a charm you have for her. Her literary judgment is very sound.'27

Florence, nicely ensconced in Max Gate that winter, was beginning to see the farcical aspect of living with the Hardys: 'The "Max Gate Menage" always does wear an aspect of comedy to me. Mrs Hardy is good to me, beyond words, & instead of cooling towards me she grows more and more affectionate.' But, on a more serious level, Florence could not be in the middle of such a tense atmosphere without feeling compassion for the unhappy couple: 'I am *intensely* sorry for her, sorry indeed for them both.'28

CHAPTER 64

The Mad Woman in the Attic?

On 23 November 1910, Dr Hawley Harvey Crippen was hanged in Pentonville Prison for the murder of his wife, Cora. The news of the murder and the execution sent shock waves around England and America, not only because of the doctor's respectability, but also because he was one of the first criminals to be captured with the aid of the wireless telegraph. Dr Crippen was American and had moved to England with his wife, who had been a music-hall singer and had openly conducted affairs. He was fired by the pharmaceutical company he worked for, as he spent too much time managing his wife's career. He soon found a new job at Drouet's Institution for the Deaf, where he hired a young typist, called Ethel Clare Le Neve. They began an affair, while his wife conducted one of her own with a lodger. In January 1910, the Crippens threw a party, after which Cora disappeared. Dr Crippen claimed that she had returned to America, died and been cremated. Meanwhile, Le Neve moved into his house, and began wearing his wife's clothes and jewellery. After a visit from Scotland Yard, Crippen and the typist fled to Canada. Cora's remains were found in the basement of the house. The captain of the ship on which Crippen and the typist sailed recognised the couple, even though Ethel was in disguise as a boy. Using the telegraph, the captain contacted Scotland Yard, who arrested Crippen as he landed in Canada. He admitted his guilt, was put on trial (all he cared about was the reputation of the typist), found guilty, and hanged.

Emma Hardy became obsessed with the idea that her husband looked like Dr Crippen, which led her to believe that she would be murdered and stashed in the cellar of Max Gate.

Florence found her employer's concern amusing: 'Mrs Hardy is queerer than ever', she wrote to Clodd: 'She has just asked me whether I have noticed how extremely like *Crippen* Mr TH is, in personal appearance. She added, darkly, that she would not be surprised to find herself in the cellar one morning. All this in deadly seriousness.' Florence alluded to her own awkward status as the third person in the marriage, comparing herself with Crippen's mistress: 'I thought it was time to depart or she would be asking me if I didn't think I resembled Miss Le Neve.'[1] Perhaps Emma did not, in fact, believe that Hardy and Florence's relationship was as innocent as it seemed. She had perhaps intuited that she was viewed as an impediment to their happiness. It was rather an unfortunate coincidence that Miss Le Neve and Florence Dugdale were both typists, and that Le Neve had once been Dr Crippen's secretary before she became his mistress.

Emma told Florence of her intention to go abroad because that would 'have a good effect on T.H.'. She knew that Hardy missed her when she was away. Florence agreed that it would be a good idea for Emma to go abroad, but was shocked when she suggested that the two women should go away together. Once again, it appears that Emma had begun to twig that something was amiss. She certainly knew that removing Florence from Max Gate would be distressing to Hardy. Florence redoubled her efforts to stay in Emma's good books. Though she was agnostic, which pleased Hardy, she amped up her image as a devout Protestant girl, knowing it would please Emma. She told her employer that she had been addressing her Protestant bible classes 'on the current danger', that is to say the anti-Catholic cause. Playing to Emma's prejudice, she stirred the anti-papist pot: 'The Roman Catholic priests all over the country have given orders to their followers to vote *Liberal*, she told her – from their powerbase in Ireland, they would become a 'stronghold of Roman Catholicism & a menace to this country'. The prime minister, Florence believed, was 'in league with the R.C.s'.[2] It was cruel and manipulative of Florence to incite Emma's fears, bigoted as they were. Later, Florence would tell the convert Betty Owen that Roman Catholicism was the best of all religious faiths: 'If one has need of a religion, that I am sure is the only one.'[3]

Florence now assured Emma that she would be delighted to accompany her to Boulogne as soon as the weather improved. Emma had written a poem about Hardy called 'A Ballad of a Boy' with the intention of publishing it, but had decided that it would 'cause annoyance'. Florence wrote that 'it is so good a poem, & so full of life & originality that I am sorry it cannot be published'. She assured Emma: 'Personally I cannot see in it one line that would identify the boy with Mr. Hardy.'[4] Engaging the services of a local printer, Emma got *Alleys*, her poetry collection, published late in 1911. Her prose volume, *Spaces,* was a religious rhapsody, with a vision of the Day of Judgement. It ends with a dialogue between God and Satan on the subject of creation. It is almost as if she is casting herself as a rebellious angel in the house and her husband as an over-weening God who thinks he is the only one with a creative imagination:

Satan   'Thou sayest Thou art from Everlasting that Thou didst
         create all things – even me. Thou sayest that Thou lovest
         all. Thou dost not love us – Thy angels love not thee. I

> love Thee not. Me they love, and my behests shall they
> obey, not Tine. My power is as great as Thine. Thou
> didst not create me.'
>
> God 'Mine they are, Mine thou wert. My love has been greatly
> given to thee, so thou are fairer than all angels and a
> large portion of my power has been upon thee – but
> thou canst not create. I have created *thee* and these my
> angels.[5]

There is something unbearably sad about Emma's attempts to
create, to get herself into print, especially when Hardy continued
to do so much to support Florence's writing, while ignoring his
wife and her literary efforts.

Upon the death of Kitsey the white cat, Florence entered
Hardy's forbidden study and found him composing a 'pathetic
little poem' to the beloved feline. She looked over his shoulder
and read the line: 'That little white cat was his only friend.' She
was infuriated: 'That was too much for even my sweet temper,
& I ramped round the study proclaiming: "This *is* hideous
ingratitude."' Florence had believed Hardy when he had told
her that *she* was his only friend. Instead of Hardy pleading
forgiveness and placating her, 'the culprit' looked 'highly
delighted with himself, & said smilingly, that he was not exactly
writing about himself but about some imaginary man in a similar
situation'.[6] It is striking that Hardy seemed to enjoy Florence's
anger at being supplanted by his dead cat. She would later
suggest that Hardy also took pleasure in Emma's cruel remarks
and insults about Hardy and his family. Lilian Gifford told
Florence that the Giffords had tongues which could 'cut to the
bone'. Florence wrote to her confidante, Clodd: 'Mr Hardy had
more than twenty years of insults, and apparently enjoyed them
very much – according to what he says now.'[7]

It was a disturbing claim, but perhaps Florence was correct in intuiting Hardy's masochistic tendencies. Emma's sharp tongue was similar to that of Jemima Hardy. He quite liked being told off by a woman. He often infuriated his friends and family by soaking up the insults that were hurled at him, never fighting back, retreating to his study. Florence reported that Emma had forbidden Hardy's family to enter Max Gate in her presence for twenty years, and Hardy had not made a word of protest. Edward Clodd expressed regret in his diary that Hardy had acquiesced to this demand of his 'half mad wife'.[8] By nature gentle and kind, he appeared to believe that cutting Emma out of his life and ignoring her anger, was the best policy. He had no idea that in her attic room, she was writing out all her rage and despair. Nor did Florence know about the secret diaries.

The pressure had been building and on Christmas Day 1910, there was a huge marital row. Florence was at the centre of the quarrel. Hardy wanted to take her to the cottage at Bockhampton to see his sisters for a seasonal visit. Emma, now dependent on Florence, refused on the grounds that Kate and Mary would 'poison my [Florence's] mind against her'. A 'violent quarrel' ensued. For once, Hardy's anger was aroused. It was an ugly fight. Fifteen years after the incident, Florence would recall: 'oh dear, oh dear *what* a scene'. Hardy stormed off alone to visit his sisters, and Emma retreated to her attic to 'write her memoirs'. Florence was left alone in the drawing room, the air full of rage and hatred. Hardy returned later in the evening. It was, Florence wrote, 'the first Christmas of the kind I had ever spent, having always been with a party of cheerful people before that'. She made a vow that 'no power on earth would ever induce me to spend another Christmas at Max Gate'. She left the house and returned to London.

In the garden of Max Gate, Emma with Gordon Gifford, Hardy with his Rover Cob

The attic room at Max Gate, as it is today

Helen Paterson, illustrator of
Far from the Madding Crowd

Florence Henniker

**The Poor Man
and the Ladies?**

Agnes Grove: frontispiece to *The Social
Fetich*, dedicated to Hardy

Rebekah Owen, with a Tess-like hat

Jemima by Mary

Hardy by Mary

Florence by Mary

With Florence at the seaside at Aldeburgh—while Emma was still alive

Emma, *c.*1904, with Kitsey the cat

Gertrude Bugler as Marty South

Hardy and Florence, *c.*1914, with Wessex the dog

The collaborators on the self-ghosted autobiography

Thomas Hardy, aged 16
1856

THE EARLY LIFE OF

THOMAS HARDY

1840—1891

COMPILED LARGELY FROM
CONTEMPORARY NOTES, LETTERS, DIARIES, AND
BIOGRAPHICAL MEMORANDA, AS WELL AS FROM
ORAL INFORMATION IN CONVERSATIONS EXTEND-
ING OVER MANY YEARS

BY

FLORENCE EMILY HARDY

New York
THE MACMILLAN COMPANY
1928

Still a lover of the bicycle, Hardy took a dislike to motor cars, which covered his apples with dust. Betty and Catherine Owen had succumbed to the rage for the automobile, and Emma desired a car and chauffeur of her own. Hardy refused. In November, Hardy had received the Order of Merit (O.M.), the most distinguished of royal honours, and, though he had turned down a knighthood, he accepted. Friends remarked on how pleased his mother would have been, had she only been alive. Jemima would have been pleased, but she would never have said so. Emma was mortified that Hardy accepted an honour that only *he* benefited from. She would have much preferred the knighthood that would have made her become Lady Hardy. Florence was asked to look after Hardy on the day of the investiture, and see that he was properly dressed. Emma stayed home. In his memoir, Hardy began to refer to Florence as 'Miss Dugdale, a literary friend of Mrs Hardy's at the Lyceum Club, whose paternal ancestors were Dorset people dwelling near the Hardys'.[9]

Following the death of yet another cat, Florence wrote to Emma with condolences: 'I hope that you have quite recovered from the shock of Marky's death. Poor little creature. I often speak of her.' She made herself even more indispensable to Emma, interviewing three candidates for the position of cook. Then in the summer the women took a seaside holiday together in Worthing. Florence sent a postcard to Mary Hardy, to whom she had grown close. She told her that she was having a 'delightful' time, sea-bathing twice a day, crossing the road 'daily in my bathing dress'.[10] No doubt Mary shared the news with her brother, and what a delight it must have been for him to imagine Florence in her bathing costume.

Florence and Henry were as close as ever, frequently writing to one another. He was handsome, straight-talking, honourable (perhaps everything his brother was not), and she appreciated his innate goodness: 'He is one of the best friends I ever had – true, strong & generous in every thought & deed – Giles Winterbourne in the flesh – or perhaps Gabriel Oak.'[11] Tom and Florence had hopes that Henry would marry her sister, Constance.

When Hardy and Florence went with brother Henry and sister Kate on another of their cathedral sightseeing trips, this time to Bath, Gloucester, and Bristol, Florence reported to Clodd that the man with the Order of Merit to his name was in the best of health and exceptionally cheerful. The Hardy siblings could not fail to notice Florence's effect on his spirits, in sharp contrast to his many 'moods of depression'.[12] Shortly after the visit, Hardy sent Florence a Christmas greeting with a quotation from the epistle to the Galatians: 'Ye have been called unto liberty' – a verse that continues 'only use not liberty for an occasion to the flesh, but by love serve one another'.[13] Hardy had been starved of love for so many years that he told Florence 'I do not ask for much – I only want a *little* affection.'[14] Florence observed that 'nothing could be more lonely than the life he used to live – long evenings spent alone in his study, insult & abuse his only enlivenment'.[15]

Mary Hardy had not accompanied her siblings on the tours, since she had been ill. Emma, too, was in poor health and considerable pain, though Hardy refused to believe it, saying that she was in 'great health and vigour'. Then on 15 April 1912, the unsinkable *Titanic* sank and two of Hardy's acquaintances died. He set about writing his poem 'The Convergence of the Twain'. While the ship was being built in the spirit of 'human vanity' and 'Pride of Life', the 'Immanent Will' that rules the universe 'Prepared a sinister mate' in 'A Shape of Ice'. The convergence of the opposing forces of life and death is unavoidable, determined by 'the Spinner of the Years'.[16] So too for Hardy: an accumulation of deaths and losses were converging with the hope of a new life brought by Florence.

The following month, Florence and Hardy were together again at Aldeburgh. Then there was another dreadful scene between Emma and Hardy during a ceremony at Max Gate when he was presented with a gold medal by the Royal Society of Literature. Poets Henry Newbolt and William Butler Yeats came down to Dorchester. During luncheon in the dining room, Emma gave Yeats 'much curious information' about her two 'very fine cats' – who sat on the table beside her plate. Newbolt wrote in his diary: 'Yeats looked like an Eastern Magician over-powered by a Northern Witch.' 'I too', he added, 'felt myself spellbound by the famous pair of Blue Eyes, which surpassed all that I had ever seen.'[17] Sadly, when it came to the actual presentation of the medal, Hardy asked his wife to leave, even though the two men and Emma herself protested. In the end, she left the room.

Few people realised that Emma was in agonising pain and taking a strong medication – opium mixed with alcohol – to alleviate her excruciating back pain caused by gallbladder prob-lems and angina. Emma had a maid, a fourteen-year-old girl from Cheslebourne, Alice Gale, who was nicknamed 'Dolly' because of her doll-like features. Gale slept in the attic bedroom next to her mistress and witnessed Emma's last year of pain and misery. Emma also suffered from painful eczema (possibly stress-related). Little Dolly would rub her back and brush her constantly itching scalp. Emma and Dolly had to climb three flights of stairs to enter the attic. Dolly would bring up break-fast and luncheon, and Emma would come down to dinner, though, according to Dolly, never a word was spoken by man or wife. On Sundays, Emma would attend Fordington church, pushed in a bath chair by the gardener. Her one comfort was her cats, who slept on her bed.

Dolly was interviewed several times about her life at Max Gate. She was fond of Emma, who sometimes scolded her for bringing up lunch late, but she 'despised' Hardy, whom she described as a 'wizen up little man' with 'shift eyes'. She saw his cold-hearted manner towards his wife. And she had heard the rumours of a mistress in London. Her parents told her that the famous writer was a man of loose morals, imploring her to leave the house immediately if he behaved improperly. Dolly reported that no matter how much pain she was in, Emma would never wake her, but would suffer through the night alone. Florence she remembered as a lovely lady with beautiful hair. She claimed that everyone in Dorchester gossiped that Florence was the London mistress.[18]

Emma was well enough to give one of her garden parties in July. According to Dolly, Florence attended the party, which was the last she ever gave. Later, Emma arranged a seaside picnic for the young women of a local Needlework Guild. Later, they returned to Max Gate, where Emma presented each of the girls with a cup and saucer. Dolly Gale described the difficulty of heating the attic. Both women attended to the fire, but it was 'either too hot or too cold', so they were continually building it up or reducing it to achieve the correct temperature. The attic rooms were tiny and modestly furnished. By contrast, Hardy had a large bedroom and his study with a view of the garden.

By the autumn of 1912 Emma's health had deteriorated severely. Records of two visits made shortly before her death shed light on the intolerable state of the marriage, and Emma's deplorable physical condition. Of her mental condition much has been made, most of which seems off the mark.

In September Edmund Gosse arrived accompanied by fellow critic and essayist A. C. Benson (author of the lyrics to Elgar's 'Land of Hope and Glory'). Arthur Benson, Master of Magdalene College, Cambridge, was the son of Mary (Minnie) Sigdwick Benson, who married a man who would become the Archbishop of Canterbury. She bore six children, none of whom married, and all of whom seemed to prefer their own sex. Mary herself had an affair with the famous composer Ethel Smyth and was also sexually involved with Lucy Tait, daughter of the previous Archbishop of Canterbury, about which she felt profoundly guilty. In 1878, she wrote in her diary: 'Once more and with shame O Lord, grant that all carnal affections may die in me, and that all things belonging to the spirit may love and grow in me. Lord, look down on Lucy and me, and bring to pass the union we have both so blindly, each in our own region of mistake, continually desired.'[19]

After her husband's death, Mary and Lucy set up house together. They were together until Mary's death and were buried together. Her son Arthur Benson never married. He and his sister suffered from mental illness, probably bipolar disorder, inherited from their father. His sister Maggie suffered from delusions and mania, tried to kill herself, and had to be restrained, ending her life in the Roehampton mental hospital, The Priory. But in an era when mental illness was shrouded in shame and secrecy, this family history did nothing to make Benson sympathetic to Emma Hardy's eccentricities. He wrote voluminous diaries, and his account of the meeting at Max Gate was full of clever, bitchy detail, such as the 'frightful ornament of alabaster' in the vestibule with its note to the maid that it should be 'dusted not touched'. His first impression of Emma was of 'a small, pretty, rather mincing elderly lady with hair curiously puffed & padded rather fantastically dressed'. Lilian was also there: 'a solid plebeian overdressed niece was presented to us'. At lunch he found it hard to speak to Emma, 'who rambled along in a very inconsequent way, with a bird-like sort of wit, looking sideways and treating one's remarks as amiable interruptions'. Emma produced cigarettes for the men, and Gosse persuaded her to try one, which she did coughing and spluttering while Hardy glared at her 'fiercely and scornfully'.[20]

For a depressive like Arthur Benson, the atmosphere of Max Gate was especially oppressive. The 'poor house' was 'uncomfortable', 'rather pretentious', and airless, dark and gloomy, 'like a house wrapped up and put away in a box'. The two women he found wanting: 'the crazy and fantastic wife' and the 'stolid niece'. Benson felt sorry for Hardy: 'It gave me a sense of something intolerable, the thought of his having to live day and night with the absurd, inconsequent, huffy, rambling old lady.' Benson and Gosse had gossiped about Mrs Hardy, and Gosse told him that Emma confessed to beating her husband. When Gosse remonstrated, she confessed that it was only with a rolled-up *Times* newspaper. That day, Emma complained of Hardy's ill treatment of her. She told Gosse that Hardy kept all his 'honours' to himself, and refused to buy a motor car, even though she found mobility difficult.[21]

Benson found her behaviour strange. Showing him around the dining room, she was almost talking to herself, and then in the garden, she began ejecting seeds from flower pods, 'with little jumps & elfin shrieks of pleasure'. Benson continued, with evident bafflement at this strange marriage: 'They don't get on together at all. The marriage was thought a misalliance for her, when he was poor and undistinguished, and she continues to resent it . . . He [Hardy] is not agreeable to her either, but his patience must be incredibly tried. She is so queer, and yet has to be treated as rational, while she is full, I imagine, of suspicions and jealousies and affronts which must be half insane.' Benson thought Hardy would have been happier 'in some little stone-built manor at the foot of the downs, in a happy circle, with children about him'.[22]

Gosse left his own report of the 'bewildered maid', the 'slovenly' house 'with incongruous objects', and Emma's 'absurdly dressed' appearance. The diaries of both men referred to the strange inscrutability of Hardy's demeanour. For the elegant, refined Benson, the epitome of a Cambridge Master, Hardy's manner was that of the dour countryman: 'The suspiciousness of the rustic, the idea that he must guard himself, not give himself away . . . There is something secret and inscrutable about him.' Likewise, Gosse: 'He remains what he has always been, a sphinx-like little man, unrelated, unrevealed, displaying nothing that the most affectionate solicitude can make use of to explain the mystery of his magnificent genius.'[23] Neither man (and Gosse was much the kinder of the two) alluded to the class question, and how awkward and inferior Hardy would have felt in the presence of the Cambridge Head of House.

One of the reasons that both men were puzzled by his marriage was because of the way that Hardy had always written so well about women. 'She [Emma] must be a singular partner for a man interested in a feminine temperament', Benson cattily observed. Gosse recalled Hardy warming up when speaking about his novels, and especially when it came to the 'Women interest'. He explained: 'But about Women; I wonder how I came to write like that. Now I know them better, I should write just the same.' He concluded: 'But I have said it all best in the poems.'[24]

Gosse found Hardy physically frail: 'At last the great man appears, grown, it seems to me, very small, very dry, very white.' Now seventy-two, Hardy had lost his pride in the house that he had built. There was a decided air of neglect about Max Gate, whose very walls had 'great patches of discoloration and damp'.[25] It was difficult for Emma, who was in such poor health, to manage the household staff. There was no electricity, even though Dorchester had an electric supply in 1901, so oil lamps and candles had to suffice. Water had to be drawn from the well in the garden, and then boiled over the kitchen fire. There was a lavatory, but a housemaid had to flush it with jugs of well-water.

Hardy's doctor, who visited him at this time, told the siblings that 'the lack of attention & general discomfort must have had a serious effect sooner or later'.[26] Benson felt that neither Emma nor Hardy seemed 'at all content'. Hardy, he felt, was 'waiting stolidly for destiny to declare itself'. He did not have to wait long.

———

It was in her attic that Emma had begun writing what Florence Dugdale would call 'her diabolical diaries'. Entitling them 'What I Think of My Husband', she poured out her frustration. Again and again, her anger was bound up with Hardy's failure to truly acknowledge her part in his literary success. A university lecturer and aspiring biographer called Frank Hedgcock, who visited Max Gate in 1910, recalled a scene at tea with the Hardys. They did not say a single word across the table, except for one comment: 'More tea, please.' Hedgcock remembered Emma talking to him about 'our books' and asking him which he preferred. He first told her he considered *Under the Greenwood Tree* to be 'a miniature masterpiece'. He then expressed his admiration of *A Pair of Blue Eyes*, which pleased his hostess greatly: 'She pronounced it one of *their* finest works and told me she had copied much of the original rough manuscript with her own hand.' She then added, with an arch glance at her husband, that she 'perhaps slipped in some emendations' of her own. Hardy made no response.[27]

Six weeks before her death, Emma wrote in her diary a passage about her father's disapproval of Hardy, and how right he had been in his estimate of the man as '*utterly worthless*'.[28] Yet even when she was condemning her husband in the most vitriolic terms and insults in the diaries, she was still able to write movingly about their courtship and marriage, despite her physical and mental pain.

It is not difficult to see why Emma has been perceived as the 'Madwoman in the Attic'. It had been a cliché of Victorian womanhood ever since Charlotte Brontë wrote *Jane Eyre*. But the visitor to Emma's boudoir at Max Gate will find it light and airy, with high windows and a table for writing and drawing. It presents a rather different picture from Mr Rochester's attic room on the third floor, where he locks up the raging and violent Bertha Mason. Bertha's madness is hereditary – her mother died in an asylum, and her brother is intellectually disabled. She is so violent that she stabs her brother and attempts to rip out her husband's throat with her own teeth. There are no records of Emma exhibiting such extreme aberrations. And yet Hardy (and certainly Florence Dugdale) came to believe that she inherited insanity from her father's side of the family. Florence had been in the position of Brontë's Grace Poole when she had looked after Lady Stoker, similarly incarcerated in an upstairs room, so she knew what true madness looked like. She knew, too, the great sadness of William Stoker, who refused to lock up his wife in an asylum and treated her always with kindness and love. So she may have developed an exaggerated sense of Emma's incapacity as an excuse for Hardy's neglect of her – and her own involvement with him.

Mary Hardy had accused her of 'errors of mind' and 'being mad' in 1896, and Hardy himself would remain convinced that he had seen signs of madness. 'I knew the family', he remarked, meaning that he knew the family history of mental illness – the brother and sister dispatched to lunatic asylums. His friend Sir Clifford Allbutt, a Commissioner in Lunacy, gave his off the record opinion that Emma was probably certifiable, though Hardy would never have locked her away.

Emma was certainly eccentric, and she had become dependent on her opium medication towards the end of her life. Hardy became convinced that she suffered from delusions. Her Dorset neighbours found Emma 'potty without qualification' but then again, they also found Hardy 'slightly potty'. Leonie Gifford, the daughter of Emma's first cousin, described Emma's paranoid tendencies: she kept a basket of food for flight in the case of a Catholic invasion of England. This would certainly accord with the thoughts of Florence Dugdale as she encouraged Emma's anti-Catholic delusions. Other friends and acquaintances attested to her strange behaviour, which was at first 'child-like' but became more sinister in old age. A convincing account by medical historian Anthony Fincham suggests that Emma was probably suffering from Schizoid Personality Disorder.[29] Individuals in this diagnosis tend to be isolated, do not desire to be part of a family, have little interest in sexual experiences, and lack close friends or confidantes. This disorder usually begins in early adulthood.

But if there is to be a posthumous diagnosis – always a speculative venture – the correct one, as featured in the authoritative *Diagnostic and Statistical Manual of Mental Disorders*, is Schizotypal Personality Disorder. This disorder has similar criteria to SPD, but includes delusions, odd beliefs, vague 'circumstantial' speech, paranoid ideation, behaviour or appearance that is odd, eccentric or peculiar, and social anxiety. Emma's speech, noted by many as odd, fits the diagnosis of 'unusual or idiosyncratic phrasing and construction . . . loose, digressive, or vague, but without actual derangement or incoherence'.[30] Eccentric choice of clothing is an especially distinctive criterion. And Emma certainly exhibited social anxiety, especially at formal occasions such as dinner parties.

It may be that Hardy knew all along that Emma suffered from some sort of hereditary mental condition, and out of loyalty, or shame, he kept it to himself. A sinister poem, 'The Interloper', hints that he may have long recognised the shadow cast on his marriage. The first stanza recalls a Cornish clifftop ride with Emma and her sister – but the poet senses an invisible interloper beside them on the 'quaint old chaise'. The second stanza has the couple sitting by the 'sweet stream' of the Stour, reading poetry together: 'But one sits with them whom they don't mark, / One I'm wishing could not be there.' The shadowy figure appears again at a dinner party in a (presumably London) mansion and during a gathering on a lawn. Is it death, the addressee of the poem wonders, the darkness that waits upon us all. No, the poet replies, 'It is that under which best lives corrode, / Would, would it could not be there!'[31] The nature of the 'it' was not made clear when Hardy included the poem in his collection *Moments of Vision*. But late in life, when he published the second edition of his *Collected Poems*, he added a motto that makes everything clear: 'And I saw the figure and visage of Madness seeking for a home'.

CHAPTER 65

Woman Much Missed

Betty Owen, though she had once felt that she had been frozen out by the Hardys, set out for Dorchester with her sister Catherine. They were to attend the Dorchester Dramatic Society's production of *The Trumpet-Major*. Betty admitted that there had been a thawing in the relationship, and she decided to make a call at Max Gate. They set off in their motor car, and the day before the show called in on the Hardys. The maid who answered the door told them that Mrs Hardy was not well, but Betty sent in her card, with the message 'Would you not see *us*?' and they were admitted. When Emma came down, the sisters thought she 'seemed very ill'. Emma insisted that they stay for tea and asked them to return after they had seen the play. She complained of 'great pains' in her back but refused to see a doctor, because 'she did not want to be cut up'. The sisters were convinced that she was suffering from 'nerves and melancholia'. She was tearful and wiping her eyes. Hardy came down and was kind to the sisters. Before they left, the sisters begged Emma to see a doctor. On the way home they discussed her condition: 'She will die or go insane, she can't go on like this.'[1] Hardy himself would recall an evening around this time when his wife sat at the piano and played a long series of her favourite tunes. At the end, she said she 'would never play more'.²

The day after she had seen the Owen sisters, she agreed to see a doctor, who thought her weak from lack of nourishment. That evening, Hardy left her to see a rehearsal of *The Trumpet-Major*. According to Florence Dugdale, during this time the couple had another bitter quarrel, which ended in their plans for a separation.³

Hardy claimed that the next morning, 27 November 1912, he asked the maid for an update on Emma's health and hastened to the attic. This is not the account left by Dolly Gale. She had checked her mistress first thing in the morning, and was alarmed to see her so sick and moaning in pain. Emma asked for Tom, and she rushed down to Hardy's study, and reported the news. Hardy simply looked at her and said, 'Your collar is crooked.' Afraid to look into his 'cold eyes', Dolly stared at a plaque on his desk. Taking his time, he climbed the stairs, but by then Emma had lost consciousness, and it was only then that he perceived the reality of the situation, crying 'Em, Em, don't you know me?' It was the first time Dolly had ever seen a person dying, and she rushed out to fetch the doctor. Emma was laid out on Hardy's bed, so that people could pay their last respects. Hardy told the servants to buy mourning dress in Genge's Department Store in Dorchester. In their black dresses and huge black hats, they looked like three mushrooms.

There was a note in Hardy's hand on Emma's desk, with a sad message scribbled in pencil: 'Mrs Hardy finds that she must have the Liq: Op: Sed: – which she knows to take.'⁴ The note gives the lie that Hardy had no idea that she was so ill. To Ellen Gosse, he wrote: 'Everybody, myself included, supposed her to have a high vitality & the soundest of constitutions.'⁵ But it was clear to her maid, and those last visitors, the Owen sisters, that she was desperately unwell. Hardy was in shock and denial, and

he continued to believe that her death was completely unexpected. He refused to cancel the performance of *The Trumpet-Major*
and an announcement was made on stage. One of the first things
he did was to send a telegram to Florence announcing Emma's
death and bidding her to come to Max Gate. Florence was
already on her way to see the play. She was well aware that there
had been gossip about her relationship with Hardy, but she
came, nevertheless. Kate and Lilian were managing the servants
and taking care of Hardy.

Emma was buried at Stinsford alongside the graves of Hardy's
parents and grandparents in the plot he had chosen for them
both. She would hardly have been happy to be buried with her
husband's low relatives in a county she did not care for, but he
claimed that she had expressed a wish not to be buried in
Plymouth alongside her own family. Hardy's wreath bore the
message: 'From her lonely Husband, with the old affection.'[6]
Emma's grave was covered in wreaths from a long list of fine
London ladies, most of whom she had disliked. In another
morbid twist, Florence was told by Hardy that he would lie
next to his wife when the time came, while a corner of the
graveyard would be reserved for her.[7] Small comfort, one suspects,
for Florence.

Soon after Emma's death, Hardy sorted her papers in the
attic. He discovered her diaries, including 'What I Think of My
Husband', in which she laid bare her misery in the marriage.
He was filled with guilt and remorse. Though Florence was
ensconced in Max Gate, she had little idea of what was in store.
She told her confidant, Clodd, that Hardy 'looks very well &
seems cheerful'. Kate told Florence that he had 'regained the
same happy laugh that he had when he had been a young man'.[8]
But Hardy had become obsessed with Emma's hurtful words
and Florence reported he 'spends his evenings in reading &
re-reading voluminous diaries that Mrs H. has kept from the

time of their marriage'. Florence was horrified: 'Nothing could be worse for him. He reads the comments upon himself – bitter denunciations, beginning about 1891 & continuing until within one or two days of her death – & I think he will end up *believing* them.'⁹

By writing down her denunciations, Emma had done the one thing that would truly resonate with the man of letters: putting it all down on paper to be read and reread. Hardy insisted on visiting the grave, and visiting his brother and sisters, but saw few of his friends. To make matters worse, Lilian Gifford refused to leave Max Gate, other than rushing up to London to sell Emma's clothes, before returning to plague Florence. Although Florence was uncertain of her position, she comforted herself that Lilian would no longer be popular at Max Gate. Like her aunt, she was 'imbued with ideas of the grandeur of the Gifford family, & the great Archdeacon, & the vulgarity of Mr Hardy's relatives'. Florence was particularly infuriated by the fact that Lilian continued the myth that 'Mr Hardy would *never* have been a great writer had it not been for her dear aunt's [sic] influence'. Florence was now locked in combat with Lilian, whom she described as 'Mrs Hardy in little'.¹⁰

To judge from a letter that Mary Hardy sent to her cousin, Lilian was in a stronger position than Florence in these early days of Hardy's life as a widower:

You have heard no doubt of the death of Tom's wife on 27th Novʳ /12. It was a great shock to him as the doctor had seen her the night before and said she was going on well, but she died suddenly the next morning. He does not recover his spirits as we should wish and yet the doctor and others assure him that it is a good thing as more trouble would have been in store for him had her life been spared. She was strange in her head and did not improve as she grew older. A niece of hers who was brought up at Max Gate lives with Tom as he feels he can't have a stranger there now that he is old. She and her brother will have what he has to give I suppose when his end comes. Perhaps not so much, as he never cared to make money, so long as he had enough to live on.[11]

It is not clear why Mary thought that the Gifford relatives would be the eventual beneficiaries of her brother's will.

If Florence believed that Emma's death would instantly liberate her from her life as a freelance writer, and make her the mistress of Max Gate, she was sorely mistaken. Hardy became obsessed with local gossip about their relationship. Florence reported that Hardy was 'extremely sensitive & says that if I am seen walking about in Dorchester with him, or even if it is known that I am staying at Max Gate, they will comment unpleasantly'. Tongues had been wagging, but Hardy insisted that things would change after a year. Florence tried her best to explain their relationship to Clodd: 'If only I had an opportunity for a longer talk with you I could have gone into that very complicated subject with enlightenment to you & much ease and relief to myself.' Florence was much less concerned about appearances than Hardy and she feared that he would not allow her to appear at Aldeburgh, the place where they had met in secret and sat closely together on the beach. Now that Florence was back in Enfield, Hardy had been going through Emma's papers again, and had told Florence that her denunciation of him was 'sheer hallucination in her, poor thing, & not wilfulness'. Florence could barely suppress her indignation: 'I feel as if I can hardly keep back my true opinion much longer.'[12]

An even more worrying sign was the beginning of Hardy's veneration of his wife's memory. 'I must say', she complained, 'that the good lady's virtues are beginning to weigh heavilly [sic] on my shoulders. I had three pages of them this morning.'

Florence was irritated to discover that 'Chief among her virtues now seems to rank her strict Evangelical views – her religious tendencies, her *humanitarianism* (to cats I suppose he means).' Florence could be amusing in her descriptions of Hardy's need for self-drama and this sudden change of heart towards the wife he had so long despised. But it made her feel rejected and worthless. She held on to Hardy's promise that she could come to stay at Max Gate in the spring: 'If I once get you here again', he wrote to her, 'won't I clutch you tight.'[13]

In early March 1913, leaving Florence alone in Max Gate with a loaded revolver in her bedroom, Hardy set off for Cornwall. It was forty-three years since he had met and courted Emma there. He started for St Juliot, stayed at Boscastle, and went on to Pentargan Bay and Beeny Cliff. Florence was horrified at the thought of him visiting the grave of Emma's father, 'that amiable gentleman' who wrote of him as 'a low-born churl who has presumed to marry into *my* family'. But Hardy would not be deterred. His plain-speaking sister Kate proclaimed: 'so long as he doesn't pick up another Gifford down there, all will be well.'[14]

Hardy explained that he was going 'for the sake of the girl he married, & who died more than twenty years ago'. His siblings had a very different view, saying '*that* girl never existed'. Florence, though, acknowledged that 'she did exist to him, no doubt'.[15] Florence was deeply worried that his tendency to 'luxuriate in misery' was bad for him. He was now speaking of Emma as – in John Milton's phrase in his sonnet about a dream of his dead wife – his 'late, espoused saint'.

Florence could not understand why this new veneration of Emma 'went side by side' with his reading of her 'diabolical diaries'. She thought he had destroyed them, but six weeks after

Emma's death, he produced one volume from his pocket and read her a passage. It was the passage from Emma's father, denigrating Hardy's lowly origins, and adding some 'repeated adjectives of abuse' from Emma's own mouth. Florence could not bear to repeat the 'poisonous' words. Once again, Florence seemed aware of Hardy's masochistic impulses – his belief that Emma was right about him – that he *was* a 'low-born churl' and that he somehow deserved her wrath. It's not clear whether he endured his wife's beatings with equanimity, but Hardy's passivity and stonewalling in the face of her ire is well recorded. Hardy was, of course, also giving Florence attention: 'I have never before realized the depth of his affection, & his goodness & unselfishness as I have done these last three months.' Nevertheless, she worried that for the rest of his life he would venerate Emma, and she would be forced to 'sit & listen humbly to an account of her virtues & graces'.[16]

Florence understood more of the man than the poet, perhaps not realising that Emma's death was inspiring his creative juices. In his memoir we hear that he was writing 'more than he had ever written before in the same space of time' and that he was 'in flower'. And, like the poet Thomas Gray, who also composed his best work writing mournful poems, Hardy's flower was 'sad-coloured'.[17] Hardy felt deep remorse for not visiting Emma's beloved Cornwall during their marriage. But his late pilgrimage did not bring him happiness. He wrote to Florence: 'The visit to this neighbourhood (i.e. Boscastle) has been a very painful one to me, & I have said a dozen times I wish I had not come – What possessed me to do it!'[18] His words placated Florence, but he knew that he was writing some of his best poetry. He told Florence he felt a great sense of sadness for the way that the marriage had turned out: 'Looking back it has seemed such a cruel thing altogether that events which began so auspiciously should have turned out as they did. And now suppose that something shd happen to you, physically, as it did to her mentally!'[19]

Back at Max Gate, Florence had to put up not only with his worship of his late wife, but also with her 'impecunious' Gifford relatives. Herself from a lowly background, Florence was incensed that Gordon and Lilian Gifford looked down on Hardy while taking his money. But Florence was also living on 'his bounty'. She began to fear for her fate as the second Mrs Hardy.

With Emma gone, four women were vying for control of the household. There was Kate, Lilian Gifford, the housekeeper Florence Griffin, and Florence Dugdale. The other Florence was soon disposed of, Kate was happy enough to return to her sister and brother, but Lilian was another matter. Hardy temporarily banished Emma's niece following some arguments about domestic arrangements, telling her that he would still pay her a salary, but that she must return to Max Gate in due course. Florence was convinced that 'she will come back *eventually*, of course'.

Because she had been the main witness to the unhappy, unhealthy marriage, Florence struggled to understand why Hardy was in his study for hours on end, writing letters to his friends, expressing his grief and loneliness. Like many people in the grip of grief, and even though the marriage had failed, Hardy could remember only the early years and the good times. In some senses, he was mourning the death of the marriage, and coming to terms with his own part in it – hence the remark about the girl who 'died more than twenty years ago'. He wrote to Clodd: 'One forgets all the recent years & differences, & the mind goes back to the early times when each was much to the other – in her case & mine intensely much.'[20]

Their Dorset friend, Mary Sheridan, who had scant love for Emma, and thought her half insane, had written a sympathy letter. Hardy's response suggests his guilt for his neglect: 'I had no suspicion whatever that there was anything precarious in her constitution, & reproach myself now for a lack of insight, which, if I had had it, might have enabled me to prolong her life a little by assiduous attention, & insistence on her taking more rest. However, that will never be known.'²¹ To his beloved Florence Henniker, he embroidered the circumstances of Emma's final moments: 'Half an hour earlier she had told the servant that she felt better. Then her bell rang violently, & when we went up she was gasping. In five minutes all was over.' There was, however, genuine sadness and remorse: 'I have reproached myself for not having guessed there might be some internal mischief at work, instead of blindly supposing her robust & sound & likely to live to quite old age.' Hardy and Florence Henniker were too firm friends for him to pretend that the marriage was happy: 'In spite of the differences between us, which it would be affectation to deny, & certain painful delusions she suffered from at times, my life is intensely sad to me now without her.'²²

Hardy told her that 'the saddest moments of all' were his evening walks in the garden, along the path where Emma would walk at dusk, with her cat 'trotting faithfull beside her'. Still in shock at her death, he half expected to see her 'coming in from the flower-beds with a little trowel in her hand'. The loyalty of Emma's cat was an uncomfortable reminder of his own lack of loyalty, most manifested in the presence of Florence. He told Mrs Henniker that Florence was at Max Gate helping him with page proofs. It was an entire coincidence, he said, that Florence happened to be on her way to Dorset to see his play at the very hour that Emma died.²³

Florence also had to bear with 'the niece' who had returned to Max Gate. Lilian had a weapon: her dead aunt. She used it to full effect. She would talk about Emma, currently Hardy's favourite subject, and Florence was forced to endure what she considered a charade: '[Lilian] knows that if she begins to talk in a sentimental way about dear Aunt, and St Juliot, and Archdeacon Gifford (whom she never saw) he is bowled over completely.' Lilian looked down on Florence's humble origins and chose every opportunity to make sneering remarks about her social superiority. There was a scene in a motor car when they passed a butcher's shop called Dugdale. Florence made a joke about her 'illustrious family' and Lilian seized on the allusion, making comments about how 'dreadfully vulgar it was to be connected with tradespeople'. For days and days, Lilian would not let it go: 'A person must be *very low down indeed* to have a butcher in the family.' Florence knew that the best corrective to Lilian's snobbery was to laugh, but she felt too humiliated to do so. Florence's sister had been to stay and had dissolved into tears following a fight with Lilian: 'This woman insulted her, behaved in fact like a mad woman.'[24]

It's hard to imagine Hardy's response to this absurd tug of war, with all of the women vying for his affection and attention. Florence suspected he rather enjoyed it: 'Mr Hardy could, I believe, stop it, if he chose', she wrote to Clodd. Rather cruelly, Clodd replied that Lilian was just like her aunt, an 'innocent, childlike creature' who said things without meaning it. Florence was unconvinced: 'She is thirty-four years old, and by no means childlike, although she puts on the air of a child of ten when talking to him.' It's hard not to admire Florence's caustic wit, though she herself was certainly not innocent of using her feminine wiles to capture Hardy's heart. Lilian appeared to be exacting her own revenge on the woman who had stolen her aunt's husband right under her nose. Florence was forced to endure daily sneers and jibes, and Lilian took to going to Dorchester 'telling tales to all the idle gossiping women in the place, and then tells me how they sympathise with her'. Lilian refused to help with the household: 'If I ask her to help me ever so little', Florence complained, her rival would say that she was 'not a servant' and had not been brought up to earn a living as a teacher or a journalist. Florence had the full support of the Hardy siblings, especially Henry. He was so incensed by Lilian's behaviour that he swore when he talked about the situation. Kate and Mary's opinion was that they had been 'through it all' themselves (with Emma). Florence tried (or pretended to try) to be sympathetic: 'Of course, her brother is an imbecile – one of them at least – and an uncle died in an asylum, and her grandfather was mad at times, so I ought to feel profoundly sorry for her – but I *can't* be that.'[25]

Above all, though, there was Hardy's continued veneration of the dead wife: 'And there is always this extraordinary idealisation of Mrs Hardy – whom now he says, and I think *believes*, was the sweetest, most gifted, most beautiful woman that ever lived.' Florence had become aware that Hardy was writing poems in Emma's memory, extraordinary poems that explored his profound guilt and remorse for his ill treatment of her and his failure to anticipate her death. This did not stop him from promising Florence that everything would change in a year: they would have people to stay and undertake more cathedral visits. But she was not convinced: 'I think he will just go on now, very quietly, writing poems about Mrs Hardy, and so forth.' She saw the irony in the switch of his subject-matter: 'It is rather funny when I remember those he used to write to me.'[26] Hardy's poem 'When Oats were Reaped' sees the poet walking to a grave in autumn and admitting his guilt: 'I wounded one who's there and now know well I wounded her.' The poet also suggests his own sense of pain and rejection: 'But, ah, she does not know that she wounded me!'[27] The trouble was that he was now wounding Florence, who was increasingly finding that she could not compete with a ghost. Emma had come to resent being married to a great writer, whereas Florence wanted to be married to a great writer.

CHAPTER 66

Mrs Florence Hardy

Emma's death made it easier for the Hardy siblings to see their brother now that the doors of Max Gate were open to them. In April 1913, Hardy was awarded an honorary doctorate of letters by the University of Cambridge and was made an Honorary Fellow of Magdalene. It was a huge achievement for the little country boy of Bockhampton who had dreamed of being at one of the great universities. Mary wrote her brother a poignant letter, knowing how much this accolade meant to him and even suggesting Moule's spiritual intervention: 'This is to congratulate you on the honour that Cambridge has now conferred on you. It seems as if it came from that dear soul whose dust, for so many years has been lying in the Fordington Churchyard. I came unexpectedly upon an old letter of his yesterday.'[1] Her letter was a reminder of the interest that Moule had taken in Hardy and his sister, and the tragedy of his death. What a delight Moule would have taken at his old pupil being honoured in this way. Mary was proud of her brother; the other siblings took less interest in his literary achievements. Hardy's delight was tempered by the deaths of Emma's pets, who 'strayed or were killed' during this time. The cats had gone, but Florence had a new puppy, a terrier called Wessex.

Florence was now in a difficult position. Her reputation had been besmirched in the summer of 1912 by the large legacy left to her by Sir William Stoker: she received twice as much as his brother Bram. According to one of Hardy's biographers, the Stoker family believed that she must have been his mistress while his mad wife was restrained in the upstairs room.[2] There's no evidence that this was in fact the case, but Stoker's death was a reminder of her having been a companion to a mentally ill elderly woman. It was all sounding too much like the narrative being peddled in Dorchester about the Hardy ménage in Emma's final years. Things came to a head when Lilian Gifford returned. The strain on the household was evident. Kate Hardy remarked that she had 'never seen such dismal "critters" in her life'.[3]

Though a secret 'compact' had been made in the summer, Florence delivered an ultimatum: 'If the niece is to remain here permanently, as one of the family, then I will not enter into that compact of which I wrote to you last summer', she wrote to Clodd. Florence gave Hardy one week to make a decision: 'if it settled that she stays I return to my own home, & *remain* there'. Henry Hardy was in full agreement, telling her 'it was the only way to avoid a life of misery'. Kate took Florence's side and agreed that the 'ménage à trois' was an impossible situation. It was an unspoken irony that Florence had been living in a similar threesome with Emma during her final years. Florence was irritated by Hardy's weakness, suggesting 'he is not the man to make [Lilian] go'.[4] Florence had her way. Lilian was sent home to her mother.

On 10 February 1914, little more than a year after Emma's death, Florence Dugdale was married to Thomas Hardy.

They had a quiet wedding in Enfield. Hardy insisted on secrecy, only allowing her sister and father to attend, along with his brother Henry: 'Tell your husband', Florence wrote to her sister Ethel, 'why it is that everything has been kept quiet. It was merely the fear of reporters & horrible snap-shotters.'[5] Florence's letters suggest relief rather than delight: 'I did indeed marry him that I might have the right to express my devotion – & to endeavour to add to his comfort & happiness. Had I not married him I realized that I should not be able to remain at Max Gate.'[6] She worried that when he most needed her care, she might not be able to be with him. Hardy had agreed to Florence's demand about Lilian, and had risen to her ultimatum, but there was another secret he had been keeping about a former great love of his life, which might have hastened his decision to marry Florence. It was one of the most tragic stories of Hardy's women; a Miss Havisham tale of his very own.

Sometime in 1913, when he was writing the astonishing collection of poems about Emma, their courtship, love and the breakdown of their marriage, he received a letter from an old lover. She had been waiting all these years, reading and collecting his novels, never marrying and hoping that one day they might reconcile. Allusions to their courtship in the poems and novels kept her hope alive. When she heard the news of the death of Emma Hardy, she wrote to Thomas, asking if they could meet at Max Gate. She had carefully preserved his photograph and the engagement ring he had given her over forty years ago. It was Eliza Nicholls, whom Hardy had treated so badly by transferring his affections to her younger sister.

She came to Max Gate, now an elderly woman in her seventies, and Hardy broke the news that he was to marry his young secretary. It was perhaps this visit that inspired Hardy to think about restoring a story from his 'Eliza' novel, *The Poor Man and His Lady*. That year, Macmillan had published the last two volumes of *The Wessex Edition*, and Hardy wrote to his publishers that he had considered restoring the original 'in my old age'. Eliza Nicholls returned home, broken-hearted. She destroyed her copies of all his novels, and letters, but she kept his ring and photograph. It would appear that Florence was unaware of the visit from his old love.

With the wedding over, Hardy and Florence returned to Max Gate to write letters telling their news. Hardy's line was that there was a 'continuity' about marrying Florence, as she had been a good friend of Emma's. Florence Henniker said she was 'surprised', which seemed to send Hardy into a tailspin: 'I rather am surprised that *you* were surprised at the step we have taken – such a course seeming an obvious one to me, being as I was so lonely & helpless.' He made the point that even during the latter years of Emma's life when she was 'unhinged', she still was fond of Florence.[7]

Most of his friends, though, seemed delighted with the union. Fellow author Mabel Robinson declared, somewhat hyperbolically, that Florence 'was so exactly one of your women that it seemed as though you had made her'.[8] Quite which heroine they thought she was remains a matter of speculation. Betty Owen sent silver spoons and Lake District daffodils. When she made a visit to Max Gate shortly after the marriage, she thought Hardy looked 'most cheerful and unworried. I have never seen him with such a happy expression.' Florence she thought 'a dear little gentle thing but what a melancholy face she has!' Betty thought Max Gate much improved with a new little conservatory to the drawing room, which was dotted with water lilies and daffodils, and was fragrant with the smell of hyacinths, 'everything redolent of comfort and peace'.[9] The Hardys had a short honeymoon in Devon and London, while the home improvements were undertaken.

Soon after the wedding, brother Henry suffered a stroke. He was 'unconscious for hours & is now slowly recovering', Florence wrote to Betty. She told her that she regarded Henry as 'a dear brother'. Now that she was married, Florence was setting aside her career in journalism and children's writings. Before her marriage she had published *The Book of Baby Beasts* (1911), *The Book of Baby Birds* (1912), and *The Book of Baby Pets* (1913). Her publisher wanted her to follow up with a sequel about dogs, and she had a pile of books to review, but she felt that it was unfair to Tom to take up outside work. She added: 'I have a feeling deep within me, that my husband rather dislikes my being a scribbling woman.'[10]

Florence now felt that Henry was a little better, but 'really a broken man'. Mary had been unwell, continuing to suffer with bad asthma. Betty Owen had never met Mary and Kate, and Florence now assured her that she would like the sisters. To Clodd, she had described Mary and Kate as 'ladylike, refined, and well-informed'.[11] They were certainly nothing like the 'stinking old sisters' and 'aged hens' later described by the poet Ezra Pound.[12] Florence confessed to gossipy Betty Owen that for twenty years the sisters had been prohibited from entering Max Gate (not altogether true, as Kate had sometimes acted as housekeeper when the Hardys were in London). Florence told Betty that their rift with Emma was a 'tragedy & the wounds are not yet healed'.[13] To Lady Hoare, Florence described the Hardy sisters as 'nervous and shy'. She herself was shy by nature, she understood the sisters, and they were delighted that she looked after their brother so well. Florence also told Lady Hoare that she married Hardy because he 'wanted a housekeeper who could be a companion & read to him etc – & so I came in'.[14]

Newly discovered letters written from Florence to one of her pupils, Harold Barlow, suggest however that the marriage did not lack love and passion. Shortly after her marriage, she wrote to Harold, who was living in Africa: 'Perhaps you have read, if you have the English papers, that I am now the proud and very

happy wife of the greatest living English writer – Thomas Hardy.'
She told Harold that although her husband was much older, 'it
was a genuine love match' and that her husband was 'one of the
kindest, most humane men in the world'.[15] Florence took enormous pleasure in their trips to Cambridge, where Hardy was
now a Fellow. 'I am full of joy to see how my husband finds
himself in his true environment here. He went off just now in
his cap and gown very *very* pleased with his adornments – to
dine in the college (Magdalene) – & he loves being Dr Hardy.'
Florence of course, as a woman, would not be permitted to dine
as his guest. Florence saw the 'simplicity' in Hardy: 'He is really
just like a boy – or a nice child.' Hardy had told Florence that
he thought 'he had never grown up'.[16] She felt that all Hardy
needed was 'affection & tenderness more than anyone I know
– for life has dealt him some cruel blows'. Despite the love
match, Florence said that Hardy treated her as father to a child,
'a feeling quite apart from passion'. And she felt towards him,
'as a mother towards a child with whom things have somehow
gone wrong – a child who needs comforting – to be treated
gently & with all the love possible'.[17] Not that passion was
absent: Hardy later boasted that he was still capable of sexual
intercourse in his eighties.

Hardy's own description of the marriage was quite different:
'That the union of two rather melancholy temperaments may
result in cheerfulness, as the junction of two negatives forms a
positive, is our modest hope.'[18] Both had depressive tendencies,
and Florence had issues of low self-esteem. The outbreak of war,
in the August after they married, plunged them into another
slough of despond, though their day-to-day lives were barely
affected, unlike some of their friends, such as Lady Hoare, who
had sons who immediately signed up for duty. On hearing of
war, Hardy and Florence were both 'almost paralysed with
horror'. Florence wrote to Betty Owen that 'the horror of this

is making a great change in him – I can see. To me, he seems ten years older. The thought of it all obsesses him.' He had stopped writing poems, Florence suggesting, rather acutely, that 'he cannot [write about the] things that he feels most deeply'.[19]

Florence shared some of the Max Gate news, including her problem with servants. Her parlour maid had persuaded her to take on her deaf and dumb sister as 'between maid' but the sister was useless, 'it's so hard to reprove a deaf & dumb girl'. Betty also sent a box of peaches to Mary and Kate, now living in the house Henry had built, Talbothays, near Dorchester. Mary wrote to Betty thanking her for the fruit and telling her how deeply affected her brother was by the war. Betty's sister Catherine had been unwell, and she died on 15 September. Florence, who loved her own sisters dearly, felt deeply sorry for Betty. She also shared the story of the death of her friend Alfred Hyatt, whom she described as 'the friend who was more to me than anything else in the world – for whom I know I would *gladly* have died'. Though so newly wed, she confessed that she would give up the rest of her life for 'just one brief hour with that one'. More worrying was her admission that she had lost 'the only person who ever loved me – for I am not lovable'.[20] Hardy had told Florence Henniker that his new young wife was a 'very tender companion & is quite satisfied with the quietude of life here'.[21] In contrast, Florence admitted to Betty Owen her 'awful loneliness' and 'the feeling that there is no one much in the world who cares whether I be happy or sad'.[22]

One wonders what on earth was making her feel so depressed just a few months after her marriage to a man she loved and deeply admired. As she said, she was the 'wife of the greatest living English writer'. The answer was the publication later that month of his poetry collection *Satires of Circumstance*. Hardy had included a section devoted to Emma, simply called 'Poems of 1912–13'. The title deliberately underplayed the emotional maelstrom unleashed on him by her death. It left Florence feeling deeply insecure and wretched. It was as if the ghost of the first Mrs Hardy would never leave Max Gate.

CHAPTER 67

Voiceless Ghost

Little wonder that the second Mrs Hardy was so mortified. The 1912–13 poems are universally admired as some of the greatest love poems in the English language. And their publication came in the first year of her marriage. Emma had been bitterly hurt by the lyrics in *Wessex Poems* which recounted Hardy's past lovers, and now Florence was feeling the same emotions about his Emma poems. They were not simply poems about Emma as a beloved first wife. They were a series of elegies, eighteen originally, with three added later, specifically about the suddenness of her death, her husband's terrible guilt, and his return to the scenes of their courtship days. The epigraph to the sequence is 'Veteris vestigia flammae' (traces of an old flame), words spoken by Dido, Queen of Carthage, at the beginning of Book IV of Virgil's *Aeneid*, when the arrival of a new lover stirs in her heart the memory of her first spouse, who has deserted her by dying.

Some of the questions that the poet-narrator asks are a response to – a defence against – the 'diabolical diaries' which left Hardy with so much guilt and remorse, and which he later burnt:

Through the years, through the dead scenes I have
    tracked you;
What have you now found to say of our past –
Scanned across the dark space wherein I have lacked
    you?[1]

'Hereto I come to interview a ghost', he wrote in early versions
of this poem, 'After a Journey', before crossing out this opening
line and substituting 'Hereto I come to view a voiceless ghost.'
Having rendered Emma voiceless by destroying her diaries, he
takes it upon himself to bring to life her 'nut-coloured hair, /
And gray eyes, and rose-flush coming and going'.

The poet laments the lost opportunity to say a proper goodbye,
to ask forgiveness from the once beloved. The stories of Tristan
and Iseult, Aeneas and Dido, and Orpheus and Eurydice are
used to illustrate his grief, but the deeply personal tone, in which
his own faults were so frankly laid bare, make these poems feel
astonishingly fresh and contemporary. No matter how elusive
he was in his personal life, Hardy was always honest in his
poems. The first few poems are full of guilt and remorse, especially of those final lost opportunities, such as the last evening.
He begins with 'The Going':

Why did you give no hint that night
That quickly after the morrow's dawn,
And calmly, as if indifferent quite,
You would close your term here, up and be gone
Where I could not follow.[2]

Racked with remorse ('Why, then, latterly did we not speak?'),
because he cannot follow her forward into the grave, he tracks
their story backwards through time to the blissful dawn of their
relationship 'By those red-veined rocks far West' in Cornwall,

where she was 'the swan-necked one who rode / Along the beetling Beeny Cliff'.

The second and third poems are called 'Your Last Drive' and 'The Walk'. Again, because 'I drove not with you' and 'You did not walk with me', he is compelled to travel to the West and re-enact their first drives and walks together.[3] Before the sequence turns to the journey, there is a poem about 'Rain on a Grave', then one about the location of that grave, which turns on a contrast between Cornwall and Dorset, 'there' and 'here'. 'I found her out there' begins with an evocation of 'the salt-edged air, / Where the ocean breaks', but then explains that Hardy brought her 'here' and buried her in Stinsford churchyard, far from the sea, so that in her final sleep she 'will never be stirred' by the sound of the waves that she loved. Guiltily recollecting that she would almost certainly have preferred to be buried in her beloved Cornwall, he then imagines that

> Yet her shade, maybe,
> Will creep underground
> Till it catch the sound
> Of that western sea
> As it swells and sobs
> Where she once domiciled,
> And joy in its throbs
> With the heart of a child.[4]

There is a wealth of complex feeling in that 'maybe'.

The memories then take over. How she would leave for London 'Without Ceremony', without so much as a goodbye – in just the manner with which she slipped into death. He is eager to remember her at her early best: 'How she would have loved / A party to-day' or 'reigned / At a dinner to-night' – as opposed to how she embarrassed him on social occasions in her last years.[5]

Perhaps the best, and certainly the most well-known, is the hauntingly beautiful poem, 'The Voice' in which the 'Emma' figure begs the poet to remember her at her best:

> Woman much missed, how you call to me, call to me,
> Saying that now are you not as you were
> When you had changed from the one who was all to me,
> But as at first, when our day was fair.[6]

In seeking to give back a voice to the voiceless ghost, he seemingly blames her alone for the change in their relationship from bliss to torment. But in the final stanza of the poem, he deliberately halts the flowing metre and offers an image of himself stumbling in the winter wind:

> Thus I; faltering forward.
> Leaves around me falling,
> Wind oozing thin through the thorn from norward.
> And the woman calling.

As with several of the poems, a date is given at the bottom: *December 1912*. Later in the sequence, there is a double date at the head rather than the foot of the poem: 'Beeny Cliff March 1870–March 1913'. Although it ends with the haunting word 'nevermore' (probably borrowed from Edgar Allan Poe's famous ballad about his dead beloved, 'The Raven'), this is the most joyous of the poems, with its long lines in rhyming triplets and its lovely image of

> O the opal and the sapphire of that wandering western sea
> And the woman riding high above with bright hair flapping
>   free –
> The woman whom I loved so, and who loyally loved me.[7]

The sequence closes with 'Where the Picnic Was', which retraces the climb to the site of an especially happy clifftop picnic. No poet before Hardy had been so bold as to yoke together two such heterogeneous images as a picnic and a grave. The poem ends in the place 'Where no picnics are, / And one – has shut her eyes / For evermore'.[8]

———

Hardy explained to Florence Henniker that he had written the poems 'just after Emma died, when I looked back at her as she had originally been, & when I felt miserable lest I had not treated her considerately in her latter life'. He told her that he would publish them 'as the only amends I can make, if it were so'.[9] No doubt he said something similar to his own Florence, but she was deeply hurt when in November 1914 the sequence appeared in print as a discrete section of the new poetry collection *Satires of Circumstance*. To Alda Hoare, she wrote: 'But I must confess to you – & I would confess this to noone else – the book pains me horribly, & yet I read it with a terrible fascination.' And yet she could not understand Hardy's own need to torture himself by rereading Emma's diaries. Florence told Alda: 'It seems to me that I am an utter failure if my husband can publish such a *sad sad* book.' The new Mrs Hardy blamed herself for Hardy's misery: 'If I had been a different sort of woman, & better fitted to be his wife – would he, I wonder, have published that volume?' Florence was worried that the world would think he was 'utterly weary of life – & cares for nothing in the world'.[10]

Alda Hoare rose to the occasion magnificently, telling Florence that she must not 'make the man responsible for what the poet writes'. To illustrate her point, Alda mentioned 'The Death of Regret', a poem that was not about Emma, but a lament for a friend. Florence knew that the poem was about Hardy's clearly beloved Horace Moule, but she also told Alda that it was written first for the death of a cat, strangled in a rabbit wire. It was Florence who advised him that it was too good a poem for a cat, and so he applied it to a person. Alda suggested that Hardy was writing out his grief and remorse, and it would be cathartic. Florence, greatly cheered, agreed: 'Oddly enough, as if to show me how right & just your letter was, he has been particularly bright & cheerful the last day or so.'[11]

But he was still retiring to his study for long stretches of time. When Florence was unwell with sciatica, he refused to take her to Bath to recuperate, but said that if she decided to go alone, he would be miserable. When she did go for a small 'nasal' operation, in London, Hardy did not visit her in the nursing home, and she was forced to pay for the operation from her own inheritance from William Stoker. While she was recuperating, the Hardy siblings had a meeting about inheritance. They were determined that Hardy's money should go to a '*Hardy born*'.[12] This conversation about inheritance might have been driven by Kate's insecurity about money.

Florence held on to the promise that she might still have a baby. She wrote to Sydney Cockerell and his wife, who had sent a picture of their three children: 'I have been trying to make up my mind as which I would choose were you to offer me one as a gift – & I am quite unable to decide, for I know that any one of those children would make me as proud & happy as any woman on earth.'[13] In the absence of an heir of his own, Hardy and Florence had previously decided on a distant cousin, Frank George. They were extremely fond of him and hoped that in Hardy's last days, he would live at Max Gate, and Hardy would have had 'that strong arm to lean upon'. But then Frank was one of the thousands killed in Gallipoli in the second year of the war. It was a devastating loss for all the family. Florence wrote to Alda Hoare with the news of Frank's death: 'He was, as my husband says, *our one.*'[14]

There was to be no baby for the Hardys. And there was more loss to come that November.

CHAPTER 68

My Poor Mary

Mary's death in the winter of 1915 was slow and painful. She suffered from emphysema and heart problems. Kate recorded her final days in her diary. At Talbothays, she and cousin Polly nursed Mary indefatigably, barely leaving her side, only to call the doctor. Kate was distraught when the doctor told her that Mary's heart was failing, and that he could do no more. Shortly before she took her last breath, she told Kate that she wanted to die so that she 'could see mother'.[1] Mary had been a mother figure to Kate for most of her life, so it was like losing her mother a second time around: 'It does not seem possible that she is gone – what am I to do without her', she wrote. Her only consolation was that Mary looked peaceful and happy in her coffin: 'how she used to look at Denchworth'. Kate rubbed along perfectly well together with Henry, with the occasional family 'fuss', but she was facing the loss of a person who was irreplaceable: 'Life now without Mary: what will it be for me?' she wondered.[2]

Mary's corpse was placed in an upstairs bed, and Tom and Florence were sent for. That evening, there was a family quarrel in which Henry shouted at his brother. Tom was adamant that he would not return to the house following the funeral, but

Kate and Henry insisted. Florence was horrified by the 'country' custom of kissing the dead corpse: 'They kept on worrying and worrying us to go up to see her, even to the last moment – and wanted us to keep on kissing her.' The day of the funeral was gloomy, with the mourners drenched by heavy rain. According to Florence, 'Katie seemed in a state of suppressed temper the whole while.' Mary was buried next to her parents, under a yew tree. Florence was saddened by the death of the gentler sister: 'I shall miss Mary very, very much for she had a more amiable and placid disposition than the others, and also she rather held them in check.'[3] Kate, an altogether more formidable woman, with a sharp tongue, appeared to frighten Florence. She was unaware of Kate's deep vulnerability and the desperate fear of being alone that is expressed in her diaries.

Tom was shattered by Mary's death. He told Florence's sister that they had visited Mary the day before she died but had not expected her to go so soon.[4] A particular blow was that she died on Emma's birthday. He told Sydney Cockerell that Mary was 'rather an unusual type, but of late years had been such an invalid that it was difficult for her to talk to people'. She was, he said, almost his 'only companion' in boyhood. Of the siblings, she was the only one who 'had a keen appreciation for literature' and he admired her facility in painting. Like her mother, Mary had grown very deaf in her older years, but she was a loner, who seemed to be happily absorbed in her remarkable paintings. As long ago as 1906, Hardy had described her as living almost like 'a hermit'. Mary attended a private art school in Dorchester, where she painted watercolours and oil portraits. As Hardy noted, she was especially accomplished at painting women. 'As a painter of portraits she had a real skill in catching the character of her sitter', he wrote. She always pleased 'sitters of her own sex'.[5]

Her death inspired many fine poems. In 'Conjecture', Hardy

talked of Mary as a third wife: 'If there were in my Kalendar / No Emma, Florence, Mary, / What would be my existence now?'[6] At her funeral, the vicar read Psalm 39, which reminded Hardy of her 'nature, particularly when she was young'. Of the verse 'I held my tongue and spoke nothing: I kept silence, yea, even from good words', he wrote. 'That was my poor Mary exactly.'[7] Hardy could not help to be reminded of her loyalty in keeping his secrets about Eliza Nicholls and the other women he had loved. A poem he wrote shortly after her death, 'A Man with a Past', speaks of her innocence and of three blows which she 'dumbly endured'. Another poem about her was called 'You Were the Sort that Men Forget'.[8]

Mary had been the sibling who had never wanted anything of him. It is never easy being the sibling of a famous person. It is easy to assume that there must be resentment about fame, money, and freedom, especially if you are a Victorian woman, whose opportunities are limited. If Mary felt jealousy or bitterness, she didn't show it. She adored her brother, and when he visited Talbothays, she would say nothing but listen intently to him with a look of adoration on her face. She had devoted herself to nursing her mother in her final years, and faithfully put flowers on her parents' graves after they had died. She had heeded her mother's advice to remain single and did not seem to resent Jemima for this. At least when she retired from the arduous work of school teaching she had time for her painting. Her fine portraits of her father, her mother, Florence, and indeed a young girl in a bonnet (a pupil, perhaps?), show the true extent of her talents. The rendering of her famous brother is, however, slightly disappointing: it was as if the intensity of her love and admiration for him was too much to translate onto canvas.

The local newspapers carried the story of the sister of Thomas Hardy, O.M. 'Her life was devoted to educational work' and she was endowed with 'a large share of the family taste and talent for art and music'. On a clipping of the obituary in his scrapbook, Hardy added: 'Under an often undemonstrative exterior she had a warm and affectionate nature.'[9] Later that month, Henry became seriously unwell, and Kate grew fearful for his life, making her feel 'dreadfully downhearted'.[10] To add to her worries, Tom was ill that December. Both recovered, but Kate felt increasingly alone. The death of their beloved cat, Winkie, was another blow: 'I feel utterly wretched at losing her. Mary and Winkie! Both gone from me.'[11] One morning, Kate awoke from a vivid dream of her sister: 'I dream I saw Mary quite plainly – today I feel very lonely without her and Tom seems to have utterly abandoned us.' She took solace in visiting her sister's grave and laying flowers: 'she seemed near me'.[12]

Florence had been troubled by Kate's behaviour after Mary died. She told Betty Owen that Kate was obsessing about Mary's inheritance. She had died intestate: 'Katie is in terror lest anybody but herself should have any of it.'[13] Florence told Betty that neither she nor Tom wanted a penny of Mary's money. Besides, much of it had been given to her by Tom. He was always generous to his sisters, buying their home in Dorchester when they were teaching and most needed it. He had given them clothes – an expensive and fashionable red silk dress for Kate – and not long before Mary's death had offered them a second-hand piano (though they stopped the delivery as they wanted a new one).

Kate complained that she did not feel very welcome at Max Gate and that her brother seemed not to want to see her. Florence reported that he was withdrawing into his shell: 'Tom – to my great dismay – says he feels that he never wants to go anywhere or see anyone else again. He wants to live on here, quite quietly, shut up in his study.'[14] She was beginning to get a taste of the treatment Hardy had doled out to Emma. Admittedly, he would ask Florence to read aloud to him in the evenings, but she felt increasingly lonely and resentful that her husband was not invventing people to Max Gate. If she were a Gifford, she complained, not unreasonably, he would happily pay for holidays and new furniture. She decided that the only way she would secure a holiday from the increasingly oppressive Max Gate, would be to 'hunt up Giffords – and I really cannot stand more of that'.[15]

Grasping the bull by the horns, she suggested a holiday in North Cornwall, 'for I believe he would rather go there than anywhere else'. So in September 1916, as thousands of young Englishmen were being mown down on the Somme, Hardy took Florence on a pilgrimage to St Juliot. She was still quietly seething about Emma's *awful* diary' that Hardy had burned. They had tea with the Rector at St Juliot, inspected the tablet erected to Emma in the church, and walked back to Boscastle along the Valency Valley. Despite the ghost of Emma, they were enjoying themselves: 'This morning we explored King Arthur's Castle here, & lay for an hour or so, on the grass, in the sunshine, with sheep nibbling around us, & no other living thing – while cliffs & greeny blue sea & white surf seemed hundreds of feet below.'[16] Florence was even beginning to *sound* like the first Mrs Hardy in her description of Tintagel. The weather was 'perfect', and their hotel room had a sea view and a view of the ruined castle.

Back in oppressive Max Gate, her spirits were soon depressed. Like the second Mrs de Winter in *Rebecca* she seemed to get into a 'muddle' – she sent for mourning clothes in London and felt that she had spent too much money. She worried about how long she should stay in mourning and panicked that she had not written letters using proper black-edged paper. She was anxious that she had been 'too hard upon Katie'.[17] Florence was feeling overwhelmed.

Since Mary's death, Hardy had been thinking about posterity. He was becoming ever more dependent on Sydney Cockerell, the director of the Fitzwilliam Museum in Cambridge, whom Hardy had appointed as his literary executor along with Florence. Florence's relationship with Cockerell had become strained, and she confessed to Betty Owen that she was afraid of him: 'Last time he was here I felt once or twice that I loathed him. I caught a hateful expression of his face . . . that dwells in my memory and has destroyed any liking I had for him.'[18] She also confessed that he was 'arrogant and masterful. He tries to take the whole household in hand, and rules my husband entirely.'[19] Florence was feeling displaced in her role as mistress of Max Gate and anxious about Cockerell's control of Hardy: 'my husband really does depend on him in a great many ways . . . an open breach with him would be rather disastrous'. The fact was that Cockerell was making Hardy a great deal of money, some of it through private printing of his poems. Florence's icy feelings thawed a little when Cockerell sent a 'munificent cheque'. 'Dear Mr Cockerell,' she wrote, 'I feel quite overwhelmed . . . we both thank you most heartily for all the trouble you have taken.'[20]

The Hardys had become a little alarmed at the prospect that they might have to billet soldiers at Max Gate to help with the war effort. Florence was concerned about what 'awful things the privates might bring with them'. One senses that she wasn't just worried about lice, but also sexual infections: 'Even officers do, I am told, who come from a camp.'[21] Florence's sister Margaret was getting married to her 'airman' on his next leave, and the Hardys had offered Max Gate for their honeymoon.

At last Hardy began to get back out in the world. In November, he paid a visit to a German prisoner-of-war camp: 'T. H's kind heart melted at the sight of the wounded', Florence reported.[22] He sent some German translations of his novels to the prisoner library, though she suspected the men had never heard of Thomas

Hardy. Hardy's relations with his siblings had improved and visits to Talbothays had resumed. There was even excitement at the prospect of another Hardy play being performed by the Dorchester Dramatic Society. No Hardy plays had been performed in 1914 and 1915 due to the war, but a production of *The Dynasts* for wartime charities was put on in 1916. Hardy had written an extra part for a young actress who had performed the part of Marty South back in 1913, when she was just sixteen years old. Her name was Gertrude Bugler, and she presented a serious threat to Florence. Having finally seen off the ghost of Emma, Florence was dismayed to find herself up against a beautiful, talented rival with whom Hardy had become infatuated.

CHAPTER 69

Gertrude Bugler

Over the years after the publication of *Tess of the D'Urbervilles*, many people searched for a living 'Tess'. Their search revolved around finding a 'peasant' girl who embodied her grace and beauty. Here and there a friend or acquaintance would claim that they had found a 'Tess' (one of the candidates was an attendant at a nursing home), but Hardy was always disappointed. Florence was cynical about those who tried: 'I don't believe there are many Tesses. Indeed I doubt if there ever was one.'[1] And then Hardy found one.

Her name was Gertrude Bugler. Her father was a Dorchester baker and confectioner, and his shop was used for rehearsals for the Dorchester dramatic society that would become the Hardy Players. Just after leaving school, Gertrude was cast in the role of Marty South in *The Woodlanders*. She was exceptionally beautiful and a talented amateur actor. Hardy was mesmerised. For the December 1916 production of *Wessex Scenes from The Dynasts* in aid of the Red Cross, Hardy extended the role of a 'waiting-woman' for Gertrude, who was now nineteen years old. He attended most of the rehearsals and was actively involved in the production, although he was in bed with a cold for the performance.[2] From the outset, Florence was jealous, and saw the teenager as a rival. Hardy's friend J. M. Barrie, the best-known playwright of the age, came to see the production, and Gertrude had hoped that he might help with her burgeoning career as an actress. Florence wrote a stern letter to Gertrude, suggesting that Barrie was not wholly impressed by her performance: 'I can only conclude that he feels that he can do nothing towards helping you on to a career on stage.' Florence confessed that she had told Barrie that Gertrude was better in *The Woodlanders*, and that 'as an amateur I am sure you will always give pleasure'. She told the young girl in no uncertain terms that she had no chance of becoming a professional actress. In an interesting Freudian slip, she ended the letter: 'I do sincerely hope that anything I may have said or done has had the effect of unsettling you.'[3] She had left out the *not*.

———

At the close of 1916, Florence wrote to Betty: 'Sometimes I feel *eighty*' while her husband seemed cheerful 'in spite of his gloomy poems . . . strangers must imagine that his only wish is to die & be in the grave with the only woman who ever gave him happiness.' The walls of the house and overcast garden seemed to have closed around her: 'I may not alter the shape of a garden bed, or cut down or move the smallest bush, any more than I may alter the position of an article of furniture.'[4] 'I have to bath in a puddle – a quart or three pints of hot water in a smallish hip bath.'[5] The portraits of Emma's grandmother and the infamous archdeacon at Max Gate seemed to glare down at her. She wrote to Alda Hoare that 'One has to go through a sort of mental hoodwinking and blind oneself to the past.'

There was little chance of escape, as Hardy disliked being left alone. But she insisted on attending her sister's marriage in Enfield in the spring of the new year. She also got her way inviting the married couple to honeymoon at Max Gate. Even Kate Hardy seemed rather amazed by that victory, writing in her diary: 'Bravo F!!!!'[6] Florence's resentment at the way that her husband indulged Lilian Gifford was another thorn in her side. Despite the operation on her nose, she continued to suffer with chronic pharyngitis and was seeing a London specialist. Hardy refused to pay her medical bills: 'Of course were I Lilian Gifford a cheque would be written joyfully', she complained to Betty Owen.[7] But that year, Florence and Hardy embarked on a new secret project together that would unite them, allow them to spend more time together. Hardy and Florence had been 'horrified' to hear that his old friend Clodd was writing his memoirs. The news threw them into a panic that Clodd might refer to the time they had spent together at Aldeburgh when Emma was still alive. Florence told Betty Owen that 'a man whom he had trusted implicitly' had been keeping a record of conversations that would 'probably be published'. Florence dispatched a stern warning letter, in which the fifty-year friendship between Hardy and Clodd was broken. Florence also worried about rumours of her friend Betty's inclination to gossip, begged her to burn all her letters: 'Some are, I fear, most horribly indiscreet.'[8]

Sydney Cockerell had been urging Hardy for some time to 'write something down about yourself'.[9] Cockerell's relationship with Florence had improved, and they were both united in their belief that Hardy should write his own life. Deeply private, and worried about how he might be judged by posterity, Hardy had finally accepted that he must put his own record straight. So began the project code-named 'The Materials': the ambitious undertaking of the life of Thomas Hardy as though written by Florence Hardy. In July 1917, she told Cockerell that she had been taking notes while her husband was revising his diaries. Hardy was finishing the proofs for another volume of poetry, *Moments of Vision*, but he promised that as soon as they were done, they would continue with the secret project. The dreadful wartime summer of 1917 had also made her think about her posterity. She had such a fear of air raids that she made her own will for fear that if she were killed, anything she owned would go to Kate and Henry rather than her 'own people'.[10]

Relations improved with the new secret project, and a short holiday to Torquay, though it turned out to include another Emma pilgrimage to her childhood town of Plymouth: Florence 'had a tiring & rather depressing time there'. Not unreasonably, she disliked visiting the graves of Emma's ancestors: 'How much better to have no neglected little plot of ground to testify to the indifference of grand-children to their grand-parents' memory.'[11] Nevertheless, they had a pleasant holiday, and her spirits seem much restored. But another shock was in store for Florence.

Moments of Vision was published at the end of November 1917. Florence was plunged back into the despair of a year earlier: 'the idea of the general reader will be that T.H.'s second marriage is a most disastrous one and that his sole wish is to find refuge in the grave with her with whom alone he found happiness.'[12] This time round, Hardy had written around thirty more poems connected with Emma, and many were inspired by her account of her childhood. Moreover, though Hardy had long been greatly irritated by Emma's insistence that she was responsible for some of his literary work, he now deliberately muddied the waters by including some of her own words, taken from *Some Recollections*. There were also allusions to the 'Emma' novel, *A Pair of Blue Eyes*, and her own novella, *The Maid on the Shore*. It was as though Hardy was now revealing that their thoughts and words in the early years were inextricably intertwined. If only he had given her that credit when she was alive, she would not have felt so miserable and undervalued. And now he was hurting his second wife. One can almost imagine Florence scouring the text looking for a poem that celebrated their love. Hardy exercised some tact in inscribing an affectionate message in Florence's copy: 'this first copy of the first edition, to the first of women Florence Hardy'.[13] But was that enough?

Florence was plunged into another of her depressions and suffered some kind of breakdown. She told Betty Owen that she had 'home worries, of a kind sufficient to break down any woman's nerve I think'.[14] She went to see Barrie's deeply moving new play *Dear Brutus* and 'wept between the acts from sheer misery (though it was a delightful play) & after the matinee when I went to tea with an old friend of my husband, I made a fool of myself, & burst into tears & sobbing when a few sympathetic questions were asked'.[15] It did not help that there was no sign of a baby for Florence.

When her sister Margaret fell pregnant, Florence concocted a '*mad* scheme' for her to come to Max Gate and have the baby at a nursing home nearby. But on reflection, she felt Hardy would be displeased: 'He is genuinely afraid of babies – & why, after all, should he be bothered with all this fuss for another man's wife and child.'[16] She added, poignantly, 'How eagerly a baby would have been welcomed in *this* house – Max Gate – years ago.'[17] When her sister gave birth to a baby boy, she called him Thomas. Florence was delighted and hoped he would resemble her husband 'in as many ways as possible – besides in name'.[18] Hardy and Florence disagreed about female emancipation in terms of childbearing. Florence felt strongly that it was a woman's duty to bring children into the world. Her husband thought otherwise, telling Florence Henniker that if he were a woman he would 'think twice before entering into matrimony in these days of emancipation, when everything is open to the sex'.[19]

Despite everything, she told Betty that she was happily married to Tom. There were moments when she felt depressed (often about the war), but then her husband would be 'wonderful

– with that inner radiance of his – a true sun-shine giver'.[20] But just a few months later she had moved her study, like her predecessor, into the Max Gate attic.

───

In 1920, by the age of eighty, Hardy had acquired a dignity and attractiveness hard to define, though several tried to do so. A friend of Sydney Cockerell, with more than a hint of condescension, believed that age has softened his peasant manners and 'decided accent', transforming him into a 'refined, fragile, gentle little old gentleman, with . . . a gentle and smooth voice and polished manners'.[21] His friend and prolific fellow-writer J. M. Barrie described his strange charisma best, saying that there was 'something about him more attractive than I find in almost any other man – a simplicity that really merits the adjective *divine* – I could conceive some of the disciples having been thus.'[22] That February Hardy went to Oxford to receive another honorary Doctorate of Letters, and to attend an Oxford University Dramatic Society production of *The Dynasts*. The Oxford don Maurice Bowra, an admirer of Hardy's poetry who had read *Moments of Vision* in the trenches, said that he carried himself well for a man of eighty and 'looked like a very good, rather shrunken English apple'.[23]

Hardy still had the mental energy for his writing. With an enormous body of work behind him, and no inclination to return to fiction after the controversy surrounding *Jude*, he concentrated on the secret memoir with Florence. Though Emma had been such a huge part of his life, she had burned most of their correspondence, so Florence was saved the pain of reading their love letters, which Hardy described as being similar to that of the Brownings. Florence was less happy that her husband had renewed his interest in Gertrude Bugler. Even though he was in his eightieth year, he developed an infatuation for Gertrude, who that same year had been cast in the role of Eustacia Vye in *The Return of the Native*. Hardy made it clear that the mumming scene, where Eustacia is cross-dressed, was a key moment. He wrote to Thomas Tilley, the Dorchester alderman who had adapted and produced the play: 'Reminder: To tell Clym & Eustacia to *speak up* very *clearly* when they first exchange words ("Are you a woman?" &c) as it is the key to the whole action.'[24] Gertrude was even lovelier now than she had been at sixteen. It would be his last infatuation.

Though the war was now over, there had been terrible casualties amongst his family and friends. There was more trauma when Lilian Gifford suffered a nervous breakdown and was incarcerated in the London County Council asylum in Essex. Florence told a friend: 'She has gone off her head, poor thing, & put in an asylum, & I am going to see her as my husband is really not fit for the journey this weather.'[25] During her visit to the asylum, Florence told Cockerell that she did not 'perceive any symptoms of insanity, but the doctor and the medical superintendent assured me that she *was* insane'.[26] Florence had consulted with Lilian's brother Gordon and his wife, who confirmed the diagnosis. Gordon told Florence that he and his wife had had a 'dreadful time' with Lilian: 'The brother's wife being a dressmaker, was not fit to associate with Lilian . . . that absurd obsession about the grandeur of the Gifford family.' Hardy had been generous with his annuity for Lilian, and he suggested that Lilian should live at Max Gate upon her release; a notion that was roundly rejected by Florence and the Hardy siblings. Florence explained that her husband was not so much upset about Lilian as annoyed at her selling the securities he had bought and invested in less secure investments without telling him. Florence reported the Medical Superintendent had said Lilian 'can never have been quite sane'.

Florence had achieved another small victory by removing the Gifford portraits: 'Grandmother Gifford & the great ARCH-DEACON have not returned, & I can well dispense with them.' She had also persuaded Hardy to install a new kitchen range. In May, a new upstairs bathroom was finally installed, and even a telephone, which made Florence feel much less isolated. Evenings were spent in the usual way, with Florence reading aloud. In the summer they worked their way through Jane Austen. First *Persuasion* and *Northanger Abbey*, then *Emma*: 'T.H. is much amused at finding he has *many* characteristics in common with Mr Woodhouse.'[27]

Florence had made a new friend in Louise Yearsley, the wife of the surgeon who had performed her nose operation. She told Louise that Hardy also had a new friend in the poet Siegfried Sassoon, 'one of the most brilliant, & handsome likeable young men I know'.[28] But, on the whole, Hardy became more and more reclusive, and not unreasonably irritated by the constant flock of visitors to Max Gate, many of whom were fans expecting admittance and an autograph from the famous man. Florence explained that he was even reluctant to see old friends, a hint to Betty Owen who believed that she was one of Hardy's oldest friends: 'The fact is – in plain English – that there are times when he doesn't care about seeing anyone, and these times tend to become more frequent.'[29] Hardy now refused to autograph any of his books, even the devoted Betty's.

As Christmas approached, the Hardy Players arranged for a performance of the mummers' scene in *The Return of the Native* at Max Gate. Christmas was always a special time for Hardy, and Henry and Kate had been invited for Christmas Day. Though he disliked company, Hardy made an exception for the Hardy Players. Despite having long cast off the role of novelist for poet, the adaptations of his novels made him fall back in love with his spirited heroines. And there was no one who performed his heroines better than Gertrude Bugler, who had the perfect Dorset accent and the required country-girl innocence. Now at twenty-four, she had grown into her beauty and word was spreading about her talent. She was the star of the Hardy Players, and she had a sweet and generous temperament to match her acting skills. The cross-dressing – in an age when the shape of a woman's legs was rarely seen – enhanced her charms. Florence was apprehensive. But she was relieved to hear that Gertrude was engaged to her cousin, Ernest Bugler, so would be off limits for her husband. Florence also hoped that marriage would distract Gertrude from her theatrical ambitions.

On Christmas Day, Florence dressed carefully in a new 'very skimpy and up-to-date' tea frock. She was determined to look her best, and her husband responded well. He teased her by calling her by the name of a character from a book they were reading together: 'Madge Asking-for-it'.[30] Florence joked that she was 'Anyone more unlike, I flatter myself . . . or perhaps regret.' It was a truly magical time, with the mummers performing in the drawing room, while musicians played the fiddle and sang Christmas carols outside: 'the *real* old Bockhampton carols', Florence relayed. Refreshments were served in the dining room, for once filled with joy. The only fly in the ointment was Gertrude 'looking prettier than ever in her mumming dress'.[31]

By now, Florence was confiding in Sydney Cockerell, who appeared to be a sympathetic ally. She told him, 'T.H. has lost his heart to her entirely, but as she is soon getting married I don't let that cast me down *too* much.'[32] She also gossiped that Gertrude's star status was upsetting the rest of the Hardy Players. Florence was too honest not to admit that her husband's spirits had been uplifted by the play: 'At the party (of the Mummers etc) last night he was so gay – & one of them said to me that he had never seen him so young & happy & excited.' With her sharp wit, she added that Hardy was inspired to write a poem 'always a sign of well-being with him. Needless to say it is a dismal poem.'

The Hardy Players were planning a single performance of *The Return of the Native* in London, much to the cast's delight, as well as performances in Dorset. Florence was forced to admit that Gertrude was 'a beautiful creature, only 24 & really nice & refined'. But she expressed a sense of puzzlement that Gertrude was telling people that Mrs Hardy had advised her not to try to become a professional actress. 'I am puzzled as to *when* I did give that advice – but I think T.H. did – he is quite crazy about her.'[33] Worse was to follow when Hardy asked Gertrude whether she might one day play Tess. Florence was astute enough to know that playing Tess spelled danger. Her depression returned. 'I know, as well as anyone, I think what depression is. Night after night I lie awake and face gloom unutterable.' When she left Max Gate, her spirits lifted: 'When I get away from here it vanishes almost entirely – in fact *quite* entirely, and also almost intolerable pains that I suffer from here – which proves that it is a matter of nerves and nothing else.'[34] But with Gertrude now settled in Dorset, Florence was afraid to stay away from Max Gate for too long.

Betty Owen, who was an ardent admirer of Gertrude Bugler, made plans to attend *The Return of the Native* at the Dorchester Corn Exchange. After the play, there was tea, and Betty managed to nab a seat next to Gertrude. But then the actor who played the part of Clym came over and asked Gertrude if she were free to speak to Mr Hardy, whisking her away from Betty's table. Hardy had eyes for nobody else than 'Eustacia'.[35]

Gertrude had asked Florence if she would attend the London performance of *Return of the Native* and provide some written impressions. Florence declined, writing a thinly veiled hostile letter in which she accused the press of making Gertrude 'a one star play' which would 'be the downfall of the Hardy plays'. The *Daily Mail* was 'booming' (puffing) the beautiful young actress, which Florence felt would be detrimental for her career and 'apt to bring ridicule upon what would otherwise have justly been acknowledged to be a very good amateur performance'.[36] She also reiterated the point that J. M. Barrie was not engaging in 'excessive laudation' of Gertrude. Florence continued to believe that Gertrude would never make it as a professional actor and lost no attempt to tell her and other people of her opinion. Her husband thought otherwise.

Florence's woes were increased that April by an operation to remove six of her teeth. Soon after, the Hardys attended a production of *Far from the Madding Crowd* with Gertrude in the part of Bathsheba. There was great excitement for the Hardy Players when 'Bathsheba' episodes were performed in the castle ruins at Sturminster Newton. Hardy held a tea for the cast in the house where he and Emma had once stayed. He insisted that Gertrude should stay over and sleep in the room in which he had written *The Return of the Native*. Things came to a head when Gertrude committed a social faux pas and called at Max Gate, requesting to see Mr Hardy rather than the mistress of the house. Gertrude had appeared at the door, and Florence had opened it, astonished by her words: 'Mr Watkins told me I might call to see *Mr Hardy*. I have much – much to tell him.' Florence was taken off guard and made it perfectly clear that Gertrude was not welcome.

Later, she penned a frosty letter: 'As you must know this is a most extraordinary thing to do. In the first place all invitations to Max Gate, naturally come from me, as is the custom, & again it is not usual in our station of life for any lady to call upon a gentleman.' It did little good that Gertrude insisted that she had been sent by William Watkins, the secretary of the Hardy Players. Florence was not appeased: 'It is simply "not done".'[37] Gertrude wrote back to explain the muddle, but Florence felt that 'misunderstanding upon misunderstanding' had resulted in 'so hopeless a tangle that it seems hopeless to remove them by a letter'. Florence had got the impression that Gertrude was spreading rumours, and that the press had got hold of the story that J. M. Barrie was a regular visitor to Max Gate. Gertrude had expressed her unhappiness that Florence had treated her like a stranger and an unwelcome visitor. Florence apologised, but marked her territory with the words 'We [Hardy and Florence] are, in fact, almost one person.'[38]

Gertrude was cast as Cytherea in the adaptation of Hardy's first published novel, now titled 'A Desperate Remedy', but she became pregnant and withdrew from the role. Florence felt sure that the play would be the last production of the Hardy Players. Gertrude's pregnancy also prevented her from taking the lead in a verse play that he had written for her, *The Queen of Cornwall*. There had been a partial reconciliation between the two women. A woman named Ethel Fare took over the role of Cytherea, but the play was a failure: 'farcical in serious parts, & the audience was convulsed with laughter when they should have been aghast', Florence recorded. Her tone had hardened: 'Poor Gertrude Bugler seems to have suffered agonies at being cut out by a rival leading lady, Ethel Fare, & the tragic climax is that she had a still-born son on the day of the performance.'[39] Florence's jibe at Gertrude's miscarriage was in extremely poor taste. When Hardy learned of the stillbirth, he secretly sent a silver vase full of carnations.

Doubtless the sight of the lovely young girl, in the throes of pregnancy, arriving at her door had been too much for Florence to endure. Other visitors to Max Gate at this time saw only the happiness between the Hardys. Florence was perceived as a loving and gentle presence, with her soulful brown eyes and quiet grace. She felt a strong sense of duty to protect Hardy from the throngs of 'pilgrims' who descended on Max Gate uninvited. One of the Max Gate parlour maids, Ellen Titterington, who was in service with the Hardys from 1920–28, left a charming picture of domestic happiness, with nutritious, homely meals, walks with Wessex the dog, and Florence reading aloud every night until the clock struck ten.[40] The novelist John Galsworthy described her 'vibrating attractive voice'.[41] Ellen recalled that although Florence Hardy was difficult to work for, she was 'devoted to her husband's comfort . . . She was like a nursemaid caring for her charge.' Ellen felt that her mistress was 'proud of being married to a man as famous as Mr Hardy'. Certainly, Florence put Hardy's needs before her own, and felt unhappy leaving him even for a few hours or to visit her family in Enfield.

Even though it had been ten years since Emma had died, she was still haunted by her presence. On the anniversary of Mary's death (and Emma's birthday), Florence had felt a little depressed. She was irritated by the fact that Hardy made so much of Emma's birthday in death, given that it was 'always forgotten during her lifetime. She told me once I was the only living person who ever did remember it.' Now Florence felt 'What a revenge did you but know it.'[42] On Emma's anniversary and birthday they would take flowers to the grave, gathered from Florence's beloved rose bushes, and place them on what Hardy insisted on calling 'our' grave. Florence was forever reminded that she, Emma and Hardy would lie together for eternity. A decade on, and Florence still felt like Dr Crippen's typist. She confided in Siegfried Sassoon, urging him to 'call me anything but Mrs Hardy. That name seems to belong to someone else, whom I knew for several years, & I am oppressed by the thought that I am living in *her* house, using *her* things – & worst of all, have even stolen her name.' Florence felt that from the moment she learned of Emma's death 'I seemed suddenly to leap from youth into dreary middle-age'.[43]

And if Florence felt that she had nipped the Gertrude problem in the bud, she was sorely mistaken. When Hardy first saw Gertrude, he had been struck by her beauty and innocence. But it was the discovery of her origins that had been overpowering. Her mother, Augusta, had been the very same milkmaid he had spotted in Dorset, and who had become an inspiration for Tess. Hardy began plans to revive the dramatisation of *Tess of the D'Urbervilles* that he had written in the 1890s. Gertrude Bugler became for him the living embodiment of the heroine he most loved.

CHAPTER 70

My Tess

Our success with 'Tess' was in the main owing to the
alluring charm of the young woman who played the part.

(Thomas Hardy to John Masefield, 4 December 1924)

Hardy had found his Tess. It was one of the most moving scenes
he had ever witnessed: the sight of the lovely young girl on the
night of her honeymoon, fatally confessing her past to her
beloved husband. At that moment, Gertrude believed that she
was Tess. First, her relief that her husband had confessed to a
murky past of his own. The twenty-four hours he had spent
with a prostitute in London. That confession released her own
misplaced guilt and shame, that her employer had seduced her
and left her with a baby. Then, Angel's disbelief, his anger, his
sadness, his rejection of his new wife who had fallen from her
pedestal. The scene ended with the sound of her 'heart-rending
sobs', followed by complete silence: 'Here was one of the world's
most eminent men of letters in the late evening of his life,
watching the heroine, whom he had himself created, come to
life in the very house of the scene which he had visualised.'[1] The
atmosphere was electric.

Hardy had arranged for some members of the Hardy Players to visit Woolbridge Manor, the ancestral home of the Turberville ancestors, where he set the dramatic confrontation between Angel Clare and Tess. Having secured the permission of the owners, they had performed the pivotal scene in a large, sparsely furnished room, with the low winter sun streaming through the mullioned windows. It was the perfect setting for the rehearsal, and all the actors felt the 'significant atmosphere of the setting, especially Gertrude Bugler'. She was 'the very incarnation of Tess Durbeyfield of the novel, and as he sat and watched he appeared to be greatly moved'.[2]

Four years before, Hardy had tried to persuade the manager of the Hardy Players to perform *Tess*, but he felt that Dorchester wasn't quite ready for a play that had a reputation for immorality. Their attitude changed, partly because of the movies.

Hardy was fascinated by the new medium of moving pictures. In 1913, one of the first feature films ever made was an American production of *Tess* with Minnie Maddern Fiske in the role of Tess. Fiske had successfully played Tess in a stage version on Broadway in 1897. Mrs Fiske was regarded as one of the most prominent American actresses. She had helped to bring Ibsen to the American stage. Her performance of Nora in *A Doll's House* launched Ibsen into fame across the Atlantic. She was also a playwright and a director.

In 1921 a silent movie of *The Mayor of Casterbridge* had been made, with Hardy's cooperation. He had visited the set when they were filming on location. Then in 1924, came the second *Tess* movie, with the aptly named Blanche Sweet in the title role. The film was successful, but Louis B. Mayer changed the climax to a happy 'Hollywood' ending, much to Hardy's chagrin. The film is now lost. It was shown in the Corn Exchange in Dorchester, with the (over-)acting causing much amusement among the Hardy Players. It was after this showing that some of the players had spoken to Hardy about the possibility of staging *Tess*. They were ready to take on his most famous novel. Little did they know that Hardy had been working on a script since the 1890s. Hardy had been waiting a long time for the opportunity.

He gave them his old script and said they could adapt it as they pleased. But there was one condition. He would only allow the production to go ahead if Gertrude took the lead role. This was awkward, since she was now married, the mother of a six-month-old baby, and breastfeeding. When she was approached by the manager to take the part of Tess, she was interested but worried about travelling to Dorchester, and childcare arrangements. A deal was struck in which her mother would help to look after the baby, and Gertrude would take the long bus ride to rehearsals. Her younger sister, Norrie, was cast in the part of Tess's sister, Liza-Lu, and she agreed to stand in as Tess when her sister was unable to get to rehearsals. Having been told that Hardy would not countenance any other actress in the role, Gertrude made the commitment. She did it for herself, for the mother who first inspired Tess, and for her fellow actors. And she did it for Hardy, whom she respected, admired and wanted to please.

He insisted on being present at rehearsals. He answered questions with sense and good humour. Often, he asked Gertrude to sit next to him and talk. He called her Tess. There was never any question that Hardy behaved inappropriately or made her feel uncomfortable. They talked only about the role, and she was pleased to see the pleasure it was bringing to the very elderly man. As for the excursion to Woolbridge Manor, he knew that it would help the actors to get into their roles, and, above all, would enhance Gertrude's performance.

To the end of her days, Gertrude repudiated the notion that Hardy was a pessimist. He was, she said, a realist, and there was nothing in Tess's experience at the hands of weak men that convinced her otherwise. The part of Alec was taken by a young man who would never forget the experience, and Hardy's kind interest in his part. He once admonished him for being too nice to Tess, but he was never overbearing or controlling. He just wanted the actors to know their lines and trust their own instincts. The production was also a reminder of Martha Brown and the guilt he felt watching the woman being hanged. He began to research the murder and the execution in the Dorchester archives to find out more about the case. The French translator of *Tess* had written to him asking for advice about translating Dorset slang. He also explained that the story had 'little foundation' in reality: 'I once saw a milkmaid something like her – who had a voice also like hers – but her history was quite different – happily! . . . A woman was hanged here more than 60 years ago for murdering her husband, but the circumstances were not similar.'[3]

Hardy was so struck by Gertrude's physical resemblance to the Tess of his imagination that when his publisher thought of bringing out a new illustrated edition of the novel, he suggested that they should use Gertrude as a model: 'But what I think would be a great help to the artist if she goes on with the work would be to see the young woman who has personified Tess in the play, who is the very incarnation of her. A meeting with her privately, which I could arrange, might perhaps suffice, but a better thing would be for her to see her in dairy costume on the stage.'[4] Gertrude herself was not fully aware of the extent of Hardy's infatuation, but naturally all of this made Florence insecure.

The cast came to Max Gate to rehearse, and for Hardy to give notes. Norman Atkins, the young man who played Alec, noticed Hardy's absorption in Tess. But he was astonished when Florence invited him back to tea, only to confess her anxiety about her husband and Gertrude. She was 'put out' by Hardy's interest, and worried that the rest of the Hardy Players were gossiping. Atkins said this was 'a bolt from the blue' and that it seemed to him 'a perfectly natural reaction of an old man toward a young and attractive woman who so ably portrayed his heroines'.[5]

The play opened on 26 November. Gertrude Bugler was a sensation. In the last scene Tess asks: 'Do you think we shall meet again', and Clare makes no response. Her last words as she was arrested were 'It is as it should be. I am glad – yes glad. This happiness with you could not have lasted.' 'There were a good many other wet handkerchiefs', Hardy wrote to Gertrude, sending her favourable press clippings. The review in *The Times* described Mrs Bugler's performance as 'full of the right sort of simplicity and breadth, and of a most moving sincerity and beauty – more beauty, one imagines, than could have been achieved by one or two of the many eminent professional actresses who have longed to play this character'.[6]

There were four performances of *Tess* in Dorchester, and a performance at Weymouth, when Hardy noticed that Gertrude had forgotten to remove her wedding ring. He offered to hold it for her, and when the performance was over, he replaced it on her finger as if he himself was marrying her. There was talk of a further performance at nearby Budmouth, but Gertrude was astonished when Hardy told them that a London producer, Frederick Harrison, was interested in bringing her to the West End.

Hardy had been in touch with the celebrated Sybil Thorndike, for whom George Bernard Shaw had recently written the role of St Joan, to explore the possibility of a London transfer, and he invited her to come to the performance by the Hardy Players.

He told her that the performance by the Dorchester amateurs 'is for our local entertainment only & has nothing to do with the question whether it is a good play or a bad one' – that could be judged from the script, which he offered to send her.[7]

But the rapturous reception of Gertrude's performance now raised the genuine possibility of her becoming a professional, unusual as that would have been for a married woman. She said that she would take the opportunity, providing she could take her sister Norrie for company. Hardy was ambivalent: 'But forgive my saying that I don't quite like the idea of your going to London (if this comes to anything, which it may not). We are so proud of you down here that we wish to keep you for ourselves, so that you may be known as the Wessex actress who does not care to go away, & who makes Londoners come to her.' But he also told her that she must make her own decision.[8] Hardy felt responsible for Gertrude. He made her a present of inscribed copies of *The Return of the Native* and *Tess of the D'Urbervilles*, writing respectively 'To Gertrude Bugler the impersonator of "Tess"/"Eustacia" With affectionate regard, Thomas Hardy.'

Florence intervened. She wrote to Gertrude, contradicting the claim that Frederick Harrison had agreed to produce, insisting that *Tess* was promised to Sybil Thorndike: 'I tried to convey this to you on Saturday evening, but had no chance. When I saw my husband so deep in conversation with you and for so long, during supper, I did not know he was making wild promises.' She reminded Florence that Hardy was in his eighty-fifth year, and 'is easily carried away when talking to any young woman and would promise anything – but verbal promises go for nothing'.[9] She hinted that Miss Thorndike might 'bring a lawsuit' if her plans to produce *Tess* were thwarted. Desperately worried about losing her status as Mrs Hardy, Florence was trying everything in her power to dissuade Gertrude from playing the part. When it became obvious that Harrison was most sincere in his offer, Florence wrote an apology note of sorts, telling Gertrude that 'the foolish trouble has blown over – for good I hope'. She tried to explain her behaviour by saying 'All my happiness lies in one direction. Unlike you I have no child to promise future happiness, no career before me – everything seems to lie behind.'[10]

Gertrude was confused by Florence's conduct because Hardy had been entirely professional in his dealings with her. It was Tess he saw, not Gertrude. All his communications with Gertrude were courteous, respectful and kind. He asked about her new baby and was sensitive to the fact that she was a young mother. He was also respectful towards her husband, who had been a captain in the war and had won the Military Cross. At no time did Gertrude feel uncomfortable with his attention. But back at Max Gate, tempers were flaring. Sydney Cockerell recorded in his diary that there was a 'cloud over the house as T.H. is absorbed in Mrs Gertrude Bugler . . . F.H. greatly disturbed about it.'[11] It was he wrote, 'a sorry business'. Florence was upset that Hardy was 'offhand' with her, an unpleasant reminder of his behaviour towards his first wife. The next day, Sydney went for a walk with her, and she unburdened her worries. His advice was, that as Hardy was eighty-four and a half, she should not take his crush seriously, but rather laugh it off. She responded that she had tried, but it was his ill treatment that hurt: 'he spoke roughly to her and showed her that she was in the way'.[12]

The next day, she asked Sydney if he would walk into Dorchester with her, and she told him that she had been 'in such a fret in the night that she thought she would go mad'.[13] The Bugler affair was tapping into her worst fears: that she would go insane like her predecessor. She simply could not shake off the ghost of Emma. Her fears were confirmed when her husband made no allusion to the fact that it was her forty-fifth

birthday. Florence had comforted Emma when Hardy had deliberately avoided mention of her birthday, and now the same thing
was happening to her.

Her jealousy of Gertrude had increased with the discovery of
a poem he had written about the young actress, which seemed
to suggest their going away together. Florence was distraught
and she burned the poem. Her pain and humiliation were
understandable, but what she did next had serious consequences
for Gertrude, which the young woman found it hard to forgive.

———

Seven decades on, Gertrude Bugler remembered the details of
an encounter when Florence Hardy turned up uninvited at her
door in a state of high anxiety. The fact that Florence had turned
Gertrude away from Max Gate when she had appeared unexpectedly was an irony lost on Mrs Hardy. She was ready to bully,
cajole, persuade, do anything to stop Gertrude from continuing
to play Tess. Florence was almost incoherent, but Gertrude
perceived that there had been some kind of incident where
Florence had discovered the poem that Hardy had written about
his feelings for Gertrude. There had also been talk about some
kind of elopement. Florence begged Gertrude not to accept the
London offer, not least on the grounds that her husband was
too old and fragile to endure the excitement. She told Gertrude
that she must refuse the offer. In her nervous excitement, she
told Gertrude that there was already gossip in Dorchester, and
that Hardy might come to her dressing room, which would excite
further gossip. Gertrude was astounded. When she eventually
found the courage to speak, she told Florence that all the arrangements had been made and that it was too late to pull out. But
the older woman was adamant. Gertrude must write to the
manager and tell him that she couldn't leave her young baby.

So that's what she did. She wrote to her manager, and to Hardy, and she lied and told them that she needed to stay at home with her baby. Hardy was very understanding: 'No doubt you have come to a wise conclusion, though I think he [Mr Harrison] is a little disappointed. Although you fancy otherwise, I do not believe that any London actress will represent Tess so nearly as I imagined her as you did.'[14] Florence followed up her uninvited visit to Gertrude's home with a letter saying that neither she nor her husband could 'stand any emotional disturbances'. She told Gertrude that she had seen a doctor over what she had feared were delusions (just as Emma had suffered from delusions), but the doctor reassured her that she was not delusional.[15] She tried to explain that other people had noticed Hardy's obsession, and that gossip had been circulating: 'You see I know all that has been said – to myself & other people.' Florence informed Cockerell that 'All is well and happy here now since Mrs B. gave up the Haymarket scheme.' She told him of her plan to put a stop to the Hardy Players, 'I cannot go through another experience like that, and it would be bad for him [Hardy] also.'[16]

Sadly for her, Hardy did not give up on persuading Gertrude to play Tess again, and he would suggest her for other performances, though the damage had been done. Bugler's blunt verdict was: 'Hardy had two jealous wives, and he knew it.'[17] Unsurprisingly, she disliked Florence and thought she was a snob. It was almost as though Florence was becoming Emma, with her own delusions and insecurities. An operation on her neck to remove a tumour in the early autumn of 1924, had left her nerves shattered, and she continued to worry about cancer. She also continued to feel that living in Max Gate was 'enough to drive anyone into an asylum'. This in part helps to explain her conduct towards the altogether innocent Gertrude Bugler, and after Hardy's death she tried to make amends, but by then it was too late for Gertrude to become a professional actor. The terrible scene at Beaminster was like something out of *Desperate Remedies*.

Gertrude saw Hardy for one last time. Following the meeting with Frederick Harrison, Hardy had walked her down the drive at Max Gate. He turned to her and said: 'If anyone asks you if you knew Thomas Hardy, say, "Yes, he was my friend".' Thoughts of Tess consumed him throughout that year and all through the next, as several actresses wanted to play the part, though Hardy continued to believe that Gertrude was the one true Tess, the 'very incarnation of her'.[18] When Philip Ridgeway, the manager of Barnes Theatre, received Hardy's permission to stage *Tess*, Hardy urged him to think of a provincial country girl, such as Gertrude. He confessed: 'I cannot *think* of any other Tess.'[19] The choice finally fell upon Gwen Ffrangcon-Davies, who was a highly successful and accomplished actress, but did not physically resemble Hardy's idea of his heroine.

CHAPTER 71

Kate & Florence

Into his eighties, Hardy continued to enthral people with his quiet charisma and nobility of visage. Siegfried Sassoon thought he resembled a 'wizard' and that he was the 'nearest thing to Shakespeare I should ever go for a walk with'.[1] He looked one moment like 'a delightful old country gentleman' but then the light would dim, and his face would be transformed into 'the wisdom of the ages in human form. For that time-trenched face in the flicker of firelight was genius made visible, superhuman in its mystery and magnificence.' Leonard Woolf, a man not easily impressed, noted: 'He is one of the few people who have left upon me the personal impression of greatness.'[2] He walked (and ran) like a man of sixty. At the age of eighty-two he rode his bicycle to Talbothays to see his siblings. Accolades continued to be showered on him: a new painting to hang in the National Gallery, and, much to the delight of the Max Gate household, a personal visit from the Prince of Wales.

Florence did her best to keep the household calm, and the visit from the prince was a great success. Kate and Henry had wanted to be there but been told that they could only come if they hid away upstairs. It was difficult for Kate not to feel resentment. Despite Florence's sense of isolation, and her description of the loneliness of her days at Max Gate, the visitors' book showed the steady string of admirers and friends who passed through the doors and came to tea. The book for 1925 registered more than a hundred visitors.[3] One of the Hardy Players who came to tea remembered the China tea, the abundance of delicious home-made cakes which were served on a three-tier cake-stand, and the thinly sliced 'microscopic' sandwiches resembling pale yellow and brown postage stamps. Florence regarded the delicacy of her sandwiches as a mark of her refinement, in contrast to the 'large Mad-Hatter sandwiches' of the first Mrs Hardy.[4]

Another visitor during the last years of Hardy's life was Virginia Woolf. She left a detailed description of Hardy in her diary. She arrived at Max Gate with her husband, Leonard. She noticed the parlour maid in her stiff cap, and the silver cake-stand with the chocolate roll. Florence was there to greet them wearing a sprigged voile dress, black shoes and a necklace. Part of the performance was waiting for Hardy to come in from his study, the very same pattern as initiated by Emma all those years ago. Indeed, just as Emma had amazed visitors by her excessive conversation about her cats, Florence talked endlessly about her pet, as though Wessie the terrier was her child: 'She has the large sad lack-lustre eyes of a childless woman; great docility and readiness, as if she had learnt her part; not great alacrity, but resignation, in welcoming more visitors.' Hardy finally made an appearance, addressing them in the manner of an 'old doctor' or 'solicitor'. He was now eighty-six, but full of cheerfulness and vigour: 'He did not let the talk stop or disdain making talk.' He had remembered seeing Virginia in her cradle as a baby. Like many others, Woolf noticed his bird-like appearance – the diminutive body, overly large head and hooked nose. He was an 'old poulter pigeon'.

Unlike many others, who liked to describe his 'simple peasant' look, Woolf, no stranger to snobbery, saw no evidence of class consciousness: 'He seemed perfectly aware of everything . . . There was not a trace anywhere of deference to editors, or respect for rank or extreme simplicity.' Woolf was mesmerised, reduced to stammering in his presence as she tried to draw him out on his writing: 'What impressed me was his freedom, ease and vitality.'[5]

For Woolf, Hardy always remained a 'Great Victorian', even as *Satires of Circumstance*, published in 1914, was 'the most remarkable book to appear in my life time'.[6] It seems extraordinary that he had lived through the age before the advent of the railway, where women wore huge crinolines, and the horse and cart was the main method of local transportation. Now women wore flapper dresses and he had access to a motor car, a wireless, a telephone. Though he wrote about rural life, and lamented the changes wrought by the modern world, he embraced it too. He was the beneficiary of a world where a man could become self-made and rise to the top through genius, education, and hard work. And he never ceased his love of writing, believing that if he stopped, the wheels would stop turning. He was happy holding a pen in his hands.

Hardy's productivity was extraordinary for a man in his eighties. During the past few years he had published two more volumes of poetry, *Late Lyrics and Earlier* (1922) and *Human Shows, Far Phantasies, Songs and Trifles* (1925), and he was preparing the collection that would be posthumously published as *Winter Words* (1928). He acknowledged that his later poems would 'never have been written if it had not been' for Florence and that he 'could never put into words his immense debt to her'.[7]

Florence and Hardy were also hard at work on 'The Materials', a huge undertaking, which involved sifting through copious diaries, notebooks, letters. More honours and degrees were heaped upon him, and there was even a suggestion of a Wessex University, with a Thomas Hardy Chair of Literature. A stage adaptation of *The Mayor of Casterbridge* in Weymouth in September 1926, saw him receive a standing ovation. The following year, he laid the first foundation stone for the new Dorchester Grammar School.

There had been deaths. That of Florence Henniker in 1923, 'After a friendship of thirty years', had hit him hard. Agnes Grove died in December 1926 and 'Beloved Wessex' was put to sleep just after that Christmas. Florence took his passing badly: 'Of course he was merely a dog, & not a good dog alway, but *thousands* (actually thousands) of afternoons & evenings I would have been alone but for him & had always him to speak to.'[8]

Hardy was finally feeling his age. He rallied from an illness in 1925, when he was 'rambling' and told Florence he felt 'so unwell & just like he used to when he was a little boy & very delicate'.[9] By Christmas 1927, he was confined to bed, with the doctor expressing worries about his heart, and forbidding visits. Florence noted that neither Kate nor Henry had offered to visit, '& perhaps that is better for him'. When the time came, Florence intended to call for her sister, Eva, who was a nurse, to assist her at his final moments. He rallied again the day before New Year's Eve, eating pheasant and drinking champagne. Kate noted that 'very deep snow' had fallen and that Tom was staying in bed.[10] She stayed up to let in the new year but felt that she could not feel cheerful: 'The Year has ended sadly.' The snow was making it impossible to travel, but Kate telephoned Max Gate for news, sometimes calling twice a day for an update. She and Henry visited on 8 January, noting that he was weak and '*very much changed*'.[11] He was pleased to see them. Eva came to Max Gate the next day, and Sydney Cockerell was called. On the eleventh, Kate went to Max Gate, writing in her diary: 'I saw Tom but I am afraid he is not going to be here long. He looks like father & altogether I can't blind myself to what is coming.'

Florence and Hardy had been writing his memoir for several years, but now they knew that only she could complete the work. Each evening, as he faded, Florence would read aloud favourite poems, such as Robert Browning's 'Rabbi Ben Ezra' and *The Rubaiyat of Omar Khayyam*. She was struck by 'the look of wistful intentness with which Hardy was listening'.[12]

Then on the morning of 11 January 1928, he asked the maid, Nellie, for a rasher of bacon to be grilled in front of the fire in his bedroom, the way that his mother Jemima had cooked it. Later in the day, he cried out 'Eva, what is this?' Florence told a friend that a look of horror passed over his face just before he died, and that before he lost consciousness he spoke a few broken sentences, one of them 'heartrending in its poignancy, showed that his mind had reverted to a sorrow of the past'.

Florence's solicitor later said that Hardy died with 'broken words' about Emma, although, according to a letter to Clodd, Florence recalled that his words about Emma occurred some time before his death. Eva Dugdale and Nellie Titterington (who was sitting in the next-door dressing room) confirmed that his last words were not about Emma, but were indeed 'Eva, Eva what is this?' Kate Hardy telephoned at eight thirty and was informed that he was weak but had taken some beef tea. Just over half an hour later, 'the end came'.[13] Cockerell just had time to phone the BBC so that an announcement on the radio could be made to the nation at the end of the nine o'clock news.

For most of his life, Hardy had been pulled between his wives and his family. His genius and his great success had brought wealth and contentment, but he had always felt displaced. One of his final thoughts, he told Florence, was his wish that if he were to live his life again, he would 'prefer to be a small architect in a country town'.[14] In the early days of their courtship and marriage, Florence had grown close to Henry and Kate, but relations had cooled over the intervening years. Now, in death, there would be a family rift about where he would be buried. Hardy's executors, Cockerell and Florence, and James Barrie, wished him to be buried in Poets' Corner in Westminster Abbey, while his family wanted him to be buried at Stinsford with his family, as he had wished. A ghastly compromise was suggested by the Stinsford vicar: to cut open the body and remove the heart, which could be buried at Stinsford, while his body could be laid to rest in the Abbey.

The day after Hardy's death was Florence's birthday, but nobody noticed. She recorded that in death her husband had 'a look of radiant triumph such as imagination could never had conceived'.[15] Cockerell, who had slept in the dining room, fully dressed, helped to dress Hardy in his doctoral robe, noting Hardy's expression was 'noble, majestic and serene – that of the Happy Warrior'. When Kate arrived later that morning, she thought 'he looked like his own people [with] the same triumphant look on his face that all the others bore – but without the smile'.[16] Almost immediately she was told that her brother should be buried at the Abbey. Kate and Henry felt 'pushed out'. When they returned the next day, they were shown her brother's body, dressed in his red ceremonial robes, with flowers all around him. Florence was now alone, and told Kate and Henry that Tom was to be cremated: 'This *was another staggering blow but we kept a* "stiff upper lip".'

Kate was furious that they had not been told of the plan, and that if they had not decided to pop in that evening, they would never have seen their brother's body again. They were told that Hardy's body was to be taken to Woking early the following morning. But worse was to come. To her intense horror, Kate was informed of the plan to remove the heart and was told the news the rest of his body would be *cremated* and his ashes buried at Westminster Abbey: 'Another Staggering blow', she wrote. She and Henry were appalled by the thought of cremation. And the siblings were to be separated for the funerals. The plan was for Kate to attend the service at the Abbey, and Henry the service at Stinsford.

On the evening of the thirteenth, a surgeon removed the heart and wrapped it in a tea towel, which was placed in a biscuit tin before being moved to the burial casket. Many years after the event, a rumour arose that Cobweb the cat discovered the heart and began to eat it. When the undertaker came, he saw what had happened. He wrung the cat's neck and buried it in the casket alongside Hardy. The story is, fortunately, a myth. It would have been astonishing for such an animal lover as Florence to have sanctioned the killing of a beloved cat. In fact, Cobweb died the following year, after an operation to remove an abscess.

Whatever did happen, the 'heart funeral' was held at Stinsford, and the ashes were interred at Westminster Abbey, with Kate and Florence as chief mourners. Kate thought the service 'very mournful & hopeless & strange'. She was deeply relieved when it was over, and they returned to James Barrie's place for a 'crumb' to eat and a 'taste of tea'. This was not how funerals were conducted in Stinsford. Henry, by contrast, was well looked after, and the weather was much better in Dorset: 'There the good sun shone & the birds sang & everything was done simply, affectionately & well.' The Stinsford church was full, and Henry threw violets on the casket. It was a 'trying ordeal' for him, but Kate noted that he got through it well.[17] With Florence in London, Gertrude Bugler was there for the funeral at Stinsford.

Florence was now alone in Max Gate: 'with all my memories. It is the hour when I used to sit & read to him – & the house is silent, save for the ticking of the clock.'[18] Hardy's death had made her a rich woman, but she was grief-stricken. 'It is all too terrible,' she wrote to Betty Owen, 'like a dreadful nightmare.' She told Betty 'Life seems absolutely at an end for me – & I wish it actually.'[19] Florence's mother had suffered heart problems, and she had gone back home to nurse her before returning to Max Gate to sort Hardy's papers, and the poems he had gathered for his final collection, which they had hoped would be published on his ninetieth birthday. Florence had told Kate and Henry about a legacy given to them, but they refused to discuss the matter.

Florence was left to complete the biography that she and Hardy had written, though she admitted that it was compiled entirely from 'extracts from his Diaries & notebooks' and other information that was required for his biography.[20] She told Cockerell that Hardy had spent 'not only weeks, but *months*, in going over & over this biography, altering & revising copiously'.[21] She told E. M. Forster that she was perpetually numb with misery, Siegfried Sassoon that her life had become 'intolerably & unalterably lonely'. That was the hardest pill to swallow 'after fourteen years of the closest companionship'. The doctor had prescribed a sleeping draught, which only seemed to render her 'numb with misery'. T. E. Lawrence had sent a kind condolence letter and she confessed to him that she would have taken her own life 'had it not been that he left me work to do'. She felt that she had failed her husband 'at every turn'. Florence told Lawrence that time would not help, 'for I know my own nature, and I shall miss him more and more. The thought of years that may have to be lived through without him fills me with terror.' At Max Gate, she was surrounded by more ghosts: 'There was really nothing in my life except T.H, nor will there ever be.'[22]

In March, Hardy's cousin Theresa died, and there was a falling-out with Kate about funeral arrangements, for which Florence offered to pay. Florence was upset that the Hardy family were blaming her for the two funerals and the separation of the heart from the body. But by May, Florence was beginning to realise 'that the close that wonderful & precious life was not so untimely as it seemed to be first'.[23] In September, she rented an apartment in Adelphi Terrace, where Hardy had once been apprenticed to Blomfield. It was close to James Barrie's home. Florence had hoped that Barrie might make a proposal of marriage, but he resisted her charms. Florence was to find, over the years, that the important men who had flocked to Max Gate for her famous teas, were not so keen to see her now that her famous husband was dead. She suffered from insomnia and felt little human connection to others. It was a pity that she and Kate Hardy did not come together during their loneliness. Henry Hardy, who had been in poor health for some time, died in December, just eleven months after his brother.

Kate's life had not turned out as she had expected. She had secrets of her own. Many years before, when she was living in Dorchester, she had entered a relationship with Charles Meech Hardy, a first cousin twice removed. Hardy liked him, but Charles had a reputation for heavy drinking. There appeared to be a kind of secret engagement – there were coded references to him in Kate's diary. But, in 1916, at the age of fifty-seven, he married another woman. By then, Kate was sixty. She resigned herself to spinsterhood, and her diary records a life of quiet desperation: churchgoing, visits to the graves of her family to lay flowers, and trips to Max Gate. More outgoing than Mary, she nevertheless recorded many home visits from female friends and neighbours. The acquisition of a motor car enabled Kate and Henry to take trips together. It was Henry who collected Florence from hospital in London after her operation and took her home to Max Gate, covered in warm rugs.

Kate nursed her brother during his final illness. She had been deeply worried about him, and one day he had slipped from his bed onto the floor, which had frightened her immensely. Unable to lift him, she had made a makeshift bed for him on the floor. By early December, he was lapsing in and out of consciousness, and the doctor confirmed that his heart was failing. Kate, usually pragmatic, was in a state of panic. By now, he did not recognise Kate, and she knew that her last sibling was dying: 'Oh dear, dear, to think after all I can do nothing to save him.'[24] Early on the morning of 9 December, just eleven months after his brother's death, Henry 'very quietly spread his wings & went to join the "Friends Beyond"'. 'So his pains are over', Kate wrote in her diary, 'and may his soul rest in peace.'[25] Like Florence after Hardy's death, Kate was overwhelmed by loneliness: 'Now life without Henry – how lonely, sad & distressful.' Her only comfort was that in death her brother's face had an expression of 'happiness, peace & content'. He looked, she wrote, 'as he looked at 25 or 30 years of age & seems as if he will speak to me'.[26] Florence, too, was deeply upset, writing of her brother-in-law a few months later, 'He was the kindest soul imaginable, & devoted to me, & I loved him.'[27] Following Henry's death, Florence made a greater effort to see Kate, and they appeared to resume their friendship.

Florence's friendship with Sydney Cockerell deteriorated after Hardy's death. He wrote a scathing attack on her, describing her as 'dull beyond description – an inferior woman with a suburban mind' who was ambitious to be wealthy. According to Sydney, Barrie '*did* propose in a moment of emotion; but, to her great chagrin, he backed out'.[28]

A newly discovered letter, written four years after Hardy's death, suggests quite a contrary view to the idea that she was a gold-digger, who was only interested in Hardy's celebrity. Sitting in the Max Gate drawing room, with her French bulldog snoring gently by the fire, she wrote that the dog was her only companion:

'It was such a wonderful thing to live in close association with that great mind & that noble personality. After having lived 14 years with such a companion it is little wonder that I feel intolerably lonely – & find the world very empty.'[29]

And she did her utmost to make amends to the woman she had wronged. In July 1929, she gave Gertrude Bugler first refusal to play Tess in a new production in London. She asked Gertrude to meet her that evening for tea, and when she arrived at Max Gate, Gertrude was waiting. The two women talked for some time. Gertrude later went to London and was 'magnificent' in the part. Florence noted that she 'is as young-looking as ever and has distinctly improved in looks'.[30] Now that Gertrude was no longer a rival, Florence did all she could to help, offering to find (and help to pay for) accommodation, and advising her to play the 'murder scene' in her own 'quiet determined way'. Florence confessed that she believed that Hardy's 'excitement' over Gertrude had weakened his heart, and, in a sense, she was right. She believed that without Gertrude's Tess, 'he might have been alive today'.[31] It was generous to make amends to the woman who had inadvertently caused her so much pain. Florence explained to Siegfried Sassoon that she did not want Mrs Bugler to regret 'that she had never had a chance to show what she can do on a London stage'.

Gertrude finally had her moment in the bright lights of London. Florence's act of contrition brought her a sense of peace: 'I am writing this in T.H.'s chair at his writing-table in the study: the pines stand black against the mysterious blue of a summer night, & a late blackbird has only just ceased whistling. The spirit of T.H. seems all around, & lately I have had a feeling that all is well.'[32]

EPILOGUE

The Well-Beloved

He is a man who all his life long is in love with love
rather than with any particular woman, and 'the well-beloved'
is his name for a sort of Platonic idea that assumes one
embodiment after another for an elusive ideal which is
the permanent element in many fleeting forms.

(W. M. Payne, review of *The Well-Beloved*
in *The Dial*, 16 May 1897)

On an unseasonably cold summer's day in August 1925, two
years before Hardy's death, Florence and Thomas made a
pilgrimage to the country house, Racedown, where William
Wordsworth had lived rent-free and first became a great poet.
They were met by the owner, Lady Hester Pinney, who showed
the pilgrims around the house, and gave them tea in the best
parlour. Lady Pinney and Hardy discussed *Tess*: 'It amused Hardy
to hear that I had seen a tail-piece of a woman hanging at the
end of a chapter of one of his stories. Was it Tess?' Racedown
was close to the village of Birdsmoorgate, where Martha Brown
lived, and the scene of the crime where she killed her husband.
Hardy and Florence signed the visitor's book, and then Florence,

who Lady Pinney thought treated her husband 'like a piece of Dresden china' hurried him away. As he was leaving, he turned to his hostess, and asked her: 'Will you find out about Martha Brown?' Lady Pinney asked who she was, and he replied: 'She killed her husband. I saw her hanged when I was sixteen. She lived over there.' Hardy pointed to the houses clustered around Birdsmoorgate.[1]

Hester Pinney was a Poor Law Guardian. After her meetings, she stayed behind to chat to the elderly people in the workhouse. She asked everyone over eighty if they knew anything about the case. Everyone, Lady Pinney recalled, knew about it – the young husband and the woman who had killed him with an axe: 'These people remembered the story of Martha Brown better than what they ate for dinner the week before.' Lady Pinney collected their stories and sent them to Hardy.[2] They contained four important eye-witness accounts, from Jim Brown, George Aplin, Mrs Trim, and Mrs Bayley. Most agreed that Martha Brown was 'a wonderful looking woman'. There were fascinating, albeit grisly, details, such as the blood stain that could never be removed from the floor and the strand of John Brown's hair found on the axe. George Aplin's mother, a midwife who also had a job laying out the dead, told her son about the murder, and was told about Martha's good looks, with her 'beautiful curls'. Mrs Trim also told Lady Pinney about Martha's 'long black curls'. All four witnesses described the black gown, though there was some disagreement as to its fabric:

An old spinster, Mary Philip[s], of Broadwindsor told me her next door neighbour Amelia Dale, (who died a year ago in the Mental Hospital) had walked all the way from Mosterton to Dorchester, with 13 others, to see Martha hung, & 'she was hung in a black silk gown' Mrs Bailey said it was satin & satin went out of fashion for some time after! Mrs Bailey tells me.[3]

Several of the witnesses blamed the 'lustful' Mary Davis, for 'upholding' a married man in her house.

Hardy wrote to Lady Pinney to thank her for the information. This was where he wrote of the indelible memory:

> My sincere thanks for the details you have been so indefatigable as to obtain about that unhappy woman Martha Brown, whom I am ashamed to say I saw hanged, my only excuse being that I was but a youth, & had to be in the town at the time for other reasons. I gather from your description that the house of the murder has quite disappeared. I daresay it was pulled down as much on account of its tragic associations as from its dilapidated state. I wonder if there are any remains of it. I remember what a fine figure she showed against the sky as she hung in the misty rain, & how the tight black silk gown set off her shape as she wheeled half-round & back.[4]

The excuse that he 'had to be in the town at the time for other reasons' was lame, and he knew it. The young Thomas Hardy had, in fact, made careful plans to witness the execution from a prime position.

Florence also wrote to her on the same day: 'The most terrible touch, & the most dramatic, is that account of Mary Davis, who was morally responsible for the whole tragedy, walking to see the hanging of the woman she had wronged. Horrible woman.'[5] Florence told Lady Pinney that her husband's account of the hanging was 'vivid, & terrible'. She thought it was a pity that a 'boy of sixteen should have been permitted to see such a sight'. Florence thanked her for all her work on the case and told her that Hardy was 'deeply interested in it'.

Hardy followed up with a visit to the County Museum to search through old copies of the *Dorset County Chronicle*. He was keen to know whether the house in Birdsmoorgate had indeed been demolished, and he was also trying to trace the full account of the trial. As he himself grew closer to death, he wanted to know more details about the event that had marked his life. At the age of eighty-six, he still felt a mixture of shame and eroticism about the hanging, and yet he also believed that at the time of the execution he felt little emotion: 'I suppose because boys are like it.'[6] He came to believe that he should not have gone.

That winter, Lady Pinney came to Max Gate, and they sat close to the open fire, 'talking about Martha and Tess as if they were in the next room'. Lady Pinney thought that his 'sympathy for these unhappy women whose stories had much in common was wonderful'. To Hardy, Tess was flesh and blood. Just as real to him as the real woman who had been hanged. It was as if he were haunted by them both.

For once, Hardy was talking freely and openly about the effect that the execution had upon him, and how he had transmuted it into his masterpiece. Pinney wrote that there were 'extenuating circumstances for both crimes'. And 'it was evident that the misadventure of seeing Martha hanged over the prison gate never left his mind and it influenced his stories'. It was almost as if Hardy himself was making the true and full connection for the first time.[7] Lady Pinney told Hardy that she thought that the ending of *Tess* was the right one. His answer was: 'I am so glad you say that; many people think I ought to have left her to die on Stonehenge. As if Tess could die on Stonehenge!' She was still so vividly real to him.[8]

The last time Lady Pinney saw him was when in the County Museum, searching amongst the old papers of the *Dorset County Chronicle* until he found the account of the trial. Perhaps for the first time, he discovered the role of Horace Moule's father, who led Martha to the gallows. Though there is no denying Florence's assertion that the execution gave a 'tinge of bitterness

& gloom' to Hardy's life's work, it also gave him the inspiration to look inside the mind and the soul of a murderess, to see the 'extenuating circumstances' and to render her a sympathetic and 'pure' woman.

He took great satisfaction from the fan letters he received in which young women thanked him for creating in Tess a character who reflected their own hard experience. Emily Pass, for example, who wrote from New York:

> I have recently read 'Tess of the d'Urbervilles', and feel I would like you to know how much it has meant to me. I am twenty years old, and am sympathetic with 'Tess', the more so because some of my own experiences in life have been not unlike hers. The book is more personal to me than any book I have ever read or I think any that I shall ever read. I loved the portrayal of Tess, and the intricate workings of her beautiful soul. I wonder at your complete understanding of a woman's soul.[9]

Or this, sent from The Hague in stumbling English, but with great heart:

> I am a Dutch girl, who just finished your above mentioned work and I cannot resist the desire to tell you how that work has moved me, how deep an impression it made upon me.
>
> I've never read a book in which I felt something of my self as in your so well-painted – Tess.
>
> I think Tess caracter so beautiful, it is never weak, she always gives and never asks . . . And after all I think it not a crime when she kills that vile wretch, and not at all a crime which ought to be punished – and not at all punished in that way. –
>
> That killed fellow was the cause of all – the cause of her miserable life (and in the same time so beautiful life)– and were not the parents indeed the cause of all?

Who deserves punishment? Tess least of all.

I think life so difficult and several troubles I have had, I met in this book. Oh, I wish that there are more people in the world as you are, for you understand a woman.[10]

As in *Tess*, it is always the case that 'The Woman Pays'. The Hardy women paid a high price for his fame and his glory. Eliza Nicholls, waiting faithfully like Miss Havisham, for her lover to return; Tryphena, with her black eyebrows like musical slurs, and her wild spirit, prevented from marrying her cousin. Emma, writing her diabolical diaries in her attic room, while her husband was falling in love with the woman who would become his second wife. Florence, whose searing jealousy of the 'living incarnation' of Tess, caused her such mental anguish. Mary, the woman whose life was so constrained that she 'came into the world . . . and went out . . . and the world is just the same . . . not a ripple on the surface left.'[11] Jemima, the fearless and outspoken matriarch, who instilled his love of books from such an early age, and who encouraged him to escape the confines of his background. All these women, and more, left more than a 'ripple on the surface'. Could there have been fictional schoolmistresses, Fancy Day and Sue Bridehead, without Tryphena, Mary, Kate and Florence? Could there have been Mrs Yeobright and Ann Dewy without Jemima Hardy? Or the quieter, unseen heroines, Marty South and Elizabeth-Jane, without Mary Hardy? Bathsheba without Martha Sharpe? Elfride Swancourt without Emma Lavinia Gifford? The list goes on.

Hardy's posthumous poetry collection *Winter Words* celebrates many of those women he had loved and lost. His tribute to Horace Moule, 'Standing by the Mantelpiece', suggests his deep love of the one man who truly inspired him and believed in his genius. That suicide was branded on Hardy's heart. His last poem, 'He Resolves to Say No More' made his position clear: 'From now always / Till my last day / What I discern I will not say.'[12] But Hardy always revealed more than he concealed, like Easter eggs hidden amongst the reams of his poetry. The American novelist and poet Louise Chandler Moulton wrote in 1892: 'I know no man who likes women better, and there is nothing that a woman could possibly do that would seem to him wrong.'[13]

If there was ever a philosophy to explain Hardy's view of romantic love, it can be found among the pages of his final and often neglected novel, *The Pursuit of the Well-Beloved*. The story spans forty years in the life of a famous sculptor, who Pygmalion-like attempts to carve in stone the ideal woman. He also spends his life searching for a woman in the flesh, falling in love with Avice, and then falling in love with Avice's daughter, and then her granddaughter, a third Avice. Each woman represents a different facet of womanhood: the ingénue, the flirt, and the shy, virginal girl. The point is that the sculptor is falling in love with an ideal that no woman can ever live up to. For Hardy, desire was often based upon the woman that was unattainable. Once she is his, the attraction dies. If only Florence had seen that Hardy's infatuation with Gertrude Bugler was just that, the search for the well-beloved, she would have saved herself a great deal of guilt and misery.

Few people could understand how 'real' Tess was to him. Lady Pinney came close when she said he talked about Tess as if she were just in another room in Max Gate. Perhaps to him she was there? And indeed Hardy had the chance, before he died, to finally meet Tess in his Max Gate drawing room. On 6 December 1925, a party of West End actors arrived at Max Gate 'laden with huge theatrical baskets of clothes and props'.

They were met in the hall and given tea. Hardy made a point of chatting to all the actors. There was a tiny audience of Florence and Hardy, Mr Tilley, and two maids in cap and apron.

By now, the room was dark, and lit by the glow of the fire and flickering candles. Tess's home was recreated using chairs and a small table, and when they were removed, the corner of the room became Stonehenge. When it came to that pivotal scene, the simplicity only added to the magic. The actress who played Joan Durbeyfield recalled Gwen Ffrangcon-Davies's 'beautiful voice and exquisite playing' and the shadows thrown by the candlelight: 'It was beautiful.'

Gwen herself felt that she had become the part of Tess: 'I found for once I was not acting but living the part.' When it came to the confession scene between Tess and Angel, 'I had a feeling of absolute reality.' The tragic scenes unfolded themselves in that dark quiet room 'under their creator's eyes'.[14] At the end of the performance Gwen gazed at Hardy, who was sitting quietly. His eyes were full of tears.

Acknowledgements

My thanks to the archivists and librarians at the Dorset County Museum, Dorset History Centre, Colby College, Eton College, and the Beinecke Library, Yale University, and to Dr Timothy Hands. Helen Gibson kindly introduced me to Marilyn and Andrew Leah who kindly sent me a copy of Emma Lavinia Hardy's novella *The Maid on the Shore.* I am indebted to the great wealth of Hardy scholarship, as cited in the endnotes, and most especially to Michael Millgate – again and again, one finds a key quotation or point of information in the primary sources and then discovers that Millgate has cited it in his authoritative biography.

Thanks to Arabella Pike, my exemplary editor and friend. This is our tenth book together, and, as always, I benefit enormously from her tact and wisdom. My thanks to Sarah Chalfant and Andrew Wylie; agents supreme! Thanks to Anne O'Brien for her excellent copy-edit, and the publishing team at William Collins: Alex Gingell, Sam Harding and Lizzy Rowles.

Since this is a book about the roles that women played in the life of Thomas Hardy, I would like to pay my own tribute to the women in my life, whose support during the last year has been invaluable. My thanks to my daughter, Ellie Bate, and my sister, Christine Beaver. And to Shelley Treadaway, Lolly Nissan, Naomi Brackett, Nicole Hudson, Amy Wesson, Michele Hammer, Nancy Melin, Shari Short, and Laura Sackis-Jones.

My final thanks are for my family. Thank you, Tom and Harry, for everything you do for me, and for all the love and laughs. My deepest thanks are reserved for my husband, Jonathan Bate. You are my first reader, and, as ever, you have the sharpest eyes and the best judgment. Thank you for sharing my enthusiasm for Thomas Hardy.

Notes

ABBREVIATIONS

CL   *The Collected Letters of Thomas Hardy*, edited by Richard
         Little Purdy and Michael Millgate, 8 vols (1978–2012), cited
         by date of letter

CP   *Thomas Hardy: The Complete Poems*, ed. James Gibson (2001)

DCM   Dorset County Museum Archive of Thomas Hardy, now in
         the Dorset History Centre, Dorchester

EH   Emma Lavinia [Gifford] Hardy, first wife

EHD   *Emma Hardy Diaries*, ed. Richard H. Taylor (1985)

FH   Florence Emily [Dugdale] Hardy, second wife

IR   Thomas Hardy, *Interviews and Recollections*, edited by James
         Gibson (1999)

KH   Katharine (Kate) Hardy, sister

LEF   *Letters of Emma and Florence Hardy*, edited by Michael
         Millgate (1996), cited by date of letter

LW   *The Life and Work of Thomas Hardy* by Thomas Hardy, edited
         by Michael Millgate (1985), bringing together 'Florence Emily
         Hardy', *The Early Life of Thomas Hardy 1840–1891* (1928) and
         'Florence Emily Hardy', *The Later Years of Thomas Hardy,
         1892–1928* (1930)

MH   Mary Hardy, sister

MM   Michael Millgate, *Thomas Hardy: A Biography Revisited* (2004)

ORFW   *One Rare Fair Woman: Thomas Hardy's Letters to Florence
         Henniker 1893–1922*, ed. Evelyn Hardy and F. B. Pinion
         (1972)

PMN   *Thomas Hardy's 'Poetical Matter' Notebook*, ed. Pamela Dalziel
         and Michael Millgate (2009)

PN   *Personal Notebooks of Thomas Hardy*, ed. Richard H. Taylor
       (1979)
RG1   Robert Gittings, *Young Thomas Hardy* (1975)
RG2   Robert Gittings, *The Older Hardy* (1978)
SR   Emma Hardy, *Some Recollections*, ed. Evelyn Hardy and
       Robert Gittings (1979)
TH   Thomas Hardy

Quotations from all but one of Thomas Hardy's novels are from the readily accessible Oxford World's Classics editions, cited by chapter (or book and chapter) number in order to allow passages to be found in other editions. The one exception is *Tess of the D'Urbervilles*, quoted from the Penguin Classics edition (2008), which is recommended for its fuller treatment of the many textual variants in Hardy's successive versions of the novel.

PROLOGUE
1. *CL*, TH to Lady Hester Pinney, 20 January 1926. See also Thomas Hardy, 'Thomas William Hooper Tolbort', *Dorset County Chronicle,* 14 August 1883.
2. Hardy's words, noted down by Elliott Felkin, 'Days with Thomas Hardy', diary extract published in *Encounter*, April 1962, p. 29.
3. Florence Hardy to Sydney Cockerell, 27 June 1918, Sydney C. Cockerell Papers, Richard L. Purdy Collection of Thomas Hardy, Beinecke Library, Yale University.
4. Quoted, MM, p. 477.
5. *CL*, 28 August 1914.
6. Sydney Cockerell to TH, 7 Dec 1915 (DCM).
7. Prefatory note to *The Early Life of Thomas Hardy 1840–1891* by Florence Emily Hardy (1928).
8. Florence Hardy to Rebekah Owen, *LEF*, 18 Jan 1916.
9. TH to Cockerell, *CL*, 5 Dec 1915.
10. To Cockerell, *LEF*, 7 Feb 1918.
11. See *The Life and Work of Thomas Hardy* by Thomas Hardy, edited by Michael Millgate (1985), p. xxi. Hereafter, references to Hardy/ Florence's two-volume biography (*The Early Life*, 1928, and *The Later Years*, 1930) will be to this compilation, cited as *LW*.

12. *CL*, TH to George Douglas, 7 May 1919. Hardy's afterthought: 'Kipling, by the way, whom I met in London, said that we all seem ghosts nowadays.'

13. Hedgcock, 'Reminiscences of Thomas Hardy', *IR*, p. 94; TH to Thomas MacQuoid, 29 October 1891.

14. Irving Howe, *Thomas Hardy* (1967), p. 131; Emma Hardy, *LEF*, 13 Nov 1894.

15. Michael Millgate, *Thomas Hardy: A Biography Revisited* (2004), cited as MM, is the authoritative biography, to which I am much indebted. Robert Gittings' two-volume life, *Young Thomas Hardy* (1975) and *The Older Hardy* (1978), remains highly readable and full of insights. Among more recent biographies, Ralph Pite's *Thomas Hardy: The Guarded Life* (2006) is especially strong on the geography of Hardy's Wessex and Claire Tomalin's *Thomas Hardy: The Time-Torn Man* (2006) is very sensitive on the two marriages, but perhaps insufficiently attuned to Hardy as a class-torn man.

16. TH to H. W. Massingham, *CL*, 31 Dec 1891, responding to a review of *Tess*.

CHAPTER 1

1. Jane Sharp, *The Midwives Book; or, The Whole Art of Midwifry Discovered* (1671), ed. Elaine Hobby (1999), p. 175.

2. *LW*, pp. 316–17.

3. *LW*, p. 19.

4. *LW*, p. 19.

5. *LW*, p. 7.

6. *LW*, p. 7.

7. *LW*, p. 316.

8. *LW*, p. 316.

9. *LW*, pp. 316–17.

CHAPTER 2

1. *LW*, p. 11.

2. *LW*, p. 7.

3. *LW*, p. 9.

4. *LW*, p. 5.

5. See John R. Doheny, 'Biography and Thomas Hardy's Maternal

Ancestors: The Swetmans', *The Thomas Hardy Journal*, 11:2 (1995), pp. 46–60 (p. 51).

6. *LW,* p. 11.
7. Eastlake was born in Plymouth, and first achieved fame from painting one of Hardy's heroes, Napoleon, on board the *Bellerophon* in Plymouth Sound. He later became President of the Royal Academy and Director of the National Gallery. See *LW,* p. 11.
8. Doheny, p. 51.
9. See C.H.S. Baxter, *Melbury Osmond – The Parish and Its People* (1966), p. 11.
10. *LW,* p. 11.
11. http://www.wessexmorrismen.co.uk/docs/TheDorsetOoser.pdf.
12. *LW,* p. 12.
13. *LW,* p. 7.
14. Doheny, p. 56.
15. *LW,* p. 11.
16. *LW,* p. 12.
17. Quoted, *The Thomas Hardy Yearbook*, 11 (1995), p. 56.
18. 17 Jan 1842, Lock Collection, DCM.
19. Doheny, p. 57.
20. https://hannfamily.org.uk/Hannfamily-0/p32.htm.

CHAPTER 3
1. See Joanna Martin, *Wives and Daughters: Women and Children in the Georgian Country House* (2004), p. 14.
2. See Rictor Norton, 'The Gay Love Letters of John, Lord Hervey to Stephen Fox', *Town and Country* (1998), http://rictornorton.co.uk/hervey1.htm.
3. 'The First Countess of Wessex' (*Harper's New Monthly Magazine*, 1889), repr. as 'Dame the First' in *A Group of Noble Dames* (1891, repr. 1919), p. 7.
4. *Wives and Daughters*, p. 83.
5. *Wives and Daughters*, p. 134.
6. *Wives and Daughters*, pp. 47–9.
7. https://www.jamesboswell.info/biography/william-obrien-actor-and-provost-master-general-bermudas.
8. *Wives and Daughters*, p. 160.

9. *PN*, pp. 26–7.
10. *LW*, p. 14.
11. *The Letters of Horace Walpole*, ed. John Wright (1840), p. 405.
12. *LW*, p. 14.
13. *CP*, pp. 263–8.

CHAPTER 4
1. *LW*, p. 12.
2. Richard Little Purdy Collection, Beinecke Rare Book and Manuscript Library, Yale University, GEN MSS III, Series IV, Box 20, Folder 626.
3. See, for example, A. James Hammerton (1992), *Cruelty and Companionship: conflict in nineteenth-century married life* (1992); Anna Clark, *The Struggle for the Breeches: gender and the making of the British working class* (1995).
4. Though Jemima herself was baptised in September 1813.
5. *LW*, p. 12.
6. *LW*, p. 19.
7. *Wives and Daughters,* pp. 138–43.
8. *LW*, p. 18.
9. *CP*, p. 252.

CHAPTER 5
1. *LW*, p. 453.
2. MM, p. 22.
3. David Clammer, 'Dorset's Volunteer Infantry 1794–1805', *Journal of the Society for Army Historical Research*, 89 (2011), pp. 6–25, http://www.jstor.org/stable/44231815.
4. *PN*, pp. 8–9.
5. *PN*, p. 9.
6. 'One We Knew, M. H. 1772–1857', *CP*, p. 275.
7. 'The Self-Unseeing', *CP*, p. 166.
8. *Two on a Tower*, chapter II.
9. Ibid.
10. *LW,* p. 20.
11. 'Domicilium', *CP*, p. 3.

CHAPTER 6

1. Census data for Puddletown and Dorchester in the time of Hardy's youth reveals the high proportion of married women listed as having occupations: see, for example, https://www.opcdorset.org/PiddleFiles/Puddletown/1841Piddletown.htm and https://www.opcdorset.org/fordingtondorset/Files2/1841CensusHTDist2.html.
2. *LW*, p. 12.
3. See https://www.badseysociety.uk/village-life/wickhamford-glove-making-the-mid-19th-century.
4. Betty Hand to Mary Hand, 17 Jan 1842 (DCM, quoted, MM, p. 21).
5. 'Logs on the Hearth: A Memory of a Sister' (December 1915), *CP*, p. 490 – the poem ends with a characteristically macabre image of her rising from her 'chilly grave'.
6. *CL*, TH to Cockerell, 5 Dec 1915.
7. MH note in *Cries of London* (DCM). See also, *LW*, p. 19.
8. See the curious phrase in his autobiography, 'This peculiarity in himself troubled the mind of "Tommy" . . . and set him wondering at a phenomenon to which he ventured not to confess' (*LW*, p. 19).
9. *Jude the Obscure*, pt I, ch 1.
10. DCM D/HAR/1/1/1, described as an imaginary or retrospective portrait of Jemima and Thomas as a baby, but conceivably an actual portrait showing his younger brother Henry.

CHAPTER 7

1. *Under the Greenwood Tree*, pt I, ch 1.
2. Ibid, pt I, ch 4.
3. *LW*, p. 16.
4. 1912 Preface to *Under the Greenwood Tree*.
5. *LW*, p. 17.
6. 1912 Preface.
7. *Under The Greenwood Tree*, pt I, ch 4.
8. Ibid, pt I, ch 8.
9. 'The House of Hospitalities', *CP*, p. 206.
10. 'The Oxen', *CP*, p. 468.

CHAPTER 8

1. Mary Hardy to Nathaniel Sparks, 18 October 1908 (Sparks Family Papers, Eton College MS 710 03/03).
2. https://www.dorsetlife.co.uk/2006/09/puddletown/.
3. See https://www.athelhampton.com/hardyatathelhampton.
4. Lois Deacon and Terry Coleman, *Providence and Mr Hardy* (1966), p. 170. She also posits the bizarre theory that Rebecca was Jemima's child.
5. *LW*, p. 501. A post-Hardy revision to the *Life*, suggested by J. M. Barrie.

CHAPTER 9

1. *LW*, p. 23.
2. *LW*, p. 23.
3. *LW*, pp. 104–5.
4. *LW*, p. 21.
5. *CP*, p. 511.
6. *PMN*, p. 16.

CHAPTER 10

1. *LW*, p. 447.
2. Walter de la Mare, *The Listener*, 28 April 1956 (*IR*, p. 163).
3. *CP*, p. 623.
4. See Tony Bradbury, 'Thomas Hardy's Hertfordshire Relatives', *The Thomas Hardy Journal*, 15:2 (1999), pp. 49–59.
5. *LW*, p. 22.
6. *LW*, pp. 21–2.
7. Bradbury, p. 51.
8. Hardy made the connection to Florence Dugdale. 'One or two of them are hard on Mrs Evans (Bathsheba) – unfairly so, as she gave the real B. quite startlingly to me, seeming just like my handsome aunt from whom I drew her' (*CL*, 18 Nov 1909).
9. *LW*, p. 22.
10. *IR*, p. 110.
11. *LW*, p. 22.

CHAPTER 11

1. *Jude*, I-ix.
2. Betty Hand to Mary Hand, 17 Jan 1842 (Lock Collection, DCM).

3. Antell's son, John, interview, MM, p. 38.
4. *FEH*, Florence Hardy to Alda, Lady Hoare, 30 July 1915.
5. *LW*, p. 28.
6. *LW*, p. 28.
7. *LW*, p. 22.
8. *LW*, p. 23.
9. Florence Hardy, 'Notes on Thomas Hardy's Life' (DCM).
10. *LW*, p. 24.
11. *LW*, p. 26.
12. *LW*, p. 23.
13. *LW*, p. 27.
14. *IR*, p. 2.
15. Ibid.
16. Ibid.
17. *LW*, p. 502.
18. Ibid.
19. *IR*, p. 1.
20. See 1851 Census. https://www.opcdorset.org/fordingtondorset/Files2/1851CensusAllSaints.html.
21. 1851 Census.
22. Martin Ray, *Thomas Hardy Remembered* (2007), pp. 131, 125.
23. F. B. Pinion, *Thomas Hardy: His Life and Friends* (1992), p. 28.
24. *LW*, p. 26.
25. *LW*, p. 24.
26. Ibid.
27. Ibid.
28. *LW*, p. 25.
29. Ibid.

CHAPTER 12
1. *LW*, p. 25.
2. *LW*, p. 24.
3. See his ballad 'The Dance at the Phoenix' (*CP*, pp. 43–8).
4. *PMN*, p. 16.
5. *LW*, p. 27.
6. *LW*, p. 29.
7. This story was added later, at the request of J.M. Barrie. See *LW*, pp. 501–2.

8. *LW,* p. 29.
9. DCM, quoted, RG1, p. 24.
10. *LW,* p. 29.
11. Ibid.
12. Ibid. Forty years later, Hardy recorded the incident in his novel *The Well-Beloved.*
13. *LW,* p. 30. Herne the Hunter was first mentioned in Shakespeare's *The Merry Wives of Windsor.*
14. *IR,* p. 110.
15. Ibid.
16. *LW,* pp. 214–15.
17. Ibid.
18. *CP,* p. 131.
19. Ibid, p. 25.
20. *LW,* p. 30.
21. *IR,* p. 3.
22. Ibid.
23. 'Louie', *CP,* p. 772.
24. *LW,* p. 20.
25. *LW,* p. 21.
26. Ibid.

CHAPTER 13
1. *LW,* p. 479.
2. Ibid.
3. *LW,* p. 235.
4. *Under the Greenwood Tree,* chapter 1.
5. *LW,* p. 8.
6. *LW,* p. 345.
7. *Tess of the D'Urbervilles,* 1.iii.
8. *PN,* p. 12.
9. *PN,* p. 14.
10. *PN,* p. 12.
11. *PN,* p. 10.
12. Ibid.
13. *PN,* p. 26.
14. *PN,* p 10.
15. *CL,* TH to Frederic Harrison, 20 June 1918.

16. Literary Notes III, DCM.
17. *LW*, p. 475.
18. Charlotte Lindgren, 'Thomas Hardy: Grim Facts and Local Lore', *Thomas Hardy Journal*, 1:3 (1985), pp. 18–27 (p. 21).
19. Summer Strevens, *Burned at the Stake: The Life and Death of Mary Channing* (2017).
20. *PN*, p. 38.

CHAPTER 14

1. Newspaper reports and reminiscences of the trial, from which quotations in this chapter are taken, are helpfully gathered in Nicola Thorne, *In Search of Martha Brown: The True Story of the Mysterious Woman Thomas Hardy Saw Hanged* (2000). See also http://www.opcdorset.org/fordingtondorset/Files2/ExecutionElizabethMarthaClarke1856.html.
2. V. A. C. Gatrell, *The Hanging Tree: Execution and the English People, 1770–1868* (1994), p. 68.

CHAPTER 15

1. Handley Moule, *Memories of a Vicarage* (1913), p. 13. This memoir is the source of most of the information in this chapter.
2. Ibid, p. 54.
3. Reported by Hardy, *CL*, 20 March 1904.
4. *LW*, p. 423.
5. *Memories of a Vicarage*, p. 58.
6. 'The Advantages of the Dry Earth System' (1868); 'The Impossibility Overcome: or the Inoffensive, Safe, and Economical Disposal of the Refuse of Towns and Villages' (1870); 'The Dry Earth System' (1871); 'Town Refuse, the Remedy for Local Taxation' (1872), and 'National Health and Wealth promoted by the general adoption of the Dry Earth System' (1873).
7. *LW*, p. 138.
8. *Memories of a Vicarage*, p. 66.
9. Ibid, p. 29.
10. Ibid, p. 62.
11. *LW*, p. 138.

CHAPTER 16

1. *LW*, p. 457. See also Fran Chalfont, 'Fellow-Townsmen: Thomas Hardy and Sir Frederick Treves', *Thomas Hardy Journal*, 6:2 (1990), pp. 62–78.
2. *LW*, p. 37.
3. See https://www.opcdorset.org/fordingtondorset/Files2/ JohnPouncy1818-1894.html.
4. *LW*, p. 31.
5. *LW*, pp. 32–4.
6. Ibid, p. 34.
7. *Thomas Hardy's Public Voice: The Essays, Speeches, and Miscellaneous Prose*, ed. Michael Millgate (2001), p. 230.
8. *CL*, 20 March 1904.
9. RG1, p. 28.
10. See John R. Doheny, 'Thomas Hardy's Relatives and their Times: some "Sparks Letters" and other Documents', *Thomas Hardy Year Book*, 18 (1989), p. 49.
11. MM, p. 59.
12. *LW*, p. 27.
13. Florence Hardy in conversation with Richard Purdy (Yale, GEN MSS 111, Series IV).

CHAPTER 17

1. Newspaper reports and reminiscences of the hanging, from which quotations in this chapter are taken, are helpfully gathered in Nicola Thorne, *In Search of Martha Brown: The True Story of the Mysterious Woman Thomas Hardy Saw Hanged* (2000).
2. *The Sketch*, 2 November 1904, pasted and annotated in Hardy Scrapbook (DCM).
3. See Elliott Felkin, 'Days with Thomas Hardy', *Encounter*, XVIII (April 1962).
4. *LEF*, Florence Hardy to Lady Pinney, 20 Jan 1926.
5. Studies in the psychology of voyeurism are commensurate with some of Hardy's peccadilloes, such as the use of a telescope, or a sexual interest in clothing, such as silk, particularly when a person is bending down. See for example https://www. psychologistanywhereanytime.com/sexual_problems_pyschologist/ psychologist_voyeurism.htm.

CHAPTER 18

1. Note in DCM.
2. Charles Moule wrote a poem for Hardy's 80th birthday, recalling their boyish pursuits in and around Dorchester. See *LW,* p. 419.
3. *Memories of a Vicarage,* p. 35. See also *LW,* p. 37.
4. Ibid (my italics).
5. *LW,* p. 38.
6. *LW,* p. 37.
7. *Tess,* chapter XVIII.
8. *LW,* p. 37.

CHAPTER 19

1. Details taken from Robert Southey's *Life of Horatio Nelson* (1813).
2. See *LW,* p. 18.
3. Ibid, p. 26.
4. Ibid, p. 33.
5. Thus the London *Times* (11 Aug): 'the wretched culprit was tried . . . for the wilful murder of a young woman named Sarah Ann Griffy, at Stoke Abbotts, on the 30th of April last, and also for having set fire to the house in which his victim resided. The prisoner is a very young man, not having reached his 20th year, and had been working as a labourer for some time past in the vicinity . . . On the day of the murder . . . when all the parties, who were farm labourers, were at work, excepting the deceased, the prisoner entered the house, and, after maltreating her, inflicted a most fearful gash in her throat, nearly five inches long, with a clasped cheese knife, and other injuries on the hands, arms, and breast, and then set fire to the house.'
6. *LW,* p. 33.
7. Ibid.
8. *LW,* p. 472.

CHAPTER 20

1. G. B. Sharpe to TH, 21 Sept 1859 (DCM, quoted, MM, p. 61).
2. *Dorset County Chronicle,* 18 November 1858.
3. Ibid.
4. *LW,* p. 38.
5. Ibid.
6. *LW,* p. 36.

CHAPTER 21

1. See Lance G. E. Jones, *The Training of Teachers in England and Wales* (1924); R. W. Rich, *The Training of Teachers in England and Wales during the 19th Century* (1933); and Christina de Bellaigue, *Educating Women: Schooling and Identity in England and France, 1800–1867* (2007).
2. TH to Sir Henry Newbolt, 21 June 1920; *Jude*, III-i.
3. See Michael Millgate and Stephen Mottram, 'Sisters: Mary and Kate Hardy as Teachers', *The Thomas Hardy Journal*, 25 (2009), pp. 4–24 (p. 7).
4. See Celia Barclay, 'Mary Hardy and Annie Lanham', *The Thomas Hardy Journal*, 12:1 (Feb 1996), pp. 57–61.
5. Mary Hardy to Nathaniel Sparks, 26 Nov 1907 (Eton MS).
6. Ibid.

CHAPTER 22

1. The best account of Thomas Hardy and religion can be found in Timothy Hands, *Thomas Hardy: Distracted Preacher?* (1989).
2. Cited, RG1, p. 49.
3. Ibid, p. 55.
4. Ibid, p. 8.
5. Constance Oliver Waight, *Thomas Hardy Proposes to Mary Waight* (1963), pp. 7–10.
6. 'The Fiddler of the Reels', in *Life's Little Ironies* [short story collection], ed. Alan Manford (1996), pp. 141–2.

CHAPTER 23

1. *LW*, p. 43.
2. Sometimes called the Great Exposition or the International Exhibition to distinguish it from the Great Exhibition of 1851. The best account of Hardy's time in London can be found in Mark Ford, *Thomas Hardy: Half a Londoner* (2016).
3. Frederick Dolman, 'An Evening with Thomas Hardy', *Young Man*, VIII (March 1894).
4. Quoted, MM, p. 74.
5. *LW*, p. 43.
6. Ibid.
7. *CP*, p. 8.

CHAPTER 24

1. 1 Kings 9–12.
2. *CL*, 17 August 1862.
3. *Athenaeum*, 3 Feb 1866.
4. *CL*, TH to MH, 17 Aug 1862.
5. *CL*, TH to MH, 3 Nov 1862.
6. See *The Mayor of Casterbridge* and Alan Chedzoy, 'Those Terrible Marks of the Beast: Barnes, Hardy and the Dorset Dialect', *The Hardy Society Journal*, 4:3 (2008), pp. 46–60.
7. *CL*, TH to MH, 3 Nov 1862.
8. Ibid.

CHAPTER 25

1. There is, for example, no mention of Eliza Nicholls in Robert Gittings' two-volume biography. Hardy's most knowledgeable and conscientious biographer, Michael Millgate, accepted the truth of the connection, but it was only after the publication of his reissued biography that more facts about the Eliza Nicholls connection emerged. Claire Tomalin was dismissive of the claim: 'Like the Mary Waight story, the entanglement with Eliza Nicholls is not much more than a family tradition . . . well-known men attract claims of this kind' (*Time-Torn Man*, pp. 71, 400).
2. The correspondence between Headley and Purdy, the photographs, and his notes regarding the interview can be found in the Beinecke Library, Yale. See Purdy Hardy Collection: GEN MSS III Box 17, Folder 549.
3. Henry Bastow to TH, May 1861 (DCM).
4. See Michael Wheeler, *Heaven, Hell, and the Victorians* (1994), p. 151.
5. Millgate and Mottram, p. 26.
6. Markings to Romans 7:23 in Hardy's 1861 Bible (DCM). I am deeply grateful to Dr Timothy Hands for sharing with me his comprehensive transcription of Hardy's markings and annotations in his religious books.
7. Sarah Headley to Richard Purdy, 26 May 1957 (Yale).

CHAPTER 26

1. TH to MH, *CL*, 10 Feb 1863.
2. TH to MH, *CL*, 19 Feb 1863.
3. MH to TH, 28 Nov 1862.

4. TH to MH, *CL*, 19 Feb 1863.
5. *LW*, p. 42.
6. Recorded by Blomfield's own nephew (RG1, p. 57).
7. *The Memoirs of Cora Pearl: The English Beauty of the French Empire* (1886), quoted, Joanna Richardson, *The Courtesans: The Demi-monde in Nineteenth-century France* (1967), pp. 28–9.
8. *LW*, p. 45.
9. *IR*, p. 171.

CHAPTER 27

1. MH Diary (DCM).
2. Millgate and Mottram, 'Sisters', p. 8.
3. TH Obituary for MH (DCM).
4. MH Diary (DCM).
5. *LW*, p. 53.
6. *LW*, p. 49.
7. 'Schools of Painting Notebook', *PN*, pp. 105–14. Recycled into the 'Indiscretion' short story: 'Rubens for his sensuous women . . . Romney was greater than Reynolds because Lady Hamilton was his model, and thereby hung a tale' – *An Indiscretion in the Life of an Heiress and other Stories*, ed. Pamela Dalziel (1994), p. 81.
8. TH to MH, 19 Dec 1863.
9. Ibid.
10. Millgate and Mottram, 'Sisters', p. 9.
11. *LW*, p. 49.
12. Ibid.
13. To Edmund Gosse, *CL*, 2 Nov 1883.
14. Dennis Taylor, 'Hardy's Copy of *The Golden Treasury*', *Victorian Poetry*, 37:2 (1999), pp. 165–91 (p. 165).
15. Moule to TH, 2 Mar 1863, 2 July 1863, 21 Feb 1864 (DCM).

CHAPTER 28

1. His elliptical marking against a passage in Hebrews: quoted, Michael Millgate and Stephen Mottram, 'Eliza Bright Nicholls: New Source, Old Problems', *The Thomas Hardy Journal*, 26 (Autumn 2010), p. 29.
2. See Sarah Headley materials, Purdy Collection, Yale (GEN MSS III, Series IV, Box 17, Folder 549).

3. *LW*, p. 47.

4. DCM.

5. Between 1865–7, there are no annotations, which biographers have concluded led to a loss of his faith.

6. Noted in MM, p. 82.

7. Sarah Headley confirmed this to Purdy (Yale).

8. Thomas Hardy's 'Studies, Specimens &c.' Notebook, ed. Pamela Dalziel and Michael Millgate (1994). See also Dalziel, 'Hardy's Sexual Evasions: The Evidence of Studies, Specimens &c. Notebook', *Victorian Poetry*, 31:2 (1993), pp. 143–55.

9. Annotation to 'For lo, I raise up the Chaldeans, that bitter and hasty nation, which shall march through the breadth of the land, to possess the dwelling places that are not theirs' (Habakkuk 1:6).

10. Annotation to 'Oh Lord, how long shall I cry, and thou wilt not hear! even cry out unto thee of violence' (Habakkuk 1:2).

11. *Studies, Specimens Notebook*, p. 62.

12. *Golden Treasury*, Book First, poem XVI.

13. *LW*. p. 50.

14. Journal Note, 2 June 1865 (*LW*, p. 52).

15. Review in *The Morning Chronicle* of Etty's *Youth on the Prow, and Pleasure at the Helm* (1832), now in Tate Britain.

16. See Phyllis Bartlett, 'Hardy's Shelley', *Keats-Shelley Journal*, 4 (1955), pp. 15–29.

17. P. B. Shelley, *The Revolt of Islam* (1818, originally published as *Laon and Cythna*, 1817), Canto II, stanza xxiii.

18. See Bartlett, pp. 16–17.

19. E. M. Forster was a great admirer of Meredith. *The Ordeal of Richard Feverel* is the novel that Leonard Bast tells Margaret is a beautiful book; Bast also quotes lines from *Modern Love*.

CHAPTER 29

1. *LW*, pp. 52–3.

2. TH to MH, 28 Oct 1865.

3. TH to MH, July 1866.

4. *LW*, p. 53.

5. *LW*, p. 55.

6. TH to MH, July 1866.

7. MH to TH (DCM).

8. To J. W. Mackail, 13 Aug 1916.
9. *LW*, p. 54.
10. Quoted, RG1, p. 98.
11. *CP*, p. 235.
12. *CP*, pp. 199–201.

CHAPTER 30
1. Letter from Sarah Headley to Richard Purdy, 29 Dec 1956 (Yale).
2. *CP*, pp. 11–12.
3. *CP*, p. 7.
4. *CP*, pp. 902–3.
5. *Modern Love* (1862), sonnet xvii.
6. *CP*, p. 15.
7. *CP*, p. 15.
8. *CP*, pp. 15–16.
9. *CP*, p. 16.
10. *CP*, p. 12 (Hardy's ellipsis).
11. *LW*, p. 53.
12. To Edmund Gosse, 30 Aug 1887.
13. *CP*, pp. 9, 14.
14. *Wessex Poems and other Verses* (1898), p. viii.

CHAPTER 31
1. Millgate and Mottram, 'Sisters', p. 12.
2. Ibid.
3. Ibid, p. 14.
4. Ibid, p. 15.
5. *LW*, p. 57.
6. *LW*, p. 58.
7. See Deacon, *Providence and Mr Hardy*, p. 32.
8. Ibid, p. 33.
9. Tryphena (signing herself 'Triffie') to James Sparks, 23 Aug 1869 (Eton).
10. *CP*, p. 296.
11. Note (DCM), cited, MM, p. 100.
12. *LW*, p. 59.

CHAPTER 32
1. Cited, Paula Byrne, *The Real Jane Austen: A Life in Small Things* (2013), p. 313.
2. *PMN*, pp. 35–6.
3. *Desperate Remedies* (1871), vol. 1, chapter 2.
4. *LW*, p. 59.
5. *LW*, p. 65.
6. *CP*, pp. 499–501.
7. *LW*, p. 64.
8. *LW* p. 65.
9. *LW*, p. 419.
10. *LW*, p. 66.
11. Deacon, *Providence*, p. 34.

CHAPTER 33
1. *LW*, p. 65.
2. *LW*, p. 60.
3. *LW*, pp. 60–63.
4. *Return of the Native*, chapter X.
5. *CP*, pp. 158–9.

CHAPTER 34
1. Nathaniel Sparks Jr, note dated 7 Nov 1955 (Eton).
2. FH to Henry Reed and KH cited by I. Cooper Willis (see MM, p. 98).
3. *CL*, TH to Mrs Smith, 6 Jan 1874.
4. Harold Hoffman was the first to discover the existence of Catherine Pole. He interviewed various people who confirmed the relationship. His papers were lost and then rediscovered by Michael Rabiger. See Rabiger, 'The Hoffman Papers', *Thomas Hardy Yearbook*, 10 (1981), pp. 20–24.
5. Stephen Mottram, 'Thomas Hardy and Cassie Pole', *The Hardy Society Journal*, 7:2 (2011), pp. 69–73.
6. *CP*, p. 450–51.
7. *LW*, p. 284.
8. Vere H. Collins, *Talks with Thomas Hardy at Max Gate* (1928), p. 24.
9. *CP*, pp. 499–501.
10. *CP*, p. 223.

11. *CP*, p. 230.
12. *Desperate Remedies*, III. i.
13. Ibid.
14 Mottram, 'Cassie Pole', p. 69.
15. *CP*, p. 224.
16. FH, typescript, 'Notes of Thomas Hardy's Life', p. 29 (DCM).

CHAPTER 35
1. *SR*, p. 14.
2. *SR*, p. 1.
3. *SR*, p. 41.
4. *SR*, p. 3.
5. *SR*, p. 20.
6. *SR*, p. 12.
7. *SR*, pp. 3–4, slightly misquoting Coleridge's poem 'Youth and Age'.
8. *SR*, p. 4.
9. *SR*, p. 6.
10. *SR*, p. 9.
11. *SR*, p. 21.
12. *SR*, p. 25.
13. *SR*, p. 24.

CHAPTER 36
1. *Records of the British and Foreign Schools Society*, quoted, Pamela Horn, *Education in Rural England, 1800–1914* (1978), p. 94.
2. Frances Widdowson, *Going up into the Next Class: Women and Elementary Teacher Training*, 1840–1914 (1980), p. 47.
3. Quoted, Mary Sturt, *The Education of the People: A History of Primary Education* (2013), p. 369.
4. Quoted, Widdowson, p. 49.
5. Ibid.
6. Deacon, *Providence*, p. 51.
7. *CP*, pp. 781–2.
8. Ibid.

CHAPTER 37
1. *LW*, p. 77.
2. *SR*, p. 30.

3. *SR*, p. 32.
4. *SR*, p. 31.
5. *LW*, p. 76.
6. *LW*, p. 78.
7. *LW*, p. 74.
8. *CP*, pp. 350–51.
9. *LW*, p. 78.
10. *LW*, p. 78.
11. *CP*, p. 433.
12. *SR*, pp. 55, 33.
13. *SR*, p. 34n.
14. *CP*, p. 312.

CHAPTER 38
1. *CP*, pp. 17–18.
2. *CP*, pp. 335–7.
3. *CP*, pp. 321–2.
4. TH Bible (DCM).
5. *PN*, Notebook entry dated 30 Oct 1870.
6. Cited, MM, pp. 116–17.
7. MM, p. 121.
8. *LEF*, EH to TH, 24? Oct 1870.
9. Quoted, R. L. Purdy, *Thomas Hardy: A Bibliographical Study* (1968), p. 5.

CHAPTER 39
1. *The Athenaeum*, 1 April 1881.
2. *Desperate Remedies*, vol. 1, chapter 1.
3. Ibid.
4. Vol. 1, chapter 6.
5. Vol. 1, chapter 6.
6. Vol. 1, chapter 6.
7. Vol. 1, chapter 6.
8. Vol. 1, chapter 2.
9. Vol. 1, chapter 3.
10. *LW*, p. 85.

CHAPTER 40

1. TH to Tinsley, 20 October 1871.
2. *CP*, pp. 315–17.
3. *CP*, p. 479.
4. *LW*, p. 89.
5. *LW*, p. 89.
6. *SR*, p. 37.
7. 'The Maid on the Shore' (MS in DCM).
8. 'The Maid on the Shore', p. 6.
9. *LW*, p. 89.
10. *LW*, p. 87.
11. The *Athenaeum* gave a generous review, especially approving the love element. The *Pall Mall Gazette* praised its originality and freshness. Horace Moule gave a long and appreciative review in the *Saturday Review* (though it was delayed until September). What the reviews had in common was criticism of the rural characters' dialogue, which all the reviewers felt was overly grand. The *Pall Mall Gazette* complained: 'the humble heroes and heroines of the tale are much too shrewd, and say too many good things to be truthful representations of their prototypes in real life'. Even Horace Moule, in the *Saturday Review*, suggested that the author had allowed his country folk to 'express themselves in the language of the author's manner of thought, rather than in their own'. See MM, p. 130.

CHAPTER 41

1. *Under the Greenwood Tree*, chapter 7.
2. Ibid, chapter 8.
3. Ibid.
4. TH, Preface to 1912 edition.
5. As recounted in Lillie May Francis, *Memories of the Hardy and Hand Families* (1968).
6. *IR*, p. 36.
7. School Log Books Plymouth, cited, Deacon, *Providence*, p. 41.
8. As told by her daughter, Eleanor, to Deacon, *Providence*, p. 40.
9. The average salary for her labouring relatives was £25.
10. Sparks Papers, Eton, cited, RG1, p. 148.

11. Quoted, *Thomas Hardy: Family History*, ed. Norman Page (5 vols, 1999), 4. 41.
12. Deacon, *Providence*, p. 43.
13. Notebook fragment (DCM), cited, MM, p. 124.
14. Part the First, chapter 7.
15. Part the Second, chapter 6.
16. Part the First, chapter 3.
17. Part the First, chapters 7, 8.
18. Part the Third, chapter 4.
19. Part the Fourth, chapter 7.
20. Part the Fifth, chapter 2.
21. Gifford, p. 154.

CHAPTER 42
1. *A Pair of Blue Eyes*, chapter XXIX.
2. Ibid.
3. Deacon, *Providence*, p. 43.
4. Cited, MM, p. 131.
5. Cited, RG1, p. 161.
6. *CP*, p. 517.
7. Vere H. Collins, *Talks with Thomas Hardy at Max Gate 1920–1922* (1928, repr. 1978), p. 26.
8. *CP*, p. 436.
9. *CP*, pp. 676–7.

CHAPTER 43
1. See Phillip Mallett, 'Leslie Stephen's Bad Five Minutes In the Alps', *The Hardy Society Journal*, 10:2 (Summer 2014), pp. 58–84.
2. *Blue Eyes*, chapter XXII.
3. *Blue Eyes*, chapter I.
4. *Blue Eyes*, chapter VIII.
5. *Blue Eyes*, chapter XIX.
6. *Blue Eyes*, chapter VII.
7. *Blue Eyes*, chapter XIII.
8. Ibid.
9. *Blue Eyes*, chapter VII.
10. *Blue Eyes*, chapter XXXVIII.
11. *Blue Eyes*, chaps. XXXVII, XXXVIII.

12. *Blue Eyes*, chapter XXXIX.
13. Quoted, *Thomas Hardy: Family History*, 4. 90.
14. Moule to TH, 21 May 1873 (DCM).

CHAPTER 44
1. Coroner's Inquest, cited, MM, p. 141.
2. *LW*, p. 96.
3. *CP*, p. 887.
4. See, for example, William E. Buckler, 'The Hardy-Moule Affair with a Reading of Four Hardy Poems', *Biography*, 5:2 (1982), pp. 136–42.
5. *CP*, pp. 12–13.
6. See Evelyn Hardy, 'Thomas Hardy and Horace Moule: Vindication of a Suicide', *Times Literary Supplement*, 23 Jan 1969, p. 89.
7. See MM, pp. 153–6.
8. *LW*, p. 96.
9. *LW*, p. 98.
10. As reported in *Cambridge Chronicle*, 27 Sept 1873.
11. H. C. C. Moule to Terry Coleman, 15 June 1965, in Deacon, *Providence*, p. 95.
12. *CP*, pp. 821–2.
13. DCM.
14. *LW,* p. 98.

CHAPTER 45
1. *Thomas Hardy's Public Voice*, pp. 260–61.
2. *LW*, p. 97.
3. *LW*, p. 97.
4. *LW*, p. 99.
5. *SR.* p. 36.
6. *LW*, pp. 98–9.
7. *LW*, p. 99.
8. *LW*, p. 99.
9. *LW*, p. 100.
10. EH to TH, July 1874 (DCM).
11. TH to Edmund Gosse, 25 July 1906.
12. *CP*, p. 621.
13. *Blue Eyes*, chapter X.

CHAPTER 46

1. *SR*, p. 37.
2. *EHD*, p. 21.
3. *EHD*, p. 22.
4. *EHD*, p. 22.
5. *LW*, TH to Henry Hardy, 18 September 1874.
6. *EHD*, p. 23.
7. *EHD*, p. 25.
8. *EHD*, p. 26.
9. *EHD*, p. 27.
10. *EHD*, p. 29.
11. *EHD*, p. 32.
12. *EHD*, p. 40.
13. *EHD*, p. 40.
14. *LW*, p. 104.
15. *EHD*, p. 54.

CHAPTER 47

1. *Far from the Madding Crowd*, chapter III.
2. Chapter IV.
3. Originally, Hardy conceived the idea of two suitors, a shepherd and a cavalryman. Boldwood was a later addition.
4. Chapter X.
5. Chapter IV.
6. See Briony A. K. McDonagh, 'Women, Enclosure and Estate Improvement in Eighteenth-Century Northamptonshire', *Rural History*, 20:2 (2009), pp. 143–62.
7. Chapter XIX.
8. Chapters XXIV, XXV.
9. Chapter XXVII.
10. Chapter XXVIII.
11. *LW*, p. 101. See also, Leslie Stephen to TH, 12 March 1874 (DCM).
12. The omission is restored for the Oxford World Classics' edition, chapter XLIII.
13. Chapter XXXVI.
14. *LW*, p. 100.
15. *LW*, p. 101.

16. *LW*, p. 103.
17. Chapter XXXIV.
18. Chapter XLI.
19. Ibid.
20. Chapter XLIII.
21. Chapter XXVII. On the real-life cavalry and infantry sword exercise, see further https://www.bl.uk/collection-items/sword-exercises.
22. Chapter LV.
23. '[Review of] *Far from the Madding Crowd*', *The Nation*, Dec 1874, repr. in Henry James, *Literary Criticism* (Library of America, 1984), pp. 1043–8.

CHAPTER 48

1. *Madding Crowd*, chaps. LI, XVIII.
2. *LW*, p. 104.
3. *LW*, p. 104.
4. *CL*, TH to Macquoid, 17 Nov 1874.
5. Macquoid to TH, 18 Nov 1874. https://hardycorrespondents.exeter.ac.uk/text.html?id=dhe-hl-h.4152.
6. *The Times*, 4 Jan 1875, p. 4.
7. *LW*, p. 105.
8. Hutton to TH, 23 Dec 1874 (DCM).
9. *LW*, p. 105.
10. *CL*, TH to George Smith, Spring 1875.
11. *EHD*, p. 56.
12. KH MSS (DCM).
13. *CP*, pp. 428–9.
14. *EHD*, p. 64.
15. *EHD*, p. 63.
16. *EHD*, pp. 66–7.
17. Letter of 26 Nov 1876 (DCM).
18. *EHD*, p. 60.
19. *EHD*, pp. 61–2.
20. *LW*, p. 110.
21. Preface to 1895 edition.
22. *Hand of Ethelberta*, chapter I.
23. Chapter VII.

24. Chapter VIII.
25. Chapter II.
26. Chapter XXIII.
27. Chapter XVII.
28. Chapter XLVI.
29. 'Sequel' [closing chapter].
30. Chapter XI.
31. Chapter XXI.
32. Chapter XXV.
33. *CP*, pp. 71–4.
34. *LW*, p. 111.
35. *LW*, pp. 111–12.
36. *EHD*, p. 80.
37. *EHD*, p. 83.
38. *LW*, p. 113
39. *LW*, p. 114.
40. *EHD*, p. 90.
41. *EHD*, p. 93.
42. *EHD*, pp. 100–101.
43. *EHD*, p. 101.
44. *EHD*, p. 103.
45. *LW*, p. 114.

CHAPTER 49
 1. *LW*, p. 115.
 2. Ibid.
 3. *PMN*, p. 4.
 4. *LW*, p. 117.
 5. *LW*, p. 122.
 6. *CP*, p. 482.
 7. *LW*, p. 116.
 8. Preface to *The Return of the Native*.
 9. Book the First, chapter III.
10. I. vii.
11. II. iii.
12. III. iii.
13. Ibid.
14. IV. vi.

15. There is also a structural influence of Shakespearean tragedy: the novel is divided into five books, like the five acts of a play (with a brief sixth book, 'Aftercourses', serving as epilogue), with each chapter being like a scene.
16. IV. vi.
17. V. i.
18. V. iii.
19. VI. iv.
20. *LW*, p. 118.
21. Ibid.
22. Ibid.
23. *LW*, p. 119.
24. *LW*, p. 122.
25. III. vi.
26. V. vii.
27. III. ii.
28. *LW*, p. 121.
29. V. i.
30. *CP*, pp. 482–3.
31. *LW*, p. 128.
32. *LW*, p. 125.
33. *LW*, p. 127.
34. *LW*, p. 139.
35. Hardy's quotation of one of his favourite poems, Wordsworth's 'Ode: Intimations of Immortality from Recollections of Early Childhood'.
36. *CP*, p. 466.

CHAPTER 50
1. *PN*, p. 21.
2. *LW*, p. 131.
3. *LW*, p. 141.
4. *LW*, pp. 142–3.
5. *LW*, p. 145.
6. *LW*, p. 150.
7. Book the First, chapter XI.
8. II. vi.
9. II. vii.

10. VI. v.
11. IV. ii.

CHAPTER 51

1. *LW*, p. 151.
2. Ibid.
3. *LW*, p. 152.
4. *CP*, p. 152.
5. MH to EH, 28 Jan 1881 (DCM).
6. Millgate and Mottram, 'Sisters', p. 17.
7. Quoted, Anne Johns and Jenny Head, *Mary and Kate Hardy: Salisbury, Wessex and Beyond* (2022), p. 82.
8. MH to EH, 28 Jan 1881 (DCM).
9. MM, p. 200.
10. *LW*, p. 154.
11. KH to EH (DCM).
12. *PN*, p. 19.
13. Chapter I.
14. Chaps. I–IV.
15. Chapter IV.
16. Chapter VI.
17. Chapter XIV.

CHAPTER 52

1. *LW*, p. 160.
2. *LW*, p. 167.
3. Havelock Ellis, 'Thomas Hardy's Novels', *Westminster Review*, April 1883, pp. 334–64.
4. *CL*, TH to Havelock Ellis, 29 April 1883.
5. Gosse to his wife Nellie, quoted, MM, p. 443.
6. Cited, Trish Ferguson, 'Trial and Error in Thomas Hardy's Legal Fictions', *The Thomas Hardy Journal*, 24 (Autumn 2008), pp. 91–105.
7. *Mayor of Casterbridge*, chapter I.
8. Chapter V.
9. Chapter XXXIII.
10. Chapter XX.
11. Chaps. IV, XVII, XXX.

12. Chapter XIV.
13. Chapter XLV.
14. Chapter XXIV.
15. Chapter XLV.

CHAPTER 53
1. *LW*, p. 171.
2. *LW*, pp. 176–7.
3. *LW*, p. 177.
4. *CL*, TH to EH, 13 March 1885.
5. *CL*, 11 May 1885.
6. *LW*, p. 179.
7. *LW*, p. 178.
8. Fanny to her mother-in-law and to Sidney Colvin, Sept 1885, in *The Letters of Robert Louis Stevenson*, ed. by Bradford A. Booth and Ernest Mehew, vol. V (1995), p. 125.
9. *LW*, p. 182.
10. See Alan Manford, 'Who Wrote Thomas Hardy's Novels? (A Survey of Emma Hardy's Contribution to the Manuscripts of her Husband's Novels)', *The Thomas Hardy Journal*, 6:2 (1990), pp. 84–97.
11. Chapter XXXVII.
12. *The Woodlanders*, chapter II.
13. Chapter VIII.
14. Quoted, Carl Weber, 'Hardy and *The Woodlanders*', *Review of English Studies*, 15:59 (1939), pp. 330–33 (p. 333).
15. Ibid.
16. Rebekah Owen, cited, Weber, p. 332.
17. Chapter XXVI.
18. Chapter XLVIII.
19. Ibid.

CHAPTER 54
1. *EHD*, p. 138.
2. *EHD*, p. 144.
3. *EHD*, p. 130.
4. *EHD*, p. 113.
5. *EHD*, p. 193.

6. *LW*, p. 209.

7. *ORFW*, p. 46.

8. *LW*, p. 219.

9. Quoted, *MM*, p. 251.

10. Raymond Blathwayt, 'A Chat with the Author of *Tess*', *Black and White*, 4 (27 August 1892), pp. 238–40, repr. in *Thomas Hardy Remembered*, p. 13.

11. *LW*, pp. 162–3.

12. Journal, 3 Sept 1887 (*LW*, p. 211).

13. *LW*, pp. 223–4.

14. *CL*, 24 Dec 1888.

15. *LW*, p. 231.

16. *CL*, TH to James Osgood, 4 Aug 1889.

17. Blathwayt, in *Thomas Hardy Remembered*, pp. 12–13.

18. Gittings suggests the former and Millgate the latter.

19. *LW*, pp. 226–9.

20. *LW*, p. 230.

21. Ibid.

22. *IR*, p. 26.

23. See 'Clive Holland' [the journalist C. J. Hankinson, who interviewed Hardy on several occasions], *Thomas Hardy, O.M.: The Man, His Works and the Land of Wessex* (1966), p. 237.

24. To Blathwayt, in *Thomas Hardy Remembered*, p. 13.

25. Gwen Ffrangcon-Davies, in *Thomas Hardy Remembered*, p. 292.

26. *CP*, p. 139.

27. *Tess of the D'Urbervilles*, chapter XIV.

28. Chapter XXIV.

29. Chapter XXXVI.

30. Chapter XXXIX.

31. Chapter V.

32. Chapter XXIV.

33. Chapter XLII.

34. Chapter V.

35. *Saturday Review*, 16 Jan 1892, pp. 73–4.

36. Chapter V.

37. *Tess in the Theatre: Two Dramatizations of Tess of the D'Urbervilles*, ed. Marguerite Roberts (2019), p. 7.

38. Ibid, p. 19.
39. See the full account of textual variants in the 'History of the Text', Notes and Appendices to the Penguin edition, *Tess of the D'Urbervilles*, ed. Tim Dolin (2008).
40. Chapter XI.
41. Chapter XII.
42. Chapter XXXIV.
43. Chapter XXXV.
44. Ibid.
45. *Tess in the Theatre*, p. 52.
46. Ibid, p. 61.
47. Ibid, pp. 68–9.

CHAPTER 55

1. *LW*, p. 234.
2. Ibid.
3. Deacon, *Providence*, pp. 48–9.
4. Ibid, p. 55.
5. Ibid, p. 65.
6. *LW*, p. 234.
7. *LW*, p. 235.

CHAPTER 56

1. The term seems to have been coined by Charles Reade in his novel *A Woman Hater* (1877).
2. When Alfred Austin died in 1913, Hardy said that his vote would be for Alice Meynell: 'there was no reason why a woman should make a worse Laureate than a man' (*Thomas Hardy Remembered*, p. 189).
3. M. Robinson to Irene Cooper Willis, 17 Dec 1937 (DCM).
4. Ibid.
5. Mowbray Morris to TH, 25 Nov 1889 (DCM).
6. *Pall Mall Gazette*, 31 Dec 1891; *Quarterly Review*, April 1892. See further, James Gibson, 'The writing, publication and initial critical reception of *Tess*', in his *Tess of the D'Urbervilles by Thomas Hardy* (1986).
7. *LW*, p. 258.
8. See Talia Schaffer, 'Malet the Obscure: Thomas Hardy, "Lucas

Malet" and the literary politics of early modernism', *Women's Writing*, 3:3 (1996), pp. 261–85.

9. M. Robinson to Irene Cooper Willis, 17 Dec 1937 (DCM).
10. Cited, MM, p. 288. Even the pleasant Millgate calls her lacking in poise and wit, and without beauty or style.
11. *LW*, p. 257.
12. *LW*, p. 259.
13. *LW*, p. 249.
14. See MM, p. 283.
15. *CL*, 6 Oct 1889.
16. *CL*, 30 Dec 1891.
17. *LW*, p. 257.

CHAPTER 57
1. *LW*, p. 270.
2. *LW*, p. 274.
3. *ORFW*, pp. xvii-xviii.
4. *CL*, TH to FH, 7 June 1893.
5. *CL*, 10 June 1893.
6. *CL*. 20 June 1893.
7. *CL*, 29 June 1893.
8. *CL*, 29 June 1893.
9. *LW*, p. 273.
10. *CL*, TH to FH, 2 July 1893.
11. Hardy's annotations and the possible influence of Egerton's short stories on *Jude the Obscure* are quoted and discussed in Shanta Dutta, 'Sue's "Obscure" Sisters', *The Thomas Hardy Journal*, 12:2 (May 1996), pp. 60–71.
12. *CL*, 13 July 1893.
13. *CL*, TH to Florence Henniker, 16 July 1893.
14. *CL*, TH to FH, 18 July 1893.
15. *CL*, 20 July 1893.
16. *CP*, pp. 719–20, 68–9.
17. *CL*, 17 Aug 1893.
18. *CL*, 16 Sept 1893.
19. Ibid.
20. *CL*, 6 Oct 1893.
21. 'An Imaginative Woman' was added by Hardy to the 1896

reprinting of his collection of short stories *Wessex Tales* (originally 1888), then transferred by him to the 1912 reprinting of his later collection *Life's Little Ironies* (originally 1894). It is most readily available in the World's Classics edition of *Life's Little Ironies*, pp. 7–32, from which all the quotations above are taken.

CHAPTER 58

1. KH to EH, 1882 (DCM).
2. Preface to first edition of *Jude the Obscure* (1895).
3. *CL*, 22 Oct 1893.
4. *LW*, p. 262.
5. *LW*, pp. 272–3.
6. *LW*, p. 216.
7. *LEF*, 20 Aug 1899.
8. *LW*, pp. 273–4.
9. *LW*, p. 257.
10. *LEF*, 20 Aug 1899.
11. *LW*, p. 248.
12. TH to FH, 18 Dec 1893.
13. TH to FH, 15 Jan 1894.
14. TH to Gosse, 20 Nov 1895.
15. TH to FH, 10 Sept 1893.
16. TH to Gosse, 10 Nov 1895.
17. *Jude the Obscure*, I-ii, I-xi.
18. *Jude*, II-iv.
19. I-xi.
20. I-ii.
21. I-iii.
22. I-vi.
23. I-x, I-xi.
24. TH to FH, 12 Aug 1895.
25. *Jude*, II-vi.
26. III-iv.
27. III-vii.
28. III-vi.
29. IV-iii, V-iv.
30. IV-v, IV-ii.
31. IV-v, III-ix, IV-ii.

32. III-ix, III-i.
33. III-iii.
34. III-i.
35. III-ii, III-iii.
36. III-iv.
37. V-v, IV-iv.
38. William Archer, *Real Conversations* (1904), pp. 40–41.
39. MS of *Jude* (Fitzwilliam Museum, Cambridge), fo. 149, cited, MM, p. 323.
40. *CP*, p. 62.

CHAPTER 59
1. *LEF*, p. 78.
2. CP, pp. 652–3. See further, Stephen Mottram, 'Hardy, Emma and the Giffords, A Re-Appraisal: *Some Recollections* Revisited', *The Hardy Society Journal*, 8:1 (2012), pp. 24–46.
3. The International Copyright Act (known as the Chace Act) ensured that British authors received payment for American publication of their work.
4. *CL*, TH to EH, 8 May 1895.
5. *LW*, p. 281.
6. *LW*, pp. 280–81.
7. *LW*, p. 265.
8. *LW*, p. 248.
9. TH to Henniker, 3 Sept 1895.
10. 'The local paper', quoted, *LW*, p. 286.
11. *CP*, p. 878.
12. *CL*, TH to Henniker, 11 Sept 1895.
13. 'Why Women Do Not Want the Ballot', by the Bishop of Albany, N.Y., in the *North American Review*, September 1895.
14. *CL*, TH to Agnes Grove, 3 Nov 1895.
15. *CL*, TH to Agnes Grove, 7 Nov 1895.
16. *CL*, TH to Edmund Gosse, 10 Nov 1895.
17. *CL*, TH to Henniker, 10 Nov 1895.
18. *LW*, p. 287.
19. *Pall Mall Gazette*, 12 Nov 1895. The reviewer summarised the novel as a story in which the reader finds 'infants hanging each other with box-cord on little pegs all round the room . . . and they all lived unhappily ever after, except Jude'.

20. *The World*, 13 (Nov 1895). Hardy wrote to a friend: 'Did you see that *The World* nearly fainted away, & the *Pall Mall* went into fits over the story?' (*CL*, 20 Nov 1895). A wide selection of reviews are gathered in R. G. Cox's valuable *Thomas Hardy: The Critical Heritage* (1979).

21. *LW*, p. 288.

22. Gordon Gifford, 'The First Mrs Thomas Hardy', *Times Literary Supplement*, 1 Jan 1944, p. 7.

23. *LEF*, 19 Feb 1897, to Rebekah Owen.

24. Sutro, *Celebrities and Simple Souls* (1933), p. 58.

25. T. P. O'Connor, quoting from a letter from Dr Frederick B. Fisher (1928), in *Thomas Hardy Remembered*, p. 99.

26. *CL*, TH to Lady Jeune, 17 Nov 1895.

27. *CL*, TH to Agnes Grove, 20 Nov 1895.

28. *CL*, TH to Henniker, 30 Nov 1895.

29. Egerton to TH, 22 Nov 1895 (DCM).

30. *CL*, 20 Nov 1895.

31. *LEF*, EH to Mary Haweis, 13 Nov 1894.

32. Ibid.

CHAPTER 60

1. EH to MH, *LEF*, 22 Feb 1896.

2. *LW*, p. 298.

3. TH to EH, 3 Feb 1896.

4. *CL*, TH to Agnes Grove, 25 Aug 1896.

5. *LW*, pp. 300–301.

6. *CL*, TH to Grant Allen, 7 Jan 1896.

7. *LW*, p. 316.

8. TH to KH, 18 June 1897.

9. TH to KH, 7 Aug 1897.

10. TH to KH, May 1898.

11. *LW*, p. 302.

12. *LEF*, 19 Feb 1897.

13. Carl J. Weber, *Hardy and the Lady from Madison Square* (1952), p. 61.

14. Ibid, p. 67.

15. Ibid, p. 68.

16. Ibid, p. 70.

17. EH to Owen, 19 Feb 1897.

18. EH to Owen, 14 Feb 1899.

19. *LW*, p. 322.

20. *Wessex Poems and other Verses* (1898), pp. 39–41.

21. *CP*, p. 17, following text of *Collected Poems* (1920). The revision was first made in *Selected Poems* (1916), p. 21.

22. *CP*, p. 57.

23. *LEF*, p. 19.

24. DCM, undated, 1899?, cited, MM, p. 365.

25. EH to Rebekah Owen, 24 April 1899 (Thomas Hardy Collection, Colby College, not in *LEF*).

26. *CP*, pp. 217–19.

27. EH to Owen, 24 April 1899.

28. EH to Owen, 14 Feb 1899.

29. Ibid.

30. EH to Elspeth Grahame, 20 Aug 1899.

31. EH to Louise MacCarthy, 3 Nov 1902.

32. See *LEF*, p. 17 and note.

33. EH to Owen, 27 Dec 1899.

34. EH to Owen, May 1900.

35. *CP*, pp. 90–91.

36. To Clodd, 27 March 1897.

37. See note to *LEF*, p. 12.

38. *LEF*, 2 Sept 1901.

39. To Owen, 4 April 1901.

40. *The Sphere*, 14 April 1900, p. 393.

41. *The Academy*, 27 April 1901, p. 355.

42. TH to EH, 6 Nov 1900.

43. TH to EH, 11 Dec 1900.

44. *Lady from Madison Square*, p. 136.

45. Ibid, p. 133.

46. Ibid, pp. 36–7.

47. 1900 was considered the last year of the old century, 1 January 1901 the beginning of the new one.

48. EH to Owen, 31 Dec 1900 (Colby College, not in *LEF*).

49. *CP*, p. 150. The idea of the restoring power of nature entering the poet 'unawares' is a classic example of Hardy's debt to

Wordsworth, who uses the same word in several of his greatest poems, such as 'There was a boy'.

50. *PN*, p. 27.
51. Larkin, 'High Windows' (1974).
52. EH to Owen, 4 March 1902.

CHAPTER 61

1. FH to Lady Hoare, 6 Dec 1914.
2. Paulin, *Thomas Hardy: The Poetry of Perception* (1975), p. 128.
3. *CP*, pp. 319–20. First published in *Satires of Circumstance* (1914). Hardy's original intention was for it to be the opening poem – see Richard L. Purdy, *Thomas Hardy: A Bibliographical Study* (2002), p. 162.
4. *CP*, p. 169.
5. *CL*, TH to Sydney Cockerell, 3 June 1917.
6. Nevinson, *Changes and Chances* (1924), p. 308.
7. *LEF*, 3 Nov 1902.
8. Sparks (Eton), quoted, MM, p. 383.
9. M. E. Bath, 'Thomas Hardy and Evangeline F. Smith', *Thomas Hardy Yearbook*, 4 (1973–4), p. 44.
10. Quoted, T. P. O'Connor, 'Men, Women, and Memories: Thomas Hardy's Funeral', *Sunday Times*, 22 Jan 1928, p. 13.
11. *SR*, pp. 14–15.
12. MH to Nathaniel Sparks Sr, Nov 1903 (DCM).
13. *CL*, 19 Oct 1903.
14. *CL*, 20 March 1904.
15. *CL*, 12 April 1904.
16. *CP*, p. 270.
17. *LW*, p. 345.

CHAPTER 62

1. *SR*, p. 19.
2. *SR*, p 10.
3. *The Collected Letters of George Gissing Volume 5 1892–1895*, ed. Paul F. Mattheisen, Arthur C. Young, and Pierre Coustillas (1994), 22 September 1895, p. 27.
4. Ibid, p. 28.
5. Ibid, p. 30.

6. B. Newcombe to N. Gosse, 8 March 1900 (DCM).

7. *IR*, pp. 46–7.

8. *SR*, p. 14.

9. *IR*, p. 41.

10. *IR*, pp. 32–3.

11. *IR*, p. 33.

12. *IR*, pp. 33–4.

13. FH to Rebekah Owen, 21 March 1916? (Colby College, not in *LEF*).

14. *CP*, pp. 309–10.

15. TH to FH [i.e. Florence Dugdale], 2 Jan 1906.

16. FH to Carroll Wilson, 20 March 1937 (Yale GEN MSS III, Series V, Box 22, Folder 699).

17. TH to FH, 21 March 1907.

18. See https://research.library.kutztown.edu/cgi/viewcontent.cgi?article=1066&context=dracula-studies.

19. https://www.irishtimes.com/opinion/green-doors-green-fools-an-irishman-s-diary-on-the-literary-history-of-ely-place-in-dublin-1.2753095.

20. See further, Robert Gittings and Jo Manton, *The Second Mrs Hardy* (1979), pp. 38–45.

21. *LEF*, FH to Edward Clodd, 11 Nov 1910.

22. *CL*, TH to FH, 29 April 1907.

23. *CL*, TH to Macmillan, 8 July 1907.

24. *LEF*, EH to Clement Shorter, 15 Sept & 3 Oct 1904.

25. *LEF*, 23 Jan 1906.

CHAPTER 63

1. https://womanandhersphere.com/2012/11/21/kate-fryes-suffrage-diary-the-mud-march-9-february-1907/.

2. *LW*, p. 356.

3. Emma Hardy, 'Women and the Suffrage', *The Nation*, 9 May 1908, p. 189.

4. Sylvia Pankhurst, *The Suffragette: The History of the Women's Militant Suffrage Movement 1905–1910* (1911), p. 248.

5. *CL*, TH to Millicent Fawcett, 30 Nov 1906. Fawcett's reply, 4 Dec 1906 (DCM).

6. EH to Rebekah Owen, 26 Dec 1906.

7. *CL*, 9 July 1907.
8. *CL*, 26 Sept 1907.
9. *Cornhill Magazine*, 97 (1908), pp. 642–53.
10. Lady Grove, *The Social Fetich* (1907), p. v.
11. To Grove, 16 Aug 1907.
12. To Emma, 6 July 1908.
13. To Clodd, 1 May 1909.
14. To Clodd, 22 July 1909.
15. *CP*, p. 310.
16. *CP*, p. 221.
17. To Elspeth Grahame, 31 Aug 1907.
18. *CP*, p. 311.
19. FH to EH, 15 July 1910.
20. FH to EH, 18 Aug & 30 Sept 1910.
21. EH to Owen, 16 June 1908.
22. FH to EH, 30 Sept 1910.
23. EH to Lady Hoare, 24 April 1910.
24. FH to EH, 4 Oct 1910.
25. FH to KH, 20 Oct 1910.
26. TH to Clodd, 15 Nov 1910.
27. TH to Henniker, 9 Dec 1910.
28. FH to Clodd, 11 Nov 1910.

CHAPTER 64
1. FH to Clodd, 19 Nov 1910.
2. FH to EH, 11 Dec 1910.
3. FH to Owen, 10 Dec 1913.
4. FH to EH, 1 Dec 1910.
5. 'Spaces', p. 31 of the manuscript, printed in Jon Singleton, '*Spaces, Alleys* and other Lacunae: Emma Hardy's Late Writings Restored', *The Thomas Hardy Journal*, 31 (Autumn 2015), pp. 48–88.
6. FH to Clodd, 19 Nov 1910.
7. FH to Clodd, 3 Dec 1913.
8. Clodd's MS diary, 13 July 1913, quoted, MM, p. 452.
9. *LW*, p. 378.
10. FH to MH, 9 Aug 1911.
11. FH to Owen, 20 Mar 1914.
12. FH to Clodd, 11 Dec 1911.

13. TH to FH, Dec 1911.
14. FH to Lady Hoare, 22 July 1914 (but saying that he made the remark 'some years ago').
15. To Clodd, 16 Jan 1913.
16. *CP*, pp. 306–7.
17. *IR*, p. 99.
18. Cited, Beryl Baigent, '80 Years Ago in the Thomas Hardy Household', *The Thomas Hardy Journal*, 8:3 (1992), pp. 69–75 (p. 71).
19. Quoted, Martha Vicinus, *Women who Loved Women: 1778-1928* (2004), p. 95.
20. *IR*, p. 105.
21. *IR*, p. 106.
22. Ibid.
23. *IR*, pp. 108–9.
24. Ibid.
25. FH to Clodd, 11 March 1913.
26. FH to Clodd, 20 April 1913.
27. *IR*, p. 92.
28. FH to Clodd, 7 March 1913.
29. Anthony Fincham, 'Emma Hardy: The (Mad) Woman In The Attic?', *The Thomas Hardy Journal*, 22 (2006), pp. 105–15.
30. *The Diagnostic and Statistical Manual of Mental Disorders, Fifth Edition, Text Revision (DSM-5-TR)* (2022), p. 745.
31. *CP*, pp. 488–9.

CHAPTER 65
1. *Lady from Madison Square*, pp. 158–62.
2. *LW*, pp. 386–7.
3. Wilfrid Blunt Cockerell, *Cockerell: Sydney Carlyle Cockerell, friend of Ruskin and William Morris and Director of the Fitzwilliam Museum, Cambridge* (1965), p. 233.
4. Details and quotations from MM, p. 446 & Alice Harvey [née Gale], 'I was Emma Lavinia's Personal Maid', *Thomas Hardy Year Book*, 4 (1974), pp. 6–9.
5. *CL*, 12 Dec 1912.
6. FH to Clodd, 30 Jan 1913.
7. FH to Clodd, 7 March 1913.

8. FH to Clodd, 16 Jan 1913.
9. Ibid.
10. Ibid.
11. MH to her cousin Nat Sparks, 15 Feb 1913, Sparks Family Papers, Eton College Library MS 710 03/03.
12. FH to Clodd, 30 Jan 1913.
13. Ibid.
14. FH to Clodd, 7 March 1913.
15. Ibid.
16. Ibid.
17. *LW*, p. 389.
18. FH to Clodd, 11 March 1913.
19. *CL*, TH to FH, 9 March 1913.
20. *CL*, TH to Clodd, 3 Dec 1912.
21. *CL*, TH to Mary Sheridan, 13 Dec 1912.
22. *CL*, TH to Henniker, 17 Dec 1912.
23. Ibid.
24. FH to Clodd, 3 Dec 1913.
25. Ibid.
26. Ibid.
27. *CP*, p. 772, dated Aug 1913.

CHAPTER 66
1. April 1913 (DCM).
2. RG2, p. 159.
3. FH to Clodd, 1 Jan 1914.
4. Ibid.
5. FH to Ethel Richardson, 9 Feb 1914.
6. FH to Sydney and Kate Cockerell, 13 Feb 1914.
7. *CL*, TH to Henniker, 6 March 1914.
8. Robinson to TH, 12 Feb 1914 (DCM).
9. *Lady from Madison Square*, p. 171.
10. FH to Owen, 20 March 1914.
11. Clodd's MS diary, 13 July 1913, quoted, MM, p. 452.
12. *Cockerell*, p. 223. Cockerell was furious about this attack on the sisters and demanded that the passage be redacted from Pound's book *Kulchur*.
13. *LEF*, FH to Owen, 5 April 1914.

14. To Hoare, 22 July 1914.
15. Quoted, Angelique Richardson, 'Life behind the Gates: newly discovered letters from Thomas Hardy's wife Florence', *TLS*, 3 April 2020.
16. To Lady Hoare, 7 May 1914.
17. To Lady Hoare, 9 Dec 1914.
18. *CL*, TH to FH, 17 Feb 1914.
19. FH to Owen, 5 Sept 1914.
20. FH to Owen, 1 Dec 1914.
21. *CL*, TH to FH, 17 July 1914.
22. FH to Owen, 1 Dec 1914.

CHAPTER 67
1. 'After a Journey', *CP*, p. 349.
2. 'The Going', *CP*, p. 338.
3. *CP*, pp. 339–40.
4. 'I Found Her Out There', *CP*, pp. 342–3.
5. 'Without Ceremony', *CP*, p. 343; 'Lament', *CP*, p. 344.
6. 'The Voice', *CP*, p. 346.
7. *CP*, p. 350.
8. *CP*, pp. 357–8.
9. TH to Henniker, 17 July 1914.
10. FH to Lady Hoare, 6 Dec 1914.
11. FH to Hoare, 9 Dec 1914.
12. FH to Owen, 30 Dec 1915 (Colby College, not in *LEF*).
13. *LEF*, 20 June 1915.
14. FH to Lady Hoare, 30 Aug 1915.

CHAPTER 68
1. KH Diary, 23 Nov 1915 (DCM).
2. Ibid, 24 Nov.
3. FH to Rebekah Owen, 3 Dec 1915.
4. *CL*, 30 Nov 1915.
5. *CL*, TH to Cockerell, 5 Dec 1915.
6. *CP*, pp. 477–8.
7. *LW*, p. 402.
8. *CP*, pp. 508–9, 433–4.
9. *Southern Times*, clipping in Lock Collection (DCM).

10. KH Diary, 30 Dec 1915.
11. KH Diary, 29 Jan 1916.
12. KH Diary, 18 Jan 1916.
13. FL to Owen, 3 Dec 1915.
14. Ibid.
15. FH to Owen, 5 May 1915.
16. FH to Sydney Cockerell, 9 Sept 1916.
17. FH to Owen, 3 Dec 1915.
18. FH to Owen, 26 Oct 1916 (Colby, not in *LEF*).
19. FH to Owen, 3 Nov 1916.
20. FH to Cockerell, 10 Nov 1916.
21. FH to Owen, 3 Nov 1916.
22. FH to Cockerell, 10 Nov 1916.

CHAPTER 69
1. *LEF*, FH to Rebekah Owen, 1 Dec 1914.
2. *LW*, p. 405.
3. FH to Gertrude Bugler, 13 Dec 1916.
4. FH to Owen, 15 May 1916 (Colby, not in *LEF*).
5. FH to Owen, 5 June 1916 (Colby, not in *LEF*).
6. KH Diary, 25 March 1917 (DCM).
7. FH to Owen, 29 July 1917 (Colby, not in *LEF*).
8. FH to Owen, 18 Jan 1916.
9. Cockerell to TH, Dec 1915 (DCM).
10. FH to Cockerell, 23 July 1917.
11. FH to Cockerell, 24 Oct 1917.
12. *Friends of a Lifetime: Letters to Sydney Carlyle Cockerell*, ed. Viola Meynell (1940), p. 296.
13. DCM.
14. FH to Owen, 13 Dec 1917.
15. Ibid.
16. To Lady Hoare, 21 April 1918.
17. Ibid.
18. FH to Louise Yearsley, 10 Nov 1918.
19. *CL*, TH to Henniker, 27 Oct 1918.
20. FH to Cockerell, 24 Feb 1918.
21. Katharine Adams to Sydney Cockerell, 4 Aug 1920, in *The Best of Friends: Further Letters to Sydney Carlyle Cockerell*, ed. Viola Meynell (1956), p. 25.

22. *Letters of J. M. Barrie*, ed. Viola Meynell (1942), pp. 175–6.
23. C. M. Bowra, *Memories, 1898–1939* (1967), p. 118.
24. *CL*, 17 Nov 1920.
25. FH to Louise Yearsley, 10 Aug 1919.
26. FH to Cockerell, 19 Aug 1919.
27. FH to Cockerell, 8 Aug 1920.
28. FH to Yearsley, 10 Nov 1918.
29. FH to Owen, 15 Oct 1920.
30. FH to Cockerell, 26 Dec 1920.
31. Ibid.
32. Ibid.
33. FH to Yearsley, 30 Dec 1920.
34. FH to Cockerell, 31 Jan 1921.
35. *Lady from Madison Square*, pp. 203–4.
36. FH to Bugler, 1 Feb 1921.
37. FH to Bugler, 13 June 1922.
38. FH to Bugler, 17 June 1922.
39. FH to Cockerell, 26 Nov 1922.
40. *IR*, p. 150.
41. *IR*, p. 121.
42. FH to Cockerell, 26 Nov 1922.
43. FH to Siegfried Sassoon, 22 June 1922 (Eton).

CHAPTER 70
1. *IR*, p. 214.
2. Ibid.
3. *CL*, TH to Madeleine Rolland, 14 March 1921.
4. *CL*, TH to Frederick Macmillan, 4 Dec 1924.
5. *IR*, p. 213.
6. *The Times*, 27 Nov 1924.
7. TH to Thorndike, 2 Nov 1924.
8. TH to Bugler, 16 Dec 1924.
9. FH to Bugler, 2 Dec 1924.
10. FH to Bugler, 22 Dec 1924.
11. 10 Jan 1925, quoted, Blunt, *Cockerell*, pp. 214–15.
12. 11 Jan 1925, p. 215.
13. 12 Jan 1925, p. 215.
14. TH to Bugler, 7 Feb 1926.

15. FH to Bugler, 7 Feb 1925.
16. FH to Cockerell, 10 Mar 1925..
17. 'An Interview with Gertrude Bugler', *Coast to Coast* (TVS Television, May 1990), https://www.youtube.com/watch?v=qooe7J4FKp8.
18. TH to Macmillan, 4 Dec 1924.
19. *CL*, 26 July 1926.

CHAPTER 71
1. *IR*, p. 127
2. *IR*, p. 121.
3. *IR*, p. 216.
4. *Thomas Hardy Remembered*, p. 178.
5. Diary entry, 25 July 1926, in Virginia Woolf, *A Writer's Diary*, ed. Leonard Woolf (1953), pp. 88–93.
6. Woolf to TH, 17 Jan 1915, https://hardycorrespondents.exeter.ac.uk/text.html?id=dhe-hl-h.5954.
7. *Thomas Hardy Remembered*, p. 275.
8. *LEF*, FH to Sydney Cockerell, 29 Dec 1926.
9. *LEF*, FH to Siegfried Sassoon, 29 Jan 1927.
10. KH Diary, 26 Dec 1927 (DCM).
11. KH Diary, 8 Jan 1927 (DCM).
12. *LW*, p. 480.
13. KH Diary, 11 Jan 1927 (DCM).
14. *LW*, p. 478.
15. *LW*, p. 481.
16. KH Diary, 12 Jan 1927 (DCM).
17. KH Diary, 16 Jan 1927 (DCM)
18. *LEF*, FH to Dorothy Allhusen, 17 Jan 1928.
19. FH to Owen, 26 Jan 1928.
20. FH to Gosse, 5 Feb 1928.
21. FH to Cockerell, 29 May 1928.
22. Replies to condolence letters from Forster, Sassoon, Lawrence, March 1928, *LEF*, pp. 272–8.
23. To Sassoon, 12 May 1928.
24. KH Diary, 8 Dec 1928 (DCM).
25. Ibid, 9 Dec.
26. Ibid, 11 Dec.

27. *LEF*, FH to William Lyon Phelps, 26 March 1929.
28. Cockerell, p. 223.
29. FH to Harold Barlow, 5 March 1932, quoted, Richardson, 'Life behind the Gates'.
30. FH to Cockerell, 8 July 1929.
31. FH to Sir Arthur Pinero, 1 Aug 1929.
32. *LEF*, FH to Siegfried Sassoon, 11 July 1929.

EPILOGUE
1. Quotations from Lady Hester Pinney's pamphlet, *Thomas Hardy and the Birdsmoorgate Murder 1856* (1966).
2. Pinney to TH, 16 Jan 1926, https://hardycorrespondents.exeter.ac.uk/text.html?id=dhe-hl-h.4750a.
3. Ibid.
4. *CL*, TH to Hester Pinney, 20 Jan 1926.
5. *LEF*, p. 235.
6. *CL*, TH to W. Stebbing, Oct 1926.
7. Thorne, *In Search of Martha Brown*, p. 95.
8. Quotations from Lady Pinney's papers, preserved in the Library of the University of Bristol. See Thorne, *In Search of Martha Brown*, p. 36 and p. 95.
9. Emily Anita Pass to TH, 3 Dec 1927, https://hardycorrespondents.exeter.ac.uk/text.html?id=dhe-hl-h.4684.
10. Louise Moog to TH, 5 July 1927, https://hardycorrespondents.exeter.ac.uk/text.html?id=dhe-hl-h.4605.
11. TH Diary, 23 Dec 1925, written on Mary's birthday, ten years after her death.
12. *CP*, pp. 929–30.
13. *IR*, pp. 35–6.
14. *IR*, p. 221.

List of Illustrations

FRONTISPIECE

Gertrude Bugler as Tess (Max Gate, © National Trust / Simon Harris)

PLATE SECTIONS

12) Nude: The Tinted Venus (Walker Art Gallery, Liverpool, photograph: Creative Commons Licence, flickr, ketrin1407)

13) Actress: Mary Scott-Siddons (public domain)

14) St Juliot Church, sketched by Emma with caption by Hardy (Berg Collection, New York Public Library)

15) Where he first met her: St Juliot Rectory sketched by Emma (Berg Collection, New York Public Library)

16) Courtship sketches (Berg Collection, New York Public Library)

17) Beeny Cliff, where she rode, he walked – and the site of the original 'cliffhanger' in *A Pair of Blue Eyes* (Shutterstock / Peter Turner Photography)

18) Her hair, her miniature portrait in a precious locket (Berg Collection, New York Public Library)

19) Emma Lavinia Gifford: the first Mrs Hardy (Dorset Museum)

20) In the garden of Max Gate, Emma with Gordon Gifford, Hardy with his Rover Cob (Alamy)

21) The attic room at Max Gate, as it is today (Alamy)

22) Helen Paterson, illustrator of *Far from the Madding Crowd* (public domain)

23) Florence Henniker: frontispiece to her story collection, *Outlines* (public domain)

24) Agnes Grove: frontispiece to her book, *The Social Fetich*, dedicated to Hardy (author's collection)

25) Rebekah Owen, with Tess-like hat (public domain)

26) Jemima by Mary (Dorset Museum)

27) Hardy by Mary (Dorset Museum)

28) Florence by Mary (Dorset Museum)

29) With Florence at the seaside at Aldeburgh (public domain)

30) . . . while Emma was still alive (public domain)

31) Emma, c.1904, with Kitsey the cat (Dorset History Centre)

32) Gertrude Bugler as Marty South (University of California, Riverside)

33) Hardy and Florence, c.1914, with Wessex the dog (public domain)
34) The collaborators (Alamy)
35) . . . on the self-ghosted autobiography (author's collection)

TEXT ILLUSTRATIONS

p.112 The Hardy Monument
p. 133 Hardy's Hourglass sketch
p. 144 'Her Initials', with Hardy's sketch
p. 163 George Meredith poses for *The Death of Chatterton*
p. 175 The lovers walk to Clavell Tower
p. 202 Lonely city: sketch by Hardy
p.225 Emma sketched by Hardy
p. 265 Hardy's illustration to 'She at his Funeral' in *Wessex Poems*
p. 340 Hardy's sketch of the Great Comet, illustrating 'A Sign-Seeker' in *Wessex Poems*
p. 350 Thomas Rowlandson, *Selling a Wife*
p. 377 George Cruikshank, *The Signal*
p. 378 Illustration for the 1891 serialization of *Tess* in *The Graphic*: the strawberry scene
p. 391 The 1891 serialization of *Tess* in *The Graphic*
p. 422 Hardy's sketch for 'Thoughts of Phena, at News of her Death'

All text illustrations are from the author's collection, except for the Hardy Monument (Shutterstock / Image Conscious) and the water-colour by Rowlandson (public domain).

Index